THE BEST PLAYS OF 1921-22

THE BEST PLAYS OF 1921-22

AND THE

YEAR BOOK OF THE DRAMA IN AMERICA

Edited by

BURNS MANTLE

SCIRE · QVOD SCIENDVM

BOSTON
SMALL, MAYNARD & COMPANY
PUBLISHERS

Second Printing, January, 1923

Printed in the United States of America.

THE MURRAY PRINTING COMPANY
CAMBRIDGE, MASS.

CONTENTS

Introduction iii

The Season in New York 1

The Season in Chicago 15

"Anna Christie" 22

"A Bill of Divorcement" 63

"Dulcy" 96

"He Who Gets Slapped" 126

"Six-Cylinder Love" 163

"The Hero" 199

"The Dover Road" 237

"Ambush" 271

"The Circle" 311

"The Nest" 346

The Plays and Their Authors 381

Casts and Synopses of Plays Produced in New York (1921-22) 387

Statistical Summary of the New York Season 557

Long Runs on Broadway 560

Birthplaces and Birth Dates of Prominent Players 561

Necrology 568

Index of Plays and Casts 572

INTRODUCTION

In this, the third volume of "The Best Plays series," we have treated that venerable and valued collaborateur, The Playgoing Public, a little shabbily. For which we offer, in lieu of an apology, an explanation that should serve further to clarify our editorial purpose.

We held originally that inasmuch as this work was intended to serve the playgoing public as a year book of the drama in America, it should represent the popular or so-called commercial theater, which is the theater of the people. To do this it should be concerned with the most popular as well as with the "best" plays judged by the higher literary standards, because it is the popular plays that represent the preferences and tastes of the public which it is our hope to reach. Parenthetically, therefore, the book's title probably should read "The Best (of the Successful) Plays" produced during the particular theatrical season recorded in its pages.

On arriving at the end of the season of 1921-22, however, after we had sat through and passed humble judgment upon approximately 196 productions, of which 130 (eliminating the dramatic revivals and the musical plays) came within the scope of this work, we found that there were several plays which had achieved long runs, and were therefore to be accepted as representing the playgoing public's choice of the type of entertainment that best reflected its taste, which we did not feel were entitled to inclusion in our list of ten. Not, at least, at the cost of leaving out certain others less successful.

There was. for example, the case of "Kiki," a comedy

from the French of André Picard. Produced in December, " Kiki," thanks to Lenore Ulric's striking impersonation of the name part and David Belasco's fine staging of the play, ran through the season and promises to continue for another, and possibly for two more seasons. It is, therefore, the outstanding comedy success of the year. But as a candidate for a place in the list of the ten best plays of the season " Kiki " offers little in the way of readable dialogue or dramatic story.

On the other hand there were two plays of literary quality written by American authors of promise on American themes. These were Gilbert Emery's searching social satire, " The Hero," and Arthur Richman's " Ambush," a vivid, if sordid, study of a common phase of American middle class life.

There were also A. A. Milne's second success of the year, " The Truth About Blayds," which reads splendidly; another comedy by the Kaufman-Connelly duo, " To the Ladies," an amusing satire; " Thank You," with a message for small-town America and its attitude toward its underpaid parsons which we felt would justify its inclusion; another powerful and original O'Neill drama, " The Hairy Ape "; a play by Owen Davis, " The Detour," which failed early in the season, it may be merely because it came early in the season, and Hartley Manners' " The National Anthem," which, though a trifle dated as to theme, also dealt with a social problem of interest to American playgoers.

We probably could have justified the choice of any of these. And yet for none of them were we willing to sacrifice any one of the ten we have selected.

" Anna Christie " is Eugene O'Neill at his uncompromising best as a dramatist of life. It won for Mr. O'Neill the Pulitzer prize of $1,000 for being what the Pulitzer judges consider the best American play of the year, the second Pulitzer award he has won in three years. It is, in many respects, the finest piece of dramatic writing O'Neill has done, and whether its ugliness repel or fascinate, because of its truth, it is a powerful drama.

Miss Dane's "A Bill of Divorcement" is another of the stronger dramas that does not offer the playgoer seeking sweetness and light and happy endings exclusively in the theater much to pin his enthusiasm to. But it, too, is a well-written, sound and impressive study of human beings in the grip of dramatic circumstances they cannot control.

"He Who Gets Slapped" is foreign in atmosphere and a little muddled, we feel, for American audiences. But it represents a type of foreign drama that we are likely to see a lot of and hear a lot about during the next few years. We include it here because it represents a particular section of the playgoing public we feel are entitled to representation, whatever our personal reaction may be to their choice of play.

"The Nest" does not, unfortunately, read as well as it plays. But it is good drama written upon a theme of universal appeal and certainly was one of the best plays of the year.

The comedies and lighter dramas are, we feel, all readable and all worth while. "Dulcy" may or may not find a big public. Its bromidic heroine is not easily recognizable as an amusing type in all sections, but she is true and furnishes an excellent subject for satirical treatment. "Six Cylinder Love" is simple and amusing and a sufficiently true, if slightly exaggerated, reflection of the home life and character of our newlyweds to deserve its success. It contains also many seeds of wisdom planted in jest.

"The Dover Road" is a light and graceful Milne comedy with just enough purpose to give it body and enough philosophy to give it weight, and "The Circle" is an entertaining and quite original study of a double triangle that should give prospective elopers pause and their less romantic friends a pleasant evening in the theater.

The record of the season includes the casts of the nearly 200 plays produced between June 15, 1921 and June 15, 1922, with a paragraphed synopsis of the plot of each. These, we hope, will give you some idea of what each play was about and be of some assistance in helping you to make up your mind as to whether or not it is the sort of play you want to see when it reaches your town.

We are duly grateful for the increased interest shown in the second volume of "The Best Plays" and are hopeful that you will find the third of the series also worthy a place on your own particular five foot shelf.

B. M.

Forest Hills, L. I.
June 15, 1922.

THE BEST PLAYS OF 1921-22

THE SEASON IN NEW YORK

IT may be that ten years from now, with producing theaters scattered all over Manhattan Island, the production of 196 new plays in the Broadway territory in a single playgoing season will not seem like much of a record.

But today it is a little startling. A world's record, in fact. We do not chronicle the fact boastfully. We merely call it to your attention as being worthy of comment as an interesting achievement, much as the proudest of New York's adopted citizens point with pride to the struggling crowds in the subway.

Quantity production should count for nothing in the theater. Quality is alone important. And yet — an average of five new plays a week is — Well, it just is. Isn't it?

There were two reasons for the increased number of plays — forty more than were produced last season and at least twenty more than were produced in any one season as far back as we have traced the statistics. One was the greater number of theaters to be filled. There have been, within the last few years, a dozen or more playhouses added to the Broadway list, and these have to be kept open. At least their owners and lessees feel that they have to be kept open, whatever the rest of us may think. And there are now fifty-five of them.

The other reason was a greater number of quick failures than usual. A quick failure is usually traceable to one of two causes—either it is too good or too bad for the public. And few are too good. This season increased competition played a part. With the price of seats still holding around $3.30 with the war tax, the buying public exercised greater care than usual in making its selections, which helped the successes and hurried the failures on their way.

The New York theatrical season, so far as this volume is concerned, runs from June 15 to June 15. Actually the season opens the first or second week in August and continues until the first weeks of the following June. June and July productions are neither numerous nor important, save for the annual production of Florenz Ziegfeld's "Follies."

Last season there were five plays offered between June 15 and August 1: "Goat Alley," a sociological study of negro life in Washington, by Ernest Howard Culbertson; the 1921 "Follies"; George White's "Scandals"; "The Skylark," reintroducing Margherita Sylva to the stage as a comedienne, with songs, and "The Teaser," one of the early flapper comedies. The negro play had but five performances, "The Skylark" gave up after sixteen, and "The Teaser" after twenty-nine. But the revues continued through till fall and were then sent touring. The "Follies" did very well, as usual, according to the road reports, but the "Scandals" fared less happily.

In August the rush started. There were twenty-two plays produced in twenty-five playing days. Of the twenty-two, two practically ran the season through: "Six Cylinder Love," which is still playing as this chapter is written, and "Tangerine," a music play starring Julia Sanderson, which continued for 337 performances. "Dulcy" was also one of the August successes, and "The Greenwich Village Follies," but few of the others successfully met the test, though there were interesting and worthy plays among them. Owen Davis' "The Detour," for one, a splendid study of character, and Zoe Akins' "Daddy's Gone-a-Hunting," a story of an irresponsible artist's search for freedom and its reaction upon his loyal wife, which Marjorie Rambeau carried to 126 performances, but was afterward forced to abandon on tour. The picturesque failures included "Honors Are Even," which had so delighted Boston the previous summer that a long run was expected for it; "The Poppy God," on which the Selwyns had also banked heavily, and "Two Blocks Away," a comedy which had lured Barney Bernard from the A. H. Woods management to that of Charles B. Dillingham, only to drop him, as it were, in the center of Broadway and leave him there. "The Nightcap," another mystery, after a three-months' run here, went touring and scored a hit in Chicago. Enough people liked Harry Wagstaff Gribble's comedy of temperaments, "March Hares," to double the predictions that some time this author will surely write a good play, and "Back Pay," glorifying the self-sacrifice of a kept lady, hung on for ten weeks, with Helen MacKellar effectively emotional at eight performances a week. In August, too, there flashed one of those encouraging signs of the time of which much is written. "Getting Gertie's Garter," a "rawr" comedy, and expected to rally the morons for a season's run, quit after fifteen weeks.

September beat the August record by two. There were twenty-four productions this month, which left four Sundays and two Saturdays with nothing for the play reviewers to do. The September productions were lively and interesting. They included Irving Berlin's "Music Box Revue," on which Mr. Berlin and Sam Harris spent a million dollars of their own and their friends' money — including the cost of a new theater — with the avowed object of out-Follying the magnificence of the "Follies." And they came as close to it as the limited size of their stage and their company would permit. As a result the "Music Box Revue" was the outstanding revue success of the year, at a top price of $5.50 a seat when there were any seats to be had outside the brokers' offices, which was not often. The million dollar investment, it is said, has all been paid off by this first success.

"The Circle," Somerset Maugham's comedy success in which Mrs. Leslie Carter was reintroduced to the stage after a seven-year retirement in France, and in which John Drew came back, after a rest of two years, also started in September and continued well into the spring. David Belasco began his season with two interesting revivals, David Warfield and "The Music Master," and Frances Starr and "The Easiest Way." Lou Tellegen, while his publicity men boldly capitalized his published quarrels with Geraldine Farrar, tried for a sensational success in "Don Juan" at the Garrick and failed. The Irish Players, after a successful season in London, brought "The White-Headed Boy" to New York and played it to the applause of the appreciative minority for eight weeks at the Henry Miller Theater. "Bluebeard's Eighth Wife," with Ina Claire, also started in September and continued until February, and "Blossom Time," which may properly be classified as the most successful of the operettas produced this season, began on the twenty-ninth a run that continued until July and was then withdrawn for a month. The Franz Schubert melodies, skilfully worked into the score, are largely responsible, and an excellent singing cast was of great assistance.

By the time October was reached, about half the plays that had been hopefully offered in August and September were, as you might say, lying on their backs waiting for the movers. So twenty-two others were rushed in to take their places. These, happily, included several which were afterwards listed with the best entertainments of the season. Clemence Dane's "A Bill of Divorcement" was one. For a fortnight this fine, but slightly depressing play struggled for its life. It was about to be cast forth from the theater in which it was being played, when another management took it over, and in another theater it ran 170 performances. Arthur Richman's "Ambush" was presented the same week. This drama also made a fine impression, disappointing only those who insist upon a steady diet of happiness in every plot.

The dramatized "Main Street" was an October production, continuing for eleven weeks at the National Theater, but never to exciting receipts, and "Lilies of the Field," an intimate history of the older "gold diggers," played a slightly forced run of 167 performances at the Klaw. This was the month that "Bombo" and Al Jolson opened the new Jolson Theater in Fifty-Ninth Street, which was built to take the place of the Winter Garden, then harboring Shubert vaudeville. But the Winter Garden is back in the revue field now, and nobody seems to know exactly what will be done with the Jolson while its titular hero is out of town. In October, John Golden produced another of the pure plays in which he takes pride, a pleasant little comedy called "Thank You," which Winchell Smith helped Tom Cushing revise, and which continued for 218 performances at the Longacre. "Thank You" pleads the cause of the underpaid parson.

Booth Tarkington's "The Wren" was one of the month's unhappy failures, and "The Love Letter," with John Charles Thomas and his fine baritone voice starred, was another. This latter disappointment drove Thomas first to vaudeville and later to an announced intention of studying for grand opera, which he is now doing. Lionel Barrymore scored a fair success in "The Claw," supporting on his own talented shoulders a somewhat soggy play, and Mr. Woods started a vast amount of censorship talk with his production of "The Demi-Virgin," which included a "strip poker" scene that gave the visiting buyers, and their friends, the resident sellers, something to talk about for 268 performances. During this run the *Times* refused to print the name of the attraction in its advertising columns. As a result, there appeared each day a tantalizing query reading: "Are you one of the 168,423 persons who have already seen the most famous play in America at the Eltinge Theater?" George Cohan's "The O'Brien Girl" was one of the musical comedy successes of the month, and "The Wandering Jew" one of the heaviest of the importations. The latter remained nine weeks and then went touring.

November was the star month of the season, with twenty-seven productions which, with the Sundays out, was a little better than one a day. It was Mr. Belasco's month, seeing that he started it with the production of "The Grand Duke" on the first and closed it with the production of "Kiki" on the twenty-ninth. "Kiki," as more fully appears in the introduction to this volume, proved the comedy success of the year, thanks to Lenore Ulric and her gifted director, and though "The Grand Duke" did not do as well as had been hoped for it, it did achieve a run of 129 performances, and then petered out on the road.

In between these two there were several successful productions. Eugene O'Neill's "Anna Christie" was among them, and "Good Morning, Dearie," which was rushed in to take the place of the unexpected "Love Letter" failure, and is still playing at the Globe. Ed. Wynn's "Perfect Fool" also started in November and lasted until June, and there was a Ziegfeld "Midnight Frolic" performance which tried again to live without liquor and died without much of a struggle after twenty weeks. There was also a Milne comedy, "The Great Broxopp," a trifle obscurely produced at the Punch and Judy Theater, which deserved better than the nine struggling weeks it got.

November was also a month of quick failures. For one, Bessie Barriscale came east from Hollywood to play a comedy written by Howard Hickman, husband, stage director and movie mentor to the lady. Together they produced "The Skirt" and it lasted one week. Another venture was an elaborate staging of " The Great Way," for which Helen Freeman supplied the inspiration and the costs. This, too, was through six days later. George Scarborough's " The Mad Dog," with Conway Tearle, hung on for two weeks, but it was not nearly so poor as that sounds. " The Title " was another two-week failure, and so was " Marie Antoinette." But the prize winner in this division was a musical piece called " Suzette," which blossomed on Thursday and was sleeping peacefully the following Saturday night.

By December the number of available plays had been considerably reduced, and only seventeen productions were the result. The list included three hits, however: "The Dover Road," "Bulldog Drummond" and "Captain Applejack." The first is included in our list of the season's most satisfying offerings, the second is an English melodrama, seriously written by " Sapper," a wartime author who has had quite a vogue in London, but generously accepted as a gorgeous burlesque by American audiences; and the third is a mechanical but amusing comedy by Walter Hackett, an American who has been doing most of his writing in London the last few years. It is still popular. The spectacular failure this month was that of " The Idle Inn," which was expected to confirm the triumph of Jacob Ben-Ami, the young Jewish actor who had scored so unmistakably the year before in " Samson and Delilah," but which lasted only three weeks. There was a revival of " Trilby " by a coöperating group of actors, which ran two weeks, and there were two more revivals, " Bought and Paid For " and " Alias Jimmie Valentine," which were played for four and five weeks respectively. William Faversham, who had been playing " The Silver Fox," tried " The Squaw Man " again, with Mrs. Lydig Hoyt, a society amateur, in Julie Opp's old role. It continued for five weeks. It was a month of revivals, in fact, but the only one of them that did particularly well was " The Chocolate Soldier," which started on the twelfth at the Century and continued for ten weeks. This was the month that Charles Wagner, famed previously as an operatic impresario, decided to make a star of Sidney Blackmer, a gifted juvenile from the South. He presented Mr. Blackmer in a comedy by Clare Kummer entitled "The Mountain Man," and though the play weakened seriously after it had passed an excellent first act, young Mr. Blackmer's characterization of a Tennessee mountaineer was so unusually good, it continued for 163 performances.

New plays were still scarce in January. The producers had evidently thrown everything they had ready into the breach. They were now breathing hard, but producing little. There were only thirteen new plays offered in January, and no outstanding success among them. True, the Theater Guild came along with "He Who Gets Slapped," adding something to its achievements as the clearing house in America for the picturesque foreign play, and Arthur Hopkins revived "The Deluge" impressively — impressively, but not successfully. For the second time a playgoing public that refuses to pay to have its feelings harrowed in the theater, whatever the benefit to its soul, refused to buy this stirring drama by Hennig Berger.

The Mannerses, J. Hartley and Laurette Taylor, having rested through the early season, now came forward with a dramatic preachment by Mr. Manners on the evils of "jazz," illustrating the evil thoughts and pastimes of our wealthiest and best young people. A good play, and interesting, but a bit belated as to theme and somewhat over-preachy in its moral propaganda. Samuel Shipman, who knows his public a lot better than do his critics, offered "Lawful Larceny," which several of the experts insisted would not last long. But "Lawful Larceny" has passed its 130th performance and is still going as I write this.

There was an interesting experiment made with a

musicalized version of "Pomander Walk," which did very well, with Peggy Wood featured, and Elsie Janis brought her ex-soldier "Gang" in for a seven-week run. This was the month, too, in which Marie Lohr arrived from London by way of Canada. The English actress had never played in America before, and there was considerable curiosity aroused by her approach. But Miss Lohr, grown matronly the last few years, was offering a repertoire of old-time theatrical melodramas, opening with a stilted affair called "The Voice from the Minaret," and her audiences were disappointed. Nor did her later revival of Sardou's "Fedora," one of her big successes at home, help any. Four weeks and she was gone.

By February the producers had recovered their second wind, so to speak, and another rush of new plays resulted. Twenty-one were produced and several of them were quite worth while. One was "The Nest," a play Grace George translated from the French of Paul Geraldy and excerpts of which we have included in this volume. Another was "To the Ladies," a bright domestic comedy touched with satire, written by the authors of "Dulcy." This was the month selected by the Theater Guild for its experiment with George Bernard Shaw's "Back to Methuselah," a play so long that it had to be divided into three parts and played as a Shaw cycle. This the Guild accomplished by playing each part one week, and then repeating each part for a second week. The public interest was piqued by the novelty and the first three weeks were practically sold out before the first performance. The second three weeks, even though the impression had by that time become fixed that the audiences were being talked into a lethargic state, were also well patronized and still another week was added in which each section of the play was given for three performances.

"The Chauve-Souris," or "Bat Theater," of Moscow, was imported in February by Morris Gest and achieved an immediate popularity that carried it through the season. This, the most unusual entertainment of many years, is a rollicking Russian vaudeville, organized originally by the actors of the Russian Art Theater in Moscow for the entertainment of each other in their off hours. They began in a basement cafe, and when the public, hearing of their informal jollifications, insisted on being admitted, they began charging admission. Later, many of these artists found themselves stranded in Paris during the war. Banding together a second time, and borrowing a little money from those refugees who had succeeded in hiding a part of their rubles from the Bolsheviki, they reorganized the "Chauve-Souris" and restaged their entertainment. Within a few weeks they were what is known as the rage of Paris. After that, one Nikita Balieff, two hundred pounds of amiability with a comedy sense plus, took over the coöperative organization and put it on a business or salary basis. When Paris audiences began to grow small he took his troupe to London, where he learned to "spik bat Eengleesh." Here the rage continued. The New York engagement followed. It began February 4. By June the engagement had turned a profit of nearly $150,000 for Mr. Gest. (And how that man needed it! He was $400,000 in debt when the season began.) For the summer the Russian entertainers were moved up to the Century roof, which was redecorated for them in the Russian style. As this is written they are still playing there, and still getting $5 a seat for the 500 seats which represent the seating capacity. They may have an off night now and then, but so far these have been rare.

The February plays also included "The Rubicon," which made decent folk blush and helped along a censorship; "Montmartre," a production financed by ten players who banded themselves together as the Theater Assembly; "Madame Pierre," a snappy little play of the boulevards made from Brieux' "Les Hannetons," which, for some reason, lasted only five weeks when it was expected to run that many months; and Mary Shaw's revivals of "Mrs. Warren's Profession" and "Ghosts," neither of which was able to stir a paying interest.

The March productions did not amount to much. There were fourteen of them; the best, A. A. Milne's "Truth About Blayds" and Eugene O'Neill's "The Hairy Ape." This last was started in the Provincetown Theater, the converted stable in Greenwich Village which is the home of the Provincetown Players, of whom O'Neill is one. The Players, who were really the means of introducing the playwright to the success he since has earned, were in a bit of a hole financially and needed help. Arthur Hopkins had bought "The Hairy Ape," but at O'Neill's request agreed to let the Provincetowners have it for a few weeks. Its immediate success as one of the striking dramatic novelties of the year drew large audiences to the Provincetown Theater for several weeks and put the Players on their feet again. After that it was transferred to the Plymouth Theater, where it continued for ten weeks. Another O'Neill play, "The First Man," was tried this month at the Neighborhood Playhouse, but not being a particularly good play to start with, and being badly miscast in an important role, it did not last long. George Cohan returned to the stage in March, producing a comedy called "Madeleine and the Movies," with his daughter Georgette in an important role. Later he joined the cast himself, playing opposite Georgette. The play did very well, but was never a big success, and after ten weeks it was sent to Chicago as "Garrison and the Girls," Donald Brian playing the leading role.

"The Truth About Blayds," the nearest Milne has come to serious drama so far, was an immediate success with what is known slangily as the *intelligencia*, and continued for fourteen weeks. It proved a charming play, tastefully staged by Winthrop Ames. Arthur Hopkins, having bought a play written by two young women from episodes in the life of Voltaire, engaged Arnold Daly for the title role, but "Voltaire" could not find a public and was shelved after two weeks. Walker Whiteside came in from the road with "The Hindu," which did fairly well at the Comedy, and the Shuberts staged a big musical play at the Century called "The Rose of Stamboul."

The nearest to a success that April's twelve productions could boast was Eddie Cantor's "Make It Snappy," a typical Winter Garden revue with better comedy than usual. Marjorie Rambeau, appearing in "The Goldfish," was personally cheered by the press, but not much was thought of her play. Her audiences liked it, however, and now, after ten weeks, it has been moved from the Maxine Elliott Theater to the Astor and is hugely popular, particularly with the ladies. Adolph Klauber added another to the list of mystery plays, producing one called "The Charlatan," which did very well for eight weeks.

A comedy called "Kempy" was the proud success of the May list; and though this most unusual season was supposed to be practically over there were sixteen new plays added to the Broadway attractions in May. "Kempy" was written by J. C. and Elliott Nugent of the vaudeville Nugents, (there are, I believe, five of them altogether). J. C., the father, is the author of innumerable sketches and has been trying to get a production for a full-length play for many years. Finally he earned his chance, and to everybody's surprise "Kempy" proved the hit of the spring season. It is a bright little domestic comedy and well played, with three Nugents, (the two authors and sister Rose, an attractive ingenue) in the cast.

The big success of the month, however, was "Partners Again," the newest of the Jules Eckert Goodman and Montague Glass Potash and Perlmutter comedies; and,

I think, the best of the series. This brought Barney Bernard and Alexander Carr together after a three-year separation and they were riotously welcomed. The Theater Guild tried a revival of Arnold Bennett's "What the Public Wants"; James Montgomery financed a revival of "Hindle Wakes," renamed "Fanny Hawthorne," a fine play, by the way, and there was a revival of "Billeted" staged in the Village. None of these did particularly well. Ethel Levey, seeking to re-establish herself as a musical comedy star, chose a terrible affair called "Go Easy, Mabel," and was through in three weeks.

The first half of June was distinguished by the arrival of the 1922 "Follies," two or three weeks earlier than usual. This "National institution glorifying the American girl," ("If it does not glorify, it certainly exposes her," declares Will Rogers) achieved its customary success with the home folks and visitors. On the fifth there was an all-star revival of "The Rivals," organized by the Players' Club, with Francis Wilson as Acres, Tyrone Power as Sir Anthony, Robert Warwick as Captain Jack, Pedro de Cordoba as Faulkland, John Craig as Sir Lucius, Henry T. Dixey as Fag, James T. Powers as David, Mary Shaw as Mrs. Malaprop, Violet Hemming as Lydia Languish and Patricia Collinge as Lucy. Allan Pollock, who had been playing the semi-demented hero of "A Bill of Divorcement" all season, felt, by June, that he should do something to convince his public that he had not lost his mind entirely, stage appearances to the contrary notwithstanding. He therefore produced, on his own, a pleasant little comedy by H. M. Harwood, which was known in England as "A Social Convenience," but which Mr. Pollock decided to rename "A Pinch Hitter." After the twenty-five performances for which his contract called, he withdrew it with the announced intention of later adding it to his repertoire.

And so we are arrived at the end of a season that;

taken all in all, was neither better nor worse than the average. Unless you figure that it must have been worse, because of the greater number of plays produced.

THE SEASON IN CHICAGO

By O. L. Hall

Dramatic Editor, Chicago Journal

AS a market for the wares of the theater, Chicago has steadily grown in importance, multiplying its playhouses, providing a refuge for many a needy management in quest of a paying public, and taking many players into citizenship for an entire season.

As a scene of theatrical experiment, Chicago's importance has steadily diminished. Shunned by managers, authors and players with something new on their hands, the metropolis of the Midwest has become merely a notable terminus for the drama outward bound from New York.

It was the habit of producing managers of a few years ago to journey to Chicago and announce their intention of converting its theaters into so many laboratories. From these were to issue the masterpieces; the interior had tastes superior to those of the seaboard. Out by the headwaters shone the lamp of promise. Occasionally came a manager with a play unknown in Stamford or the New Jersey coast resorts, and the city by the lake became for a night a producing center. If the play promised to thrive, the owner began telegraphing to New York for a theater; if it were an ailing thing, it ultimately was led out on the prairie to die.

That was yesterday. Today is scantier still of adventure. The managers say it costs too much to transport the drama, for them to risk experiment far from the storehouse. The Midwest otherwise views the situation; it believes that the constant and insistent demand for attractions for over-theatred Manhattan Island so engrosses the attention of the producers that they have neither the time nor the material to supply even the major cities of the hinterland.

The great playgoing public of the Midwest takes pride in its independence, which is more imaginary than real. It is a chauvinistic public, eager and willing to sustain local enterprise. It regards with an amused toleration the East's pretentions to infallible judgment in the theater, and it is thrilled by the spectacle of an eastern semi-failure finding large popular success in the West. Likewise it takes a lively interest in the Chicago failure of a play that has been loudly acclaimed in the East.

Whatever the emotions of the public of the interior may be, it does rely in a degree upon the accolade of the drama's capital. The travelers between Chicago and New York are legion. Word of success at the port is quickly borne to the corn country, and word of failure, too. The tastes of the average midwestern theatergoer differ not at all from the tastes of the average easterner. In his fondness for the make-believe of the stage the human creature holds to type from coast to coast.

So, most of the plays which are thought by New Yorkers to be good one season are thought to be good in Chicago a season later, or the season after that. Seven of Mr. Mantle's ten best plays of the New York season of 1920-21 reached Chicago in 1921-22, and to five of the seven — "Enter Madame," "The Emperor Jones," "Nice People," "The Bad Man" and "Liliom" — the latter city gave hearty support. It took a lively interest also in a sixth play in the list, "The Skin Game," and generously applauded it despite the fact that it was atrociously acted.

Sir James Barrie's play, "Mary Rose," accorded a position of honor in the East, was a Chicago failure, mystifying its second-season public and coming short of its approval. The three remaining plays in Mr.

Mantle's list, "Deburau," "The First Year" and "The Green Goddess," are unknown to the second city. "Deburau" will remain merely a rumor; "The First Year" will seek the great central market in the season to come, bringing new players; "The Green Goddess" is between seasons merely an expectation.

Fifty plays and thirty musical shows were acted in Chicago in the past season. The plays had a total of about 360 weeks and the musical shows filled an aggregate of about 190 weeks in runs of various length. The sum of the attendance at these plays and shows was about 4,500,000. These figures represent clearly enough the importance of Chicago as a theatrical market, and any manager capable of wielding a lead pencil may quickly arrive at them. Yet these figures are well-nigh futile as an invitation to original effort in play production.

Leo Ditrichstein, acting "That Homely Henriquez," Walker Whiteside, producing his own play called "The Hindu," and Miss Grace George, staging "The Exquisite Hour" and "Me and My Diary," did about all for Chicago that was done in the way of experiment. The two actors afterward conveyed their slender dramas to the East; the actress carried her plays but a little ways from the scene of production.

"The Exquisite Hour" revealed in Margaret Wright a new candidate for the fame and emoluments of dramatic authorship. The play readily betrayed her inexperience; it made little headway under the propulsion of Miss George's best effort. It dealt, in a manner somewhat new, with a crisis in the married life of a well-matched couple. The title, and in a measure the theme, were suggested by Paul Verlaine's "L'Heure Exquise," and those verses were sung in the play to the familiar music of Reynaldo Hahn.

The Ashtons had been married for a number of years. He was prosperous, maintained a fine home, and apparently made every provision for his wife's comfort and happiness. She, too, thought so. She was an idler, centering her interest in social activities, giving little heed to her husband's affairs and drifting along with a sense of security. Her placid life was suddenly and unexpectedly disturbed. A young lady telephonist arrived from Ashton's office demanding to see her employer, and, failing to find him, blurted out in a moment of terror the startling information that her fiance, not incorrectly, believing himself wronged, had threatened to kill Ashton. The homicidal emotion had given way, however, to a plan for reprisals, and the muscular workman even then was on his way to invade the Ashton home.

So came to Mrs. Ashton the first intimation that her husband was unfaithful, and being a woman of wit, if not of very much sense, she speedily determined to steer the situation to her own advantage. She sent the girl away to meet her husband, and herself awaited the arrival of the raging lover, name o' Barry. In he stormed to inform Mrs. Ashton in halting but unmistakable language why he had come. She told him she was as much hurt as he, and that they together would take their revenge. She ordered the servants to array the uncouth and bellowing mechanic in her husband's best dinner clothes, and then, dispatching a note to Ashton apprising him of the rendezvous, the injured pair set out for a suburban bungalow on a mission which Mrs. Ashton meant, of course, to be entirely harmless.

Scarcely had they reached the bungalow when Ashton and the girl appeared, none too soon to save the adventurous wife from possibly regrettable consequences of her rash action. There the play fell down. Explanations were ready and trite, Barry was packed off with the girl, and Ashton remained for his wife's lecture. Somewhere in this lecture was hidden the purpose of the play. Mrs. Ashton sought, employing the device of question and answer, to learn from her husband why she had failed to hold him. Had she given too much or too little, too readily or too reluctantly? What was a wife's duty to her husband; his to her? Were they incompatible? What could the matter be?

The answer never appeared. The duologue ran on for many minutes; the questions were numerous and direct, and sometimes embarrassingly frank. But the author had no solution. However, it did appear, after the husband and wife had passed the night separately, that the answer to the riddle of their disunion came in their awakening to the necessity of mutual understanding. The Ashtons, full of forgiveness, greeted each other at dawn. That, apparently, was the exquisite hour. Miss George's brittle style, her sparkle, her skill in give and take were not enough to make an entertainment of the play which probably is having its eternal sleep.

Interest in "The Exquisite Hour" not rising to flood tide, Miss George was moved to give American staging to "Me and My Diary," a satirical comedy in one act, written by Gertrude E. Jennings, Englishwoman, and dealing with the literary eccentricities of Margot Asquith. This opuscule was deficient in spirit and wit, but with better acting it might have wrought an effect. The principal actress did not appear to attempt a characterization; at least, she did not achieve it.

The events of this little play pass on a day quickly following the publication of the sensational memoirs. A titled government official telephones to protest the penwoman's grave betrayal of the secrets of Downing Street and in pour her friends and acquaintances, old and new; one to complain that she is scandalized on this page and that, another to berate the author for passing her by entirely. A parlor maid, inferentially in the book, comes to demand recompense for her injured feelings. This scene is designed to exhibit the heroine's tact and wit, but it comes off awkwardly. An old lover, long lost in the Congo, puts in an appearance and gives the autobiographer a thrill, but quickly disillusions her with an offer of help in grammar. The reviews, read in the play, also make much of the literary lady's disregard of the rules of syntax. As in the case of "The Exquisite Hour," any word concerning Miss Jennings' comedy also probably is necrological.

Reference may be made, in passing, to "The Love Chef," a comedy devised by Edgar Selwyn as a medium for the dialectic gift of Leo Carillo. It oscillated unsteadily between comedy and burlesque and its use of the expedient of making a servant of a titled foreigner had insufficient novelty to recommend the play to interest. Its life was brief.

The season saw the production of several musical shows: "Love Birds," "Under the Bamboo Tree," "Lola," "Molly Darling" and "The Hollywood Follies." The lamented Bert Williams was the nominal star of "Under the Bamboo Tree," a regulation musical comedy of the palm-fringed island sort. "Love Birds" and "Lola" died very young with their finances involved.

It is not possible to go further with the history of the season's enterprises in the Midwest. The amateurs of the neighborhood repertory companies, acting in halls, homes, schools, churches and abandoned stables, have gone farther in exploration of new drama than the commercial managers, so-called. But their field is circumscribed, their influence parochial and evanescent. Their disclosures neither ask nor merit admission to a list of the ten best plays of the season.

A list of the ten best plays of the theatrical year in Chicago may seem a ghoulish roster to a drama lover of the East, for the list must contain the names of some antics which were old long ago. But here are the ten:

"Lightnin'"
"Nice People"
"The Bad Man"
"Anna Christie"
"The Intimate Strangers"
"Enter Madame"

"The White-Headed Boy"	"Mr. Pim Passes By"
"The Detour"	"Liliom"

The foregoing ten were not equally successful with the lakeside public, but considering their locations and the quality of the acting bestowed upon them, all but two found perhaps the favor to which they were entitled. There was at no time in the season a dearth of drama of fair quality; there was at no time a plethora of plays worth while. Throughout the season the drama fared better than the various examples of lyric folly, yet good acting more often than good writing was the theater's lure.

Chicago, rapidly increasing the number of its theaters, is hastening to a time when experiment will be much more frequent, if not constant. Last season saw production at its nadir.

"ANNA CHRISTIE"

A Drama in Three Acts

By Eugene O'Neill

EUGENE O'NEILL, upon whom we have come to depend as a regular contributor to the best plays of the season, told his friend, George Jean Nathan, before "Anna Christie" was produced that whatever the reception of the play might be he would have not a single alibi to offer. The cast, said he, was perfect; the direction of Arthur Hopkins had brought more out of the play than even he, the author, had imagined was there, and the Robert Edmund Jones' settings were strikingly true to the atmosphere with which he had labored to surround his drama.

The play was first presented at the Vanderbilt Theatre, November 2, 1921, and, as it happened, no alibi was called for. The discriminating playgoers who had learned what to expect of O'Neill were enthusiastic in their endorsement. It is a rough play in that it is a story of rough characters. Much of its dialogue may prove offensive to playgoers of superfine sensibilities, and those readers who fear a similar reaction are reminded that it is the story of a coal barge captain, a prostitute, and a steamship stoker. These do not speak the language of the drawing room. But it is also one of the big dramas of the day, soundly human, impressively true in characterization and, in its bigger moments, intensely dramatic.

The opening scene reveals the bar and a section of a small back room in "Johnny-the-Priest's" saloon near South Street, New York. There is a partition running down the center of the stage, through which a swinging half-door lets into the " sitting room " from the bar. A second door is from the " family entrance " on the adjoining side street. It is typical of what the water-front saloon was in the pre-Volstead days, dark, grimy, forbidding, sordid. Its principal hangers-on are sailors and longshoremen, with the " sitting room " devoted to the better acquaintance of the women of the district and their prospective patrons. At the bar " Johnny " himself presides. " With his pale, thin, clean-shaven face, mild blue eyes and white hair, a cassock would seem more suited to him than the apron he wears." Two longshoremen get their drinks and return to their jobs. Larry, the barkeeper, returns from his lunch, prepared to relieve the boss. A postman brings in a letter. It is addressed to " Christopher Christopherson " in care of the saloon proprietor. " A square head " name, laconically observes the postman. " Old Chris, that's who," decides Larry.

Chris Christopherson is the captain of a coal barge who has been doing most of his drinking at " Johnny the-Priest's " hospitable saloon for several years, whenever he is in port. Johnny hasn't seen him for some months now, so he is likely to pop in at any time. The letter is postmarked St. Paul. It might be from old Chris's daughter, seeing he is supposed to have a girl out west somewhere.

They are still idly considering the possibility when Chris himself comes lurching through the street doors. " He is a short, squat, broad-shouldered man of about fifty, with a round, weather-beaten, red face from which his light blue eyes peer short-sightedly, twinkling with a simple good humor. His large mouth, overhung by a thick, drooping, yellow mustache, is childishly self-willed and weak, of an obstinate kindliness. A thick neck is jammed like a post into the heavy trunk of his body . . . . He is dressed in a wrinkled, ill-fitting, dark suit of shore clothes, and wears a faded cap of gray cloth over his mop of grizzled, blond hair. . . ."

Old Chris has been drinking and is of a mind to treat the world generously, particularly his old friends, Johnny and Larry, the barkeeper. As they drink he would regale them with song. He is just in from Norfolk and the "vedder" has been "dirty" — "yust fog, fog, fog all bloody time," which has resulted in a slow voyage.

There is an insistent ring at the back door, which reminds Chris that he had left his lady friend, "Marthy," waiting at the family entrance. And Marthy is not one to wait patiently. He rushes now to let her in, and apologize. Marthy "might be forty or fifty. Her jowly, mottled face, with its thick red nose, is streaked with interlacing purple veins. Her thick gray hair is piled anyhow in a greasy mop on top of her round head. Her figure is flabby and fat; her breath comes in wheezy gasps," but aside from that she is fairly presentable. "There still twinkles in her bloodshot blue eyes a youthful lust for life which hard usage had failed to stifle, and a sense of humor, mocking but good tempered. She wears a man's cap, double-breasted man's jacket and a grimy, calico skirt. Her bare feet are incased in a man's brogan several sizes too large for her, which gives her a shuffling, wobbly gait."

It takes several scoops of lager and ale to mollify the angry Marthy, and while she drinks them the muddled Chris reads laboriously through his letter. And as he reads "his face lights up with an expression of mingled joy and bewilderment. . . . Suddenly he pounds his fist on the table with happy excitement."

CHRIS — Py Yimminy! Yust tank, Anna says she's comin' here right avay! She got sick on yob in St. Paul, she say. It's short letter don't tal me much more'n dat. (*Beaming*) Py golly, dat's good news all at one time for ole fallar! (*Then turning to Marthy, rather shame-*

facedly) You know, Marthy, Ay've tole you Ay don't see my Anna since she was little gel in Sveden five year ole.

MARTHY — How old'll she be now?

CHRIS — She must be — lat me see — she must be twanty year ole, py Yo!

LARRY — (*surprised*). You've not seen her in fifteen years?

CHRIS — (*suddenly growing somber — in a low tone*). No. Ven she vas little gel, Ay vas bo'sun on vindjammer. Ay never gat home only few time dem year. Ay'm fool sailor faller. My voman — Anna's mother — she gat tired vait all time Sveden for me ven Ay don't navar come. She come dis country, bring Anna, dey go out Minnesota, live with her cousins on farm. Den ven her mo'der die ven Ay vas on voyage, Ay tank it's better dem cousins keep Anna. Ay tank it's better Anna live on farm, den she don't know dat ole davil sea, she don't know fader like me.

Suddenly there begin to loom before Chris the new problems that Anna's coming will put upon him. She must, for one thing, be kept clear of the sailor's life; the thought of his daughter's marrying one of his calling is maddening to old Chris. Then there is Marthy. Something must be done about Marthy. Perhaps he can tell her a lie that will get her ashore and off the barge before Anna comes! Failing this — But Marthy saves him from further worry, though for a time she takes malicious joy in teasing him until he is utterly miserable with fear of what she may do. Then she bursts into raucous laughter in her enjoyment of the situation.

MARTHY — (*chuckling, scornfully*). A squarehead tryin' to kid Marthy Owen at this late day! After me campin' with barge men the last twenty years. I'm wise to the game up, down, and sideways. I ain't been born and dragged up on the waterfront for nothin'. Think I'd make trouble, huh? Not me! I'll pack up me duds and beat it. I'm quittin' yuh, get me? I'm tellin' yuh I'm sick o' stickin' with yuh and I'm leavin' yuh flat, see? There's plenty of other guys on other barges waitin' for me. Always was, I always found. (*She slaps the astonished Chris on the back*) So cheer up, Dutchy! I'll be offen the barge before she comes. You'll be rid o' me for good — and me o' you — good riddance for both of us. Ho-ho!

Chris is ready to celebrate with several more whiskies at the happy outcome of this particular complication. He can let his imagination soar now as to just what his little girl will be like. "What you tank she look like, Marthy? Ay bet you she's fine, good, strong gel, pooty like hell! Living on farm make her like dat. And Ay bet you some day she marry good, steady land fallar here in East, have home all her own, have kits — an' den Ay'm ole grandfadder, py golly! An' Ay go visit dem every time Ay gat in port near!"

He would sing a song to express his joy, and pound the tables, and Marthy's back. But Marthy warns him that celebrating is dangerous at the moment. Much better for him if he would go around the corner and "put a feed" into himself. "Listen, yuh old nut! Yuh don't know what time yer kid's liable to show up. Yuh want to be sober when she comes, don't yuh?" He does, of course, and is soon on his way in quest of food. Chris is little more than out of the room before the family entrance bell rings again and Larry opens the door to admit "a tall, blond, fully developed girl of twenty, handsome after a large, Viking daughter fashion, but now run down in health and plainly showing all the outward evidences of belonging to the world's oldest profession. Her youthful face is already hard and cynical beneath its layer of make-up. Her clothes are the tawdry finery of peasant stock turned prostitute."

She shuffles a little uncertainly and weakly into the room and sinks into a chair by the table. Larry waits expectantly. "Gimme a whisky — ginger ale on the side," she says. As he turns to go, she adds, with a forced smile: "And don't be stingy, baby!" A moment later she has downed the liquor at a gulp. "Gee," she says, smiling across at the curious Marthy, "I needed that bad, all right, all right!"

"Where'd yuh come from?" demands Marthy. "St. Paul — out in Minnesota," answers the girl. And the older woman bursts into hoarse, ironical laughter. "So this is Chris' 'little gel!' Gawd!"

They are acquainted, presently, these two. Anna has a little money and a parched throat, after a day and a half on the train. She sat up all night in the day coach, and she is willing to buy drinks as long as her money lasts. Besides, she's pretty weak, being just out of a hospital.

ANNA — (*leaning over to Marthy, confidentially*). The joint I was in out in St. Paul was raided. That was the start. The judge gave all us girls thirty days. The others didn't seem to mind being in the cooler much. Some of 'em was used to it. But me, I couldn't stand it. It got my goat right — couldn't eat or sleep or nothin'. I never could stand bein' caged up nowheres. I got good and sick and they had to send me to the hospital. It was nice there. I was sorry to leave it, honest.

MARTHY — (*after a slight pause*). Did yuh say yuh got to meet someone here?

ANNA — Yes. Oh, it's not what you mean. It's my old man I got to meet. Honest! It's funny, too. I ain't seen him since I was a kid — don't even know what he looks like — yust had a letter every now and then. This was always the only address he give me to write him back. He's yanitor of some building here now — used to be a sailor.

MARTHY — (*astonished*). Janitor!

ANNA — Sure. And I was thinkin' maybe, seein' he ain't never done a thing for me in his life, he might be willin' to stake me to a room and eats till I get rested up. (*Wearily*) Gee, I sure need that rest! I'm knocked out. (*Then resignedly*) But I ain't expectin' much from him. Give you a kick when you're down, that's what all men do. (*With sudden passion*) Men! I hate 'em! — all of 'em! And I don't expect he'll turn out no better than the rest. (*Then with sudden interest*) Say, do you hang out around this dump much?

Marthy does, off and on. And she knows "Old Chris." — A funny old nut, but, "Yuh can bet your life, kid, he's as good an old guy as ever walked on two feet. That goes!"

But Marthy is obliged to explain to Anna that Chris is not a janitor. He is the captain of a barge — a coal barge. And it is probably on the barge that he will expect his daughter to live.

ANNA — (*scornfully*). Me? On a dirty coal barge! What d'you think I am?

MARTHY — (*resentfully*). What d'yuh know about barges, huh? Bet yuh ain't never seen one. That's what comes of his bringin' yuh up inland — away from the old devil, sea — where yuh'd be safe! Gawd!

ANNA — (*angrily*). His bringing me up! Is that what he tells people! I like his nerve! He let them cousins of my old woman's keep me on their farm and work me to death like a dog.

MARTHY — Well, he's got queer notions on some things. I've heard him say a farm was the best place for a kid.

ANNA — Sure. That's what he'd always answer back — and a lot of crazy stuff about staying away from the sea — stuff I couldn't make head or tail to. I thought he must be nutty.

Marthy — (*casually*). He is, on that one point. So yuh didn't fall for life on the farm, huh?

Anna — I should say not! The old man of the family, his wife, and four sons — I had to slave for all of 'em. I was only a poor relation, and they treated me worse than they dare treat a hired girl. (*After a moment's hesitation — somberly*) It was one of the sons — the youngest — started me — when I was sixteen. After that, I hated 'em all so I'd killed 'em if I'd stayed. So I run away — to St. Paul.

Marthy — I've heard Old Chris talkin' about your bein' a nurse girl out there. Was that all a bluff yuh put up when yuh wrote him?

Anna — Not on your life, it wasn't. It was true for two years. I didn't go wrong all at one jump. Bein' a nurse girl was yust what finished me. Takin' care of other people's kids, always listenin' to their bawling and crying, caged in, when you're only a kid yourself and want to get out and see things! At last I got the chance — to get into that house. And you bet your life I took it! (*Defiantly*) And I ain't sorry, neither. (*After a pause — with bitter hatred*) It was all men's fault — the whole business. It was men on the farm ordering and beating me — and giving me the wrong start. Then, when I was a nurse, it was men again hangin' around, bothering me, trying to see what they could get. (*She gives a hard laugh*) And now it's men all the time. Gawd, I hate 'em all, every mother's son of 'em! Don't you?

Marthy — Oh, I dunno. There's good ones and bad ones, kid. You've just had a run of bad luck with 'em, that's all. Your old man, now — Old Chris — he's a good one.

Anna — (*skeptically*). He'll have to show me.

Now old Chris is back from his lunch. Marthy hears him as he comes into the bar. She goes to the swinging door to warn him, as well as she can, that Anna has arrived and that she (Marthy) is going down to the barge to get her clothes and get out.

Chris " stands before the door to that back room in an agony of embarrassed emotion — then he forces himself to a bold decision, pushes open the door and walks in. He stands there, casts a shy glance at Anna whose brilliant clothes, and to him, high-toned appearance, awe him terribly. He looks about him with pitiful nervousness as if to avoid the appraising with which she takes in his face, his clothes, etc.— his voice seeming to plead for her forbearance."

CHRIS — Anna!

ANNA — (*acutely embarrassed in her turn*). Hello — father. She told me it was you. I yust got here a little while ago.

CHRIS — (*goes slowly over to her chair*). It's good — for see you — after all dem years, Anna. (*He bends down over her. After an embarrassed struggle they manage to kiss each other.*)

ANNA — (*a trace of genuine feeling in her voice*). It's good to see you, too.

. . . .

ANNA — (*resentfully*). But why didn't you never come home them days? Why didn't you never come out West to see me?

CHRIS — (*slowly*). Ay tank, after your mo'der die ven Ay vas avay on voyage, it's better for you you don't never see me. Ay don't know, Anna, vhy Ay don't never come home Sveden in ole year. Ay vant come home end of every voyage. Ay want see your mo'der, your two bro'der before dev vas drowned, you ven you vas born — but — Ay don't go. Ay sign on oder ships — go South America, go Australia, go China, go every port all over vorld many time — but Ay never go aboard ship sail for Sveden. Ven Ay gat money pay for passage home as passenger den — (*He bows his head guiltily*)

Ay forgat and Ay spend all money. Ven Ay tank again it's too late. (*He sighs*) Ay don't know vhy but dat's way with most sailor faller, Anna. Dat ole devil sea make dem crazy fools with her dirty tricks. It's so.

ANNA — (*Who has watched him keenly while he has been speaking. With a trace of scorn in her voice*). Then you think the sea's to blame for everything, eh? Well, you're still workin' on it, ain't you, spite of all you used to write me about hatin' it. That dame was here told me you was captain of a coal barge — and you wrote me you was janitor of a building!

CHRIS — (*embarrassed, but lying glibly*). Oh, I work on land long time as yanitor. Yust short time ago Ay got dis yob 'cause Ay vas sick, need open air.

ANNA — (*skeptically*). Sick? You? You'd never think it.

CHRIS — And, Anna, dis ain't real sailor yob. Dis ain't real boat on sea. She's yust ole tub — like piece of land with house on it dat float. Yob on her ain't sea yob. No. Ven your mo'der die, Ay keep my word, py yingo!

. . . .

CHRIS — (*eagerly*). But Ay gat place, Anna — nice place. You rest all you want, py yimminy! You don't never have to vork as nurse gel no more. You stay with me, py golly!

ANNA — (*pleased by his eagerness*). Then you're really glad to see me — honest?

CHRIS — (*pressing one of her hands in both of his*). Anna, Ay like see you like hell, Ay tal you. An' don't you talk no more about getting yob. You stay with me. Ay don't see you for long time, don't forgat dat. (*His voice trembles*) Ay'm gatting ole. Ay got no vone in vorld but you.

ANNA — (*touched — embarrassed by this unfamiliar emotion*). Thanks. It sounds good to hear someone — talk to me that way. Say, though — if you're so lonely

— it's funny — why ain't you never married again?

CHRIS — (*shaking his head emphatically — after a pause, slowly*). Ay love your mo'der too much for ever do dat, Anna.

ANNA — (*impressed, slowly*). I don't remember nothin' about her. What was she like? Tell me.

CHRIS — Ay tal you all about everything — and you tell me all tangs happen to you. But not here now. Dis ain't good place for young gel, anyway. Only no good sailor fallar come here for gat drunk. (*He gets to his feet quickly and picks up her bag*) You come with me, Anna. You need lie down, gat rest.

But Anna is still of a mind to hang back. She cannot quite reconcile herself to the thought of a coal barge as a fit home for a convalescent, even of her kind. But Chris' enthusiasm inspires her with some little hope. Life on a coal barge is not as grimy as it sounds, according to his description. "Tug come an' ve gat towed out on voyage — yust water all around, and sun, and fresh air, and good grub for make you strong, healthy gel." She is still thirsty, she tells him, and he orders a little port wine for her that she may celebrate "dis vun time."

In the bar Chris gets the drinks. "Who's the blonde?" demands Larry. And Chris answers proudly, "Dat vas Anna, Larry . . . Don't you tank she vas pooty gel?" To which Larry replies embarrassedly that she sure is; a peach, in fact.

In the sitting room Anna has collapsed again. She has tried, with Chris away, to take her bag and "beat it," and found her strength unequal to the venture. Sadly she sinks into a chair, covers her face with her hands and sobs. She recovers hurriedly when Chris comes again with the drinks, however, though he looks at her searchingly.

CHRIS — You look tired, Anna. Vell, Ay make you take good long rest now. (*Picking up his beer*) Come, you drink vine. It put new life in you. (*She lifts her glass — he grins*) Skoal, Anna! You know dat Svedish word?

ANNA — Skoal! (*Downing her port at a gulp like a drink of whiskey — her lips trembling*) Skoal? I guess I know that word, all right, all right!—The curtain falls.

ACT II

Ten days later the deeply-laden barge, *Simeon Winthrop,* is at anchor in the outer harbor of Provincetown, Mass. " It is ten o'clock at night. Dense fogs shroud the barge at all sides, and she floats motionless on a calm. . . . To the right of the visible section of the barge is the cabin, its misty windows glowing wanly with the light of a lamp inside. The chimney of the cabin stove rises a few feet above the roof. The doleful tolling of the bells, on Long Point, on ships at anchor, breaks the silence at regular intervals."

Anna is standing on a coil of rope on which a lantern rests. " She looks healthy, transformed, the natural color has come back to her face. She has on a black, oilskin coat, but wears no hat. She is staring out into the fog astern with an expression of awed wonder. The door is pushed open and Chris appears. He is dressed in yellow oilskins — coat, pants, sou'wester — and wears high sea-boots."

Chris would have Anna come in. The fog is bad, " vorst one of her (the sea's) dirty tricks." But Anna loves it. " It's so funny and still. I feel as if I was out of things altogether," she muses, feelingly. She has come to like the sea, too — as much as she has seen of it.

CHRIS — (*glancing at her moodily*). Dat's foolish talk, Anna. You see her more, you don't talk dat vay.

(*seeing her irritation he hastily adopts a more cheerful tone*) But Ay'm glad you like it on barge. Ay'm glad it makes you feel good again. (*With a placating grin*) You like live like dis alone with ole fa'der, eh?

ANNA — Sure I do. Everything's been so different from anything I ever run across before. And now — this fog — Gee, I wouldn't have missed it for nothing. I never thought living on ships was so different from land. Gee, I'd yust love to work on it, honest I would, if I was a man. I don't wonder you always been a sailor.

CHRIS — (*vehemently*). Ay ain't sailor, Anna. And dis ain't real sea. You only see nice part. (*Then as she doesn't answer, he continues hopefully*) Vell, fog lift in morning, Ay tank.

ANNA — (*the exultation again in her voice*). I love it! I don't give a rap if it never lifts! (*After a pause*) It makes me feel clean — out here — 's if I'd taken a bath.

But Chris won't give up. If he cannot make her come in, out of the fog, he can at least do something to kill this growing interest in the sea which she is showing. So he talks with her of its treacheries and of the dirty tricks it has played him all his life. And little by little she learns much of his life that she had not known before. "Was the men in our family always sailors?" she asks; "as far back as you know about?"

CHRIS — Yes. Damn fools! All men in our village on Coast, Sveden, go to sea. Ain't nutting else for dem to do. My fa'der die on board ship in Indian Ocean. He's buried at sea. Ay don't never know him only a little bit. Den my tree bro'der, older'n me, dey go on ships, den Ay go too. Den my mo'der she's left all 'lone. She die pooty quick after dat — all 'lone. Ve vas all avay on voyage when she die. (*He pauses sadly*) Two my bro'der dey gat lost on fishing boat same like your bro'ders vas drowned. My oder bro'der, he save money, gave up sea, dan he die home in bed. He's only one dat ole devil don't kill. (*Defiantly*) But me, Ay bet you Ay die ashore in bed, too! . . . Dey're all fool fallar, dem fallar in our family. Dey all vork rotten yob on sea for nutting, don't care nutting but yust gat big pay day in pocket, gat drunk, gat robbed, ship avay again on oder voyage. Dey don't come home. Dey don't do anytang like good man do. And dat ole devil, sea, sooner, later, she svallow dem up.

ANNA — (*with an excited laugh*). Good sports, I'd call 'em. (*Then hastily*) But say — listen — did all the women of the family marry sailors?

CHRIS — (*eagerly — seeing a chance to drive home his point*). Yes — and it's bad on dem like hell vorst of all. Dey don't see deir men only once in long while. Dey set and vait all 'lone. And vhen deir boys grow up, go to sea, dey sit and vait some more. (*Vehemently*) Any gel marry sailor, she crazy fool! Your mo'der she tal you same tang if she vas alive.

But Anna is not depressed. Rather she is exalted by her belated contact with the sea. "But why d'you suppose I feel so — so — like I'd found something I'd missed and been looking for — 's if this was the right place for me to fit in? And I seem to have forgot — everything that's happened — like it didn't matter no more. And I feel clean, somehow — like you feel yust after you've taken a bath. And I feel happy for once — yes, honest! — happier than I ever been anywhere before! It's nutty for me to feel that way, don't you think?" "Ay tank Ay'm damn fool for bring you on dis voyage, Anna," he answers, a grim foreboding in his voice.

From the port side of the barge comes the hail of a man's husky, exhausted voice: "Ahoy!" Evidently "some sailor fallar who has lost his course in the fog."

grunts Chris, as he goes to lend a hand. For a moment Anna resents the intrusion. "Why don't that guy stay where he belongs?" she mutters, staring again into the fog in an effort to recover the mood that has been lost.

There is much scuffling up forward and some muffled orders. Then "Chris appears from around the cabin to port. He is supporting the limp form of a man dressed in dungarees, holding one of the man's arms around his neck. The deckhand, Johnson, a young, blonde Swede follows him, helping along another exhausted man in similar fashion. Anna turns to look at them."

CHRIS — (*stopping for a second*). Anna! You come help, will you? You find vhiskey in cabin. Dese fallars need drink for fix dem. Dey vas near dead.

ANNA — (*hurrying to him*). Sure — but who are they? What's the trouble?

CHRIS — Sailor fallars. Deir steamer gat wrecked. Dey been five days in open boat — four fallars — only one left able stand up. Come, Anna.

Now they are all aboard, save one, and Johnson has gone to help him. Then "Mat Burke stumbles in around the port side of the cabin. He moves slowly, feeling his way uncertainly. . . . He is stripped to the waist; has on nothing but a pair of dirty dungaree pants. He is a powerful, broad-chested, six-footer; his face handsome in a hard, rough, bold, defiant way. He is about thirty, in the full power of his heavy-muscled, immense strength. . . . He finds his way to the coil of hawser and sits down on it in an attitude of spent weariness."

His mind still wanders as he talks aloud to himself. He is still in the boat, urging, cursing, ordering the men to row. Anna comes out of the cabin with a tumbler a quarter full of whiskey for him. The light from the door falls upon his naked dirtiness and she instinctively recoils, but overcomes her first feeling of repulsion and hands him the drink.

Lifting his head slowly Burke looks upon Anna as upon a vision. " Is it dreaming I am?" he mutters. Is she a mermaid come out of the sea to torment him? The drink sets him straight. " 'Tis rale flesh and blood she is!"

BURKE — And what is a fine, handsome woman the like of you doing on this dirty scow?

ANNA — (*coldly*). Never you mind. (*Then half-amused, in spite of herself*) Say, you're a great one, honest — starting right in kidding after what you've been through.

BURKE — (*delighted — proudly*). Ah, it was nothing — aisy for a rale man with guts to him, the like of me. (*He laughs*) All in the day's work, darlin'. (*Then more seriously, but still in a boastful, confidential tone*) But I won't be denyin' 'twas a damned narrow squeak. We'd all ought to be with Davy Jones at the bottom of the sea, by rights. And only for me, I'm tellin' you, and the great strength and guts is in me, we'd be being scoffed by the fishes this minute!

ANNA — (*contemptuously*). Gee, you hate yourself, don't you? (*Then turning away from him, indifferently*) Well, you'd better come in and lie down. You must want to sleep.

BURKE — Lie down and sleep, is it? Divil a wink I'm after having for two days and nights and divil a bit I'm needing now! Let you not be thinking I'm the like of them three weak scuts come in the boat with me. I could lick the three of them sitting down with one hand tied behind me. They may be bate out but I'm not — and I've been rowing the boat with them lying in the bottom not able to raise a hand for the last two days we was in it. (*Furiously, as he sees this is making no impression upon her*) And I can lick all hands on this tub wan by wan, tired as I am!

ANNA — (*sarcastically*). Gee, ain't you a hard guy! (*Then with a trace of sympathy as she notices him swaying from weakness*) But never mind that fight talk. I'll take your word for all you've said. Go on and sit down out here, anyway, if I can't get you to come inside. (*He sits down weakly*) You're all in, you might as well own up to it.

But Mat is not one to admit to weakness. He's a fine man, and a strong man, and he knows it, and she knows it, too. And he would be after stealin' a kiss from her, seeing it is plain she is too fine a girl for the likes of the old squarehead that owns the scow! But Anna will have none of that and pushes him away with such force that in his weakened condition he falls heavily and, for a moment, is completely knocked out. Frightened now, she kneels beside him, " raising his head to her knee and staring into his face anxiously for some sign of life."

He's far from dead, is Mat, though 'twas a powerful push she gave him. " There's not a man in the world can say the same as you, that he seen Mat Burke lying at his feet and him dead to the world!"

ANNA — (*rather remorsefully*). Forget it. I'm sorry it happened, see? (*Burke rises and sits on the bench — then severely*) Only you had no right to be getting fresh with me. Listen, now, and don't go gettin' any more wrong notions. I'm on this barge because I'm making a trip with me father. The captain's my father. Now you know.

BURKE — The old square — the old Swede, I mean?

ANNA — Yes.

BURKE — (*rising and peering into her face*). Sure I might have known it, if I wasn't a bloody fool from birth. Where else'd you get that fine yellow hair; it's like a golden crown on your head.

ANNA — (*with an amused laugh*). Say, nothing stops

you, does it? (*Then attempting a severe tone again*) But don't you think you ought to be apologizing for what you said and done yust a minute ago instead of trying to kid me with that mush?

BURKE — (*indignantly*). Mush! (*Earnestly*) Indade, and I will ask your pardon a thousand times — and on my knees, if ye like. I didn't mean a word of what I said or did. (*Resentful again for a second*) But divil a woman in all the ports of the world has ever made a great fool of me that way before.

ANNA — (*with amused sarcasm*). I see. You mean you're a lady-killer and they all fall for you.

BURKE — Leave off your fooling! 'Tis that is after my getting my back up at you. 'Tis no lie I'm telling you about the women. Though it's a great jackass I am to be mistaking you, even in anger, for the like of them cows on the waterfront is the only women I've met up with since I was growed to a man. (*As Anna shrinks away from him at this, he hurries on pleadingly*) I'm a hard, rough man, and I'm not fit, I'm thinking, to be kissing the shoe-soles of a fine, decent girl the like of yourself. 'Tis only the ignorance of your kind made me see you wrong. So you'll forgive me, for the love of God, and let us be friends from this out. (*Passionately*) I'm thinkin' I'd rather be friends with you than have my wish for anything else in the world. (*He holds out his hand to her shyly.*)

ANNA — (*looking queerly at him, pleased in spite of herself*). Sure!

Now Mat would know more of Anna and of her life ashore. But she is not inclined to talk of herself. She's a governess, she tells him; "I take care of kids for people and learn them things." But let them not talk of her; let him tell her about the wreck and how he came to be saved, when so many were drowned. It was, of course, because of the great strength of him, and his rowing for two days with the three others in the bottom of the boat, dead to the world.

It was a terrible end for those who were drowned, thinks Anna. It would be, agrees Burke, for "them swabs does live on land, maybe. But for the like of us does be roaming the seas a good end, I'm telling you — quick and clane." "Yes, clean," she answers, struck by the word. "That's yust the word for — all of it — the way it makes me feel." "That's the way with the sea," Burke agrees. "I'm thinking you have a bit of it in your blood, too." And soon he is "kidding again" and all but asking her to marry him.

BURKE — It's a hard and lonesome life, the sea is. The only women you'd meet in the ports of the world who'd be willing to speak you a kind word isn't woman at all. You know the kind I mane, and they're a poor, wicked lot, God forgive them. They're looking to steal the money from you only.

ANNA — (*her face averted — rising to her feet — agitatedly*). I think — I guess I'd better see what's doing inside.

BURKE — (*afraid he has offended her*). Don't go, I'm saying. Is it I've given you offense with my talk of the like of them? Don't heed it at all! I'm clumsy in my wits when it comes to talking proper with a girl the like of you. And why wouldn't I be? Since the first day I left home for to go to sea punching coal, this is the first time I've had a word with a rale, decent woman. So don't turn your back on me now, and we beginning to be friends.

ANNA — (*forcing a smile*). I'm not sore at you, honest.

BURKE — (*gratefully*). God bless you!

ANNA — But if you honestly think the sea's such a rotten life, why don't you get out of it?

BURKE — Work on land, is it? (*She nods. He spits*

scornfully) Digging spuds in the muck from dawn to dark, I suppose? I wasn't made for it, Miss.

ANNA — (*with a laugh*). I thought you'd say that.

BURKE — But there's good jobs and bad jobs at sea, like there'd be on land. I'm thinking if it's in the stoke-hole of a proper liner I was, I'd be able to have a little house and be home to it wan week out of four. And I'm thinking that maybe then I'd have the luck to find a fine, dacent girl — the like of yourself, now — would be willing to wed with me.

. . . .

ANNA — (*held by his eyes for a moment, shrinks back from him with a strange, broken laugh*). Say — are you — going crazy? Are you trying to kid me? Proposing — to me! — for Gawd's sake! — on such short acquaintance!

"Chris comes out of the cabin and stands staring blinkingly astern. When he makes out Anna in such intimate proximity to this strange sailor, an angry expression comes over his face."

BURKE — (*following her — with a fierce, pleading insistence*). I'm telling you there's the will of God in it that brought me safe through the storm and fog to the one spot in the world where you was! Think of that now, and isn't it queer —

CHRIS — Anna! (*He comes toward them, raging, his fists clenched*) Anna, you gat in cabin, you hear!

ANNA — (*all her emotions immediately transformed into resentment at his bullying tone*). Who d'you think you're talking to — a slave?

CHRIS — (*hurt — his voice breaking*). You need gat rest, Anna. You gat sleep. (*She does not move. He turns on Burke, furiously*) What you doing here, you sailor fallar? You ain't sick like oders. You gat in fo'c'stle. Dey give you bunk. (*Threateningly*) You hurry, Ay tal you.

ANNA — But he is sick. Look at him. He can hardly stand up.

BURKE — (*straightening and throwing out his chest — with a bold laugh*). Is it giving me orders ye are, me bucko? Let ye look out, then! With wan hand, weak as I am, I can break ye in two and fling the pieces over the side — and your crew after you. (*Stopping abruptly*) I was forgetting. You're her old man and I'd not raise a fist to you for the world. (*His knees sag, he wavers and seems about to fall. Anna utters an exclamation of alarm and hurries to his side.*)

ANNA — (*taking one of his arms over her shoulder*). Come on in the cabin. You can have my bed if there ain't no other place.

BURKE — Glory be to God, is it holdin' my arm about your neck, you are? Anna! Anna! Sure it's a sweet name is suited to you.

ANNA — Ssssh! Ssssh!

BURKE — Whist, is it? Indade and I'll not. I'll be roaring it out like a foghorn over the sea! You're the girl of the world and we'll be marrying soon and I don't care who knows it.

ANNA — Ssssh! Never mind that talk. You go to sleep.

" They go out of sight into the cabin. Chris, who has been listening to Burke's last words with open-mouthed amazement, stands looking after them hopelessly."

CHRIS — (*turning suddenly and shaking his fist out at the sea — with bitter hatred*). Dat's your dirty trick, damn ole devil, you! (*In a frenzy of rage*) But, py God, you don't do dat! Not while Ay'm living! No, py God, you don't!

The curtain falls

ACT III

The scene is the interior of the cabin on the *Simeon Winthrop,* " a narrow, low-ceilinged compartment, the walls of which are painted a light brown with white trimming. . . . White curtains, clean and stiff, are at the windows. A table with two cane-bottomed chairs stands in the center of the cabin. A dilapidated wicker rocker, painted brown, is also by the table.

" It is afternoon of a sunny day about a week later " and the barge is at dock in Boston Harbor. " Anna is seated in the rocking chair by the table with a newspaper in her hand. She is not reading, but staring straight in front of her. She looks unhappy, troubled, frowningly concentrated in her thoughts. Chris wanders about the room casting quick, uneasy side glances at her face." He sings dolefully of his friend " Yosephine " in an attempt to cover his apparent uneasiness concerning Anna. The singing irritates her. " Gee," she exclaims finally, " I sure wish I was out of this dump and back in New York!"

Chris, too, is tired of lying around, but he can't quite understand why Anna is so restless. She has been having a good time in Boston, going ashore every night with Mat Burke — to picture shows. . . . Evidently it is an old quarrel with these two, and Anna resents its recurrence. Hasn't she been back on board every night at eleven? What right has he to be suspicious of her? Or Mat?

Chris is not suspicious — of her. " Yust worried." He knows " what kind of fallar those stokers are " — " de dirtiest, rough gang of no-good fallars in vorld." Strong, for fight, it may be, but there are other ways of fighting them than with fists. And Mat Burke had better have a care — which makes Anna laugh.

ANNA — (*suddenly changing her tone — persuasively*). Aw, come on, be good. What's eating you, anyway?

Don't you want no one to be nice to me except yourself?

CHRIS — (*placated*). Yes, Ay do, Anna — only not fallar on sea. But Ay like for you marry steady fallar what got good yob on land. You have little home in country all your own.

ANNA — Oh, cut it out. (*Scornfully*) Little home in the country! I wish you could have seen the little home in the country where you had me in jail till I was sixteen. Some day you're going to get me so mad with that talk, I'm going to turn loose on you and tell you — a lot of things that'll open your eyes.

CHRIS — (*alarmed*). Ay don't vant —

ANNA — I know you don't; but you keep on talking yust the same.

CHRIS — Ay don't talk no more den, Anna.

ANNA — Then promise me you'll cut out saying nasty things about Mat Burke every chance you get.

CHRIS — Vhy? You like dat fallar — very much, Anna?

ANNA — Yes, I certainly do! He's a regular man, no matter what faults he's got. One of his fingers is worth all the hundreds of men I met out there — inland.

CHRIS — (*his face darkening*). Maybe you tank you love him, den?

ANNA — (*defiantly*). What of it if I do?

CHRIS — Maybe — you tank you — marry him?

ANNA — No! (*Chris' face lights up with relief. Anna continues, slowly, a trace of sadness in her voice*) If I'd met him four years ago — or even two years ago — I'd have jumped at the chance, I tell you that straight. And I would now — only he's such a simple guy — a big kid — and I ain't got the heart to fool him. (*Breaking off suddenly*) But don't never say again he ain't good enough for me. It's me ain't good enough for him.

She must be crazy to talk that way, thinks Chris. Well, Anna agrees, perhaps she is. There have been times the last two or three days when she has thought so. . . . Now she has gone to walk to the end of the deck. Out the window of the cabin Chris shakes his fist in the direction of the sea. "Dirty ole davil, you!" he mumbles.

The door is flung open by Mat Burke. " Chris scowls at the intruder, and his hand instinctively goes back to the sheath knife on his hip. Burke is dressed up — wears a cheap blue suit, a striped cotton shirt, a black tie and black shoes newly shined. His face is beaming with good humor. For this, as he has planned it, will be his wedding day.

" I'll take this chance when we're alone to have a word with you," he tells the scowling Chris; " and that word is soon said. I'm marrying your Anna before this day is out and you might as well make up your mind to it, whether you like it or no."

" That's easy to say," sneers Chris. But as it happens Anna has told him differently. She will never marry fallar like him.

BURKE — I'll not believe it. 'Tis a great old liar you are, and a divil to be making a power of trouble if you had your way. But 'tis not trouble I'm looking for, and me sitting down here. (*Earnestly*) Let us be talking it out now as man to man. You're her father, and wouldn't it be a shame for us to be at each other's throats like a pair of dogs, and I married with Anna. So out with the truth, man alive. What is it you're holding against me at all?

CHRIS — (*a bit placated by Burke's evident sincerity*). Vell — I don't vant for Anna to gat married. Listen, you fallar. Ay'm ole man. Ay don't see Anna for fifteen years. She vas all Ay gat in vorld. And now vhen she come on first trip — you tank Ay want her leave me 'lone again?

BURKE — (*heartily*). Let you not be thinking I have no heart at all for the way you'd be feeling.

CHRIS — (*pleading*). Dan you do right tang, eh?

You ship avay again, leave Anna alone. (*Cajoling*) Big fallar like you dat's on sea, he don't need vife. He gat new gel in every port, you know dat.

BURKE — (*angry for a second*). God stiffen you! (*Then calmly*) I'll not be giving you the lie on that. But divil take you, there's a time comes to every man on sea or land isn't a born fool, when he's sick of the lot of them cows and wearing his heart out to meet up with a fine dacent girl, and have a home to call his own and be rearing up children in it. 'Tis small use you're asking me to leave Anna. She's the wan woman of the world for me and I can't live without her now, I'm thinking.

But there's no agreement in them. Chris will not be beaten, neither by no-good sailor fallar like Burke, or by that ole davil, sea. And for all Burke's struggle to keep his temper, they're soon hurling curses at each other. And now Chris, in a towering rage, springs at Burke with his sheath knife in his hand. He's no match for the younger man, however, and is flung back, empty-handed, against the cabin wall. Before they can resume the fight Anna has entered the cabin. Like whipped boys they try to lie themselves clear of her suspicion that they have been at each other's throats.

But Burke is in no mood to let the argument pass entirely. It may be as well finished one time as another. Especially as Anna is demanding an explanation. So "he draws a deep breath, and then plunges in boldly."

BURKE — The whole of it's in a few words only. So's he'd make no mistake, and him hating the sight of me, I told him in his teeth I loved you. (*Passionately*) And that's God's truth, Anna, and well you know it!

CHRIS — (*scornfully — forcing a laugh*). Ho-ho! He tal same tang to gel every port he go!

ANNA — (*resentfully*). Shut up, can't you? (*Then to Burke*) I know it's true, Mat. I don't mind what he says.

BURKE — God bless you.

ANNA — And then what?

BURKE — And then — and then I said — I said I was sure — I told him I thought you have a bit of love for me, too. (*Passionately*) Say you do, Anna! Let you not destroy me entirely, for the love of God!

ANNA — (*deeply moved*). So you told him that, Mat? No wonder if he was mad. (*Forcing out the words*) Well, maybe it's true, Mat. Maybe I do. I been thinking and thinking — I didn't want to, Mat, I'll own up to that — I tried to cut it out — but — (*she laughs helplessly*) I guess I can't help it anyhow. So I guess I do, Mat. (*Then with a sudden joyous defiance*) Sure I do! What's the use of kidding myself different? Sure I love you, Mat!

CHRIS — (*with a cry of pain*). Anna!

BURKE — God be praised!

ANNA — And I ain't never loved a man in my life before, you can always believe that — no matter what happens.

BURKE — Sure I do be believing ivery word you iver said or iver will say. And 'tis you and me will be having a grand, beautiful life together to the end of our day.

With that he tries to kiss her, and though at first she turns away, she yields finally, " overcome by a fierce impulse of passionate love. She takes his head in both her hands and holds his face close to hers, staring into his eyes. Then she kisses him full on the lips."

Then " pushing him away from her and forcing a broken laugh," she cries " good-by!" and starts for the door. It is mystifying to Burke, this " good-by," now that they have just been pledged to each other with full understanding. But Chris begins to understand. And there is a " foolish hope in his eyes " as he refuses to shake hands with the exultant Burke, or to consider the matter settled. " 'Tis a rotten bad loser ye are, divil mend you!" cries Burke. "Ay don't lose," answers Chris. "Anna says she like you little bit, but you don't hear her say marry you, Ay bet."

Nor does he; for Anna, quiet now, but determined, confirms his hope. She cannot marry Mat; the kiss was really her "good-by." But why, he demands; why?

ANNA — (*resolutely*). I can't tell you — and I won't. I got a good reason — and that's all you need to know. I can't marry you, that's all there is to it. (*Distractedly*) So, for Gawd's sake, let's talk of something else.

BURKE — I'll not! (*Then fearfully*) Is it married to someone else you are — in the West maybe?

ANNA — (*vehemently*). I should say not.

BURKE — (*regaining his courage*). To the divil with all other reasons then. They don't matter with me at all. (*Masterfully*) I'm thinkin' you're the like of them women can't make up their mind till they're drove to it. Well, then, I'll make up your mind for you bloody quick. (*He takes her by the arm, grinning to soften his serious bullying*) We've had enough of talk! Let you be going into your room now and be dressing in your best and we'll be going ashore.

CHRIS — (*aroused — angrily*). No, py God, she don't do dat! (*He takes hold of her arm.*)

Anna, instinctively repelled by Mat's new tone of authority, draws away from him. Where does he get that stuff? What right has he to be ordering her about? Or Chris? Or any man? She'll have none of either of them, if it comes to that. And stung finally by their ugly quarreling over possession of her she turns defiantly, "blazing out at them passionately."

ANNA — You can go to hell, both of you! (*She laughs wildly*) You're yust like all the rest of them — you two!

Gawd, you'd think I was a piece of furniture! I'll show you! Sit down now! (*As they hesitate — furiously*) Sit down and let me talk for a minute! You're all wrong, see? Listen to me! I'm going to tell you something — and then I'm going to beat it. (*To Burke — with a harsh laugh*) I'm going to tell you a funny story, so pay attention. (*Pointing at Chris*) I've been meaning to turn it loose on him every time he'd get my goat with his bull about keeping me safe inland. I wasn't going to tell you but you forced me into it. What's the dif? It's all wrong, anyway, and you might as well get cured that way as any other. Only don't forget what you said a minute ago about it not mattering to you what other reason I got, so long as I wasn't married to no one else.

BURKE — (*manfully*). That's my word and I'll stick to it!

ANNA — (*laughing bitterly*). What a chance! You make me laugh, honest! Want to bet you will? Wait 'n' see! (*She stands looking from one to the other of the two men with a hard, mocking smile. Then she begins, fighting to control her emotion*) First thing is, I want to tell you two guys something. You was goin' on 's if one of you had got to own me. But nobody owns me, see? — 'cepting myself. I'll do what I please, and no man, I don't give a hoot who he is, can tell me what to do! I ain't asking either of you for a living. I can make it myself — one way or another — I'm my own boss, so put that in your pipe and smoke it! You and your orders!

BURKE — (*protestingly*). I wasn't meaning it that way at all and well you know it. You've no call to be raising this rumpus with me. (*Pointing to Chris*) 'Tis him you've a right —

ANNA — I'm coming to him. But you — you did mean it that way, too. You sounded — yust like all the rest.

(*Hysterically*) But, damn it, shut up! Let me talk for a change!

BURKE — 'Tis quare, rough talk, that — for a dacent girl the like of you!

ANNA — Decent? Who told you I was? (*Chris is sitting with bowed shoulders, his head in his hands. She shakes him violently*) Don't go to sleep, Old Man. Listen here, I'm talking to you now.

CHRIS — (*with frightened foreboding*). Ay don't vant for hear it. You vas going out of head, Ay tank, Anna.

ANNA — (*violently*). Well, living with you is enough to drive anyone off their nut. Your bunk about the farm being so fine! Didn't I write you year after year how rotten it was and what a dirty slave them cousins made of me? What'd you care? Nothing! Not even enough to come out and see me. That crazy bull about wanting to keep me away from the sea don't go down with me. You yust didn't want to be bothered with me. You're like all the rest of 'em.

CHRIS — (*feebly*). It ain't so —

ANNA — But one thing I never wrote you. It was one of them cousins that you think is such nice people — the youngest son — Paul — that started me wrong. (*Loudly*) It wasn't none of my fault, I hated him worse'n hell and he knew it. But he was big and strong (*Pointing to Burke*) like you.

BURKE — (*half springing to his feet — his fists clenched*). God blarst it!

CHRIS — (*in a cry of horrified pain*). Anna!

ANNA — (*to Chris*). That was why I run away from the farm. That was what made me get a yob as nurse girl in St. Paul. And you think that was a nice yob for a girl, too, don't you? With all them nice inland fellers yust looking for a chance to marry me, I s'pose. Marry me? What a chance! They wasn't looking for marrying. I'm owning up to everything fair and square. I was caged in, I tell you — yust like in yail — taking care of other people's kids — listening to 'em bawling and crying day and night — when I wanted to be out — and I was lonesome — lonesome as hell! (*With a sudden weariness in her voice*) So I gave up finally. What was the use?

She stops and looks at the two men. Both are motionless and silent. Chris seems in a stupor of despair, his house of cards fallen about him. Burke's face is livid with the rage that is eating him up but he is too stunned and bewildered yet to find a vent for it.

ANNA — You don't say nothing, either of you — but I know what you're thinking. You're like all the rest! (*To Chris*) And who's to blame for it, me or you? If you'd even acted like a man — if you'd even been a regular father and had me with you — maybe things would be different!

CHRIS — (*in agony*). Don't talk dat vay, Anna! Ay go crazy! Ay von't listen! (*He puts his hands over his ears.*)

ANNA — (*infuriated by his action*). You will too listen! (*She pulls his hands from his ears*) You — keeping me safe inland — I wasn't no nurse girl the last two years — I lied when I wrote you — I was in a house, that's what! — yes, that kind of a house — the kind that sailors like you and Mat goes to when you're in port — and your nice inland men, too — and all men, God damn 'em! I hate 'em! I hate 'em!

" She breaks into hysterical sobbing, throwing herself into the chair and hiding her face in her hands on the table. The two men have sprung to their feet," stunned by the revelation. In mocking bitterness Anna turns to Mat to remind him of his promise — that nothing would count with him so long as she wasn't married already. " So I suppose you want me to get dressed and go ashore?" Her laugh mocks the suggestion. " Yes you do," she adds, sneeringly. " God stiffen you," he moans.

Anna tries to keep up her hard, bitter tone as she continues, but gradually, in spite of her, a note of pitiful pleading creeps in.

" I s'pose if I tried to tell you I wasn't — that — no more—you'd believe me, wouldn't you? Yes, you would! And if I told you that yust getting out in this barge, and being on the sea had changed me, and made me feel different about things, 's if all I'd been through wasn't me and didn't count and was yust like it never happened — you'd laugh, wouldn't you? And you'd die laughing sure if I said that meeting you that funny way that night in the fog, and afterwards seeing that you was straight goods stuck on me, had got me to thinking for the first time, and I sized you up as a different kind of man — a sea man as different from the ones on land as water is from mud — and that was why I got stuck on you, too. I wanted to marry you and fool you but I couldn't. Don't you see how I'd changed? I couldn't marry you with you believing a lie — and I was ashamed to tell you the truth — till the both of you forced my hand, and I seen you was the same as all the rest. And now, give me a bawling out and beat it, like I can tell you're going to."

" She stops, looking at Burke. He is silent, his face averted, his features beginning to work with fury. She pleads passionately." " Will you believe it if I tell you that loving you has made me — clean? It's the straight goods, honest!" He makes no reply. " Like hell you will! You're like all the rest!"

With his voice trembling with passion, Burke arouses himself from his stupor. " The rest, is it?" he shouts. " God's curse on you! Clane is it, you slut you? I'll be killing you now!"

" He picks up the chair on which he has been sitting,

and swinging it high over his shoulder springs toward her. Chris rushes forward with a cry of alarm, trying to ward off the blow from his daughter. Anna looks up into Burke's eyes with the fearlessness of despair."

BURKE — (*throwing the chair away into a corner of the room*). I can't do it, God help me, and your two eyes looking at me. (*Furiously*) Though I do be thinkin' I'd have a good right to smash your skull like a rotten egg. Was there ever a woman in the world had the rottenness in her that you have, and was there iver the man the like of me was made the fool of the world, and me thinking thoughts about you, and dreaming dreams of the fine life we'd have when we'd be wedded! (*His voice high-pitched in lamentation*) Yerra, God help me! I'm destroyed entirely and my heart is broken in bits! I'm asking God Himself was it for this He'd have me roaming the earth since I was a lad, only to come to black shame in the end, where I'd be giving a power of love to a woman is the same as outhers you'd meet in any hooker-shanty in port with red gowns on them and paint on their grinning mugs, would be sleeping with any man for a dollar or two.

ANNA — (*in a scream*). Don't Mat! For Gawd's sake! (*Then raging and pounding on the table with her hands*) Get out of here! Leave me alone! Get out of here!

BURKE — (*his anger rushing back on him*). I'll be going, surely! And I'll be drinking sloos of whiskey will wash that black kiss of yours off my lips; and I'll be getting dead rotten drunk so I'll not remember if 'twas iver born you was at all; and I'll be shipping away on some boat will take me to the other end of the world where I'll never see your face again!

CHRIS — (*grasping Burke by the arm*). No, you don't go! Ay tank maybe it's better Anna marry you now.

BURKE — (*shaking Chris off ——furiously*). Lave go of me, ye old ape! Marry her, is it? I'd see her roasting in hell first! I'm shipping away out of this, I'm telling you! (*Pointing to Anna*) And my curse on you and the curse of Almighty God and all the Saints! You've destroyed me this day and may you lie awake in the long nights tormented with thoughts of Mat Burke and the great wrong you've done him!

Crying out in anguish Anna starts to run after him as he strides out the door. As she stops suddenly and hides her face in her outstretched arms, sobbing, old Chris tries to comfort her. "Ain't your fault, Anna; Ay know dat," he says. "It's dat ole davil sea do dis to me. . . . It's her dirty tricks! It was all right on barge with yust you and me. Den she bring dat Irish fallar in fog, she make you like him, she make you fight with me all time! If dat Irish fallar don't naver come, you don't naver tal me dem tangs, Ay don't naver know and everytang's all right. (*He shakes his fist again*) Dirty ole davil!

ANNA — (*with spent weariness*). Oh, what's the use? Go on ashore and get drunk.

CHRIS — (*goes to the door, silent and stupid — then turns*). You vait here, Anna?

ANNA — Maybe — maybe not. Maybe I'll get drunk, too. Maybe I'll — but what the hell do you care what I do? Go on and beat it.

Chris turns stupidly and goes out. Anna is sitting at the table staring straight in front of her as the curtain falls.

ACT IV

Again the cabin, "about nine o'clock of a foggy night two days later." Anna, dressed again in the clothes she wore into Johnny-the-Priest's saloon the day she arrived from St. Paul, is ready to leave. Her suitcase is packed and sitting in the center of the floor. "Her face is pale and she looks terribly tired and worn, as if the two days just past had been ones of suffering and sleepless nights. She stares before her despondently, her chin in her hands."

There is a knock on the door, followed by the shuffling entrance of old Chris. "He is in a bleary, bedraggled condition, suffering from the after-effects of his drunk." In his hand he carries a pail of beer. Shiftily he avoids Anna's direct gaze, and winces when she speaks to him.

She is not without sympathy for him, in spite of the contempt she affects, and his attitude toward her is one of great pity. Even when she confesses that although she has been ready to go back to New York for two days, with her ticket bought and all, she has waited and waited — hoping against hope that she may see Mat Burke again. "If he did come back it'd only be 'cause he wanted to beat me up or kill me, I suppose. But even if he did I'd rather have him come than not show up at all. I wouldn't care what he did."

Chris understands now. "Ay'm sorry for you lak hell he don't come, Anna. . . . Ay'm sorry for everytang Ay do wrong for you, Anna. Ay vant for you be happy all rest of your life vor make up. It make you happy marry dat Irish fallar, Ay vant dat, too."

ANNA — (*dully*). Well, there ain't no chance. But I'm glad you think different about it, anyway.

CHRIS — (*supplicatingly*). And you tank — maybe — you forgive me sometime?

ANNA — (*with a wan smile*). I'll forgive you right now.

Chris — (*seizing her hand and kissing it — brokenly*). Anna lilla! Anna lilla!

ANNA — (*touched, but a bit embarrassed*). Don't bawl about it. There ain't nothing to forgive, anyway.

It ain't your fault and it ain't mine and it ain't his, neither. We're all poor nuts and things happen, and we yust get mixed in wrong, that's all.

CHRIS — (*eagerly*). You say right tang, Anna, py golly! It ain't nobody's fault! (*Shaking his fist*) It's dat ole davil, sea!

ANNA — (*with an exasperated laugh*). Gee, won't you ever can that stuff?

Chris doesn't attempt to answer her. He has intimated that he has fixed something for her so that whatever else happens she will never again have to return to her old life, and she is curious to know what it is. He is "shipping away on sea again," he tells her. He has signed as a bosun on a steamer sailing next day for Cape Town, Africa. It is the best way, he thinks. He does not want to spoil her life, as he had her mother's, and, perhaps, if "the ole davil sea" gets him back it will leave Anna alone. And he has arranged with the men in the steamship office to pay over to her each month all his wages.

To Anna, this is the worst possible thing Chris could do, to leave her alone, as he had left her mother before her; to go on dodging his responsibilities — "But what's the use of talking. You ain't right, that's what," she concludes, a little pitifully. "I'll never blame you for nothing, no more. But how could you figure out that was fixing me —"

. . . .

Chris has gone to lie down in his cabin. All that he can think to do he has done. Anna has forgiven him and a little embarrassedly permitted him to kiss her good-night. Now she is walking distractedly up and down the cabin "trying desperately to banish her thoughts." There is a heavy step on deck outside the cabin. A moment later, as Anna crouches back in a corner of the cabin, Mat Burke appears in the doorway. "He is in bad shape, his clothes torn and dirty, covered with sawdust, as if he had been groveling or sleeping on barroom floors." His face and hands are bruised; his eyes are bloodshot and carry an expression of "wild, mental turmoil, of impotent animal rage baffled by its own abject misery."

He stands for a moment in the doorway as he announces his presence. "Let you not be hiding from me, whoever's here — though 'tis well you know I'd have a right to come back and murder you. . . . There's no one here, I'm thinking, and 'tis a great fool I am to be coming. . . . Yerra, Mat Burke, 'tis a great jackass you've become, and what's into you at all, at all? She's gone out of this long ago, I'm telling you, and you'll never see her face again."

Anna steps out of the shadow. In her hand she holds a revolver she has found in Chris' coat, but it has no frightening effect on Mat. He walks into it directly, in spite of the girl's warning. "Let you shoot, then," he challenges, with a "sudden, wild grief." "Let you shoot, I'm saying, and be done with it! Let you end me with a shot and I'll be thanking you, for it's a rotten dog's life I've lived the past two days since I've known what you are, 'till I'm after wishing I was never born at all."

ANNA — (*overcome — letting the revolver drop to the floor*). What d'you want coming here? Why don't you beat it? Go on! (*She sinks down into the rocking chair.*)

BURKE — 'Tis right you'd be asking me why did I come. (*Then angrily*) 'Tis because 'tis a great weak fool of the world I am, and me tormented with the wickedness you'd told of yourself, and drinking oceans of booze that would make me forget. Forget? Divil a word I'd forget, and your face grinning always in front of my eyes, awake or asleep, till I do be thinking a madhouse is the proper place for me.

ANNA — (*glancing at his hands and face — scorn-*

fully). You look like you ought to be put away some place. Wonder you wasn't pulled in. You been scrapping, too, ain't you?

BURKE — I have — with every scut would take his coat off to me! (*Fiercely*) And each time I'd be hitting one a clout in the mug, it wasn't his face I'd be seeing at all but yours; and me wanting to drive you a blow would knock you out of this world where I wouldn't be seeing or thinking more of you.

. . . .

ANNA — (*resentfully*). Then get out! No one's holding you!

BURKE — (*bewilderedly*). And me listen to that talk from a woman like you and be frightened to close her mouth with a slap! Oh, God help me, I'm a yellow coward for all men to spit at! (*Then furiously*) But I'll not be getting out of this till I've had me word. (*Raising his fist*) And let you look out how you'd drive me! (*Letting his fist fall*) Don't be angry now! I'm raving like a real lunatic, I'm thinking, and the sorrow you put on me has my brains drowned in grief. (*Grasping her arm intensely*) Tell me it's a lie, I'm saying! That's what I'm after coming to hear you say.

ANNA — (*dully*). A lie? What?

BURKE — (*with passionate entreaty*). All the badness you told me two days back. Sure it must be a lie! You was only making game of me, wasn't you? Tell me 'twas a lie, Anna, and I'll be saying prayers of thanks on my two knees to the Almighty God!

ANNA — (*terribly shaken — faintly*). I can't, Mat. (*As he turns away imploringly*) Oh, Mat, won't you see that no matter what I was I ain't that any more? Why listen! I packed up my bag this afternoon and went ashore. I'd been waiting here all alone for two days, thinking maybe you'd come back — thinking maybe you'd think over all I'd said — and maybe — oh, I don't know what I was hoping! But I was afraid to even go out of the cabin for a second, honest — when you didn't show up I went to the railroad station. I was going to New York. I was going back.

BURKE — (*hoarsely*). God's curse on you!

ANNA — Listen, Mat! You hadn't come and I'd gave up hope. But — in the station — I couldn't go. I'd bought my ticket and everything. (*She takes the ticket from her dress and tries to hold it before his eyes*) But I got to thinking about you — and I couldn't take the train — I couldn't! So I came back here — to wait some more. Oh Mat, don't you see I've changed? Can't you forgive what's dead and gone — and forget it?

BURKE — Forget, is it? I'll not forget till my dying day, I'm telling you, and me tormented with thoughts.

Mat, too, has " signed on " and is sailing at noon the next day, and by another of the sea's tricks, it may be, he is sailing on the same ship with old Chris for Cape Town. The irony of it fills Anna with bitter laughter, the like of which he cannot understand. Nor will she explain. It's a secret he'll learn soon enough.

ANNA — (*cynically*). What kind of a place is this Cape Town? Plenty of dames there, I suppose?

BURKE — The divil with them. Is it no shame you have at all? I'm a fool to be wasting talk on you and you hardened in badness. I'll go out of this and lave you alone forever. (*He starts for the door — then stops to turn on her furiously*) And I suppose 'tis the same lies you told them all before that you told to me?

ANNA — That's a lie! I never did!

BURKE — (*miserably*). You'd be saying that, anyway.

ANNA — Are you trying to accuse me — of being in love — really in love — with *them?*

BURKE — I'm thinking you were, surely.

ANNA — (*furiously*). You mutt, you! I've stood

enough from you. Don't you dare! — (*With scornful bitterness*) Love 'em! Oh, my Gawd! You damn thick-head! Love 'em? (*Savagely*) I hated 'em, I tell you! Hated 'em, hated 'em, hated 'em! And may Gawd strike me dead this minute, and my mother, too, if she was alive, if I ain't telling you the honest truth!

BURKE — If I could only be believing you now!

ANNA — (*distractedly*). Oh, what's the use? What's the use of me talking? What's the use of anything? (*Pleadingly*) Oh, Mat, you mustn't think that for a second! You mustn't! Think all the other bad about me you want to and I won't kick, 'cause you've a right to. But don't think that! (*On the point of tears*) I couldn't bear it! It'd be yust too much to know you was going away where I'd never see you again — thinking that about me!

BURKE — (*after an inward struggle — tensely*). If I was believing — that you'd never had love for any other man in the world but me — I could be forgetting the rest, maybe.

ANNA — (*with a cry of joy*). Mat!

BURKE — (*slowly*). If 'tis the truth you're after telling, I'd have a right, maybe, to believe you'd changed — and that I'd changed you myself till the thing you'd been all your life wouldn't be you any more at all.

ANNA — (*hanging on his words — breathlessly*). Oh, Mat! That's what I've been trying to tell you all along!

BURKE — For I've a power of strength in me to lead men the way I want, and women; and I'm thinking I'd change you to be a new woman entirely so I'd never know, or you either, what kind of a woman you'd been in the past at all.

ANNA — Yes, you could, Mat! I know you could!

BURKE — And I'm thinking 'twasn't your fault, maybe, but having that old ape for a father that left you to grow up alone, made you what you was. And if I could be believing 'tis only me you —

ANNA — You got to believe it, Mat! What can I do? I'll do anything, anything you want to prove I'm not lying.

So it occurs to Mat that if Anna will swear an oath, "a terrible, fearful oath," that would send her soul straight to the divils in hell if she was lying—he might be able to forgive her. She is eager for the test, as he takes from his pocket an old, battered crucifix and bids her swear on that.

"Swear I'm the only man in the world iver you felt love for! . . . That you'll be forgetting from this day all the badness you have done and never do the like of it again. . . . And may the blackest curse of God strike you if you're lying!" To all of which Anna feelingly subscribes.

"Oh, glory be to God, I'm after believing you now!" shouts Mat Burke, beaming with joy — till a second terrible doubt assails him. Is she a Catholic? Does taking an oath on a Catholic cross mean anything to her?

"I ain't nothing," admits Anna. "What's the difference? Didn't you hear me swear?"

For a moment he hesitates, and then the great passion of him overcomes all his doubts. "Oath or no oath, 'tis no matter!" he shouts defiantly, as if challenging fate. "We'll be wedded in the morning with the help of God." And then, still more defiantly, he adds: "We'll be happy now, the two of us, in spite of the divil!" as he "crushes her to him and kisses her fiercely."

From the cabin door old Chris appears. For an instant there is the old look of hatred for Mat Burke in his eyes; "then a look of resignation and relief takes its place," and he bravely offers to share his beer with them that they may all drink in celebration.

It is then that Mat learns for the first time that he and Chris are to be shipmates. His first reaction is one of resentment — that Chris should think of sailing again and leaving Anna alone. But the girl assures him it is better that way. "You got to go, too. We'll need the money. . . . I'll get a little house somewheres and I'll make a regular place for you to come back to, wait and see . . .!"

But Burke is still a little troubled in his mind. There's the thought of Anna's lack of religion, and —

"It's funny," ventures old Chris moodily, and speaking "with somber premonition," "it's queer, yes — you and me shipping on same boat dat vay. It ain't right. Ay don't know. It's dat funny vay ole davil, sea, do her vorst dirty tricks, yes. It's so."

"I'm fearing maybe you have the right of it for once, divil take you," admits Mat gloomily.

"Gee, Mat, you're not agreeing with him, are you?" cries Anna, her gaiety just a little forced. Into their glasses she pours what is left of the beer. "Come on!" she calls, her arm around his shoulder; "Here's to the sea, no matter what! Be a game sport and drink to that. Come on!"

They gulp down the liquor, as from the window, where Chris is standing "looking out into the night, lost in his somber preoccupation," comes a mumbled prophecy.

"Fog, fog, fog, all bloody time! You can't see vhere you vas going, no! Only dat ole davil sea, she know!"

Mat and Anna are staring at him, it may be a little frightened, as from the harbor comes the "muffled, mournful wail of steamers' whistles," and the curtain falls.

"A BILL OF DIVORCEMENT"

A Drama in Three Acts

By Clemence Dane

MANY interesting incidents cluster around the story of "A Bill of Divorcement" and its production in America. The author of the play, Clemence Dane, is an English actress, and her play was a feature of the 1920-21 season in London. Discharged from hospital about the time of the play's production, after having spent the better part of three years being literally made over by the war surgeons, Allan Pollock, an English actor, attended the performance. At this time Mr. Pollock had practically given up returning to the stage, but the character of Hilary Fairfield fascinated him. He, too, had been a victim of the war; he, too, had spent weary months in the care of the medics. And though there never had been any doubt as to his mental condition, which is the basis of Fairfield's tragedy, he felt that he was in a much better position to judge the temperamental reactions of Miss Dane's leading character than most other actors. Within the week following he had convinced the owners that he could play Hilary, and had bought from them the American rights to the drama.

Charles B. Dillingham, while this was happening in London, was making up his mind to have a fling at the production of dramatic plays in New York during the approaching season. He had previously confined his attention to elaborate musical comedies. And just as he had decided to try his hand at drama along came Mr. Pollock's proposition that he undertake the direction of an American tour of "A Bill of Divorcement," to which he agreed.

The play was presented in New York the evening of October 10, 1921. It was one of the busiest weeks of the fall season and there were several other plays opening against it. The play reviewers were therefore scattered, the greater number attending the first performance of a new American comedy by Booth Tarkington. Most of the assistant reviewers who were assigned to cover the "Divorcement" play wrote favorable reports of the opening, but with a guarded enthusiasm. Later in the week the leading reviewers began dropping in upon the performance, and by Sunday their columns were overflowing with their praise of it.

The playgoing public, however, did not immediately respond. Pollock, though he had played in America before the war, was little known; Miss Dane was not known at all, and the impression had spread that "A Bill of Divorcement" was a war play and unpleasant. Being early in the season, there was a long list of more promising entertainments to choose from.

For two weeks, it may be three, the play languished. It was, the lessees of the theatre declared, a failure, a "critics' success," than which there is no other kind of success that gives the commercial manager such severe pain. Another attraction was booked to follow "A Bill of Divorcement" the succeeding week, and the storehouse doors were yawning.

Then something happened. Almost overnight a change took place in the public's attention. People began to buy seats and demand to know why the play was being withdrawn. Another firm of managers, with a theatre free, put in a bid for the attraction. "A Bill of Divorcement" was moved from the Cohan Theatre to the Times Square and for the next several months it was the biggest kind of a success.

This play was written by Miss Dane at a time when a divorce bill, intended to make such changes in the existing English laws as seemed necessary to correct current abuses, many of them growing out of the hasty "war marriages," was under discussion. She asks her audiences, therefore, to imagine that the divorce bill has become the law of the land and sets the time of the action of the play ahead to 1933.

The scene is in the hall, "obviously used as the common room," of a small country house in England. It is Christmas day and the Fairfields — Miss Hester Fairfield, "one of those twitching, high-minded, elderly ladies in black, who keep a grievance as they might keep a pet dog — as soon as it dies they replace it by another," and her niece by marriage, Margaret Fairfield, are at breakfast.

"Such a little, pretty, helpless-looking woman as Margaret has generally half-a-dozen big sons and a husband to bully; but Margaret has only a daughter, and her way of looking at even the chair in which that daughter ought to be sitting, is the way of a child whose doll has suddenly come to life. For the rest, she is so youthfully anxious and simple and charming that the streak of gray in her hair puzzles you. You wonder what trouble has fingered it. It does not occur to you that she is quite thirty-five."

At the moment Margaret Fairfield is doing what she can to allay the aunt's irritation, caused not alone by the non-appearance of the seventeen-year-old daughter of the house, Sydney Fairfield, but by the very thought that the girl had danced until three in the morning — and on Christmas day, too! Margaret, it appears, is to be married on New Year's to Gray Meredith, and though Miss Fairfield is severely pained by the prospect she finds some consolation in the thought that Sydney, at least, will benefit from the discipline of a step-father, "if you can call him a step-father when her father's still alive."

When Sydney does come out of her room she is seen to be "physically a bigger, fairer edition of Margaret," but there the likeness ends. "Her manner is brisk and decided. She is very sure of herself, but when she loses her temper, as she often does, she loses her aplomb and reveals the schoolgirl. Her attitude to the world is that of justice untempered, except where her mother is in question, by mercy. But she is very fond of her mother."

Also she is extremely annoyed by the constant hectoring and criticism of her aunt. She is seventeen; she has left school; she is about to become engaged, and with the confidence and assurance of her years she purposes to come pretty close to ordering her own life from then on. To which emphatic statement of intention her mother interposes a gentle objection. "I don't know what you mean, Sydney — but don't!" she pleads.

SYDNEY — I mean that I'm not going to let Aunt Hester interfere in my affairs like she does in yours. That's what I mean.

MISS FAIRFIELD — These are the manners that they teach you at your fine school, I suppose.

SYDNEY — Never mind, auntie, I've had my lessons in the holidays, too. You needn't think I haven't watched the life you've led mother over this divorce business.

MARGARET — (*distressed at the discussion*). Sydney! Sydney!

SYDNEY — (*remorselessly*). Well, hasn't she? What prevented you from marrying Gray ages ago? Father's been out of his mind long enough, poor man! You knew you were free to be free. You knew you were making Gray miserable and yourself miserable — and yet, though that divorce law has been in force for years, it's taken you all this time to fight your scruples! At least, you call them scruples! What you really mean is Aunt Hester and her prayer book. And now, when you have at last consented to give yourself a chance of being happy — when it's Christmas day and you're going to be married at New Year's — still you let Aunt Hester sit at your own breakfast table and insult you with talk about deadly sin. It's no use pretending you didn't, auntie, because mother left my door open and I heard you.

MARGARET — (*with a certain dignity*). Sydney, I can take care of myself.

SYDNEY — (*oblivious of it*). Take care of yourself! As if everybody didn't ride roughshod over you when I'm not there.

MARGARET — Yes, but my pet, you mustn't break out like this. Of course your aunt knows you don't really mean to be rude —

SYDNEY — I do mean to be rude to her when she's rude to you.

MARGARET — My dear, you quite misunderstood your aunt.

SYDNEY — Oh, no, I didn't, mother!

It is a little too much for Margaret, all this family bickering. She can't quite help feeling that she should tacitly endorse the conventions as they are represented by Miss Fairfield, and yet her heart pleads earnestly for the sympathy and understanding of Sydney. She wants to believe that she is doing right in marrying Gray, that she did right in availing herself of the divorce law to free herself from the incompetent Hilary. And yet there is a lingering twinge of conscience that frightens her.

But to Sydney "it's morbid to have a conscience." "If father had been dead fifteen years, would you say, 'I hope I'm doing right!'" she demands of her mother. "And he *is* dead. His mind's dead. You know you've done all you can and you're frightfully in love with Gray . . . and he with you. So what's the worry about? Aunt Hester? What people like Aunt Hester choose to think? I call it morbid!"

Still Margaret is troubled. For one reason, because Sydney gets so excited; because she is at times so much like her father. For another, she can't quite reconcile herself to the thought of Sydney being engaged — at seventeen. True, Margaret had thought herself in love with Hilary at seventeen; had married at that age, in fact. But that was because of the war.

SYDNEY — It's extraordinary to me — whenever you middle-aged people want to excuse yourselves for anything you've done that you know you oughtn't to have done, you say it was the war. How could a war make you get married if you didn't want to?

MARGARET — (*groping for words*). It was the feel in the air. They say the smell of blood sends horses crazy. That was the feel. One did mad things. Hilary — your father — he was going out — the trenches — to be hurt. And he was so fond of me he frightened me. I was so sorry. I thought I cared. Can't you understand?

SYDNEY — No. Either you care or you don't.

MARGARET — (*passionately*). How can you know until it happens to you? How was I to know there was more to it than keeping house and looking after Hilary — and you? How was I to know?

SYDNEY — (*doubtfully*). Is there so much more to it?

MARGARET — Yes.

SYDNEY — I don't believe there is for some people. Why, it's just what I want — to look after Kit and a house of my own and — oh, at least half-a-dozen kids.

The frankness of the rising generation is sometimes a little frightening to Margaret. She is never exactly easy with Sydney. And the girl knows it and laughs. "If you had to choose between me and Gray," she says,, "it wouldn't be Gray who'd lose you." To which Margaret a little doubtfully replies, "I hope I'd do right!"

The bell announcing the arrival of Gray Meredith

sends Margaret flying to dress for church, and leaves Sydney to receive him. "He is about forty, tall, dark, and quiet, very sure of himself, and quite indifferent to the effect he makes on other people. As he is a man who never has room in his head for more than one idea at a time, and as, for the last five years, that idea has been Margaret, the rest of the world doesn't get much out of him. But mention her and he behaves exactly like a fire being poked."

He accepts good-naturedly Sydney's banter, thanks her for the Christmas tie and sends her scurrying to the car in search of the gift he has brought for her and left outside with Kit — Kit being the rector's son to whom Sydney is engaged.

He turns then to Margaret, coming down the stairs flushed with happiness, and, it may be, a little conscious of the new gown she is wearing. It is not altogether new to Gray, however, seeing that he and Sydney had stolen it away while they took it downtown to match it with the silver fox furs which are Gray's gift to her.

Now she has the furs on, and is radiant — save for a shadowless fear that seems to be stalking her this morning. She feels it when Gray calls her "Meg." It is his idea of a pet name that shall be his own for her, one that no one else uses. But someone else has called her "Meg," and she would have him make a name for her that shall be new — all new — a name that no one else has ever used. She is a little afraid of her happiness — and yet for the first time in her life she is really happy. Through an opened door the bells of the church are heard faintly. They sound like wedding bells to Margaret.

"I suppose you think I'm sentimental," she says to Gray, who is smiling a little amusedly at her. "No, but you're pure nineteenth century," he answers. And then, as the telephone rings and the old look of apprehension steals over Margaret's face, he adds: "There goes the twentieth. Don't you see how it makes you jump?"

It is only a mistake by central, but it is significant to Margaret that the church bells stopped ringing as the 'phone bell began! She draws her new furs closely about her, as though she had felt a sudden chill, as they start for church.

. . . .

Young Kit Pumphrey, the rector's son, "is a good-looking, fair-haired boy who may be twenty-two, but is nevertheless much younger than Sydney, whom he takes as seriously as he takes everything else in life. It is part of her charm for him that he finds it a little difficult to keep up with her." This morning he is plainly worried about something. His manner is not quite easy as Sydney settles down on the couch beside him with a sigh of relief.

SYDNEY — I thought they'd never get off. Mother has a way of standing around and gently fussing — I tell you I'll be glad when next week's over.

KIT — So'll I. I haven't had a look in lately.

SYDNEY — (*with an intimate glance*). Not last night? But it has been a job, running mother. I'm bridesmaid and best man and family lawyer and Juliet's nurse all rolled into one — and a sort of lightning conductor for Aunt Hester into the bargain. That's why I've had so little time for you. It's quite true what Gray was saying just now — mother *is* nineteenth century. She's sweet and helpless, but she's obstinate, too. My word, the time she took making up her mind to get that divorce!

KIT — It's just about that I've been wanting to talk to you. You see —

And then, with a little stammering and hesitating, the young man finally succeeds in telling her that when he arrived home from the dance the night before he found his reverend father sitting up for him. There had been a bit of a row in consequence and during the row the rector had learned for the first time, not only that he (Kit) and Sydney were engaged, but that her father was still alive. He had always thought Margaret Fairfield a widow — otherwise he never would have agreed to officiate at her approaching marriage to Gray Meredith on New Year's, which news disgusts Sydney utterly. The old rector knew all about it and was perfectly willing to perform the ceremony. What right had a new man to come into the parish and refuse — however —

SYDNEY — It's no use being sorry. We've got to do something.

KIT — (*hopelessly*). When once the old man gets an idea into his head —

SYDNEY — He'd better not let it out in front of mother. Gray'd half kill him if he did. And I tell you this, Kit, what Gray leaves I'll account for, even if he is your father. Poor little mother!

KIT — Well, I'm all on your side, you know that. But of course, Sydney, a clergyman needn't remarry divorced people. It's in that bill. The governor was quoting it today.

SYDNEY — But doesn't he know the circumstances?

KIT — He only knows what I do.

SYDNEY — One doesn't shout things at people, naturally. But it's nothing to be ashamed of. It's only that my unfortunate father's been in an asylum ever since I can remember. Shell shock. It began before I was born. He never came home again. Mother had to give up going to see him even; it excited him so frightfully.

KIT — Pretty tragic.

SYDNEY—Oh for years now he hasn't known anyone, luckily. And he's well looked after. He's quite all right.

KIT — (*uncomfortably*). You're a queer girl.

SYDNEY — But he is.
KIT — Yes —but —
SYDNEY — What?
KIT — Your own father —
SYDNEY — (*impatiently*). My dear boy, I've never even seen him. Oh, of course, it's very sad, but I can't go about with my handkerchief to my eyes all the time, can I? I hate Kant.

In reply to which Kit leans toward her, accusing her playfully of being "a little brute" and "as hard as nails," and kisses her as she turns her face inquiringly up to his. At which inappropriate moment Miss Fairfield passes through the hall. "Really, Sydney!" she protests. The idea of such a thing happening is quite distressing to Aunt Hester. And before lunch, too!

Something tells Kit that he will not be able to stand much of Aunt Hester after he has married into the family, but he will have to stand his share, Sydney assures him. And he will have to accustom himself to the thought that she, Sydney, is going to have things pretty much her own way. Marriage is a "sort of mutual show," of course, but, "My dear boy, if you want a doormat you'd better look out for some one — some one like poor, dear mother, for instance." To which Kit replies that she is like her mother. "Me?" says Sydney. "Do you think I'd let my daughter run me the way I run mother? Not much!"

The reappearance of Miss Fairfield, driven out of the drawing room, she says, by the cold, finally breaks up their tete-a-tete. Now Kit has gone and Miss Fairfield and Sydney are having none too jolly a time seeking to make the best of their enforced companionship. Suddenly they are again startled by the ringing of the telephone, and this time there is someone with a message. Sydney takes it — and her face blanches as she repeats the gist of it to her aunt.

The call is from the sanitarium at Bedford. *Hilary Fairfield has escaped!* He would, it seems, probably have been released regularly within a few days, seeing that he had improved wonderfully of late and was apparently entirely cured. But, knowing this, he had taken French leave — and the authorities were eager that he should return and comply with certain formalities attending a patient's discharge. The assumption is that Hilary will make straight for his old home. Sydney promises to let them know if her father should put in an appearance there.

She is as one stunned as she turns from the 'phone. The thing is incredible, and yet it has happened!

SYDNEY — Their theory is that he has suddenly come to himself. Is it possible, auntie? Can it happen? After sixteen years?

MISS FAIRFIELD — It's quite possible. It does. It was the same with my poor sister, Grace. After ten years, that was.

SYDNEY — But the doctors said incurable.

MISS FAIRFIELD — The Almighty's greater than the doctors. And nerves — nerves are queer things. I nursed your Aunt Grace. Well, I always told your mother to wait.

SYDNEY — (*struck*). Is that a fact about Aunt Grace? Was she out of her mind too?

MISS FAIRFIELD — She never had to be sent away.

SYDNEY — Nobody ever told me.

MISS FAIRFIELD — There's something in most families.

SYDNEY — But with father — wasn't it shell shock?

MISS FAIRFIELD — It was brought on by shell shock.

SYDNEY — D'you mean that in our family there's insanity?

MISS FAIRFIELD — (*fidgeting*). That's not the way to talk. But we're nervy, all of us, we're nervy. Your poor father would have been no worse than the rest if it hadn't been for the war.

SYDNEY — (*slowly*). What do you mean, "nervy?"

MISS FAIRFIELD — (*with a sidelong glance*). I mean the way you're taking this.

SYDNEY — (*sharply*). How am I taking it?

MISS FAIRFIELD — (*irritated*). Well, look at you now.

SYDNEY — (*coldly*). I'm perfectly under control.

MISS FAIRFIELD — That's it. It's not natural.

SYDNEY — (*slowly*). You mean I shouldn't bother to control myself if —

MISS FAIRFIELD — (*hastily*). You're too young to think about such things.

SYDNEY — — if I weren't afraid, you mean. Did mother know — when she married?

MISS FAIRFIELD — I tell you there are troubles in every family, but one doesn't talk about them.

SYDNEY — But she *did* know the trouble was insanity?

MISS FAIRFIELD — (*shortly*). I don't know.

SYDNEY — Did father?

MISS FAIRFIELD — One always knows in a general sort of way.

SYDNEY — (*relentlessly*). Am I nervy?

MISS FAIRFIELD — Young people don't have nerves.

SYDNEY — Insanity! A thing you can hand on! And I told Kit it was shell shock!

MISS FAIRFIELD — I don't see what difference it makes to Christopher.

SYDNEY — You don't see what difference —? You don't see—? (*To herself*). But I see—

Pathetically she turns to Miss Fairfield for comfort and advice. Suppose her father really gets well? Whatever will he do? It is more a question as to what Margaret will do, insists the older woman. But it can't have anything to do with her mother, replies Sydney. Whatever else happens it must be kept off mother. "Auntie, if you'd only be decent — if I only knew what to do!"

But Miss Fairfield, refusing to discuss such a problem with one so young, flounces out of the room, and Sydney is left alone. She is still a little dazed. She thinks some of telephoning, possibly to some dependable family friend, but thinks better of it. Finally she throws herself upon the sofa, furrowing her brow as she tries to think it out. And then —

" She is roused by the click of a latch as the French window in the inner room is softly opened, and Hilary Fairfield steps over the threshold. He is a big, fresh-colored man with gray hair and bowed shoulders. In speech and movements he is quick and jerky, inclined to be boisterous, but pathetically easy to check. This he knows himself, and he has, indeed, an air of being always in rebellion against his own habit of obedience. He comes in, treading softly, his bright eyes dancing with excitement, like a child getting ready to spring a surprise on some one. Something in the fashion of the empty room (for he does not see Sydney crouching in the cushions) disconcerts him. He hesitates. The happy little smile fades. His eye wanders from one object to another, and he moves about, recognizing a picture here, fingering there an unfamiliar hanging, as it were, losing and finding himself a dozen times in his progress round the room. He comes to a stand at last before the fireplace, warming his hands; then he takes out a pipe and with the other hand feels absently along the mantelpiece. Sydney, who has been watching him with a sort of breathless sympathy, says softly —

SYDNEY — What are you looking for?

HILARY — They've moved my — (*with a start*) Eh? (*He turns sharply and sees her.*) Meg! It's Meg! (*With a rush*) Oh, my darling!

SYDNEY — (*her confidence in her power to deal with the situation suddenly gone*). I — I'm not Meg.

HILARY — (*boisterously*). Not Meg! Tell me I don't

know Meg! (*Sydney gives a nervous schoolgirl giggle.*) Eh? (*Then, his voice changing completely*) No, it's not Meg. (*Uneasily*) I beg your pardon. I thought you were — another girl. I've been away a long time.

SYDNEY — Whom do you want?

HILARY — (*startled again*). There, you see, it's her voice too. Who are you?

. . . .

SYDNEY — (*slowly*). I think I'm your daughter.

HILARY — (*stares at her blankly — then he bursts out laughing*). Daughter! Daughter! By God, that's good! My wife isn't my wife, she's my daughter! And my daughter's seventeen and I'm twenty-two.

SYDNEY — You're forgetting what years and years —

HILARY — Yes, of course. It's years and years. It's a lifetime. It's my daughter's lifetime. What's your name — daughter?

SYDNEY — Sydney.

HILARY — Sydney. Sydney, eh? My mother was Sydney. I like Sydney. I — (*Catching at his dignity*) I suppose we're rather a shock to each other — Sydney?

SYDNEY — No. You're not a shock to me. But I'm afraid —

Gently she tries to meet and satisfy his impatient questioning as to Margaret. Told that she is at church, he would go and meet her, but is finally dissuaded. They talk a little ramblingly of the changes "Meg" has made in the house furnishings; of everything that has changed, "except Aunt Hester." Again Hilary insists on going to meet his wife, and again meets the immovable opposition of his daughter. Her mother is not to be frightened. "Meg understands," he insists, softening under her firm stand. "So do I understand!" she replies, jealously.

HILARY — I believe you do. You got wild all in a

moment. That's my way, too. It means nothing. Meg can't see that it means nothing. But it makes a man wild, you know, to be dragooned when he's as sane as — my God, I *am* sane! That's all over, isn't it? I *am* sane. Daughter!

SYDNEY — (*watching him*). Father?

HILARY — Don't let me get — that way. It's bad. Help me to go slow. I'm as well as you are, you know. But it's new. It only happened today — like a curtain lifting.

A little proudly he tells her how he had outwitted the guards at the sanitarium; how he was "led, like Peter, out of prison," took the first taxi he saw and promised the driver double to drive him home; the taxi is even now clicking away added tuppences at the lower gate. Then the bell rings and Sydney knows that Margaret has come. She runs to meet and to warn her mother. Soon Margaret enters and faces Hilary.

HILARY — (*like a man who can't see*). Meg! Is it Meg? Meg, I've come home.

MARGARET — (*terrified*). Sydney, don't go away!

SYDNEY — It's all right, mother!

HILARY — Meg!

MARGARET — But they said — they said — incurable. They shouldn't have said — incurable.

HILARY — What does it matter? I'm well. I'm well, Meg! I tell you — it came over me like a lantern flash — like a face turning to you. I was in a garden, you know — lost. I was a lost soul — outcast! No hope. I can never make anyone understand. I was never like the rest of them. I was sane, always; but — the face was turned away.

SYDNEY — What face?

HILARY — The face of God.

MARGARET — Sydney — is he —?

SYDNEY — It's all right, mother! That isn't madness. He's come to himself.

MARGARET — Then — then — what am I to do?

HILARY — What's that? (*He comes nearer.*)

MARGARET — I — I —

HILARY — (*staring at her*). You don't say a word. One would think you weren't glad to see me. Aren't you glad to see me?

MARGARET — Of course — glad — you poor Hilary!

HILARY — If you knew what it is to say to myself — "I'm at home!"

. . . .

MARGARET — But you didn't know me.

HILARY — My voice didn't — and my speech and my actions didn't. But *I* knew you. Meg — behind the curtain — behind the dreams and the noises, and the abandonment of God — I wanted you. I wanted — I wanted— (*He puts his hand to his head.*) Look here — we mustn't talk of these things. It's not safe, I tell you. When I talk I see a black hand reaching up through the floor — do you see? — there — through the widening crack of the floor — to catch me by the ankle and drag — drag —

SYDNEY — Father — father — go slow!

MARGARET — (*terrified*). Sydney!

SYDNEY — It's all right, mother! We'll manage.

HILARY — (*turning to her*). Yes, you tell your mother. I'm all right! *You* understand that, don't you? Once it was a real hand. Now I know it's in my mind. I tell you, Meg, I'm well. But it's not safe to think back — yet. Not safe to think about anything but — Oh, my dear, the holly and the crackle of the fire and the snow like a veil of peace on me — and you like the snow — so still — (*He comes to her with outstretched arms.*)

MARGARET — (*faintly*). No — no — no —!

HILARY — (*exalted*). Yes — yes — yes! (*He catches her to him.*)

MARGARET — For pity's sake, Hilary —!

BASSETT — (*entering*). Lunch is served, ma'am!

MARGARET — (*helplessly*). Sydney —

SYDNEY — Lay an extra cover. This — my — this gentleman is staying to lunch.

HILARY — (*boisterously*). Staying to lunch! To lunch! That's a good joke, isn't it? I say, listen! I'm laughing. Do you know, I'm laughing? It's blessed to laugh. Staying to lunch! Yes, my girl! Lunch and tea and supper and breakfast, thank God, and for many a long day!

The curtain falls

ACT II

It is early afternoon of the same day. The scene is Margaret's drawing-room, "furnished in gentle, white-walled, water-color-in-gold-frame fashion." The maid, having shown in Gray Meredith, is explaining that the family is still at lunch, having been kept late by the unexpected appearance of a visitor—a strange gentleman.

Margaret is the first to come to him. Excitedly she tells him what has happened — that Hilary has come back, that he is well, that he knows nothing of what has transpired within the last fifteen years. "His hair's gray and he talked as he talked at twenty. It's horrible."

Over the first shock of the news, Gray is for immediate action. Certainly there can be no middle course so far as Margaret is concerned. Hilary must be told, must be made to see that he no longer has any claim on her; that she is no longer his wife; that she belongs to him (Gray), as Margaret admits, in her heart, she does. But she must do nothing to hurt Hilary, she insists, nothing that might bring back the old trouble upon him.

GRAY — We'll go straight up to town and get married at once. That'll settle everything.

MARGARET — You mustn't rush me. I've got to do what's right.

GRAY — It is right. There's nothing else to be done. You can't stay here.

MARGARET — No, I can't stay here. Don't let me stay here!

GRAY — Come with me. The car's outside. You say Alliot will be here in ten minutes. Leave him a note. He's an old friend as well as a doctor. Let him deal with it if you won't let me.

MARGARET — Oh, can't you see that I must tell Hilary myself?

GRAY — (*angrily*). Women are incomprehensible!

MARGARET — It's men who are uncomprehending. Can't you feel that it'll hurt him less from me?

GRAY — It'll hurt him ten thousand times more.

MARGARET — But differently. It's the things one might have said that fester. At least I'll spare him that torment. He shall say all he wants.

. . . .

GRAY — (*deliberately matter-of-fact*). Listen to me! I am going home now. There are orders to be given. I must get some money and papers. But I shall be back here in an hour. I give you just that hour to tell him what you choose. After that you'll be ready to come.

MARGARET — If — if I've managed —

GRAY — There's no if. You're coming.

MARGARET — Am I coming, Gray?

HILARY — (*entering from the hall*). Meg, Sydney said you'd gone to your room. Hullo! What's this? Who's this? Doctor, eh? I've been expecting them down on me. (*To Gray*) It's no good, you know. I'm as fit as you are. Any test you like.

MARGARET — Mr. Meredith called to see me, Hilary! He's just going.

HILARY — Oh, sorry! (*He walks to the fire and stands*

warming his hands, but watching them over his shoulder).

GRAY — (*at the door, in a low voice to Margaret*). I don't like leaving you.

MARGARET — You must! It's better! But — come back quickly!

GRAY — You'll be ready?

MARGARET — I will.

It isn't easy for Margaret to tell Hilary the truth, and less easy for him to grasp it. He suspects that Gray Meredith, about whom he pointedly inquires, is in love with Margaret. He can see it in his manner. And he can't blame him. Rather he is inclined to blame Margaret for luring him on with her look and her smile. She is, he believes, more beautiful than she was when he went away. And yet he misses something. "Something you used to have," he tells her wistfully; "kind — kind of a way with you — the child's got it. Sydney — my daughter, Sydney! She's more you than you are. You — you've grown right up — away — beyond me — haven't you?" "Yes, Hilary," she answers simply.

But he will catch up with her, he cries exultantly. If she will but wait for him he will catch up with her; if she will but hold out her hands. "I can't, Hilary," she cries. "My hands are full!"

MARGARET — (*pitifully*). I've done nothing wrong. I'm trying to tell you. I only want to tell you and make you understand. Hilary, fifteen years is a long time —

HILARY — (*dully*). Yes. I suppose it's a long time for a woman to be faithful.

MARGARET — That's it! That's the whole thing! If I'd loved you it wouldn't have been long —

HILARY — (*violently, crying her down*). You did love me once.

MARGARET — (*beaten*). Did I — once? I didn't know — (*There is a silence.*)

HILARY — (*without expression*). What do you expect me to do? Forgive you?

MARGARET — (*stung*). There's nothing to forgive. (*Softening*) Oh, so much, Hilary, to forgive each other, but not that.

HILARY — (*more and more roughly as he loses control of himself*). Divorce you, then? Because I'll not do that! I'll have no dirty linen washed in the courts.

MARGARET — (*forced into the open*). Hilary, I divorced you twelve months ago.

The shock of her announcement throws the unhappy man into a state bordering hysteria. "She's mad," he shouts. She had no cause to divorce him. She's only trying to pull the wool over his eyes; to drive him mad again. Wildly he calls for all in the house to come and listen to him. And when they come he demands that they shall side with him; that Sydney shall stand away from her mother and with him and understand that her mother is "poisoning him."

HILARY — (*raving*). I tell you she's pouring poison into my ear. You remember that fellow in the play — and *his* wife? That's what she's done. If I told you what she said to me you'd think I was mad. And that's what she wants you to think. She wants to get rid of me. She's got a tame cat about the place. I'm in the way. And so she's come to me, d'you see, and tells me — what do you think? She says she's not my wife. What do you think of that?

MISS FAIRFIELD — (*grimly*). You may well ask.

MARGARET—(*to Sydney*). He won't listen—

SYDNEY — Sit down, darling! You're shaking.

MARGARET — He's always had these rages. It's my fault. I began at the wrong end. Hilary — it's not — I'm not what you think.

HILARY — Then what was that man doing in my house?

MARGARET — In a week I'm going to marry him.

HILARY — D'you hear her? To *me* she says this! Is she mad, or am I?

MARGARET — (*desperately*). I tell you there's been a law passed —

The arrival of Dr. Alliot, the family physician, for whom Sydney had 'phoned, happily relieves the tenseness of the situation. Dr. Alliot "is a pleasant, roundabout, clean little old man . . . but behind his comfortable manner is a hint of authority which has its effect, especially on Hilary," of whom, in a sense, he now takes charge.

He understands all that Hilary would tell him, he insists. He has heard the particulars of his cure from the sanitarium, and while he (Hilary) may have to go back to comply with certain formalities, he has no doubt that he is quite well again. Frequently an expression of reasonable doubt creeps into his kind eyes at some slightly wild statement on Hilary's part. He is of a mind to humor Hilary, and yet he seems to realize that the truth must be told, and it were better that it be told directly and without attempt at softening it. He is reminded of a quotation in his attempt to clarify his position and that of the others. "It is expedient that one man should die for the people." A hard word, but a true one.

Gently, when he finally secures Hilary's attention, he recalls to the sick man the agitation against the marriage laws and the passage of certain laws that followed which were, probably, traceable directly to the war and the war marriages.

HILARY — (*lowering*). So that's where I come in! Margaret, is that where I come in?

DR. ALLIOT — Never, I suppose, in one decade, were there so many *young* marriages. Happy? That's another thing! Marry in haste —

MARGARET — They weren't all happy.

DR. ALLIOT — But they were *young,* those boys and girls who married. As young as Kit, and as impatient as Sydney. And that saved them. That young, young generation found out, out of their own unhappiness, the war taught them, what peace couldn't teach us — that when conditions are evil it is not your duty to submit — that when conditions are evil, your duty, in spite of protests, in spite of sentiment, your duty, though you trample on the bodies of your nearest and dearest to do it, though you bleed your own heart white, your duty is to see that those conditions are changed. If your laws forbid you, you must change your laws. If your church forbids you, you must change your church. And if your God forbids you, why then, you must change your God.

MISS FAIRFIELD — And we who will not change?

MARGARET — Or cannot change — ?

DR. ALLIOT — Stifle. Like a snake that can't cast its skin. Grow or perish — it's the law of life. And so, when this young generation — yours, not mine, Hilary — decided that the marriage laws were, I won't say evil, but outgrown, they set to work to change them.

MISS FAIRFIELD — You needn't think it was without protest, Hilary. I joined the anti-divorce league myself.

DR. ALLIOT — No, it wasn't without protest. Mrs. Grundy and the churches are protesting still. But in spite of protest, no man or woman today is bound to a drunkard, an habitual criminal, or —

HILARY — Or —?

DR. ALLIOT — Or to a partner who, as far as we doctors know —

HILARY — But you can't be sure!

DR. ALLIOT — I say as far as we know, is incurably insane — in practice, is insane for more than five years.

HILARY — And if he recovers? Look at me!

DR. ALLIOT — (*with a sigh*). "It is expedient — "

HILARY — And you call that justice!

MARGARET — At least call it mercy. All the days of your life to stand at the window, Hilary, and watch the sun shining on the other side of the road — it's hard, it's hard on a woman.

DR. ALLIOT — At least call it common sense. If a man can't live his normal life, it's as if he were dead. If he's an incurable drunkard, if he's shut away for life in prison —

HILARY — But I'm not a drunkard. I'm not a convict. I've done nothing. I've been to the war, to fight, for her, for all of you, for my country, for this law-making machine that I've called my country. And when I've got from it, not honorable scars, not medals and glory, but sixteen years in hell, then when I get out again, then the country I've fought for, the woman I've fought for, they say to me — "As you've done without her for seventeen years, you can do without her altogether." That's what it is. When I was helpless they conspired behind my back to take away all I had from me.

He is still rebellious, but quiet. Nor can he rise heroically to Dr. Alliot's suggestion that, however hard the situation may be, he must face it like a man. "One of you must suffer," Alliot tells him. "Which is it to be? The useful or the useless? The whole or the maimed? The healthy woman with her life before her or the man whose children ought never to have been born?"

It is a speech that hurts Hilary — and Sydney, as well. For it is confirmation of the thought that has been assailing her ever since her father's return, whenever she thought of marrying Kit.

The Pumphreys are announced — young Kit and his father, the rector. "The rector is an insignificant man with an important manner and a plum in his mouth." And he has come to say, he finally manages after much bush-beating, that he cannot remarry a divorced person.

Nor can he willingly give his consent to his son's marrying "the child of a woman who remarries while her husband is still alive."

He does not contend that the church does not "wink" at such practices, but — He is concerned only with his own conscience, and that will not permit him to act otherwise than as he has suggested. Told that Hilary Fairfield is again well, that he has returned from the sanitarium healed in mind and body, the rector is highly pleased. That, to his mind, will settle everything.

RECTOR — Providence! It's Providence! (*With enthusiasm*) I never knew anything like Providence. Changed indeed, Miss Fairfield! My objection goes. Dear little Sydney! Ah, Mrs. Fairfield, in a year you and your husband will look back on this — episode as on a dream — a bad dream —

MARGARET — (*stonily*). I have no husband.

RECTOR — Ah! The remarriage — a mere formality —

MISS FAIRFIELD — Simpler still — the decree can be rescinded.

MARGARET — (*stunned*). Aunt Hester, knowing his history, knowing mine, is it possible that you expect me to go back to him?

MISS FAIRFIELD — He's come back to you.

RECTOR — A wife's duty —

MARGARET — (*slowly*). I think you're wicked. I think you're both wicked.

RECTOR — Mrs. Fairfield!

MISS FAIRFIELD — Control yourself, Margaret!

MARGARET — (*with a touch of wildness in her manner*). You — do you love your wife?

RECTOR — Mrs. Fairfield!

MARGARET — Do you?

RECTOR — Mrs. Pumphrey and I — most attached —

MARGARET — Suppose you weren't. Think of it — to want so desperately to feel — and to feel nothing. Do you know what it means to dread a person who loves you? To stiffen at the look in their eyes? To pity and — shudder? You should not judge.

Margaret is still determined to go with Gray when he comes, and Dr. Alliot approves of that course. He will, meantime, take Hilary home with him, that, together, they may make all things right with the sanitarium. Also he has made Hilary see the situation a little more clearly — and fairly. And yet when Hilary comes, and he is alone with Margaret for their farewells, there is a wild pleading in his voice. He realizes that it is too late; he knows, as Alliot says, that she has made a new life for herself — but isn't there, couldn't there be room in it for him? "Suddenly he throws himself down beside her, catching at her hands, clinging to her knees."

HILARY — Oh! Meg, Meg, Meg, isn't there just a chance?

MARGARET — (*faintly*). Hilary, I can't stand it.

HILARY — (*and from now to the end of the scene he is at full pelt, tumbling over his words, frantic*). Yes, but listen to me! Listen to me! You don't listen. Listen to me! I've been alone so long —

MARGARET — Gray! Gray! Why don't you come?

HILARY — I'll not trouble you. I'll not get in your way — but — don't leave me all alone. Give me something, the rustle of your dress, the cushion where you've lain — your voice about the house. You can't deny me such little things, that you give your servants and your dog.

MARGARET — It's madness —

HILARY — It's naked need!

MARGARET — What good should I be to you? I don't love you, Hilary — poor Hilary. I love him. I never think of anything but him.

HILARY — But it's me you married. You promised —

you promised — better or worse — in sickness, in health. You can't go back on your promise.

MARGARET —(*helpless*). It isn't fair!

HILARY — Anything's fair. You don't know what misery means.

MARGARET — I'm learning.

HILARY — But you don't *know*. You couldn't leave me to it if you knew. Why, I've never known you hurt a creature in all your life! Remember the rat hunts in the barn, the way we used to chaff you? And the starling? And the kitten you found? Why, I've seen you step aside for a little creeping green thing on the path. You've never hurt anything. Then how can you hurt me so? You can't have changed since yesterday —

MARGARET — (*in despairing protest*). It's half my life ago —

HILARY — It's yesterday, it's yesterday!

MARGARET — (*with the fleeting courage of a half-caught bird*). Yes, it is yesterday. It's how you took me — yesterday — and now you're doing it again!

HILARY — (*catching at the hope of it*). Am I? Am I? Is it yesterday — yesterday come back again?

MARGARET — (*in the toils*). No — no! Hilary, I can't!

HILARY — (*at white heat*). No, you can't. You can't leave me. You can't do it to me! You can't drive me out — the wilderness — alone — alone — alone! You can't do it, Meg — you can't do it — you can't!

MARGARET — (*beaten*). I suppose — I can't.

HILARY — You — you'll stay with me? (*Breaking down utterly*). Oh, God bless you, Meg, God bless you, God bless you — (*She resigns her hands to him while she sits, flattened against the back of her chair, quivering a little, like a crucified moth.*)

MARGARET — (*puzzling it out*). You mean — God help me!

The curtain falls

ACT III

It is tea time, the same afternoon. In the hall that furnished the setting for the first act, Hester Fairfield and Sydney are trying not to quarrel more than is their custom over Sydney's suggestion that it is too early for tea, seeing that lunch was late. In the background, Kit, manœuvring to have a talk with Sydney, if it is possible to dislodge Aunt Hester, slips quietly up the stairs. The tea question having been settled Sydney's way, Aunt Hester finally decides to search out Margaret, who is still "talking and talking" with Hilary, seeking some adjustment of their problems.

Now Margaret comes "dragging into the room, shutting the door behind her." Her blanched features frighten Sydney. But she refuses to talk with her daughter. She has come to ask Kit to wait until she can write a note to Gray Meredith. "Do you want Gray to come here?" Sydney asks. "I want him not to come here," replies Margaret, and goes to write the note.

Kit is in a playful mood. He doesn't at all agree with his father in his attitude toward the marriage, though it is evident that he has given the matter serious thought. Sydney is of no mind to fool with him. She wants to talk seriously. She introduces the subject of eugenics, in which they are both interested, and on which she has been helping Kit prepare a paper.

SYDNEY — (*slowly*). Kit, talking of that paper — I read somewhere — suppose now — is it true it can skip a generation?

KIT — It? What?

SYDNEY — Oh — any illness. Suppose — *you*, for instance — suppose you were a queer family — a little, you know. And say your mother was queer — and you weren't. You were perfectly fit, you understand, perfectly fit —

KIT — Well?

SYDNEY — What about the children?

KIT — I wouldn't risk it. Thank the Lord your father's only shell shocked.

SYDNEY — But isn't there a school that says there's no such thing as heredity?

KIT — Well, all I know is I wouldn't risk it.

SYDNEY — It's — it's hard on people.

To which Kit agrees. That's the reason, he reminds Sydney, that Dr. Alliot has never married — because he loved a woman in whose family there had been insanity. Yet they had gone on being pals.

KIT — Rotten for her.

SYDNEY — Rottener for him! What did she go on being pals with him for?

KIT — Why shouldn't she?

SYDNEY — Well, it stopped him marrying anyone else. She oughtn't to have let him.

KIT — You can't stop a person being fond of you.

SYDNEY — When it's a man you can.

KIT — My dear girl, you don't know what you're talking about?

SYDNEY — My dear boy, if a girl finds out she can't marry a man, it's up to her to choke him off.

KIT — Rot!

SYDNEY — Well, I think so.

KIT — Couldn't be done.

SYDNEY — Couldn't it just?

KIT — Any man would see through it.

SYDNEY — As if any man ever saw through anything.

She knows what to do now. She must force a quarrel with Kit and send him away without his suspecting her real reason, which she does, letting one word bring on another until she has convinced him she is jealous of a certain other girl to whom he has been a bit attentive. Finally it dawns on the unhappy Kit that he is, in effect, being sent away. "You want me to go?" he demands. "Yes," she answers. "For good?" "Yes." "Honest?" "Yes." "Right!" and he flares out of the room without waiting for the letter Margaret wanted him to give to Gray. Margaret calls him back and as he starts again for the door Sydney calls.

SYDNEY — (*in spite of herself, softly*). Kit!
KIT — (*quickly*). Yes?
SYDNEY — (*recovering herself, impishly*). You'll give her my love?
KIT — You're a beast, Sydney Fairfield! (*He goes out with a slam.*)
SYDNEY — (*in a changed voice*). You'll give her *my* love. (*Running to the door*) Kit!

"The door opens again, but it is Gray Meredith who comes in." Kit has gone on with a rush and forgotten to deliver the note after all.

Gray has come for Margaret. Pitifully she faces him, knowing that now she must tell him all she had struggled so hard to write. "She sways where she stands. Gray goes to her, and half clinging to him, half repulsing him, she sits down with her arm on the table and her head on her arm." Two or three times she tries to speak, but Gray will not listen. They have a fifty-mile drive before them, he reminds her, and she must hurry. If Sydney will get her mother's wraps — Then Margaret manages to speak. She cannot go with him. Hilary — won't let her go. "He won't — won't he?" Gray will see about that. "Where is he?"

MARGARET — Leave him alone. It's me you must punish. I've made up my mind. Oh, how am I to tell you? He convinced me. He — cried, Gray. (*Then, as*

Gray makes a quick gesture) You mustn't sneer. You must understand. He's so unhappy. And there's Sydney to think of. And Gray, he won't marry us.

GRAY — What's that?

MARGARET — The rector. He's been here.

GRAY — My God, why wasn't I?

MARGARET — And Aunt Hester — she made it worse. (*Despairingly*) You see what it is — they all think I'm wicked.

GRAY — Damned insolence!

MARGARET — But it's not them — it's Hilary. I did fight them. I can't fight Hilary. I see it. It's my own fault. I ought never to have let myself care for you.

GRAY — Talk sense.

MARGARET — But there it is. It's too much for me. I've got to stay with him.

GRAY — (*for the first time taking her seriously*). Say that again, Margaret, if you dare —

MARGARET—I've got to—stay— (*With a sharp, crying note in her voice*) Gray, Gray, don't look at me like that!

Still Gray refuses to be convinced. Either Margaret loves him, and has loved him for five years; either she wants to marry him now, or all that she has said has been untrue. He knows that is not so, declares Margaret. But — there is Hilary. "I've got to put him first because — because he's weak. You — you're strong."

"Not strong enough to do without my birthright," he answers. "I want my wife and children. I've waited a long while for you. Now you must come."

Still he would not have her do what she conceives to be wrong. "You're to do as you choose," he tells her. "I shan't force you. I'm not your turnkey. I'm not your beggar. We're free people, you and I. It's for you to say if you'll keep your — conscience, do you call it — and lose — "

MARGARET — I've lost what I love. There's no more to lose.

GRAY — You sing as sweetly as a toy nightingale. Almost I'd think you were real.

MARGARET — (*wounded*). I don't know what you mean.

GRAY — "What you love!" You don't know the meaning of the notes you use.

MARGARET — (*very white, but her voice is steady*). Don't deceive yourself. I love you. I ache and faint for you. I starve —

SYDNEY — (*appalled, whispering*). What is it? I don't know her.

MARGARET — I'm withering without you like cut grass in the sun. I love you. I love you. Can't you see how it is with me? But —

GRAY — There's no "but" in love.

MARGARET — What is it in me? There is a thing I can't do. I can't see such pain.

GRAY — (*hoarsely*). Do you think *I* can't suffer?

MARGARET — I *am* you. But he — he's so defenseless. It's vivisection — like cutting a dumb beast about to make me well. I can't do it. I'd rather die of my cancer.

GRAY — (*the storm breaking*). Die then — you fool — you fool! . . . D'you think I bear you malice? It's not I. Why, to deny me, that's a little thing. I'll not go under because you're faithless! But what you're doing is the sin without forgiveness. You're denying — not me — but life! You're denying the spirit of life! You're denying — you're denying your mate!

From the stairway at back Sydney has overheard them. Now she advances into the room and goes to her mother, protectingly. She will not permit such sacrifice.

MARGARET — (*sitting down, with a listless gesture*). There's no way out.

SYDNEY — There is. For *you* there is. I've thought it all along, and now I know. Father — he's my job, not yours.

MARGARET — (*with a last flicker of passion*). D'you think I'll make a scapegoat of my own child?

SYDNEY — (*sternly*). Can you help it? I'm *his* child. (*She throws herself down beside her*) Mother! Mother darling, don't you see? You're no good to him. You're scared of him. But I'm his own flesh and blood. I know how he feels. I'll make him happier than you can. Be glad for me. Be glad I'm wanted somewhere!

MARGARET — (*struggling against the hope that is flooding her*). But Kit, Sydney — Kit?

SYDNEY — (*with a queer little laugh that ends, though it does not begin, quite naturally*). Bless him, I'll be dancing at his wedding in six months.

MARGARET — But all you ought to have —

SYDNEY — (*jumping up, flippantly*). Oh, I'm off getting married. I'm going to have a career.

MARGARET — — the love — the children —

SYDNEY — (*strained*). No children for me, mother. No children for me. I've lost my chance forever.

For a little Margaret stands out against them both. But finally she is convinced and gives way. She will go with Gray. "He takes the cloak and throws it around her. They go out together. As Sydney, forgotten, stands looking after them, Bassett enters with the tea tray."

When Hilary comes Sydney tells him — and Aunt Hester — what has happened. They are incredulous, at first, and angry; angry with her for having jilted Kit; angry because she has let Margaret go with Gray. "I pray you get your punishment," says Aunt Hester. "Your prayers will surely be answered," replies the girl. Now she is beside her father on the sofa, comforting him.

HILARY — (*broken*). I don't see ahead. I don't see what's to become of me. There's no one.

SYDNEY — There's me.

HILARY — (*not looking at her*). I should think you'd hate me.

SYDNEY — I need you just as badly as you need me.

HILARY — (*fiercely*). It's your damn clever doing that she went. D'you think I can't hate you?

SYDNEY — (*close to him*). No, no, father, you want me too much. We'll make a good job of it yet.

HILARY — (*his head in his hands*). What job?

SYDNEY — (*petting him, coaxing him, loving him, her hands quieting his twitching hands, her strong will already controlling him*). Living. I've got such plans already, father — father, dear! We'll do things. We'll have a good time somehow, you and I — you and I. Did you know you'd got a clever daughter? Writing — painting — acting! We'll go on tour together! We'll make a lot of money! We'll have a cottage somewhere! You see, I'll make it up to you! I'll make you proud of me!

MISS FAIRFIELD — (*surveying them*). Proud of her! D'you see, Hilary! That's all she thinks of — self — self — self! Money — ambition — and sends that poor boy away! A parson's son! Not good enough for her, that's what it is! She's like the rest of the young women — hard as nails! Hard as nails!

SYDNEY — (*crying out*). Don't listen to her, father! Father, don't believe her! I'm not hard! I'm not hard!

"His arm goes round her with a gesture, awkward, timid, yet fatherly."

The curtain falls

"DULCY"

An American Comedy in Three Acts

By George S. Kaufman and Marc Connelly

AFTER a preliminary run in Chicago at the Cort Theatre, beginning there February 20, 1921, "Dulcy" was given an early season start at the Frazee Theatre in New York on August 13, 1921. It was hailed with enthusiasm by the particular public for which it was written, *i.e.*, the followers of the Franklin P. Adams ("F. P. A.") column, at that time a feature of the *New York Tribune's* editorial page, but since transferred to the *New York World.*

Some years back, Mr. Adams, seeking an imaginary character through which he could satirize the super-bromidic feminine with a single-track mind (and that track a bit rusty) took Dulcinea away from Don Quixote and recreated her for the joy of his readers.

Later, the Messrs. Kaufman and Connelly, having developed a great fondness for Dulcinea, conceived the idea of building a play around her. "Dulcy" is the result. For the play they accept credit, but for the character they make friendly and graceful obeisance to her creator.

It was assumed at the time of "Dulcy's" playhouse début that after she had attracted and entertained her own particular friends and acquaintances she would find the larger public a little cold to her charms, and her individual expression of humor. But either the multitude is capable of analyzing and appreciating the Dulcineas of its respective little groups, or they find her entertaining as a literal and easily recognizable acquaintance. At any rate the business continued excellent through a run that carried the play into the spring season.

If Dulcy were writing a brief note of acknowledgment to her playwrights she would sign herself (Mrs.) Gordon Smith, and she would have her stationery engraved, a bit elaborately, to indicate that the Smiths lived, quietly but with due regard for the social obligations of the best people, in Westchester County and within easy commuting distance of New York.

The scene of all three acts is the living room of this home. "It is a room that is splashing rather than merely striking," explain the authors. "The furniture, for no particular reason, is old Italian, but most of it is hidden beneath beautiful and variously colored batiks and drapes. . . . In a word the room is Dulcy. If there were a telephone Dulcy would have it covered with a cute little doll — but there is no telephone."

The time is just before dinner Friday evening — the particular Friday evening on which Dulcy has arranged to entertain at dinner a number of guests she has invited out for the week-end. These are to include Dulcy's younger brother, "Bill" Parker, as sophisticated as the sister is naïve; Mr. and Mrs. C. Rogers Forbes, Mr. Forbes being a leading competitor of Dulcy's husband in the imitation jewelry business; their daughter, Angela Forbes; Schuyler Van Dyck, of *the* Van Dycks, whom Dulcy has met at one or two fashionable affairs, and who plays the piano *wonderfully,* and Vincent Leach, the well-known "scenarist."

Dulcy has planned it all, very craftily, to help her husband. She knows there is a business merger being planned, with Forbes at its head, into which Gordon is to be taken on a 16 2-3 per cent basis. And she figures that if she can only —

But Dulcy has planned and figured before, rather disastrously for Gordon, and he is inclined to be apprehensive as to the outcome of her most recent activities. Also he can't just understand why, at a simple week-end party for the Forbes, there should be nine guests.

GORDON—What are you trying to do—solve the housing problem?

DULCY—(*picking up a vase of flowers*). Just wait, darling! You'll be so excited! (*Breaking the big news over Smith's shoulder*) Vincent—is coming!

GORDON—(*at sea*). Vincent?

DULCY—Yes. Isn't it *wonderful?*

GORDON—(*trying to recall*). Vincent—Vincent—who the devil is Vincent?

. . . .

DULCY—*Vincent Leach?* Don't you remember? You and I met him at Mrs. Peabody's last week—you know, the big scenario writer.

GORDON—(*faintly recalling*). Oh, yes. Is *he* coming here?

DULCY—Yes! Isn't it wonderful? (*picks up bowl from the table and starts toward the piano with it.*)

GORDON—But look here now—Dulcy, will you leave those flowers alone, and come here and talk to me?

DULCY—Just a minute, darling. (*She replaces the vase on the piano with the bowl, then takes the vase back and places it on the table*) A time and a place for everything. There! (*She seats herself on his lap.*)

GORDON—But, dear, why do you want to mix this man Leach up with Forbes? Van Dyck may be all right, but—

DULCY—Ah! That's the secret!

GORDON—I don't like—secrets. This isn't a—game.

DULCY—Promise you won't tell ! Cross you heart!

GORDON—Yes, yes.

DULCY—Well, then—Vincent and Angela (*Kisses him*)—like each other.

GORDON—You mean—Forbes' daughter?

DULCY—(*nodding*). Isn't it wonderful? So I invited them both here so they'll have the whole week-end together. And at the same time he can meet her parents. You never can tell what will happen.

GORDON — But, Dulcy, dear, you don't know Angela so well, and — this man Leach — what do you know about *him?*

DULCY — I know all about him. He's a big scenario writer, and just the man for Angie. He's — he's so practical, and she's a dreamer. Opposites should marry — you know that, darling.

GORDON — But, Dulcy, now —

DULCY — And what else do you think? I'm going to get him to help me with some of *my* scenarios while he's here.

GORDON — But why, dear —

DULCY — To make them better.

GORDON — No, no — I mean — why are you trying to match this fellow Leach with Angela? What do *you* care about it?

DULCY — Don't you see?

GORDON — No.

DULCY — Can't you guess?

GORDON — No.

DULCY — Well, if Angie *likes* Mr. Leach, and marries him —

GORDON — Yes?

DULCY — And *I* fix it —

GORDON — Well?

DULCY — Well — I'm your wife — (*Gordon springs up in alarm, dropping Dulcy off his lap.*)

GORDON — Now, Dulcy dear —

DULCY — That will make Mr. Forbes so grateful that he'll have to give you more than sixteen and two-thirds of the percentage.

GORDON — Good heavens, Dulcy! Now —

DULCY — (*ecstatically*). I figured it all out myself!

GORDON—But, now wait! (*He paces the floor.*)

DULCY — Gordon, darling — don't be upset about it. I know they ought to marry — I just know it. It's a woman's intuition. (*A pause*) Just as I knew I ought to marry you, dear. (*Gordon stops*) It was because I loved you, darling, and wanted to help you, and — and — .

Gordon is appreciative and he knows that Dulcy means well. He tells her so as he embraces her. But — they have been all through this before and Dulcy has agreed *not* to interfere in Gordy's business. She promised that much three months before when they came back from their honeymoon — just after she had discharged Gordon's secretary because she did not believe any man could wear a heavy black mustache and be honest. But Dulcy refuses to give way.

DULCY — Mr. Forbes *is* taking advantage of you and I'm not going to let him — that's all!

GORDON — (*desperately*). But that isn't the point. In the position that I am I have to go ahead with it. I wouldn't want anything to happen. (*Pleading affectionately*) Don't you see, dear! If I'm not in that merger, I'll lose — everything!

DULCY — But only sixteen and two-thirds per cent — it's such a funny number, too. I don't see why you couldn't get a nice even number — like twenty-five. (*She pauses*) Or fifty! (*Bill enters.*)

BILL — Well, has she fixed it?

DULCY — We've been all through it quietly, Willie, and it's settled.

GORDON — Now, Dulcy, you must listen.

DULCY — Now — now — not another word. Just let — let — sleeping dogs lie and everything is bound to come out all right. It always does.

Schuyler Van Dyck is the first of the guests to arrive.

"He is aristocratic and well dressed," and he is very glad to be there, though a little hesitant about accepting Mrs. Smith's kind invitation because business matters may call him suddenly back to the city. If, in such emergency, they will be so good as to excuse him — They certainly will. "We all understand business here," Dulcy assures him. "Don't we Gordon, darling? Business before pleasure! Henry, show Mr. Van Dyck to his room."

Henry, the butler, is an interesting type. Particularly interesting to Dulcy's brother, Bill, who has heard rumors. He watches Henry now, as he disappears upstairs with the Van Dyck bags.

BILL — Dulcy!

DULCY— Well, Willie?

BILL — When you took this butler out of Sing Sing —

DULCY — (*rising*) — Sing Sing? He wasn't in Sing Sing.

BILL — You didn't go way out to Leavenworth, did you?

DULCY — Now, I know just what you're going to say, but it isn't true. Just because Henry made one false step doesn't mean he's going to make another. If you ask me, I think there's enough sorrow in the world without trying to make things worse. Every cloud has a silver lining, and, so has Henry.

BILL — Yes. The question is, how did he get it?

DULCY — It doesn't matter in the least — he's all right now. He promised me. Besides, he has to report to the probation officer every week, and tell him everything he does.

BILL — Oh, he *has* to tell him everything?

DULCY — Every week.

BILL — You don't think he has any — secrets?

DULCY — You must be more tolerant, Willie. You know, there's so much good in the best of us —and so much bad in the worst of us — well, it ill behooves the best of us — (*She flounders, but is saved by the door-bell.*)

GORDON — Here are the Forbeses!

DULCY — Wait — Gordon — let that poor Henry answer. The trouble with the world, Willie, is that it doesn't give the underdog a chance. Live and let live — is my motto.

The Forbeses are typical — he of the pushing, successful, humorless business man; she of the distinctly feminine, and a little flighty, society woman. She is the second Mrs. Forbes, and Angela's step-mother. Angela is an attractive girl passing a little excitedly through her late teens, and greatly enamored of romance.

Dulcy is in her element as a reception committee, inquiring the adventures of the journey, the way they came, the state of the weather, their opinion of the scenery, etc. The introductions, too, she manages, buoyantly. Her greatest concern, as a perfect hostess, is that they should all be happy — and see everything.

DULCY — Gordon, darling, you must show Mr. Forbes and the others over the grounds. (*She is shepherding Mrs. Forbes and Angela toward the stairs*) You get a beautiful view from the lawn, Mr. Forbes. And don't forget to show him the garden, darling — all our vegetables are out of our own garden, Mr. Forbes. Then later you must see the garden, Mrs. Forbes — and Angie. You know, there's nothing like country life, is there? Out next to Nature, you know. We're like gypsies — regular gypsies. New York is a wonderful place to visit, but I wouldn't like to live there. (*They exeunt upstairs.*)

Mr. Forbes, we gather, has been a little reluctant about coming. He is well past the week-end age, and inclined to be a bit high and mighty about demanding and expecting his own way. He is impressed, however, with Schuyler Van Dyck. Everybody is. There is something mysteriously grand about this representative of an old and extremely wealthy family.

With the guests variously disposed Gordon and Forbes gradually approach the subject of their prospective business relations. But they get no farther than the approach, for Dulcy is right after them. "Well, here we are! No more business now! It's time to play! (*To Mr. Forbes*) You know one thing poor Gordon has never learned is how to play. He takes everything so seriously. Now, what I like to do is to cut loose once in a while — just be children again."

She maneuvers them around until she manages to get Mr. Forbes to herself. And then she twists the conversation until she is able to bring Gordon and the new business into it. "I don't suppose he's told you, Mr. Forbes, but he's really got a lot of things on hand!" Which is news to Mr. Forbes.

DULCY — It's really asking too much of him to make him give up all these other things to come into the jewelry combination — that is, unless it were made worth his while. (*Dulcy effects her master stroke*) of course, if he just got sixteen and two thirds per cent, he couldn't afford to give up all his time to it — no! He'd have to look after his other things, too, and you'd be the loser.

The arrival of Vincent Leach, the scenarist, interrupts her, and it requires a little time to get Vincent properly placed with the other guests. He is rather a forward young man, but with the carefully studied restraint of the artist. He is greatly enamored of Angela Forbes, knowing something of her father's business connections, but his soul is really wrapped up in his art. The motion picture business, he contends, is still in its infancy, the surface has hardly been scratched, but the possibilities are at least limitless.

LEACH — You'd be surprised! Yes, we're going to do some of Shakespeare's things next.

DULCY — Shakespeare's? Well — (*Her arms are around her husband's shoulders and she shakes him to pick up the cue.*)

GORDON — (*coming to*). Really!

LEACH — Yes, I'm at work on his continuity now. I was telling my director yesterday — I said, you know, Shakespeare had a tremendous feeling for plot. Of course, the dialogue is stilted for modern audiences — but then, you don't have to listen to that in the pictures. But he's still the master.

DULCY — He's going to organize his own company next.

BILL — Who — Shakespeare?

DULCY — No, Willie! Mr. Leach.

LEACH — Yes — The Vincent Leach Productions, Inc. The stock will be placed on the open market very soon.

DULCY — Mr. Van Dyck can tell how to do it! He owns lots of moving picture companies — don't you, Mr. Van Dyck?

LEACH—(*really interested*). Is that so?

VAN DYCK — (*modestly, as always*). Well, I'm interested in a small way.

LEACH — I'd enjoy talking to you about it later. (*To Mr. Forbes*) And how about you, Mr. Forbes? Didn't I hear that *you* were interested in pictures?

FORBES — (*turning away and smothering the line*). I don't care a damn about pictures.

LEACH — (*not believing his ears*). What's that?

FORBES — I said, I make jewelry.

LEACH — Well, of course, that's very necessary too, in its way.

Dulcy calms the threatening storm by again shuffling her guests. She organizes a rubber of bridge, into which she tries to inveigle Mr. Forbes, though that now thoroughly ruffled gentleman assures her that he does not play. She sends Mr. Leach and Angela into the garden to see the view, which is a further cause of irritation to Mr. Forbes, who storms off to the garage to see if his car is still there. Gordon, worried at Forbes' apparent anger, follows, but not before he has given Dulcy one awful look. "You know," remarks Bill, "this is probably going to be the first week-end party on record that ended on Friday night."

Mr. Forbes is still irritated when, returning from the garage, he discovers Mrs. Forbes and Mr. Van Dyck engaged in what is plainly a most sympathetic conversation. By that time he is ready and eager to leave the house party flat, a state of mind he hoarsely makes known to Mrs. Forbes the moment they are alone.

FORBES — I tell you this whole place is going to drive me crazy. I didn't want to come here anyhow. I had the backache and I wanted to stay home and rest.

MRS. FORBES — But you couldn't refuse —

FORBES — And instead of that I've got to get up at some ungodly hour in the morning and go out and play golf. If there is one thing I hate more than anything else in the world, it's golf — unless it's bridge or moving pictures.

MRS. FORBES — Now, Charlie, dear — when you're here as a guest —

FORBES — If I could think of a good excuse, I'd go back to town tonight with Sterrett, and take Angela and you with me.

MRS. FORBES — (*alarmed*). But Charlie, you can't do that when —

FORBES — Don't you suppose I see that woman's plan to throw Angela and that —that film thing together!

MRS. FORBES — But I tell you he's a most charming man.

FORBES — And I tell you, if it weren't for Smith and our business relations I *would* go back tonight!

MRS. FORBES — But, Charlie — you can't be so rude! (*Enter Gordon*).

FORBES — Sh! That reminds me — Oh, Smith. (*Smith comes down to Forbes.*)

GORDON — Yes, sir.

FORBES — Mr. Smith, Mrs. Smith has been telling me something of your other business activities.

GORDON — Other business activities? Why —

FORBES — And it came as something of a revelation to me.

GORDON — But Mrs. Smith couldn't have meant — (*Enter Van Dyck, who joins Mrs. Forbes.*)

FORBES — As you may have been aware, my agreement to admit you on a sixteen and two-thirds basis was founded on the expectation that you would give all your time to the new enterprise.

GORDON — Yes, of course, Mr. Forbes.

FORBES — In the circumstances your business and your services would hardly be worth that amount to me.

GORDON — But, my dear Mr. Forbes — you — you don't understand. Mrs. Smith —

But Dulcy is quite unperturbed. Now that everybody is there they can probably go on with their bridge game. Chatting merrily she puts them all in their places — the glowering Mr. Forbes, Mr. Sterrett, his advertising man, who has drifted into the party; Gordon and herself.

"Is everybody happy?" she calls cheerily. "And somebody tell me — which is higher — a heart or a spade? I never can remember. And do you discard from strength or weakness, Mr. Sterrett? Of course it doesn't matter — "

The curtain falls

ACT II

It is evening of the same day. From the dining room, at the left, come the sounds of table conversation. Nothing can be heard clearly, though during an appreciable pause we do hear Vincent Leach explaining definitely to some one his complete grasp of the motion picture business. "I said to Mr. Breitenstein, 'Don't you worry about those German films —!'" But that is all.

With her guests reassembled in the living room Dulcy tries again to see that everybody is made comfortable. For Mr. Forbes she finds a nice, big, soft chair, though he has tried so very hard to tell her that he prefers one with a stiff back. She maneuvers Mrs. Forbes and the constant Mr. Van Dyck into position, much to the disgust of Mrs. Forbes' husband. She starts Angela and Mr. Leach towards the French windows, that they may have a good view of the moon.

She grows restless again just as Mr. Forbes and Gordon are beginning to talk business at the side of the room, where they are comparing Gordon's newest creation in imitation pearls with Angela's real string, an incident that worries brother Bill excessively when he sees the suspected Henry taking part in the transfer of the jewels from Angela to her father.

Now Mr. Van Dyck must play something for Dulcy and her guests — just any thing. And while Mr. Van Dyck plays, Dulcy thoughtfully passes a box of candy and manages to rattle the paper coverings of the bonbons most distractingly. And suddenly — quite suddenly — she has another inspiration. Let Vincent Leach tell them the story of his newest picture while Mr. Van Dyck plays the music for it!

DULCY — It'll be just like a moving-picture theatre!

LEACH — (*with fake modesty*). Oh, but really — I don't think that I should — of course, it *would* be interesting.

ANGELA — Oh, please tell it. Vincent!

MRS. FORBES — I'd love to hear it, and so would my husband. (*She throws her husband a look.*)

DULCY — Well, now you can't refuse.

LEACH—(*with no thought of refusing*). Since you demand it.

DULCY — Oh, good! Now everybody take their places. Mr. Van Dyck, you go back to the piano. (*They all take seats*) Mr. Leach, you tell him what kind of music you want. (*Bill stands motionless and noiseless*) Be quiet, Willie. Now, I'll sit here.

BILL — Mr. Leach. (*A pause*) How many reels is this picture?

LEACH — There are eight. (*Bill sinks into his chair*) It's an extra-super-feature, not released on the regular programme!

BILL — How long does each reel take?

LEACH — Oh, about fifteen minutes.

FORBES — (*looks up*). Two hours?

BILL — To tell it?

LEACH — Oh, no, to show it. I can give you what *we* call an outline in half an hour — well, three-quarters at the most.

BILL — That's much better — three-quarters. That's fine!

DULCY — Now keep quiet, Willie, or he won't tell it. What's the name of the picture, Mr. Leach?

. . . .

LEACH — (*waiting a moment until every one is quiet*). The name of the picture —

DULCY — (*lifting an arm, and thus rattling her bracelets*). Quiet, everybody!

LEACH — Is — " Sin." (*This to the men. Forbes and Bill exchange a look*) "Sin." (*To the women.*)

DULCY — (*doing her bit*). " Sin." (*Van Dyck starts the Rachmanioff Prelude. Leach steps up and stops him.*)

LEACH — Not yet. And when I'm ready, just a soft accompaniment. (*Starting with enthusiasm*) This is really something quite new in films. I am going to show Sin — throughout the ages.

DULCY — (*with anticipation*) — Well!

LEACH — In the beginning the picture is symbolic. I open with a quotation from Hawthorne — (*For the men's benefit*) Nathaniel Hawthorne.

BILL — (*raising his hand*) — Who's the director and the cameraman?

DULCY — Willie!

LEACH—(*squelching him*). The director is Frank Heming Stratton.

BILL — Oh! (*Bill prepares for as comfortable a nap as possible.*)

LEACH — It begins — with the setting out — of Noah's Ark. (*Leach signals Van Dyck, who starts "Sailing, Sailing." Leach considers the music for a second, decides it will do and continues*) We see Noah, a man of advanced years; his wife, his sons, the animals — of each of its kind two. We see the Ark setting out upon its journey — we see the waters rise and rise and rise. For forty days it rains. (*Van Dyck changes to "Rustle of Spring."*) Civilization is all but wiped out — it is kept alive — and Sin is kept alive — only in the Ark. (*At "Sin" Van Dyck changes to "Kiss Me Again."*)

DULCY — (*in hoarse whisper to Mrs. Forbes*). "Kiss Me Again."

LEACH—Then comes a calm. (*Van Dyck changes to "Morning Mood," Grieg*). The dove is sent forth — it returns, unable to find a lighting place. (*Suiting action to the word, Forbes strikes a noisy match and lights his cigar, unmindful of Leach's glare*) And then a second dove — and it returns — and then a third — and it does not return — for somewhere in the great beyond it had found land. (*A quick signal to Van Dyck*)

Land! (*Van Dyck goes into "My Country 'Tis of Thee" loudly. Dulcy automatically rises, ever patriotic. Leach is about to begin again, looks at her surprised. Dulcy giggles her apology, then sits. Leach continues as the curtain slowly falls.*)

LEACH — Many years pass — we are now at King Solomon's Court — his wives are bathing in the fountain —

The curtain is lowered to indicate the passing of thirty minutes, during which time Mr. Leach has continued with his thrilling recital. When it is raised the scenarist, somewhat dishevelled, is still at it. The men are all asleep, all except Forbes, who is "chewing the stump of a cigar viciously, breathing heavily and seems to be wondering how many seconds he can stand it before he commits murder." Van Dyck is all but exhausted, but the three women are still "eating it up." Leach is nearing the end of his recital as the curtain rises.

LEACH — Frances rushes to the edge of the cliff, and looking over, sees an inert, lifeless form. The "Weasel" is dead. (*Leach pantomines his excuses hurriedly and takes a drink from glass of water on piano. Henry enters to clear away the coffee cups.*)

DULCY — Not yet, Henry. How many times — (*Henry exits*) Yes, Mr. Leach, the Weasel is dead —

LEACH — (*picking up the story*). And then — then the Zeppelin and Jack's automobile go into the final stretch neck and neck. On— on they speed! We get another close-up of Jack in the driver's seat! We see his face — tense — and putting into the car everything that he has, he forges — slowly — slowly ahead! Then more and more! The goal is nearer and nearer! Back in New York, Charley is seen leaving the Chinese restaurant! On the corner he meets Fanny, who throws the money in his face. (*For emphasis he touches Forbes' arm. Forbes jumps*) Then flash back to Jack — nearer and nearer — HE WINS!

BILL — (*rudely awakened*). What?

LEACH — (*explaining*). He wins!! (*Bill returns to his chair and nap with a manner of a man annoyed at being called too early. Van Dyck strikes a chord.*) Gradually he stops. The Zeppelin makes a landing. Coralie gets out of the dirigible and rushes to Jack to forgive him. Just as he takes her in his arms, her father arrives with the afternoon paper, which makes everything clear and vindicates Albert. Then the father clasps Jack's hand and apologizes to him for having thought *him* a thief. And to keep the symbolism to the end, just as Jack kisses Coralie there in Chicago, Marc Anthony is shown kissing Cleopatra in Ancient Egypt and George Washington kissing Martha Washington at Mt. Vernon. And so at the end of the Dream Trail we fade into a long shot of Jack and Coralie, once more in their South Sea bungalow, with the faithful old Toota Heva waiting to greet them in the sunset — and fade out.

"Van Dyck finishes with a loud chord. Leach is exhausted with his labors. The women rise. Leach rushes to them, his hands outstretched, anticipating their congratulations. The women take his hands, chattering. Van Dyck gets up, raising his arms and exercising his fingers. Bill awakes and rises, but finds his foot asleep. He gradually wakes himself up by some shakes and half-exercises, and awakens Smith, who also has to exercise and stretch his legs and arms. Sterrett likewise awakes. Forbes has risen and holds his back. Henry enters, clears the cups and saucers, and exits."

DULCY — (*when the excitement has died down a little*). Oh, that was the most wonderful picture I ever saw. (*The women echo this*) I mean heard! Eight marvelous reels!

BILL — What a picture! My God, what a picture!

FORBES — (*through his teeth*). And now, Eleanor, they might enjoy hearing one of *your* scenarios. In fact, I'm going upstairs to get one!

MRS. FORBES — Charlie — you — you're not really going to get one of mine!

FORBES — So help me God!

But Mr. Forbes is finally restrained from anything resembling a summary revenge. Instead he is induced to try a game of billiards — as soon as they can find the balls. Dulcy never can remember where she had them last.

Meantime the developing affair between Angela and Vincent reaches a climax. He is very much in earnest, is Vincent, and rather emotional.

LEACH — Oh, those deep burning eyes! The mystery of your hair! Angela, you're wonderful! I love you! Almost from the first moment I saw you, I've loved you — wanted you — longed for you! Why, I patterned my newest heroine just after you! To be with you is to breathe the perfume of exaltation! Angela!

ANGELA — (*breathlessly*). Vincent!

LEACH — I am offering you myself — everything that I am — oh, it's true that I've knocked about some — (*Modestly*) A good many girls have loved me, but I have never loved anyone but you, dearest. (*He kneels*) Say that you love me — a little — even though that love is now no greater than the glow of a single firefly in the fading day!

ANGELA — (*rising*). Oh, Vincent—my genius! (*Leach rises.*)

LEACH — (*clasping her in embrace*). My sweetheart! (*He kisses her and then holds her off, looking at her*) My wonder girl! Will you marry me? (*Angela's head drops in assent*) And the day? (*Embracing her again*) Love cries for its own!

ANGELA — Whenever you say — Vincent.

Vincent would not delay and he therefore suggests an elopement. At first Angela is fearful, but gradually the idea appeals to her — if Vincent will let her tell her mother and Dulcy. Vincent doesn't care whom she tells so long as she doesn't tell her father. So they tell Dulcy and find her ready and eager to help them. An elopement would be so romantic! But she agrees it would be best to let it come as a great surprise; no one should know, unless it be Mrs. Forbes. So she tells brother Bill first.

Bill is outwardly calm, but inwardly perturbed. He had known Angela in the old days and there had been some sort of an understanding between them for a while — but that is all over now, and Bill is eager to do his part in making the elopement a success. He does most of the planning, in fact, seeing that he knows the borough clerk in Bronxville. He can take them there in Mr. Forbes' car, and —

The arrangements for the elopement are no more than set when Mr. Forbes returns from his billiard game in anything but a nice temper. He had enjoyed his billiards — as a novelty. It was rather amusing to play up and down hill. But as a game —

He is just in the right mood to take Mrs. Forbes to task for flirting with Van Dyck and to demand to know where Angela is and what she is doing. "If I find this Leach person actually making love to Angela, why, I'm — I'm going to raise hell, that's all! It's been nothing but a series of aggravations — annoyances — ever since I came into this house. Eleanor, I can truthfully say that in all my fifty-three years I have never spent an unhappier evening."

MRS. FORBES — Oh, Charlie!

FORBES — But I'm not going to spend another! I am

not going to stay here and ride golf and play horseback!

MRS. FORBES — What are you going to do?

FORES — I am going — home!

MRS. FORBES — Charlie!

FORBES — I am going upstairs and pack! I promised Sterrett I'd drive him in tonight, and I'm not coming back! There's another thing! The way they're treating Sterrett! (*Starting up the stairs*) Good *night!*

MRS. FORBES — Charlie — you can't do that!

FORBES — Maybe I can't, but I'm going to! You can stay here with Van Dyck and watch Angela carrying on with that Leach person if you want to. BUT — mark my words — if anything comes out of this — if Angela and that fool *are* infatuated with each other, and try to do anything silly — I don't want ever to see *you* or *her* again! That — is all!

As he storms up the stairs Dulcy comes skipping in to announce that the young people are well on their way. Nothing so exciting has ever happened to her before, and she can't understand why Mrs. Forbes should suddenly turn upon her as one who is about to cause the complete breaking up of a happy home. "If my husband ever knows that — that I knew they were eloping, and didn't stop it, why — he'll — he'll — oh, I don't know what he'll do!" And she breaks down, sobbing. Then in bursts Forbes with the announcement that he is returning to town and that, so far as the jewelry merger is concerned, he is not at all sure he will be ready to go ahead with it — certainly not on the terms formerly suggested. Mr. Van Dyck's sudden decision to play a little Sicilian love song on the piano does not tend to quiet Mr. Forbes, and he stalks out. Gordon follows, in the hope that he may save something, at least, from the threatened break.

Things look rather blue for Dulcy, with her house party about to be shot all to pieces, her husband's business venture hanging by a thread, and the news of the elopement yet to be told — when Schuyler Van Dyck comes wonderfully to the rescue. He has listened a little and observed a great deal, and it occurs to him that if he can be of some use he would like to be. He would be glad to back Mr. Smith, for instance, in any jewelry merger he would like to start — in opposition to Mr. Forbes, if necessary.

VAN DYCK — Why doesn't he beat Mr. Forbes at his own game?

DULCY — Why — why — I never thought of that. But Mr. Forbes has all the money — and — and Gordie hasn't any.

VAN DYCK — That's it exactly! Now, I've always wanted to take a little flyer in the jewelry business. Suppose I financed Mr. Smith — suppose he and I set out to beat Mr. Forbes together? How would that be?

DULCY — (*incoherent*). Be? Be? Why, it would be incredible — unbelievable! (*Tearfully*) You — do you really mean it?

VAN DYCK — I do. I'll put up my check the moment your husband says the word.

DULCY — (*crying with joy*). Oh, Mr. Van Dyck, you've — you've made me thc proudest woman in all the world! You let me break the news to him, won't you?

VAN DYCK — Why — of course, if you wish it.

DULCY — And to think I introduced you to him! Now what will he think of me!

Then Mr. Forbes finds his car gone, and learns of the elopement. He is struggling with a barely suppressed rage when he returns to the house. Mrs. Forbes is trembling in fear of what may happen. But the Forbes' attention is focussed on Dulcy.

FORBES — Mrs. Smith — (*Turning*) and Mr. Smith. I'm measuring my words very carefully. Since — my car — is gone — and the last train — is gone, it seems that I shall be compelled to remain in this house — over night. (*He pauses. His eyes find Dulcy*) I shall — endeavor not to commit a murder.

GORDON — My dear Mr. Forbes, I'm sure this can be fixed up in some way.

DULCY — Yes. Of course it can. (*The old Dulcy for a second*) You know, an angry word spoken in haste —

FORBES — Please! (*To Mr. Smith*) Mr. Smith, in the circumstances, I don't see how we can possibly get on in business together. I don't like your methods!

GORDON — But, Mr. Forbes —

FORBES — I shall not call the matter off entirely, but any arrangement which we might eventually make would necessarily differ from our tentative discussions as to percentage. (*Gordon starts to speak*) I'm sorry, but that's my decision. The percentage would have to be adjusted. And now I wish you good night! (*He makes for the stairs.*)

MRS. FORBES — Oh, Charlie, mayn't I come with you?

FORBES — It is a matter of utter indifference to me *where* you go!

Dulcy's news of Van Dyck's offer is at first doubtfully and then exultantly received by Gordon. Now he can do what he has always wanted to do; now he can talk up to Forbes as that gentleman deserves to be talked up to; now —

His chance is not long in coming. Mr. Forbes comes back from his room to announce with a little something resembling sarcasm that he regrets being compelled to announce that on top of everything else Angela's pearl necklace has disappeared. And Henry cannot be found. But Gordon is too full of his new news to care much about a paltry string of pearls.

GORDON — Before you go, Mr. Van Dyck — (*Van Dyck halts*) And just a second, Mr. Forbes — (*Stopping*

Forbes) We'll straighten out about the necklace later. Mr. Van Dyck, I understand that you have offered to back me with unlimited capital in an independent jewelry merger? (*Dulcy sits on sofa, enjoying the situation.*)

FORBES — WHAT?

GORDON — Am I correct?

VAN DYCK — You are! Mrs. Smith has interested me very much in this matter. I'll put up the necessary capital, provided, of course, we can agree on the details.

GORDON — (*willing to agree to anything*). Oh, there'll be no difficulty about that. (*With dignity*) I accept your offer. Mr. Forbes, you said a minute ago that you were not certain whether or not our deal was off. Well, I've decided. It *is* off! I am going to line up with Mr. Van Dyck and fight you — fight you till one of us is forced to the wall. But before I do it, I'm going to tell you *why* I'm fighting you! I'm fighting you because you tried to take advantage of me!

FORBES — Advantage?

GORDON — Yes, advantage! By offering me less than you knew my business was worth. You knew I was in a hole, and now you're going to get just what you deserve. You're going to get a first rate licking!

DULCY — Oh, Gordie!

Mr. Forbes is a little startled, but of no mind to admit it. He can fight too, and if Gordon and Van Dyck want a fight, very well; they can have it. But Dulcy and Gordon are gloriously happy.

DULCY — (*rising and going to Gordon*). Gordie, darling, you were wonderful! (*Embraces him*) But the necklace! Do you think Henry —

GORDON — (*impatiently*). What's the difference whether he did or not? I feel like a new man.

DULCY — Gordie, you see — I *was* of some use after all.

GORDON — Use! You were wonderful! (*Taking her in his arms*) The best — the finest little wife in the world. (*He kisses her*) I'm going to beat Forbes, dear — I'm going to succeed — and I'll owe it all to you.

DULCY — Wasn't it lucky, my finding Mr. Van Dyck?

GORDON — Lucky! It was an inspiration!

DULCY — And I *am* a real helpmate?

GORDON — My darling! (*She is again in his arms.*)

DULCY — My Gordie! (*The door bell rings*) That's the door bell. You'll have to answer it, darling, since Henry isn't here.

The unexpected caller is a Mr. Blair Patterson, "a man somewhat under middle age, well groomed and with quite an air of authority." Mr. Patterson is an attorney and he is seeking a friend he thinks may be one of the Smith guests. Have they a Mr. Morgan stopping with them? Or a Mr. Ford? A Mr. Vanderbilt, possibly? No? A Mr. Astor? No? That's strange.

PATTERSON — H'm. Well, let me ask you — is one of your guests — tall, good-looking, plays the piano, interested in various — ah — investments —?

DULCY — (*proudly*). Oh, you mean Schuyler Van Dyck?

PATTERSON — (*thoughtfully*). Schuyler — Van Dyck.

DULCY — *He's* here.

PATTERSON — (*slowly*). Yes, I think I do mean Schuyler Van Dyck. I'm his cousin. (*Gordon and Dulcy exclaim cordially*) I — I've come for him.

DULCY — Come for him?

PATTERSON — Yes. His real name is Patterson — Horace Patterson. He has an hallucination that he's a millionaire. Goes round forming big companies — but I assure you he's perfectly harmless. (*He taps his head significantly as the curtain falls.*)

ACT III

The party is not particularly gay as it assembles next morning for breakfast. Mr. Forbes, for one, is distinctly not fit. He has not slept. He cannot find a cigar and he is still worried about Angela's elopement. Already he sees the flaring headlines: "Daughter of C. Rogers Forbes Elopes With Nut."

Even Dulcy is somewhat subdued as she comes, a little hesitantly, down the stairs. She is dressed in the brightest of sport clothes, however, and is ready for a busy day.

DULCY — Good morning, everybody. All ready for breakfast? It's a lovely day, isn't it? Has anyone been out? The sun is shining; it's just good to be alive. How do you feel this morning, Mrs. Forbes?

MRS. FORBES — I'm rather depressed.

DULCY — Depressed? Well, you mustn't be. I have some wonderful news for you. It's a surprise. Who do you think will be here inside an hour?

FORBES — A couple dozen reporters, I suppose.

DULCY — (*almost singing it*). A bridal party.

FORBES — So they *are* married!

DULCY — Yes. Willie 'phoned me just now. He said they had trouble getting in touch with the license clerk. I suppose all these people are like policemen — when you want one you never can find one. Anyway, they got him up at last and they were married at midnight.

MRS. FORBES — (*romantically*). Midnight!

FORBES — By a justice of the peace?

DULCY — No, indeed. By Dr. Carmichael — he's one of the finest ministers in Westchester. Willie knows him awfully well, so I suppose he did it as a special favor. Wasn't it nice of him?

FORBES — Yes, I appreciate it.

DULCY — So now you have a genius in the family, Mr. Forbes.

FORBES — Is he returning the car?

DULCY — Oh, of course — they'll be here any minute now — the happy couple.

Blair Patterson is one of the few who has slept well, though naturally he has worried somewhat about the trouble he has caused the Smiths in breaking in upon their party in order to retrieve his eccentric cousin, "Schuyler Van Dyck." He explains as much to Gordon when they meet on the way to the breakfast room.

PATTERSON — I'll take Mr. Patterson home with me just as soon as he can get his things together.

GORDON — There's no hurry — any more. Have you — told him?

PATTERSON — No, he hasn't seen me yet. I'll not have any difficulty; it's happened before.

GORDON — He's — a cousin, I believe you said?

PATTERSON — A distant cousin — it's really too bad. Brilliant chap — agreeable — obliging —

GORDON — He certainly is.

PATTERSON — Quite all right. Lives on Long Island with his mother and sister. Just this one hallucination.

GORDON — That's all he has?

PATTERSON — Oh, yes. Now and then he wanders off alone like this, but happily he never causes any real trouble.

GORDON — He doesn't, eh? That's fine.

PATTERSON — It's a little hard on *me* — being compelled to round him up at intervals. I have to divide my activities as a lawyer with those of a truant officer.

GORDON — Yes, it must be hard on you.

PATTERSON — (*looking about and approaching Smith*). Ah — I might ask a small favor?

GORDON — Certainly.

PATTERSON — I hope none of your guests has learned about my cousin's weakness?

GORDON — I don't think so. (*With a look toward the windows*) I hope not.

PATTERSON — If I may suggest it, it might be better to wait until I've taken him home, in case you wish to explain to anyone. It will save embarrassment. (*Van Dyck comes downstairs.*)

GORDON — I won't say anything.

PATTERSON — Thank you.

For a time it doesn't appear that Mr. Patterson is going to have an easy time convincing " Schuyler " that he should go home and leave all his Van Dyck interests at sixes and sevens, as it were. " We had all sorts of wonderful things planned," he protests; " my share alone would have been eight and a half millions. Besides, we were going to play golf."

But Patterson warns him that unless he goes, and goes peaceably, he (Patterson) will " never go through with that two hundred million dollar aeroplane company " they have been talking about, which has a most soothing effect on Schuyler.

With the Smiths the situation seems to become increasingly difficult as the morning wears on. Dulcy is not exactly at her wits' end, not having any wit, but Gordon is desperately worried.

GORDON — Dulcy — do you realize — exactly what has happened?

DULCY — Well, I — I don't know — I think so. Oh, Gordie, I didn't mean to —

GORDON — (*simply and kindly*). You must listen quietly, dear, until I finish.

DULCY — (*momentarily subdued*). Yes, darling.

GORDON — The time has come when — I must speak — frankly. (*A pause*) Do you know what Mr. Forbes is going to say to me when he learns who Van Dyck really is? (*Dulcy shakes her head; she cannot speak at the moment*) He is going to tell me that my factory and my services are of no use to him. Mr. Forbes thinks

— that he has been made a fool of, and — he's right. Our future success — depended entirely on him.

DULCY — But — but — we haven't really done anything to him. Just because we — we asked for more.

GORDON — It wasn't — our asking for more.

DULCY — Oh, you mean the elopement? (*She considers*) He doesn't like pictures?

GORDON — That was the crowning mistake.

DULCY — It was me again. It was me as usual. Oh, dear — how will it all end. (*She sits on the sofa.*)

GORDON — (*slowly*). Forbes will probably force me out of business. Then I'll have to start in all over again without — (*He glances around the room*) Without — this.

DULCY — (*forcing herself to say it*). And without me?

GORDON — (*dispassionately*). Dulcy, I love you. I shall always love you. I don't know whether it's because you have the soul of a child, or in spite of the fact that you act like one. (*He turns away*) I don't know what the future is going to do to us. You mean well, but you just don't stop to think.

DULCY — I guess, I don't think — I just think I think. (*Rising and speaking bravely*) I'll let you go, darling — if you want me to. I'm just — all wrong. I'm — a false note. I always wondered how I'd be able to make a man like you care for me — it seems so absurd for a man like you ever to love — a false note. And now — we're finding out — he can't.

GORDON — (*carried away for a second*). Dulcy, we can't end everything like this! You're not a false note — you're a melody — a whole tune. (*A pause. He reverts to his previous mood*) But I don't know what to do.

Dulcy is willing to do her best to reform. She is not sure that she can — but she is willing to try. She might, she thinks, make out a sort of budget of things not to do, like the one they tried for the housekeeping expenses. But Gordon hasn't much faith in the plan. At any rate she can promise again — promise never, never to interfere in Gordon's business affairs —

And she keeps her promise — until Mr. Forbes wants a car to get back to the city, and Gordon is hoping he can't find one until there has been some settlement of the merger problem. Then Dulcy perks up and agrees to get Mr. Forbes a car immediately. And Gordon is forced to apply the muffler again.

Then Mr. Forbes meets Mr. Patterson for the first time and recognizes him as one of the Van Dyck attorneys. Certainly if he is there — and has come all the way to Westchester to consult with Schuyler Van Dyck — there must be something in Gordon's threat of forming an independent merger after all. Briefly, Mr. Forbes is worried — but Dulcy soon does all she can to relieve his mind.

DULCY — Oh, Mr. Forbes — I'm sorry — (*She pauses a second*) Sorry about — the elopement, I mean, (*There is no response from Forbes*) and everything.

FORBES — (*annoyed*). It's quite all right, Mrs. Smith — quite all right.

DULCY — And I'm sorry about the business deal, too. But it's going to come out all right.

FORBES — What's that?

DULCY — I say the business deal between you and Gordie is going to come out all right.

FORBES — Oh, is it?

DULCY — Yes. Gordie will go in with you after all. Because Mr. Van Dyck isn't Mr. Van Dyck after all.

MRS. FORBES — What?

FORBES — What's that?

DULCY — No — he has something wrong up here. (*She taps her head*) He only *thinks* he's a millionaire.

FORBES — (*keeping calm*). Oh — so Mr. Van Dyck is — not Mr. Van Dyck!

DULCY — No.

FORBES — I see.

DULCY — (*after a pause*). So everything's all right now, isn't it?

FORBES — Oh, yes. Splendid!

But Mr. Forbes is sarcastic. They might think they can fool him, but they can't. He knows a thing or two or three — and one of them is that Blair Patterson is a Van Dyck attorney and that he is there on business. Therefore — he proposes to hold Gordon Smith to his original verbal agreement: the merger will be put through as planned, and Smith will take his sixteen and two-thirds per cent or —

Before Gordon can get hold of himself and accept this now most surprising offer the elopers burst through the door. Or at least half the eloping party. Angela and Bill are there.

FORBES — Where is Leach?

ANGELA — (*with a half smile*). I don't know, father.

FORBES — You — don't know? (*To Bill*) Well, perhaps you can tell us!

BILL — (*shaking his head*). I'm sorry.

FORBES — Didn't you help to arrange this wedding?

BILL — Why — yes.

FORBES — Well, don't you know where the groom is?

BILL — Sure — I'm the groom!

And, sure enough, Bill is. "It was just the most romantic thing that ever happened in the world!" according to Angela. "William — William just kidnapped me, that's all! Oh, William!" And she melts into Bill's arms.

Dulcy is ecstatically happy. Didn't she introduce

them? And isn't everything working out beautifully? With Henry back! And the lost necklace returned, and everything! The necklace? Oh, Henry found it just before he had to go and make his report to the probation officer, and he didn't have time to give it back to anyone then. It had slipped down between the cushions where Mr. Forbes was sitting, and Henry thought it best to take charge of it, with so many people in the house.

DULCY — (*she goes up between Bill and Angela, an arm around each*). It's upstairs for you, Angie, dear. Think of Angie being a married woman, and Willie a married man! Now, Mr. Forbes, you know, sixteen and two-thirds per cent isn't very much — for a relation, a brother-in-law.

FORBES — Well, I wasn't very generous about that deal of ours, or very just. Smith —

GORDON — Yes, sir.

FORBES — What do you say to coming in with me for twenty per cent?

DULCY — Twenty!

FORBES — (*anticipating further objections*). Well, then, twenty-five?

GORDON — Dulcinea, that satisfies *me!*

DULCY — Does it? Well if it satisfies Gordon — (*She turns to him*) I didn't mean to interfere, dear. I never will again. You can rely on me. A burnt child dreads the fire. Once bitten —

Gordon is embracing her and stops her with a kiss as the curtain falls.

"HE WHO GETS SLAPPED"

A Tragi-Comedy in Four Acts

By Leonid Andreyev

THE Theatre Guild, which, in this theatrical gateway to the American theatre, is becoming a sort of clearing house for the unusual foreign play, elected in January to produce Leonid Andreyev's "He Who Gets Slapped." Not only was the manuscript promising to the Guild's readers, but their success a season back with Molnar's "Liliom" gave them added encouragement. Nor were they disappointed.

"He" was produced at the home theatre of the Guild, the Garrick, January 10, 1922. It was continued there until February 11, when it was transferred to the Fulton to permit of the staging of Bernard Shaw's cycle play, "Back to Methuselah." "He" continued at the Fulton from February 13 till May 20, and, the demand still being strong, it was taken back to the Garrick, where, at this writing, it is threatening to run through the summer.

It is a colorful and interesting, if occasionally obscure, tragi-comedy extracted from the lives of the performers in one of those permanent continental circuses for which we have no duplicate in America. The scene (as the author saw it) is "a very large, rather dirty room with whitewashed walls. . . . The room is used for many purposes. It is the office of Papa Briquet, manager of the circus. Here he keeps his little desk. It is the cloak-room of some of the actors. It is also the room where the cast gathers between calls, during rehearsals or performances. Again, it is the check room for circus property, such as gilt armchairs, scenery for pantomimes and other wares of the circus household. The walls are covered with circus announcements and glaring posters."

The only outside window of the room opens on a courtyard. "The light from it is so dim that even by day the electricity has to be turned on." At the top of the back wall is a row of small, dusty windows high toward the ceiling. "At night, when the performance is going on, a bright light shines through. By day they are dark. . . . On the right is a high, wide, arched doorway which leads to the stables and the ring." The circus is established in "one of the large cities of France."

Into this circus greenroom the audience is admitted on a certain morning while a rehearsal is in progress in the circus hall proper. Offstage, the cracking of the riding-master's whip punctuates his shouted instructions to the performers. Two clowns come ambling down the runway leading to the ring entrance playing penny whistles and rehearsing a series of mincing steps that are to illustrate a "March of the Ants."

Also from the circus hall come Papa Briquet, the manager, followed by the Count Mancini. Briquet is "a stout, quiet man of average height; his bearing is hesitant." Mancini, "gnawing at the knob of his gold-mounted cane," is tall and slight. "The seams of his coat are worn and he keeps his coat buttoned tight. He assumes extremely graceful manners, takes affected poses, and has a special fondness for toying with his cane. When he laughs, which happens often, his thin, sharp face takes on a special resemblance to a satyr."

Just now he surveys with a cynical grin the activities of the clowns. Briquet is making sundry remarks that finally stir the circus man to protest.

Briquet — You make me sick, Count Mancini. You poke your nose into everything, you disturb the artists in their work. Some day you'll get a thrashing, and I warn you that I shan't interfere.

MANCINI — A man of my association and education cannot be expected to treat your performers as equals! You see that I do you the honor of speaking with you quite familiarly, quite simply. What more can you ask, Papa Briquet?

BRIQUET — (*slightly threatening*). Really!

MANCINI — Never mind my joke. What if they did dare attack me — ever seen this, Briquet? (*He draws a stiletto out of his cane and advances it silently*) Useful little thing. By the way, you have no idea of the discovery I made yesterday. A little girl in one of the suburbs. Such a girl! — oh, well! All right, all right — (*he hums "Barber of Seville"*) I know you don't like that kind of sport. But look here, you must give me a hundred francs!

BRIQUET — Not a sou.

MANCINI — Then I'll take away Consuelo—that's all—

BRIQUET — Your daily threat!

MANCINI — My threat! And you would do the same, if you were as hard up as I am. Now look here, you know as well as I do that I have to live up to my name somehow, keep up the family reputation. Just because the tide of ill-fortune which struck my ancestors compelled me to make my daughter, the Countess Veronica, a bareback rider — to keep us from starving — do you understand — you heartless idiot!

BRIQUET — You run after the girls too much! Some day you'll land in jail, Mancini!

MANCINI — In jail? Oh, no! Why, I have to uphold our name, the splendid tradition of my family, haven't I? The Mancinis are notorious all over Italy for their love of girls — girls! Is it my fault if I must pay such awful prices for what my ancestors got free? You're nothing but an ass, a parvenu ass. How can you understand family traditions? I don't drink — I stopped playing cards after that accident! No, you need not smile. Now if I give up the girls, what will be left of

Mancini? Only a coat of arms, that's all — in the name of family traditions, give me a hundred francs!

But Briquet is not interested in family traditions to that extent and flatly refuses the loan, even with Mancini pretending to cry because of the cruelty. How can Briquet treat him so — when he (Mancini) makes it a point to leave half of Consuelo's salary absolutely untouched. He is still pleading for his francs when Zinida arrives from the ring. Zinida is the lion tamer of the show and "burningly beautiful." Also she is Briquet's "unmarried wife."

She has no more sympathy for Mancini than has Briquet, even when the count turns to wheedling and flattery to move her. She has her suspicions of Mancini. She has heard that he has engaged a teacher for Consuelo. What does that mean? It means, explains Mancini, that his daughter — the Countess Veronica — can barely read, and he counts that a crime. Now she must study and learn. She must know literature, mythology, orthography — but he has a time with her. The student he first engaged had promptly fallen in love with Consuelo and it had been necessary to throw him out. He is an artful person, Zinida concludes.

BRIQUET — (*as the room begins to fill with performers*). You are stupid, Mancini. What do you do it for? (*In a didactic tone*) What do you want her to learn? What does she need to learn? What does she need to know about life? Don't you understand? What is geography? If I were the government I would forbid artists to read books. Let them read the posters, that's enough. Right now, your Consuelo is an excellent artist, but just as soon as you teach her mythology, and she begins to read, she'll become a nuisance, she'll be corrupted, and then she'll go and poison herself. I know those books, I've read 'em myself. All they teach is corruption, and how to kill oneself.

FIRST ACTRESS — I love the novels that come out in the newspapers.

BRIQUET — That shows what a foolish girl you are. You'll be done for in no time. Believe me, my friends, we must forget entirely what is happening out there. How can we understand all that goes on there?

MANCINI — You are an enemy of enlightenment, you are an obscurantist, Briquet.

BRIQUET — And you are stupid. You are from out there. What has it taught you? (*The actors laugh*) If you'd been born in a circus as I was, you'd know something. Enlightenment, education is plain nonsense — books are nonsense! Ask Zinida. She knows everything they teach out there — geography, mythology — does it make her any happier? You tell them, dear.

ZINIDA — Leave me alone, Louis.

Their attitude irritates Mancini. Their willingness to give up the world " out there " and all their asinine philosophy angers him. He is of a mind now to skin them for more than a paltry hundred francs. Briquet is an old skinflint who pays starvation wages, and Consuelo is his greatest star. What is it that has been drawing the crowds? Not Zinida and her lions! Not a couple of musical donkeys! But Consuelo and Bazano, her partner, and their amazing tango on horseback! The horseback tango is something even His Holiness, the Pope, would applaud!

Mancini is of a temper now that impresses them and they give him, not a hundred, but twenty francs, though Zinida is still suspicious of him. Why doesn't he borrow the money from his baron — "You're plotting something artful," she tells him. "I don't know you very well, but I guess you're an awful scoundrel." But Mancini only laughs at her. "Such an insult from such beautiful lips," he protests. . . .

Outside, a gentleman has asked to see Briquet. "A

gentleman from beyond the grave," reports the athlete who brings the word; one who looks like a "drunken ghost." Briquet is for sending the stranger away, but it may be as well to see him. The athlete brings the stranger to the top of the runway, points out Briquet and leaves him.

"The gentleman is not young, and he is ugly, but his rather strange face is bold and lively. He wears an expensive overcoat with a fur collar and holds his hat and gloves in his hand."

THE GENTLEMAN — Have I the pleasure of addressing the manager?

BRIQUET — Yes. Won't you sit down, please? Tilly, bring a chair.

GENTLEMAN — Oh! Don't trouble. (*Looks around*) These are your artists? Very glad —

MANCINI — (*Straightening and bowing slightly*). Count Mancini —

GENTLEMAN — (*Surprised*). Count?

BRIQUET — (*Indefinitely*). Yes, Count. And whom have I the honor of —

GENTLEMAN — I don't quite know myself — yet. As a rule you choose your own names, don't you? As yet, I haven't chosen mine — we can decide that later. I have an idea of one already, but I am afraid it sounds too literary.

BRIQUET — Literary?

GENTLEMAN — Yes! Too sophisticated. (*They all look surprised*) I presume these two gentlemen are clowns? I am so glad. May I shake hands with them? (*Stands up and shakes hands with clowns, who make silly faces.*)

BRIQUET — Excuse me — but what can I do for you?

GENTLEMAN — (*with the same pleasant, confident smile*). Oh! You do something for me? No. I want to do something for you, Papa Briquet.

BRIQUET — Papa Briquet? But you don't look like —

GENTLEMAN — (*reassuringly*). It's all right. I shall become " like." These two gentlemen just made remarkable faces. Would you like to see me imitate them? Look! (*He makes the same silly faces as the clowns.*)

BRIQUET — You are not drunk, sir?

GENTLEMAN — No. I don't drink as a rule. Do I look drunk?

POLLY — A little.

GENTLEMAN — No — I don't drink. It is a peculiarity of my talent.

BRIQUET — Where did you work before? Juggler?

GENTLEMAN — No. But I am glad you feel in me a comrade, Papa Briquet. Unfortunately I am not a juggler, and have worked nowhere — I am — just so.

MANCINI — Just so! But you look like a gentleman.

GENTLEMAN — Oh, you flatter me, Count. I am — just so.

BRIQUET — Well, what do you want? You see I am obliged to tell you that everything is taken.

GENTLEMAN — That's immaterial. I want to be a clown, if you will allow me.

The actors smile, and Briquet is not pleased with the suggestion. He has little time to waste on such applicants as this. But the gentleman is still quite eager and not at all discouraged. True, he knows nothing about being a clown, and knows nothing he might do. But something might be invented. " From literature?" sneers Briquet. " Possibly," the gentleman admits. He might try a speech on a religious topic, for example — with a debate among the clowns. Or, if that is too academic, some sort of joke about the creation of the world and its rulers. . . .

Now, Jackson, the leading clown of the circus, has joined the group, and Briquet suggests that he look over the stranger and decide if anything in the clown line can be made of him. Jackson is not at all hopeful. The gentleman's appearance is all right, but he probably can't even turn a somersault. No, the gentleman admits he can't. And he is thirty-nine years old, which is pretty old for a clown. Jackson is inclined to turn away and let the matter drop, but Zinida, who has been quietly watching the examination, suddenly speaks in his favor, to Briquet's annoyance. The question of the gentleman's employment, however, is still unsettled when Consuelo and Bazano come down the runway.

Consuelo is a dainty little thing of seventeen or eighteen, touched but lightly with the veneer of her environment. She is in riding costume, as is Bazano, a stalwart, serious, handsome young man of twenty-odd, who is her riding partner. With considerable pride, Count Mancini presents Consuelo to the stranger.

MANCINI — My daughter, sir, Countess Veronica. Known on the stage as Consuelo, "The Bareback Tango Queen." Did you ever see her?

GENTLEMAN — I have enjoyed her work. It is marvelous!

MANCINI — Yes! Of course! Everyone admits it. And how do you like the name, Consuelo? I took it from the novel of George Sand. It means "Consolation."

GENTLEMAN — What a wonderful knowledge of books!

MANCINI — Despite your strange intention, I can see, sir, that you are a gentleman. My peer! Let me explain to you, that only the strange and fatal misfortunes of our ancient family — "sic transit gloria mundi," sir.

CONSUELO — It's a bore, Daddy — where's my handkerchief, Alfred?

BAZANO — Here it is.

CONSUELO — (*showing the handkerchief to the gentleman*). Genuine Venetian. Do you like it?

GENTLEMAN — (*again bowing*). My eyes are dazzled, how beautiful! Papa Briquet, the more I look around me, the more I want to stay with you. (*Makes the face of a simpleton*) On the one hand a count, on the other —

JACKSON — (*nods approval*). That's not bad. Look here, think a bit — find something. Everyone here thinks for himself. (*Silence.*)

GENTLEMAN — (*stands with a finger on his forehead, thinking*). Invent something — invent something — Eureka!

POLLY — That means found! Come!

GENTLEMAN — Eureka — I shall be known among you as the one who gets slapped. . . .

There is general laughter at the suggestion, which proves, the gentleman insists, that it is a good idea. It isn't bad, the veteran Jackson admits: "He Who Gets Slapped" isn't at all bad. And he will be known simply as "He," the gentleman continues. Sounds a little like a dog, thinks Consuelo.

Suddenly Jackson swings around and slaps the gentleman soundly in the face. He starts back, his face flushing, but even as he does so he realizes it is a sort of test and meets it smilingly, and the crowd is delighted. "Take him, Papa Briquet," advises Jackson, "he will make good." And so it is arranged. . . .

Mancini is anxious. He has promised a certain Baron Regnard that he will bring Consuelo to lunch today, and now the girl refuses to go. She must rehearse. Alfred (Bazano) says she must rehearse, and Alfred's wishes are of much more importance than the baron's luncheon. Let the count go alone to meet Regnard. Mancini tries to bully her, but it is of no use, and he storms out angrily, with the amused clowns following after, playing a funeral march. . . .

HE — . . . All the people about you are so nice, Papa Briquet. I suppose that good-looking bareback rider is in love with Consuelo, isn't he?

ZINIDA — (*laughs*). It's none of your business. For a newcomer you go poking your nose too far. How much does he want, Papa?

BRIQUET — Just a minute. See here, "He." I don't want to make a contract with you.

HE — Just as you please. Don't let us talk about money. You are an honest fellow, Briquet; you will see what my work is worth to you, and then —

BRIQUET — (*pleased*). Now that's very nice of you. (*In a whisper*) Zinida, the man really doesn't know anything.

ZINIDA — Well, do as he suggests. Now we must write it down. Where's the book?

BRIQUET — Here. (*To "He"*) We have to put down the names of the actors, you know — it's police regulations. Then if anyone kills himself, or —

ZINIDA — What is your name?

HE — (*smiling*). He. I chose it, you know. Or don't you like it?

BRIQUET — We like it all right — but we have to have your real name. Have you a passport?

HE — (*confused*). A passport? No.

ZINIDA — Then we can't take you. We cannot quarrel with the police, just on your account.

BRIQUET — She is my wife. I hadn't told you. She's right. You might get hurt by a horse, or hurt yourself — or do something. We don't know you, you see. I personally don't care, but out there, it's different, you see. For me a corpse is just a corpse — and I don't ask anything about him. It's up to God or the devil. But they — they're too curious. Well, I suppose it's necessary for order. I don't know — got a card?

HE — . . . you understand that I don't want my name to be known?

BRIQUET — Something like that, eh?

HE — Why can't you imagine that I have no name? Can't I lose it as I might lose my hat? When a stray dog comes to you, you don't ask him his name — you simply give him another. Let me be that dog.

BRIQUET — The Dog!

ZINIDA — Why don't you tell us your name, just the two of us. Nobody else need know it. Unless you should break your neck —

HE — (*hesitates*). Honestly? (*Zinida shrugs her shoulders.*)

BRIQUET — Where people are honest, their word is good. One sees you come from out there.

Zinida gives a start as she reads the name on the card and passes it quickly to Briquet. He, too, is startled. " If you are really what is written here — " he begins. But the gentleman checks him. " For heaven's sake — this does not exist," he says indicating the card, "it is just a check for an old hat. I pray you to forget it as I have. I am ' He ' who gets slapped — nothing more."

Briquet is still convinced the stranger must be at least a little drunk. If he isn't — well, as Zinida says, it is his own business. And together they go into the circus room that " He " may see the animals and the arena. . . .

Zinida sends for Bazano. People keep telling her that he is in love with Consuelo and she would know the truth. Bazano is evasive. He and Consuelo work together well — as for love; " I do not love anybody. No, I love nobody. How can I? Consuelo? She is here today, gone tomorrow, if her father should take her away. And I? Who am I? An acrobat. The son of a Milanese shoemaker. She? I cannot even talk about it. Like my horses, there's nothing I can say. Who am I to love?"

To Zinida the boy means a great deal. For him she is willing to lower her pride, to declare her passion, to plead for favor. But he will not listen. " When you say you love as if you were cracking me with your whip," he shouts at her. " You know it is disgusting — " And he goes.

" He " has been standing in the doorway. He has heard and seen Zinida's failure. Now he steps forward hesitantly to beg her pardon for having intruded.

ZINIDA — There you are again, poking your nose into everything, " He." Do you really want a slap?

HE — (*laughing*). No. I simply forgot my overcoat. I didn't hear anything.

ZINIDA — I don't care whether you did or not.

HE — May I take my coat?

ZINIDA — Take it, if it's yours. Sit down, " He." (" *He* " *sits*) Now tell me, " He," could you love me?

HE — (*laughing*). I? I and Love? Look at me, Zinida. Did you ever see a lover with a face like this?

ZINIDA — One can succeed with such a face —

HE — That's because I am happy — because I lost my hat — because I am drunk — or perhaps I am not drunk. But I feel as dizzy as a young girl at her first ball. It is so nice here — slap me, I want to play my part. Perhaps it will awaken love in my heart, too — Love — (*As if listening to his own heart with pretended terror*) do you know — I feel it! (*In the circus the tango is played again.*)

ZINIDA — (*listening too*). For me?

HE — No. I don't know. For everyone. (*Listens to the music*) Yes, they are dancing — how beautiful Consuelo is. The boy — he looks like a Greek god — he looks as if he'd been fashioned by Praxiteles. Love! Love! (*Silence, music.*)

ZINIDA — Tell me, " He " —

HE — At your service, Queen!

ZINIDA — " He," what shall I do to make my lions love me?

" He " is looking quizzically at her as the curtain falls.

ACT II

During an evening performance, some days later, Consuelo and Baron Regnard are visiting between her appearances. " The Baron is a tall, stout man in evening dress, a rose in his buttonhole. Grasping the ground with feet well apart, he gazes at her with convex, spider-like eyes."

Consuelo is not at all dismayed by the Baron's attitude. She seems rather to enjoy it, in fact, fencing deftly with all his inquiries. She is very sorry her father had made her return the baron's jewels. She even cried a little. But she will not let the baron call her father a beggar and a charlatan for all that. Nor will she let the baron kiss her hand. It isn't proper, except at greeting and at parting. The baron has neither just come, nor is he preparing to depart. Everybody is in love with Consuelo. The baron is sure of that. Even that new clown they call "He" — But "He" is not in love with her, Consuelo insists. "He" is just a jolly good friend — and ever so funny. "He" got fifty-two slaps yesterday! Think of that!

BARON — And Bazano, Consuelo — do you like him?

CONSUELO — Yes, very much. He is so good-looking. "He" says that Bazano and I are the most beautiful couple in the world. "He" calls him Adam, and me, Eve. But that's improper, isn't it? "He" is so improper.

BARON — And does he speak to you very often?

CONSUELO — Yes, often — but I don't understand him. It seems as if he were drunk.

BARON—"Consuelo!" That means in Spanish, Consolation — Consuelo, I love you!

CONSUELO — Talk it over with father.

BARON — (*angry*). Your father is a swindler and a charlatan. He should be turned over to the police. Don't you understand that I cannot marry you?

CONSUELO — But father says you can —

BARON — No, I cannot. And what if I shoot myself? Consuelo, silly girl, I love you unbearably — unbearably, do you understand? I am probably mad — and must be taken to a doctor, yanked about, beaten. Why do I love you so much, Consuelo?

CONSUELO — Then, you'd better marry.

BARON — I have had a hundred women, beauties, but they meant nothing to me. You are the only one, and I don't see anyone else. Who strikes man with love, God or the devil? The devil struck me. Let me kiss your hand.

CONSUELO — No. (*She thinks a while and sighs.*)

BARON — Do you think sometimes? What are you thinking about now, Consuelo?

CONSUELO — (*with another sigh*). I don't know why, I just felt sorry for Bazano. (*Sighs again*) He is so nice to me when he teaches me and he has such a tiny little room.

BARON — (*indignant*). You were there?

CONSUELO — No, he told me about it. (*smiling*) Do you hear the noise in there? That's "He" getting slapped. The intermission is coming soon.

Before she realizes what he is doing, the baron has sunk to his knees and is imploring her to love him. She begs him to get up before the others come. "It's disgusting! You're so fat!" And finally he flounders to his feet just as the performers troop in, led by the clowns and "He," in his make-up, followed by the riders and acrobats, actors, actresses, etc. They are shouting congratulations to "He." A hundred slaps he has earned, and Jackson is quite sure, now, he will have a career. "He" is pleased, but his mind is not on his success tonight. He is interested in the baron. He has approached him, now, with easy familiarity, and spoken to him. The baron may not recognize him, "He" suggests, but he is the young man who had brought back the jewels the baron had given to Consuelo. Upon which statement the baron turns his back, and "He" laughs uproariously. . . .

Briquet would warn his new clown. "He" has been doing very well, but he must not press his advantage. He must not go so far the audiences feel the bite of his slaps. Jackson is inclined to back Briquet up in this. He, too, has warned the newcomer to beware his success.

HE — Don't be angry, Jim. It's a play, don't you understand? I become happy when I enter the ring and hear the music. I wear a mask and I feel humorous. There is a mask on my face and I play. I may say anything like a drunkard. Do you understand? Yesterday, when I, with this stupid face, was playing the great man, the philosopher, I was walking this way, and was telling how great, how wise, how incomparable I was — how God lived in me, how high I stood above the earth — how glory shone above my head. Then you, Jim, you hit me for the first time. And I asked you, "What is it, they're applauding me?" Then, at the tenth slap, I said: "It seems to me that they sent for me from the Academy?"

"He" is looking around him "with an air of unconquerable pride and splendor," and the audience of his fellows is enjoying the memory of the incident related. They laugh appreciatively — all but Jackson. The old clown turns suddenly and gives "He" a real slap. "Why?" demands the clown. "Because you are a fool, and play for nothing!" At which there is more laughter.

The scene bell has rung and the performers have trooped back to the stage. Only "He" remains — "He" and Mancini. Mancini is depressed. He invites the clown to buy him a bottle of wine, that he may become cheerful. It appears the Count is in trouble. That little suburban affair of his — The girl's parents are inclined to cause trouble.

HE — Isn't there a way of settling it somehow?

MANCINI — Is there a way of getting money, somehow?

HE — And the baron?

MANCINI — Oh, yes! He's just waiting for it, the bloodsucker! He'll get what he's after. Some day, you'll see me give him Consuelo for ten thousand francs, perhaps for five!

HE — Cheap!

MANCINI — Did I say it was anything else? Do I want to do it? But these bourgeois are strangling me. They've got me by the throat. " He," one can easily see that you're a gentleman, the only one here to understand me. I showed you the jewels which I sent back to him. Damn honesty — I didn't even dare change the stones, put false ones —

HE — Why?

MANCINI — It would have spoiled my game. Do you think he didn't weigh the diamonds when he got them back?

HE — He will not marry her.

MANCINI — Yes, he will. You don't understand. (*Laughs*) The first half of his life, this man had only appetites — now love's got him. If he does not get Consuelo, he is lost, " He " — like a withered narcissus. Plague take him with his automobiles. Did you see his car?

HE—I did—Give Consuelo to the circus-rider.

MANCINI — To Bazano? (*laughs*) Are you crazy? What nonsense you do talk! Oh, I know. It's your joke about Adam and Eve. But please stop it. It's clever, but it compromises the child. She told me about it.

HE — Or give her to me.

MANCINI — Have you a billion? (*Laughs*). Ah, " He," I'm not in the proper mood to listen to your clownish jokes —

Mancini grows garulous as the wine flows, and " He " the more attentive. The baron will never marry Consuelo, " He " insists: she is not educated; she is not polished; off her horse she has no better manners than a servant girl. But these things, Mancini answers, are not necessary to a pretty woman. Consuelo is an unpolished jewel. It is best to keep jewels that way—to fool the thieves. The diamond merchants of Amsterdam knew that. Once he had tried to polish Consuelo, but soon she was learning too much and too fast. It was dangerous.

He — The sleep of a diamond! She is only sleeping, then. You are wise, Mancini.

Mancini — Do you know what blood flows in the veins of an Italian woman? The blood of Hannibal and Corsini — of a Borgia — and of a dirty Lombardi peasant — and of a Moor. Oh! An Italian woman is not of a lower race, with only peasants and gypsies behind her. All possibilities, all forms are included in her, as in our marvelous sculpture. Do you understand that, you fool? Strike here — out springs a washerwoman or a cheap street girl whom you want to throw out because she has a screechy voice. Strike there — but carefully and gently, for there stands a queen, a goddess, the Venus of the Capitol, who sings like a Stradivarius and makes you cry, idiot! An Italian woman —

He — You're quite a poet, Mancini! But what will the baron make of Consuelo?

Mancini — Make of her? A baroness, you fool! What are you laughing at? I don't understand you at any rate. But I am happy that this lovesick beast is neither a duke nor a prince — or she would be a princess and I — what would become of me? A year after the wedding they would not let me even into the kitchen — (*Laughing*) not even into the kitchen! I, Count Mancini, and she a — a simple —

He — (*jumping up*). What did you say? You are not her father, Mancini?

Mancini — Tss! — the devil — I am so nervous today! Heavens, who do you think I am? "Her father?" Of course — (*Tries to laugh*) how silly you are — haven't you noticed the family resemblance? Just look, the nose, the eyes — (*Suddenly sighs deeply*) Ah, "He." How unhappy I am! Think of it! Here I am, a gentleman, nearly beaten in my struggle to keep up the honor of my name, while there in the parquet — there sits that beast, an elephant with the eyes of a spider — and he looks at Consuelo — and —

HE — Yes, yes, he has the motionless stare of a spider — you're right!

MANCINI — Just what I say — a spider! But I must, I shall compel him to marry her. You'll see — (*Walking excitedly up and down, playing with his cane*) you'll see! All my life I've been getting ready for this battle.

A note is brought in from Baron Regnard. It is for Mancini, and it fills him with the greatest joy. He may have to borrow ten francs from his friend today, but within a month he will be driving his own car! The baron has decided to marry Consuelo. . . .

In the ring outside an awesome silence envelops the audience. Zinida, in the cage with her lions, is acting like a mad woman. Poor old Briquet cannot stand the strain of watching her. She seems possessed with the idea that she must conquer the beasts to prove their love of her. . . . She comes now, looking "like a drunken bacchante, or like a mad woman. . . . She is like the living statue of a mad Victory." The company stands awkwardly about, startled into respectful silence by her staring eyes. Suddenly her eyes meet those of Bazano and she cries out exultantly: "Bazano! Alfred! Did you see? My lions do love me!" But without answering her, Bazano hurriedly leaves the stage. Zinida's victory has been for naught. She "seems to wither and grow dim, as a light being extinguished." Briquet is puzzled. Why should Zinida want those beasts to love her? Those hairy monsters with diabolic eyes! Whom can they love? Only their equals, "He" believes. . . .

They have taken Zinida home. The performers have

drifted back into the arena. "He" and Consuelo are alone. "He" is in a bantering mood, tempered by a gathering melancholy. Consuelo is saddened by the thought of Zinida.

CONSUELO — It's all so sad here, today. "He," are you sorry for Zinida?

HE — What did she do?

CONSUELO — I didn't see. I had closed my eyes, and didn't open them. Alfred says she is a wicked woman, but that isn't true. She has such nice eyes, and what tiny cold hands — as if she were dead. What does she do it for? Alfred says she should be audacious, beautiful, but quiet, otherwise what she does is only disgusting. It isn't true, is it, "He"?

HE — Zinida loves Alfred.

CONSUELO — Alfred? My Bazano? (*Shrugging her shoulders, and surprised*) How does she love him? The same as everyone loves?

HE — Yes — as everyone loves — or still more.

CONSUELO — Bazano? Bazano? No — it's nonsense. (*Pause; silence*) What a beautiful costume you have, "He." You invented it yourself?

HE — Jim helped me.

CONSUELO — Jim is so nice! All clowns are nice.

HE — I am wicked.

CONSUELO — (*Laughs*). You? You are the nicest of all. Oh, goodness! Three acts more! This is the second on now. Alfred and I are in the third. Are you coming to see me?

HE — I always do. How beautiful you are, Consuelo.

CONSUELO — Like Eve? (*Smiles.*)

HE — Yes, Consuelo. And if the baron asks you to be his wife, will you accept?

CONSUELO — Certainly, "He." That's all father and I are waiting for. Father told me yesterday that the baron will not hesitate very long. Of course I do not love him. But I will be his honest, faithful wife. Father wants to teach me to play the piano.

HE — "His honest, faithful wife." Are those your own words?

CONSUELO — Certainly, they are mine. Whose could they be? He loves me so much, the poor thing. Dear "He," what does "love" mean? Everybody speaks of love — love — Zinida, too! Poor Zinida!

But "He" cannot answer her query about the meaning of love. Perhaps there is an answer in the lines of her hand. He puzzles over these; "lucky" lines, some of them — but there is one line that is not lucky — a strange, winding line about which the stars are whispering. "Their voices are distant and terrible; their rays are pale, and their shadows slip by like the ghosts of dead virgins. Their spell is upon thee, Consuelo! Beautiful Consuelo! Thou standest at the door of eternity."

CONSUELO — I don't understand. Does it mean that I will live long?

HE — This line — how far it goes! Strange! You will live forever, Consuelo.

CONSUELO — You see, "He," you did tell me a lie, just like a gypsy!

HE — But it is written — here, silly — and here. Here you have eternal life, love, and glory; and here, listen to what Jupiter says. He says: "Goddess, thou must not belong to any one born on earth," and if you marry the baron — you'll die, Consuelo.

CONSUELO — (*laughing*). Will he eat me?

HE — No — you will die before he has time to eat you — don't laugh, Consuelo. You stand at the gates of eternity. Your die is cast, and your Alfred, whom you love in your heart, even though your mind is not aware of it, your Alfred cannot save you. He, too, is a stranger on this earth. He is submerged in a deep sleep. He, too, is a little god who has lost himself, and, Consuelo, never, never will he find his way to heaven again — Consuelo, do you know who can save you? The only one who can save you? I! — look! It is written — "H."

CONSUELO — He Who Gets Slapped? Is that written here, too?

HE — That, too. The stars know everything. But look here, what more is written about him. He is an old god in disguise, who came down to earth only to love you, foolish little Consuelo.

CONSUELO — (*laughing and singing*). Some god!

HE — Don't mock! The gods don't like such empty laughter from beautiful lips. The gods grow lonely and die when they are not recognized. Oh, Consuelo! Oh, great joy and love! Do recognize this god and believe in him. Think a moment, sometimes they go mad, too.

. . . .

CONSUELO — I don't like it. What language are you speaking? I don't understand —

HE — I speak the language of thy awakening. Consuelo, accept this god who was thrown down from the summit like a stone. Recognize the god who fell to the earth in order to live, to play, and to be drunk with infinite joy. Awake, goddess!

CONSUELO — (*tortured*). "He" — I cannot understand. Let my hand alone.

HE — Sleep. Then awake again, Consuelo! And when thou wakest — remember that hour when, covered with snow-white sea-foam, thou didst emerge from the sky-blue waters. Remember heaven, and the slow eastern wind, and the whisper of the foam at thy marble feet. . . . You see the waves playing. You hear the song of the sirens, their sorrowful song of joy. You hear the sun singing, like the strings of a divine harp spreading its golden rays. You hear the mountains, in the blue cloud of incense, sing their hymns of glory. Remember, oh,

Consuelo, the song of the mountains, the prayer of the sea. Remember — remember —

Consuelo — (*opening her eyes*). No! "He," I was feeling so happy, and suddenly I forgot it all. Yet something of it all is still in my heart. Help me again, "He." Remind me. It hurts; I hear so many voices. They all sing "Consuelo — Consuelo." What comes after?

From the ring comes the music of a tempestuous circus gallop. It is Alfred's music, and Consuelo is happy at the sound of it. But "He" is angry. "Forget Bazano!" he commands. Suddenly he is on his knees before her. "I love you, Consuelo! I love you!"

But she will not listen. In quick temper she slaps him soundly. "You forget who you are!" she says, angrily. "You are He Who Gets Slapped! A god — with such a face! Was it with slaps they threw you down from heaven, god?"

He recoils from the blow — but quickly recovers his clown's spirits. "I was only playing, queen. . . ."

But he had no right to play so that she believed him, she answers. She is sorry she slapped him. "I did not want to, really, but you were so — so disgusting. And now you are so funny again. You have great talent, "He" — or, are you drunk?"

He is but playing the fool, he says, and Consuelo is his queen. Every queen has a fool and he is very much in love with her. Sometimes there are many fools, "and the sound of slaps does not cease. . . . Fool 'He' can have no rival! Who is there who could stand such a deluge of slaps, such a hailstorm of slaps, and not give in? 'Have pity on me. I am but a poor fool!'"

At the top of the runway another stranger from "out there" has appeared. At sight of him Consuelo runs away.

He — (*in a depressed voice*). What can I do for you?

GENTLEMAN — Is this you?

HE — Yes! It is I. And you?

GENTLEMAN — Is this you, Mr.—

HE — (*in a rage*). My name here is "He." I have no other name, do you hear? He Who Gets Slapped. And if you want to stay here, don't forget it.

GENTLEMAN — Your manner — such familiarity — you used to be —

HE — We are all familiar here. (*Contemptuously*) Besides, that's all you deserve, anywhere.

GENTLEMAN — (*humbly*). You have not forgiven me, "He"?

HE — Are you here with my wife? Is she in the audience?

GENTLEMAN — (*quickly*). Oh, no! I am alone. She stayed there!

HE — You've left her already?

GENTLEMAN — (*humbly*). No. We have — a son. After your sudden and mysterious disappearance — when you left that strange and insulting letter —

HE — (*laughs*). Insulting? You are still able to feel insults? What are you doing here? Were you looking for me, or is it mere chance?

GENTLEMAN — I have been looking for you for half a year — through many countries. And suddenly, today — by accident, indeed — I had no acquaintance here, and I went to the circus. We must talk things over — "He," I implore you. (*Silence.*)

HE — Here is a shadow I cannot lose! To talk things over! Do you really think we still have something to talk over? All right. Leave your address with the porter, and I will let you know when you can see me. Now, go! Go!

"The stranger bows and leaves. 'He' does not return the bow but stands with outstretched hand, in the pose of a great man who shows a boring visitor the door."

The curtain falls

ACT III

It is a few days later — the morning appointed by "He" for his talk with the stranger. It is before the rehearsal hour and no one is about. "He" is striding up and down waiting. "He wears a broad, parti-colored coat and a prismatic tie. His derby is on the back of his head and his face is clean-shaven like that of an actor."

The Gentleman enters. "He is dressed in black and has an extremely well-bred appearance. His thin face is yellowish and when he is upset his colorless, dull eyes often twitch."

"He" is not inclined to waste time with the fellow. Let there be no manners and let them get through with what they have to say to each other as quickly as possible. But the Gentleman finds it difficult to proceed. Everything is so strange, so weirdly strange. And strangest of all — the thought of "He" as a clown in a circus. "It is true," he says, "when everybody there decided that you were dead I was the only man who did not agree with them. I felt that you were still alive. But to find you among such surroundings — I can't understand it."

HE — You say you have a son. Doesn't he look like me?

GENTLEMAN — I don't understand.

HE — Don't you know that widows or divorced women often have children by the new husband which resemble the old one? (*Laughs*) And your book, too, is a big success, I hear.

GENTLEMAN — Are you insulting me again?

HE — What a restless, touchy faker you are! Please sit still; be quiet. It is the custom here to speak plainly. Why were you trying to find me?

GENTLEMAN — My conscience —

HE — You have no conscience. Or were you afraid

that you hadn't robbed me of everything I possessed, and you came for the rest? But what more could you take from me now? My fool's cap with its tinkling bells? It's too big for your head! Crawl back, you book-worm!

. . . .

GENTLEMAN — I am a very unhappy man. You must forgive me.

HE — Explain it to me. You say yourself that your book is a tremendous success; you are famous; you have glory. There is not a yellow newspaper in which you and your thoughts are not mentioned. Who knows me? And my heavy abstractions? You — you are the great vulgarizer! You have made my thoughts comprehensible even to horses! With the art of a great vulgarizer, a tailor of ideas, you dressed my Apollo in a barber's jacket; you handed my Venus a yellow ticket, and to my bright hero you gave the ears of an ass. And then your career is made, as Jackson says. And wherever I go, the whole street looks at me with thousands of faces, in which — what mockery — I recognize the traits of my own children. Oh! How ugly your son must be if he resembles me! Why then are you unhappy, you poor devil? (*The Gentleman bows his head, plucking at his gloves*) The police haven't caught you, as yet. Is it possible to catch you? You always keep within the limits of the law. You have been torturing yourself up to now because your marriage to my wife was not legal. A notary public is always present at your thefts. What is the use of this self-torture, my friend? I died! I'm dead! You are not satisfied with having taken only my wife? Let my glory also remain in your possession. It is yours. Accept my ideas. Assume all the rights, my most lawful heir! I died! And when I was dying (*making a stupidly pious face*) I forgave thee!

. . . .

GENTLEMAN — I am respected and I am famous, yes?

I have a wife and a son, yes? (*Laughs slowly*) My wife still loves you; our favorite discussion is about your genius. She supposes you are a genius. We, I and she, love you even when we are in bed. Tss! It is I who must make faces. My son! Yes, he'll resemble you. And when, to have a little rest, I go to my desk, to my inkpot, my books — there, too, I find you. Always you! Everywhere you! And I am never alone. And when at night — you, sir, should understand this — when at night I go to my lonely thoughts, to my sleepless contemplations, even then I find your image in my head, your damned and hateful image!

He — What a comedy! How marvelously everything is turned about in this world. The robbed proves to be a robber and the robber is complaining of theft, and cursing! I was mistaken. You are not my shadow. You are the crowd. You live by my creations, you hate me; you breathe my breath, you are choking with anger. And choking with anger, hating me, you still walk slowly on the trail of my ideas. But you are advancing backward, advancing backward, comrade! Oh, what a marvelous comedy! Tell me, would you be relieved if I really had died?

Gentleman — Yes! I think so. Death augments distance and dulls the memory. Death reconciles. But you do not look like a man who — I certainly do not dare to ask you — to ask you to die, but tell me — you'll never come back there? No, don't laugh. If you want me to, I'll kiss your hand. Don't grimace! I would have done so if you had died.

He — (*slowly*). Get out, vermin!

But the gentleman lingers. He must be sure. The performers begin to arrive. Awkwardly the Gentleman meets them. Guardedly he again approaches "He." "You did not answer my question? . . . Will you ever come back?" he demands. "Never, never, never!" shouts

"He." Let the gentleman go — and live in peace. At least, comparative peace!

Count Mancini arrives. To him "He" presents the stranger. "Prince Poniatovsky, Count Mancini!" . . .

Consuelo is to have a benefit performance before she leaves the circus. The baron has bought up all the parquet seats to guarantee its success. But it is not a happy time for Consuelo. Even Alfred Bazano is cross and sharp with her these last days. She comes running from the ring even now protesting that he had yelled at her and hit her — or almost hit her — with his whip. But she doesn't want him reprimanded for it. She has already forgiven him. Poor Alfred! No wonder he was angry. She was much too nervous to work today.

Consuelo — Hello, "He." Come and lie down at my feet and tell me something cheerful — you know when you paint the laughter on your face you are very good-looking, but now, too, you are very, very nice. Come on, "He," why don't you lie down?

He — Consuelo! Are you going to marry the baron?

Consuelo — (*indifferently*). It seems so.

He — And do you remember my prediction?

Consuelo — What prediction?

He — That if you marry the baron, you'll die.

Consuelo — Oh, that's what you're talking about — but you were making fun.

He — Nobody can tell, my queen. Sometimes one makes fun, and suddenly it turns out to be true. Suppose suddenly you should die?

Consuelo — And what is — death?

He — I do not know, my queen. Nobody knows. Like love! Nobody knows. You will be away from here. And the music will play without you, and without you the crazy Bazano will be galloping and Tilly and Polly will be playing on their pipes without you; tilly-polly, tilly-polly . . . tilly-tilly, polly-polly. . . .

CONSUELO — Please don't, " He," darling. I'm so sad, anyway — tilly-tilly, polly-polly. . . .

HE — You were crying, my little Consuelo? Give me back the image of my beautiful goddess!

CONSUELO — Ah, I don't know. There is something here. (*Presses her hand against her heart*) I don't know, " He." I must be sick. What is sickness? Does it hurt very much?

HE — It is not sickness. It is the charm of the far off stars, Consuelo. It is the voice of your fate, my little queen.

CONSUELO — Don't talk nonsense, please. What should the stars care about me? Nonsense, " He "! Tell me rather another tale which you know. About the blue sea and those gods, you know — who are so beautiful. Did they all die?

HE — They are all alive, but they hide themselves, my goddess.

. . . .

HE — (*slowly*). Consuelo, my queen! Don't go to the baron today.

CONSUELO — Why?

HE — I don't want you to.

CONSUELO — (*getting up*). What? You don't want me to!

HE — (*bowing his head low — imploringly*). I — I shall not allow it — I beg you!

Bazano comes for Consuelo. There is still more practicing to be done. He is confused. Evidently a memory of their quarrel still lingers. But Consuelo is happy and soon puts him at his ease. . . . They are a handsome couple standing side by side, says " He." " Like Adam and Eve." Consuelo remembers his foolish joke. She is laughing happily now. But her father and the baron — aren't they coming to get her? " He " inquires. They are, but they can wait, says Consuelo. They are not very important people. Now she has flown away to change her slippers that she may ride with Alfred, and Bazano waits.

HE — Bazano — you love her? (*Silence.*)

BAZANO — You allow yourself too many liberties, "He." I don't know you. You came from out there — the street.

HE — But you know the baron. She loves you. Save her from the spider! Or are you blind, and don't see the web which is woven in every dark corner. Get out of the vicious circle in which you are turning around like a blind man. Take her away, steal her, do what you want — kill her, even, and take her to the heavens or to the devil! But don't give her to this man! He is a defiler of love. And if you are timid, if you are afraid to lift your hand against her — kill the baron! Kill!

BAZANO — (*with a smile*). And who will kill the others, to come?

HE — She loves you.

BAZANO — Did she tell you that herself?

HE — Why don't you want to believe me? But look, look yourself. Look in my eyes. Do such eyes lie? (*Bazano bursts out laughing*) What are you laughing at, youth?

BAZANO — You look now as you did that evening in the ring. You remember? When you were a great man, and they sent for you from the Academy and suddenly — hup! He Who Gets Slapped!

HE — (*laughing the same way*). Yes, yes, you are right, Bazano. There is a resemblance. He Who Gets Slapped. (*With a strained expression, taking a pose*) "It seems to me they sent for me from the Academy!"

BAZANO — (*displeased*). But I don't like this play. You can present *your* face for slaps if you want to, but not me! (*Turns to go.*)

HE — Bazano!

BAZANO — And don't you ever talk to me again about Consuelo!

Bazano is angrily slapping his boot top with his whip as he dashes from the room. There is a wrathful, tortured expression on "He's" face, but he does not call Bazano back.

The count and the baron are soon there, a little disappointed to find Consuelo not ready. Mancini will fetch her, if "He" will entertain the baron for a few moments.

"The baron sits with his legs spread apart and his chin on the top of his cane. The silk hat remains on his head. He is silent."

"In what way would you like me to entertain you, Baron?" "He" inquires. "In no way!" growls the baron. "I don't like clowns!" "Nor I barons," agrees "He."

There is a silent moment and then "'He' puts on his derby hat, takes a chair with a large gesture and puts it down heavily in front of the baron. He sits astride of it, imitating the pose of the baron, and looks him in the eyes."

HE — Can you be silent very long?

BARON — Very long.

HE — (*taps on the floor with his foot*). And can you wait very long?

BARON — Very long.

HE — Until you get it?

BARON — Until I get it. And you?

HE — I too.

They glare at each other silently, their heads close together. From the ring one hears the strains of the tango as the curtain falls.

ACT IV

It is the night of Consuelo's benefit. The assembly room is in a state of great disorder, though there are flowers everywhere. Inside the arena they say the ring is practically covered with the baron's roses. They are like a carpet — for Consuelo to gallop over.

Zinida is rather pleased that Consuelo is going. It is not good for a cast to have in it so beautiful — and so accessible a girl. But "He" takes issue with the statement. Consuelo's marriage with the baron is an honest one. It may be. Zinida doesn't care. . . .

ZINIDA — When did you see a beauty clad in simple cotton? If this one does not buy her, another will. They buy off everything that is beautiful. Yes, I know. For the first ten years she will be a sad beauty who will attract the eyes of the poor man on the sidewalk; afterward she will begin to paint a little around her eyes and smile, and then will take —

HE — Her *chauffeur* or butler as a lover? You're not guessing badly, Zinida!

ZINIDA — Am I not right? I don't want to intrude on your confidence, but today I am sorry for you, "He." What can you do against Fate? Don't be offended, my friend, by the words of a woman. I like you; you are not beautiful, nor young, nor rich, and your place is —

HE — On the side-walk, from which one looks at the beauties. (*Laughs*) And if I don't want to?

ZINIDA — What does it matter, your "want" or "don't want"? I am sorry for you, my poor friend, but if you are a strong man, and I think you are, then there is only one way for you. To forget.

HE — You think that that's being strong? And you are saying this, you, Queen Zinida, who want to awaken the feeling of love, even in the heart of a lion? For one second of an illusory possession you are ready to pay with your life, and still you advise me to forget! Give me your strong hand, my beautiful lady; see how much strength there is in mine and don't pity me.

Count Mancini, resplendent in his reception finery, reports the desire of the baron and the countess to bid farewell to the entire cast during the intermission. They will please gather, therefore, in the assembly room — but they must not make it too crowded. And there will be a basket of champagne — if "He" will be good enough to order it from the buffet. . . .

From the arena, Jackson brings the report that the performance is going wonderfully, save for the laughs. Do what he will he cannot make them laugh. The orchestra seems filled with barons and Egyptian mummies. . . . But Bazano is a crazy success; daring, audacious, wonderful. . . . And Consuelo! The audience cannot make enough of her! They are cheering her now — as she finishes her waltz — and the applause sounds as though a broken wall were tumbling down. . . .

Now the circus folk come rushing in from the ring to have a part in Consuelo's farewell — and get a part of the champagne. Consuelo is flushed and happy — but timid, too. The applause, the excitement of her friends unnerves her. She tries to make them a speech, but can get no farther than: "Friends — my dears — "

They are all quite flustered when it comes to speech-making. Only Mancini is calm and full of words. He insists upon speaking of his daughter, the Countess Veronica — when, as she tearfully insists, she is just Consuelo, and always will be Consuelo to her old friends. Even Alfred insists upon calling her countess which makes her unhappy. Only the old leader of the orchestra understands —

"Consuelo," he says, when he comes to present the compliments of his men: "Consuelo! They call you Countess here, but for me you were and *are Consuelo*. . . . Consuelo! My violins and bassoons, my trumpets and drums, all are drinking your health. Be happy, dear child, as you were happy here. And we shall conserve forever in our hearts the fair memory of our light-winged fairy who guided our bows so long. I have finished. Give our love to our beautiful Italy, Consuelo!"

Consuelo is near to tears by that time, but when the orchestra begins to play her tango she quickly gets hold of herself and wants to dance. Who will dance with her? Alfred? But Bazano turns sadly away. Who, then? "The baron," shouts the crowd. Let the bridegroom dance! "I do not know how to dance," admits the baron, planting himself firmly in the center of the floor, "but I shall hold tight!"

Consuelo can't dance that way. She takes a few awkward steps and gives it up. The crowd roars with laughter. The clowns imitate the sorry baron. "He" makes his way to the front of the crowd to suggest a toast to the baron's dancing. No? To those who know how to wait, then? Doesn't the baron like that, either? Then let them drink to "the very small distance which will always remain 'twixt the cup and the lip." The baron turns his back on him. Mancini is disgusted. The bell rings. The performers go back to their show.

CONSUELO — "He," dearie, how are you? I thought you didn't want even to come near me. (*In a low voice*) Did you notice Bazano?

HE — I was waiting for my turn, Queen. It was so difficult to get through the crowd to approach you.

CONSUELO — Through the crowd. (*With a sad smile*) I am quite alone. What do you want, Father?

MANCINI — Child! The baron —

CONSUELO — Let me alone. I'll soon be — come here, "He." What did you say to him? They all laughed. I couldn't understand. What?

HE — I was joking, Consuelo.

CONSUELO — Please don't, "He." Don't make him

angry; he is so terrible. Did you see how he pressed my arm? I wanted to scream. He hurt me!

HE — It's not too late yet. Refuse him.

CONSUELO — It *is* too late.

HE — I will take you away from here.

CONSUELO — Where to? Ah, my dear little silly boy, where could you take me to? All right. Be quiet. How pale you are! — I was still a little cheerful, but when they began to speak so nicely — I thought I should begin to cry. Don't talk, don't talk, but drink to — my happiness — to my happiness, "He." What are you doing?

HE — I am throwing away the glass from which you drank with the others. I shall give you another one — "

. . . .

HE — Here is your glass. Drink to your happiness, to your freedom, Consuelo!

CONSUELO — And where is yours? We must touch glasses.

HE — Save half for me!

CONSUELO — Must I drink so much? "He," dearie, I shall become drunk. I still have to ride.

HE — Dear little girl, did you forget that I am your magician? I charmed the wine. My witchery is in it. Drink, goddess.

CONSUELO — What kind eyes you have. But why are you so pale?

HE — Because I love you. Look at my kind eyes and drink. You shall fall asleep, and wake again, as before. And you shall see your country, your sky —

CONSUELO — (*bringing the glass to her lips*). I shall see all this; is that true?

HE — And when you awake, goddess, and remember the snow-white sea-foam and the sky-blue waters — remember heaven, and the low eastern wind, and the whisper of the foam at thy marble feet —

CONSUELO — (*drinking*). There! Look! Just a half!

Take it. But what is the matter with you? Are you laughing or crying?

HE — I am laughing and crying.

Mancini is losing patience. Why will Consuelo not join the baron? Tired? She is not too tired to stay there drinking wine and chatting with a clown!

But poor little Consuelo can hardly move. They find a chair for her, and everybody gathers in sympathy. She smiles, as at the recollection of a pretty scene, and the clowns play a little tune on their pipes to cheer her. "He" sits quietly in a corner with his back turned. The baron, his thick legs spread, looks down at Consuelo with bulging uncomprehending eyes. Mancini is rushing madly about protesting to the baron that nothing like that had ever happened before. Briquet is calling for a doctor. Only "He" is calm.

"It is death, Consuelo, my little queen," says "He." "I killed you! You are dying!"

His voice is loud and bitter. "Consuelo, with a scream, closes her eyes and becomes silent and quiet. All are in terrible agitation. The baron is motionless and sees only Consuelo."

"You are lying!" shouts Mancini, furiously. "Damned clown! What did you give her? You poisoned her! Murderer! Bring a doctor!"

"A doctor will not help," calmly answers "He." "You are dying, my little queen — I killed you!"

CONSUELO — (*in a dull and distant voice*). You are joking, "He"? Don't frighten me. I am so frightened. Is that death? I don't want it! Ah! "He," my darling "He," tell me that you are joking. I am afraid, my dear, golden "He."

HE — (*pushing away the baron with a commanding gesture*). Yes, I am joking. Don't you hear how I laugh, Consuelo? They all laugh at you here, my silly child. Don't laugh, Jim. She is tired and wants to sleep. How can you laugh, Jim? Sleep my dear, sleep my heart, sleep my love.

CONSUELO — Yes, I have no more pain. Why did you joke that way and frighten me? Now I laugh at myself. You told me, didn't you, that I — should — live — eternally?

HE— Yes, Consuelo! You shall live eternally. (*Lifts up his arms as if straining with all his forces to lift her soul higher*) How easy it is now! How many lights are burning about you?

CONSUELO — Yes, light — is that the ring?

HE — No, it is the sea and the sun. Don't you feel that you are in the foam, white sea-foam and you are flying to the sun?

CONSUELO — I am flying. I am the sea-foam and this is the sun. It shines — so strong — I feel well.

Poor little Consuelo dies, and a heavy silence settles over the group of watchers. "He" stands for a moment with his arms uplifted, gazing intently down at the dead girl. Then, trembling and unsteady, he goes off to one side to "struggle lonesomely with the torpidity of coming death."

Slowly the tragedy of Consuelo's passing settles upon them. Zinida and Jackson, the clown, are in tears. Briquet has gone to stop the music in the ring. Bazano, struggling to control his grief, gives way to bitter sobbing.

Mancini, as he awakes from his stupor, grows hysterical. The police! Let the police be called! Let them take this murdering "He" and cut off his head!

The baron, too, crushing in his fat hands the red rose he was to wear at his wedding, grows suddenly alive. He will go for the police himself! He was a witness! He saw! "I saw how he put poison — I — " He staggers off the stage.

JACKSON — (*clasping his hands*). Then it is all true?

Poisoned? What a vile man you are, "He." Is this the way to play? Now wait for the last slap of the executioner!

ZINIDA — Leave his soul alone, Jim. He was a man and he loved. Happy Consuelo!

A shot is heard in the corridor. They stand aghast as tragedy follows tragedy in this once happy circus. An attendant rushes in, his face pale, his eyes staring, his hand pointing dramatically to his head.

THOMAS — Baron — Baron — his head — he shot himself!

BRIQUET — God! What is it? The baron? What a calamity for our circus!

MANCINI — The baron? The baron? No! What are you standing here for?

BRIQUET — Calm down, Count. Who would have believed it? Such a respectable — gentleman!

HE — (*lifting his head with difficulty*). What more? What happened?

THOMAS—The baron shot himself! Honestly! Straight here! He's lying out yonder.

HE — (*thinking it over*). Baron? (*Laughs*) Then the baron burst?

JACKSON — Stop it! It's shameless! A man died and you — what's the matter with you, "He"?

Slowly "He" "is lifted to his feet by the last gleam of consciousness and life." He speaks "strongly and indignantly."

"You loved her so much, Baron? And you want to be ahead of me even *there?* No! I am coming! We shall prove then whose she is to be — forever — "

He falls on his back, clutching at his throat. The startled group gathers around him. There is general agitation as the curtain falls.

"SIX CYLINDER LOVE"

A Comedy in Three Acts

By William Anthony McGuire

NOT all the plays that come to Broadway heralded as certain successes live up to the promise inspired by their trial performances out of town. "Six Cylinder Love," however, was even a greater success with its first New York audience than it had been with the boardwalk crowds at Atlantic City. Produced at the Liberty Theatre, August 25, 1921, it achieved an immediate popularity and played through the season.

It is another of those little dramas of home life among the newlyweds that, being thoroughly American, have a wide appeal in the native theatre. Somewhat extravagant as to story, its characters are purposely exaggerated to give it a farcical trimming, and thus punctuate its proceedings with laughter. The basic dramatic situations however, and the impelling motives that inspire its principal characters, are sincerely and convincingly human.

In a Long Island suburb the Richard Burtons and the Gilbert Sterlings are next door neighbors. The opening scene reveals their adjoining back yards, separated by a high board fence. It is Sunday morning and the Burtons, middle-aged folk with a daughter in her teens, are in their yard idly watching father puttering with a handsome, though not new, six-cylinder touring car. Mr. and Mrs. Burton, having been out to a late party the night before, are suffering the morning-after consequences and are inclined to snap at each other at the slightest irritation. Mrs. Burton is particularly unhappy, as it transpires, because the family fortunes are at an extremely low ebb. As a matter of fact, the house has been sold to pay an accumulation of debts brought on by their living much beyond their means. The fault, she insists, lies entirely with Mr. Burton. He had no right to mortgage their attractive little home over their heads, and certainly it would never have been necessary if he had possessed even an average allotment of brains and any business acumen whatsoever.

Mr. Burton, however, refuses to bear alone the onus of failure. Why, he demands, did he mortgage the house "over their heads"? "To put an automobile under their feet," that's why! And who was it demanded the automobile? Mrs. B. and daughter Phyllis, as they very well know. And all the trouble they have had since then has been directly traceable to the expense of maintaining the car. If —

But Mrs. Burton is not fond of post-mortems. What has happened, has happened, and she, for one, is perfectly willing to do her part in helping to straighten matters out. They will give up their suburban home and go back to the city to live. They will get a nice little apartment on Riverside Drive, and —

The first thing they will do, interrupts Burton, will be to sell the car. Then, perhaps, they can eventually get back on their feet.

MRS. BURTON — (*amazed*). Sell the car? Do we have to dispose of our one and only luxury?

BURTON — We do!

MRS. BURTON — Harold Winston is quite devoted to Phyllis; I won't have her embarrassed just now.

PHYLLIS — I'm sure father understands the situation.

BURTON — That's just the difficulty, father does understand it, but neither of you do. Now let's get down to a few facts. First — this is no longer our house. Second — we have to move, evacuate, as it were, before Friday.

Third — we do not move to Riverside Drive. In my present frame of mind it wouldn't be safe for me to live that close to a river. Fourth — I couldn't pay the rent if we did. And fifth — if I don't sell the car immediately I won't have the money to move at all, and I'll find myself a prisoner in the midst of a lot of collectors, process servers, and what not.

MRS. BURTON — Well, judging from those remarks, you must be rather short of money.

BURTON — Good God!

PHYLLIS—I wouldn't want Harold, or the Rogerses, to know that we were in such serious circumstances.

BURTON — They're friends of ours, aren't they?

PHYLLIS — Yes, of course. Very dear friends.

BURTON — We've toured them all over this part of the country; Harold has driven my car more than I have; I think he busted the radiator. (*Phyllis turns away from him angrily*) We've snubbed everybody around here in favor of Harold and his crowd. I've spent all my money on them.

MRS. BURTON — Don't brag about yourself, Richard, it's such poor taste. These people need never know our real condition; that's one thing women learned long before the war — the value of camouflage.

BURTON — I don't see the necessity of it.

MRS. BURTON—You know at times I'm not nearly so much surprised at your *losing* all your money, as I am *amazed* that you ever *made* any to lose.

PHYLLIS—If we could only keep the car for a while—

BURTON — It's impossible, Phyllis. I've already sent for Will Donroy; expect him here any minute.

Donroy is the automobile salesman who sold Burton the car and has long been a friend of the family. In fact, before they acquired the "classier" friends the automobile brought them he was an accepted suitor for Phyllis' hand. Since then she has quarreled with him and isn't eager even to see him again. The argument has no weight with Burton. Donroy is a good salesman; he knows the car and he is the best man to sell it.

The arrival of the Burton's friends, Harold Winston and the Rogerses, typical of the "smart set" of suburban towns, interrupts the quarrel. They come to exchange reminiscences of the previous night's party and to plan the outing for the day. Incidentally they are much in need of a "bracer," and have called upon their "jolly old host" to provide it. Likewise they could do with a little breakfast.

On the back porch of the Gilbert Sterlings' house next door, young Mr. Sterling appears in search of his Sunday morning paper. He is a good-looking young man in his late twenties, rather undersized, and bravely uncomfortable in a new house jacket that evidently formed a part of his "trousseau." From the house the voice of his bride is heard softly calling to tell him that she had forgotten to order the cream. Would her "baby" mind running down to the delicatessen store to get some? Her baby is not keen about it, but he will go, of course.

MARILYN — (*giving him his hat*). Will you hurry back, dear?

GILBERT — Yes, dear.

MARILYN — I'll have your coffee ready for you, sweetheart.

GILBERT — All right, dear. (*He pauses and turns back*) Oh, Marilyn!

MARILYN — Yes, dear?

GILBERT — Don't bother about making any biscuits this morning.

MARILYN — Why, it's no bother to make them for you, dear. Don't you like my biscuits?

GILBERT — Why of course I do, dear. I just didn't want my baby to overwork herself, that's all. I'll be right back.

MARILYN — Gilbert!

GILBERT — Yes, dear?

MARILYN — You forgot to kiss me good-bye.

GILBERT—Oh, I didn't mean to, dear. (*He comes back and kisses her*) There!

MARILYN—Thank you, dear.

GILBERT — You're welcome, dear.

On the Burton side of the fence everybody is convulsed at the cooing of the turtle doves. Everybody except Mrs. Burton. She finds the Sterlings "disgustingly intimate." They must be very "ordinary people," so ordinary, in fact, that she has had nothing to do with them, in which convulsion Harold Winston bears her out. He has heard that before she was married little Mrs. Sterling was a stenographer, think of that! And young Sterling started life as a newsboy. The idea of such people living in *that* neighborhood! You never know who your neighbors are nowadays!

With the arrival of William Donroy, auto salesman, the cat is out of the bag. It is the first intimation the friends have that the Burtons even contemplated selling the car. Of course, Mrs. Burton explains, they expect to buy another, a newer model, which pleases the listening friends, but excites Mr. Burton to a silent sneer. With the family in the house dancing to the victrola's jazz, Burton freely explains the situation to Donroy, even though Donroy, his mind still on Phyllis, hears but little of what he says.

BURTON — Remember when I got the car, Donroy?

DONROY — (*still looking in the house*). Yes, of course I do.

BURTON — I'm sorry now you sold it to me.

DONROY — I'm sorry now you bought it.

BURTON — (*pacing slowly up and down*). Think of it! I saved for ten years to get this place here. It takes a salaried man a long time to accumulate real money, Donroy.

DONROY — You said something.

BURTON — You know I said something.

DONROY — I said you did.

BURTON — I did.

DONROY — (*still looking in house*). Phyllis seems kind of crazy about this bird, doesn't she?

BURTON — A man's a fool to put even a small mortgage on his home just to buy a machine. Of course, I figured I'd be able to pay it off within the year. Instead, I borrowed more. Aren't you interested in my troubles?

DONROY — Sure.

BURTON — You ought to be, you caused most of them.

DONROY—Don't blame me for selling you the car. If I hadn't, someone else would have. Besides, that's my business, and there's no sentiment in business nowadays. Believe me, Burton, if you want success you've got to take out this thing in here — (*indicating his heart*) and put in a carburetor.

BURTON — You said it that time.

DONROY — You know I said it.

BURTON — I said you did.

DONROY—I did. Of course, I don't think you're justified in blaming all your difficulties on the cost of the car.

BURTON — It's not the cost of the car, Donroy. It's the upkeep.

DONROY — Upkeep? Why that isn't an expensive boat to run, is it?

BURTON — No, I can go about forty miles on five gallons of gas, a quart of oil, three or four quarts of Scotch, chicken dinners for five or six, theatre tickets, cigars and cigarettes for the bunch.

DONROY — And do you pay for it all?

BURTON — When a man buys an automobile he purchases the permanent position of host, and none of his friends ever question his right to it.

DONROY — And you mean to say that you've stood for

that sort of thing? (*Burton nods*) Then it's your own fault.

BURTON — Agreed. But we've had a good time, my family enjoy it, and —

DONROY — Do they know the facts?

BURTON — Yes. That is, in a sort of way. In the past week I've tried to tell them, but I don't think they realize even now.

DONROY — Too bad, Burton. Have you many debts?

BURTON — Donroy, if there's anybody in this world I don't owe money to, he's holding out on me.

DONROY — I'm sorry, Burton.

BURTON — Donroy, I've got to get some quick money. Will you sell it for me?

DONROY — Sure, without commission. But there's two ways of selling; first you can take it to a sales garage, allow them a certain percentage and they bear the expense of the advertising, or we can find a minute man.

BURTON — A minute man?

DONROY — That's what we call a fellow that buys a car just because he wants to buy one — whether he can afford it or not. Like yourself.

BURTON — But why do you call us minute men?

DONROY — Because there's one born every minute.

BURTON — *Oh!*

DONROY — How about your friends inside? This fellow Winston seems interested in automobiles.

BURTON — Don't waste your time on him. He's what you call a social chauffeur, always willing to drive *your* car anywhere *he* wants to go.

DONROY — Does Phyllis really like him?

BURTON — All the women do. He knows all the latest dance steps. Every time I pound a few sensible ideas into my wife, he comes along with a new shimmy dance and shakes them all out of her.

They decide that they should get eighteen hundred

dollars for the car, which Donroy insists is a lot of cash — unless they can find another "minute man." . . . And a moment later the minute man is heard from!

Gilbert Sterling has returned from the delicatessen's with his sweetheart's half-pint of cream. Soon both the Sterlings, having taken their morning exercise in the nice, fresh air, are eating their breakfast on their little back porch. At least "sweetheart" is eating and "baby" is pretending. He tries the coffee and finds it quite as bad as it had been the day before, so he surreptitiously pours his cupful into a handy flowerpot. He tries the biscuits, and promptly hides them in the pockets of his jacket. But otherwise he enjoys his morning's meal very much. . . .

Now they are out in the "garden," trying to pick out the radishes from the stones and wondering why the recently planted asparagus hasn't begun to sprout.

MARILYN — Isn't it all beautiful, Gilbert? Do you know, I'm awfully proud of our little home.

GILBERT — Are you, dear?

MARILYN — Indeed I am, and I'm always going to make it a happy one for you, dear.

GILBERT — I know you will, dear.

MARILYN — And no matter how much money you make, I'm always going to take care of you and my home myself. Make your coffee, and cook your meals, and —

GILBERT — No dear, I wouldn't think of letting you do that. That is, when we can really afford a —

MARILYN — (*interrupting*). But I will, dear.

GILBERT — Oh.

MARILYN — And then, perhaps some day we'll sit out here and watch little Gilbert romping around.

GILBERT — And perhaps little Marilyn.

MARILYN — Perhaps. Then our home will be complete, won't it? Do you know, mother still has the baby carriage she used to wheel me around in.

GILBERT — What do you think of that. Has she, dear?

MARILYN — Yes, dear.

BURTON — (*sotto voice on the other side of the fence*). If little Gilbert is any smaller than *big* Gilbert they can wheel him around in a sardine box.

MARILYN — Gilbert, don't you think that when a woman lives just for her husband and home, and a man struggles just for his wife and children, that happiness always follows?

GILBERT — It's bound to, dear.

MARILYN — I think so, too. And I believe a woman should be proud of her home. I am. And I'll always keep it clean and neat. And in the evenings, I'll always be waiting for you at the door with a smile, no matter how tired I am.

GILBERT — And I'll always run to meet you, dear, no matter how tired I am. And in the evenings I'll take you to the movies.

MARILYN — No, dear, we'll stay in our little home, and if it's summer we'll sit out here and you'll tell me all about your day's work.

BURTON — And entertain the mosquitos.

MARILYN — And if it's winter, we'll sit before the fireplace and through the glow of the dying embers we'll read the future together.

Which impresses the listening Donroy a lot. A moment later, when he hears Gilbert grandly promising that not only will he always love his little sweetheart, but always give her whatever her little heart desires, he knows there stands a minute man in the Sterling yard. "If there's anything you ever wish for, you just ask your baby for it," proudly coos Gilbert, "and you shall have it!" And within the next five minutes Mr. Donroy has that particular little sweetheart wishing with all her might for an automobile.

He accomplishes this, first, by talking in a loud tone of voice to Mr. Burton of the prospects of his being "induced" to sell the car, or to trade it in. "I know you will like our limousine and the firm will allow you two thousand dollars in trade for this car. . . . But why not do some good friend a favor. I tell you it's a real bargain. This machine is just as good as new."

On the other side of the fence little Mrs. Sterling is listening with all her ears, and Gilbert is trying his best not to hear.

"It's a classy looking machine, streamline body, wire wheels — why, if I were married I'd buy it myself, just so my wife could drive it!" continues Donroy. "You know, I think a woman looks wonderful at the wheel. I don't know why it is, but every time I see a girl driving a car I say, there goes a regular girl, full of snap, full of pep; that's what a regular fellow admires in a wife!" . . .

DONROY — Don't you know some friend out here who might appreciate this opportunity? (*Raising his voice*) You know people living in these suburbs are simply isolated, and their lives become so monotonous that in time they even get tired of each other. (*He pauses and listens; Gilbert again looks up, Marilyn is listening intently*) Think of the wife who works in the house all day. She prepares the evening meal and gets so tired of waiting for her husband to come home and eat it, that finally she hopes he doesn't. Think of the poor husband, tired out from business, standing up in a crowded suburban train, reading the evening newspaper, getting astigmatism in both eyes. When he gets home he has to walk fifteen blocks to his house. (*He rises and stands facing the fence*) Result, two cranky people, maybe a fight. (*He pauses*) How is it with an automobile? *Ah!* (*Gilbert becomes exasperated, turns a page of his paper angrily, folds it, turns his back toward the fence and tries to read. Marilyn is much impressed with what Donroy has said*) Poor little wifey, after she gets through her work takes herself out for a drive, becomes so refreshed that she doesn't mind meeting husband at the station. He's so glad to see the automobile that he kisses his wife. She drives him home. Result, happiness. (*Donroy stops and listens.*)

MARILYN — (*rising and crossing to porch*). Gilbert.
GILBERT — Yes, dear?
MARILYN — Did you hear what that man says?
GILBERT — Well, who could help hearing him? Instead of having an automobile show, they ought to let him hire Madison Square Garden.
MARILYN — I suppose it would be sort of nice to have an automobile. Ethel Howard wouldn't come out here today on account of the long train ride. If we had an automobile I suppose we could have called for her, couldn't we, dear?
GILBERT — Yes, yes, I suppose we could, dear, but, we have our home, let's be content.
MARILYN — Oh, I am contented, dear. Did you ever hear me say I was discontented, dear?
GILBERT — Why no, dear.
MARILYN — Well, I'm not, dear.
GILBERT — Of course you're not, dear. (*Smiles and resumes his reading.*)
MARILYN — (*after a pause*). Mother can't get out very often, either.
GILBERT — Well, we have lots to be thankful for. (*Marilyn looks at him quickly*) I mean, we should be satisfied for a while.
MARILYN — Oh, I am satisfied, dear. Don't I always seem satisfied, dear?
GILBERT — Why yes, dear.
MARILYN — Well, I am, dear.
GILBERT — I know you are, dear.
He smiles amiably and pinches her small chin, trying to resume his reading as though nothing had happened. But Donroy knows. "If you only knew them, I could

close the deal in five minutes," he whispers to Burton; "she's sold already."

And she is. Gilbert has no more than straightened out his paper than Marilyn is at him again. Of course, if they *did* have a car they could drive occasionally up-state to Aunt Jane's. And Aunt Jane is a wonderful cook! Or they could tour on Sundays and take their lunch! And, naturally, Gilbert could get to the office sooner —

But Gilbert is determined not even to look at Mr. Burton's car. In the first place he has seen it, and in the second place he certainly has no intention of accepting any kind of attention from a man who has consistently snubbed him ever since they have lived in the town.

Still, Marilyn reminds him, the man said the car was a *great bargain!* At which point Donroy gets his great inspiration. He will force a meeting with the Sterlings!

The next minute he is sitting in the car and has started the motor, despite the protests of the startled Burton. Now Donroy has thrown in hte clutch, honked the horn and *started!* And the next minute he has crashed into the fence, pushed it over and stopped the car practically on the Sterlings' back porch! With a cry Marilyn has flown to Gilbert's arms and, very much frightened, the two of them stand trembling on the porch.

GILBERT — Good heavens, this is terrible!

DONROY — (*turning off the motor*). Terrible? I think it's wonderful. Imagine a car having that much power!

MARILYN — My poor garden.

BURTON — Sterling, I'm very, very sorry this happened. Mr. Donroy must have lost control of the wheel. Whatever the damage is, I'll pay for it.

GILBERT — (*coming down from the porch*). That's all right, Mr. Burton, that's quite all right. Accidents will occur.

DONROY — (*getting out of the car, crossing to Gilbert,*

grabbing his hand and shaking it). I'm really very sorry, but you see I hardly stepped on her, this car picks up so quickly. The light clutch action is one of the features of this machine, a gentle pressure and it shoots forward. Well, you saw for yourself. Went right through your fence! If I'd really stepped on her I'd have gone right through your house. But that isn't the fault of the brakes; no, I'm —

At which point Mr. Burton thinks perhaps it will be just as well if he introduced the eager salesman to his prospective victim. The greetings over, Donroy continues the campaign. Soon he has little Mrs. Sterling sitting in the front seat of the car. Craftily, with Marilyn's help, he gets Gilbert in beside her.

DONROY — Now take the wheel; how about it? Great, eh?

GILBERT — Feels kind of nice.

MARILYN — Do you like it, Gilbert?

GILBERT — I never held a steering wheel before. Gives you kind of a thrill, doesn't it?

BURTON — I've had lots of fun out of it.

MARILYN — Oh, Gilbert, just suppose this were our car, and we were really going out for a long drive, just you and I.

DONROY — All right, suppose it. But here, let's do it right. Put this on. (*He takes a cap from the back seat and puts it on Gilbert's head, backwards*) There!

MARILYN — Gilbert, you look too cute for anything.

DONROY — Looks just like Barney Oldfield.

GILBERT — Yes? (*Gives a pleased chuckle.*)

DONROY — Now imagine you're at Forty-Second Street and Fifth Avenue. It's ninety-nine in the shade! You're suffocating! Now drive up Fifth Avenue very carefully. Look out for the red light! Now you're on Fifty-Ninth Street! Now you're going across Queensborough Bridge You get the first slight whiff of the river breeze. (*He takes off his hat and starts to fan Gilbert and Marilyn. They both sink down in their seats*) Now you're down on Long Island! You're doing thirty miles an hour! You come to a clear stretch of the road. *Step on her!* You're going forty! *Step on her again!* Look at that car pick up! *Step on her again!* You're going — (*Gilbert blows the horn excitedly*) What's the matter?

GILBERT — I nearly ran over a chicken.

Now Gilbert understands. It certainly is great sport. "You get the fresh air. And the exercise. I suppose everyone should have one. How much do you want for her, Mr. Burton?"

"Two thousand!" promptly responds Donroy.

But Burton is a little conscience-stricken at that suggestion. He will take nineteen hundred dollars, allowing one hundred dollars for the damage done the fence. For a moment more Gilbert hesitates. But — well, Marilyn really wants the car and he wants her to have everything she wants. And it does seem like a fine chance to get a good car at a reasonable figure, and — The upshot being that Gilbert buys the car, gives Burton a check for two hundred dollars — Donroy just accidentally having both a blank check and a fountain pen with him — and promises to pay the remaining seventeen hundred dollars in a few days. Of course, he may have to put a small mortgage on his house. But — oh, well, he can clear that off in a year — easy!

Now the jazz friends have come from the house. They are surprised, not to say startled, by the news that greets them. The car sold! The idea! And to that funny little Mr. Sterling! Whoever would have thought it possible. But their interest in the Sterlings is vastly intensified. Harold Winston, the one Burton described as the "social chauffeur," is especially nice about it.

HAROLD — Well, congratulations, Sterling. You've got a mighty fine machine.

GILBERT — Yes, she's a good little boat.

BERTRAM — (*crossing over to Gilbert*). You know, I think I've met you somewhere, Mr. Sterling.

GILBERT — Why yes, I used to deliver papers at your father's home.

BERTRAM — Fancy that, a newsboy, and now you own your own automobile. (*Pats him on the back*) Well, well, well. (*He turns and talks to Marilyn who is in the car.*)

MARGARET — (*Crossing over to Gilbert and speaking very sweetly*). Men like Mr. Sterling are to be admired, Bertram.

GILBERT — (*embarrassed by their friendliness — looking straight ahead of him*). Well, thank you, but I don't feel that I deserve any particular credit, you see when a man —

MARGARET — (*to Marilyn*). Do you drive, dear?

MARILYN — Neither Mr. Sterling nor I ever drove a car.

HAROLD — No? I'll teach you if you like.

MARILYN — Oh, I wish you would!

BERTRAM — Why, he's the finest driver on Long Island, Mrs. Sterling.

GILBERT — (*turning up to the car*). Is that so? That's fine, because I don't know — (*He sees that they are paying no attention to him and moves over to talk to Burton. Burton is busy talking to Donroy. He starts to speak to Mrs. Burton but she turns her back on him.*)

HAROLD — It's really very simple, you hold the wheel like this—no, more this way; that's right; gives you more elbow action. Now place your foot here, that's the clutch. (*Phyllis watches her friends gathered around Marilyn, realizes that they have deserted her and runs sobbing into the house.*)

MARILYN — Oh, I'm just crazy about it. I wish I could drive now.

HAROLD — You'll learn in no time. There are lots of good roads around here and we'll practice every day.

Gilbert, meantime, is more or less forgotten. The Rogerses are engrossed in watching Harold show Marilyn how the car should be managed, and the Burtons have gone in the house. He finally gets up on the running board in his effort to see over Mr. Rogers' shoulder, but the latter thoughtlessly moves and pushes him off. Disconsolately he sits down on the running board and drops his chin into his hands. He is only the owner.

The curtain falls

ACT II

The scene is the attractively furnished living room of the Sterling home several months later — an empty living room at the moment, though there are soon to be heard the sounds of an approaching automobile, the lights from which shine through the windows as the car comes to a stop.

Marilyn has been driving and there is some discussion as to whether she has been able, going sixty miles an hour or thereabouts, to shake off the motor policeman who attempted to follow her and her party, consisting of the Rogerses and Harold Winston. They are just back from a tea dance.

Gilbert is not home yet and Marilyn is a little worried, though she concludes that business of some sort has detained him. They will meet the next train, Winston assures her, and take him over to their favorite Pelham roadhouse for a dinner and a "*regular* party." Meantime the boys suggest that a little of Gilbert's Scotch would not be unwelcome. Knowing where it is they are privileged to help themselves, agrees Marilyn — and they do. Now Marilyn and Margaret Rogers are alone, and

Marilyn, suffering a twinge of conscience whenever she thinks of Gilbert, is beginning to worry again. Of course, she likes a good time, and she loves to dance with Harold, seeing that Gilbert has never learned to step so very well, but —

MARILYN — Poor Gilbert must be tired out. It was five o'clock when we got in this morning.

MARGARET—Must have been. It was quarter to, when you dropped us off.

MARILYN — And he has to leave for the office at seven-thirty. And think of it, we've been keeping this up for weeks. It was after four yesterday morning.

MARGARET — I know it, but your little husband simply revels in it.

MARILYN — Do you really think so?

MARGARET — Of course he does, silly.

MARILYN — I'm not so sure. At times, lately, he hasn't looked so well, and I often have to coax him to take us out. I don't think he's ever been quite this late before. Never on a Saturday.

MARGARET — He'll be here on the next train.

MARILYN — I suppose I could have bought something, and prepared dinner at home tonight.

MARGARET — My dear, don't teach him bad habits. You know I cautioned you about that before. Cooking isn't part of the domestic bargain any more. Why you can't even hire *cooks* to cook nowadays, so why expect wives to do it?

MARILYN — Oh, I don't do it. Why we haven't had dinner at home in ages, and we get to bed so late every night since we got the car, I simply can't get up to cook breakfast.

MARGARET — Why should you?

MARILYN — Oh, I don't mind the cooking so much, but I won't wash dirty dishes.

MARGARET — Ditto.

MARILYN — Especially, when it's so easy to drive to the Country Club, or into town, or to go to one of the roadhouses. I hate housework, anyway.

MARGARET — Ditto, again.

MARILYN — I simply can't sew, and if there's one thing I *won't* do, it's to darn socks.

MARGARET — And you're perfectly right, dear. When a woman marries to slave for a man, she generally succeeds in being just a slave.

MARILYN — I think so, too.

By the time the boys have the highballs ready, and have drunk to good old Gilbert, and glorious old prohibition, "that made every man his own barkeeper," it is time to meet Gilbert's train, and they are on their way.

Again the living room is momentarily in half-darkness, with the moonlight streaming through the window. Then another car is heard approaching the house. This one, it transpires, carries Gilbert and his employer, Mr. Stapleton, who has driven him out from town. Gilbert is appreciative of both the honor and the lift, but he is a little anxious about Mr. Stapleton's motives and he would be just as well pleased if he could get his employer out of the way before anything happens — anything, for instance, resembling an investigation of his (Gilbert's) living conditions.

Stapleton, however, is of a different mind, and without pretending to have heard Gilbert's hearty "good-night," pushes his way into the living room and allows that he thinks he will stop off for a minute or two. He is rather eager to meet Mrs. Sterling and he is interested in the house, too. Nice place. Does Gilbert own it?

Yes, *sir* — that is, Gilbert practically owns it. There is a small incumbrance — Nice furniture, too. Does Gilbert own that? Yes, *sir* — well, almost! The 'phone rings. Evidently someone is inquiring about a certain settlement for an automobile accident in which the Sterlings have figured; an accident that cost them five thousand dollars — because they had no liability insurance. Which brings Mr. Stapleton to the subject that he had been so guardedly approaching.

STAPLETON —Sterling, I'm going to tell you now why I drove you home tonight.

GILBERT — I'm certainly very anxious to find out, sir.

STAPLETON — Up to now you've been doing your work very well. I've been gradually piling responsibilities on your shoulders, until now you're in line for something real.

GILBERT — I'm glad to hear you say so, sir.

STAPLETON — Sterling, I'm about ready to retire from the active management of my business. That is, I want someone to help share the responsibilities. I don't suppose I could ever quit entirely, but the daily routine is getting to be too much for me.

GILBERT — Why, you're still a very young man, sir.

STAPLETON — Thanks, but I'm not. Now there are only two men in my employ that I'd trust the reins to. You're one of them.

GILBERT — Thank you, sir, I've always tried to —

STAPLETON — Like everyone else, I have a few little ideas that I take great pleasure in working out. Idiosyncracies, I guess you'd call them. Well, the one that concerns you is my firm belief that a man's business career is in most cases a reflex of his home life. For instance, I don't believe that a man who neglects his home, who has no domestic pride, can ever have a good business conscience. Understand what I mean?

GILBERT — Yes, I think I do, sir.

STAPLETON — Now I've told you that you were one of two —

GILBERT — And I appreciate your confidence in me, sir.

STAPLETON — The other is Jackson.

GILBERT — He's a fine fellow and a very valuable man.

STAPLETON — I'm glad to hear you say that. Well, you seem to have the right idea here. I hope you don't look upon my peculiar method as an intrusion.

GILBERT — (*notices the empty high-ball glasses on the table and, very carefully, so as not to attract Stapleton's attention, covers them with a motor duster he finds on the divan*). No, no indeed. On the other hand I think it's a splendid idea. I suppose a fellow's home habits do affect his business life.

STAPLETON — Why of course they do. I admire the man who uses his salary to establish a home, but I have no confidence in the fellow who dissipates his fireside hours, because he'll never make the most of his office hours. That's why you and Mrs. Sterling ought to be very proud of this little place.

Oh, they are, Gilbert admits, terribly proud of their little house. Mrs. Sterling, in fact, is so proud of it that she does practically all her own work and is tremendously enthusiastic about it. Their car? Oh, they drive that very little; Mrs. Sterling had much rather stay at home and sew, for one thing, and then gasoline is so high they feel they must economize.

That's the proper spirit, agrees Mr. Stapleton; economy and right living, plenty of fresh air and exercise and a quiet, simple home life — those are the things that lay the foundations for a substantial success. Well, Mr. Stapleton decides he must be going. Sorry not to have met Mrs. Sterling. Where did Gilbert say she was? Oh, yes — at the choir meeting! Practicing! That's fine! It is certainly encouraging to find young people living such economical, moral and ethical lives —

At which moment the Sterling car returns with Marilyn and party aboard. They have been to meet the "seven-ten," and not finding Gilbert, have picked up Donroy, the automobile salesman, who has come out to visit another prospect in the suburb. Now, seeing Gilbert, but not seeing Mr. Stapleton, who has moved to the rear of the room, they are all talking at once — telling the young man, before he can stop them, and despite his pantomimed protests, all the wild things they've been doing — dancing and drinking up his booze and racing away from motor cops! The Sterling boom has busted!

Desperately, now, Gilbert tries to recover the lost ground. With a flourish he introduces Marilyn to Mr. Stapleton, and with obvious effort he tries to laugh off the things his friends have been saying. "You mustn't pay any attention to what any of my friends say, Mr. Stapleton," he says, providing a homely picture by drawing Marilyn to him and swinging his arm across her shoulders. "They always like to kid Marilyn and me about drinking and dissipating. I suppose it is because we lead such old-fashioned lives." He laughs a little nervous laugh and his friends are at a loss to understand what he is driving at until finally they get it through their thick pates that he is talking for Stapleton's benefit. Then their interest increases. "And you people shouldn't joke about such things," he continues, turning to the crowd. "I've told you so before. You give out a wrong impression. What if we don't like to stay out late, and what if we don't care for drinking and dancing, and all that rough sort of thing? We're happy in our simple life, and that's everything!"

But the effort is not very successful. Mr. Stapleton continues to frown ominously, despite the humorous Donroy's deft efforts to turn the subject to automobiles. Finally he announces a wish that he might be permitted to talk with Gilbert alone, if the friends will excuse them. And then the storm breaks.

STAPLETON — So, you stay in the house too much; get up too early?

GILBERT — Well, I —

STAPLETON — Often up and around the place at five in the morning.

GILBERT — Yes, sir, I really am.

STAPLETON — Yes, you are — when you get in at that time. You and your friends never drink? As long as it's the law you believe in obeying it?

GILBERT — Well sir, I'm awfully sorry that I exaggerated things that way, but I did it because I wanted you to have a good opinion of me. I don't think you ought to rub it in.

STAPLETON — I don't see how you manage it on your salary.

GILBERT — Well, sir, I do.

STAPLETON — Do you?

GILBERT — After all, this is our home, and what we do here is our own affair.

STAPLETON — Oh, no, not entirely. When my books show a mysterious shortage of several thousand dollars, and just about the time when you've paid out five thousand to cover an automobile accident! That seems to be more than a coincidence.

GILBERT — (*taken aback*). Why, sir, I —

STAPLETON — You can't live the sort of life you're living on the salary I pay you. If I didn't have any real suspicion before investigating your conduct, I have enough evidence now to at least convince me of your unworthiness. As far as the shortage is concerned, that rests beween you and Jackson. That's all I've got to say to you, Sterling. (*He moves to the door and opens it.*)

GILBERT — Mr. Stapleton, (*Stapleton pauses in doorway*) I'm responsible, not Jackson.

STAPLETON — (*closing the door*) . You admit that you stole the money?

GILBERT — No sir, I didn't steal.

STAPLETON — Didn't you just confess as much?

GILBERT — No sir, that is, I didn't look at it in that

way. I'll tell you. I had arranged for a second mortgage on my home. I expected the money yesterday, but they disappointed me. I mean, it's been delayed for a few days, and I did use your money in the emergency, knowing that I could repay it. I've always handled large amounts for you, and many times when I've been too late for the bank I've thousands of dollars in bonds and checks right here over the week-end. I never make a settlement until the end of the month, and you see I knew that I could repay it. Why, sir, you know I wouldn't steal.

STAPLETON — You can call it what you like, but you've taken money that didn't belong to you, and that's theft.

GILBERT — No it isn't, if I repay it.

STAPLETON — Well, perhaps embezzlement would be a better word, but nevertheless you've committed a felony. The fact that you needed the money doesn't justify the act, and your intention to repay it doesn't excuse you. When you found you couldn't raise this mortgage money in time, why didn't you borrow it elsewhere, from your friends? You couldn't, because you've already borrowed up to the limit to keep up this false system of living. Why didn't you put your cards on the table and come to me with your trouble? I was fond of you, and would have helped you. But you were afraid I would ask you what you'd been doing with the salary I've been paying you, and you didn't want me to know how you'd squandered it. But I knew it just the same. When you began neglecting your work, I began watching you. I had a lot of big things for you, Sterling. I was going to give you every opportunity. But you weren't square. You wouldn't play fair, and I'm through with you. . . . I'm going to see that you get exactly what you deserve.

He turns and starts toward the door just as the door opens and Richard Burton walks into the room. Mr. Stapleton continues on his way. It certainly is the psychological moment for the former owner of the automobile to arrive, but Gilbert is in no mood to appreciate it. Burton, of course, knows nothing of what has happened and chatters blithely of his own experiences, assuming that Gilbert has been one of the lucky ones able to keep his head above water and maintain a decent home in a decent, if somewhat expensive, community.

"Do you know," muses Burton, "this is the third time in four months that I've spent Saturday afternoon out here, just sort of hanging around the old place. And when I sold it I thought I was glad of it. (*He sighs*) But I've missed it. When I think of that place I'm living in now — no yard, no sunshine — home! Huh! Four dismal walls that keep saying to me—'You're here because you didn't appreciate a good home.' And at night when I climb the stairs, each one of the rickety old steps creaks out—'Go on, climb you failure, climb! You were up once, but you couldn't stay there, so go on, climb the rest of your life, you poor boob.' It's tough, Sterling."

Gilbert allows that it is. Of course, if he can do anything for Burton — He can, Burton admits; he can relieve his mind, if he will. And then he admits that ever since he sold Gilbert the car he has suffered from a guilty conscience. Not because the car was not worth the money, but because of what went with it. "Sterling," he says, "I've often thought of you. Like me you mortgaged your home to buy a luxury, and it's a mistake, and I feel responsible. That is really why I came here tonight — to let my experience be a warning to you before it's too late. I hope you understand."

The sounds of the jazz music to which the friends are dancing in the next room are heard. They remind Burton of what he has come to do, and that is to warn Gilbert against "skidding into the ditch," and particularly against the bunch of friends that seem to have successfully transferred themselves to the Sterling home. "When I sold you the car, I didn't mean to throw in all those accessories," Burton explains, and he wants to apologize. Let Gilbert beware of them. They are fair-weather friends, all of them. They will be loyal and lovely so long as the graft is good, but once the break comes they will treat Gilbert just as they treated him. A statement that Gilbert knows to be true, though he tries to resent it.

Now the dancers are back from the other room, and finding their old friend Burton there, receive him with that thinly-veiled rudeness characteristic of their kind. Gilbert asks him to stay to dinner, but he admits that he has given up parties, which rather amuses the crowd. He is gone now, to the relief of the friends who proceed to pity him for the poor old thing that he is — a failure.

"Old Burton is just a poor fool, that's all," is Harold's opinion. "Good old wagon, but done broke down," agrees Rogers. Well, they had better get started. Everybody's starved. But they are reckoning without their host.

"I'm not going," announces Gilbert, by way of hurling a bombshell into the center of the party.

They argue with him, plead with him, and Marilyn grows quite peevish with him. But he sticks to his statement. He is not going. Why? Well, for one reason, he thinks they treated Burton contemptibly. And if Burton deserves that sort of thing from them, so does he.

GILBERT — I've been just as much of a fourflusher as he ever was. The only difference between him and me, is, that I'm not going to wait for you backbiters to quit me — I'm going to have the fun of quitting you.

MARILYN — (*coming to him*). Why dear, what are you saying?

HAROLD — Just a minute, Gilbert.

GILBERT — (*moving toward them*). No, you listen to me, please. I'm not going with you tonight because I can't afford your company. I haven't any more money to spend on you. I'm in debt now.

MARGARET — Gilbert, don't get so excited. If we've said anything to hurt your feelings I'm sure we didn't mean it.

HAROLD — Why no, our remarks weren't directed at you, old fellow. Come on, forget it, and let's go.

BERTRAM — Yes, let's go. (*He starts toward the door, Margaret follows.*)

MARILYN — Gilbert dear, I think you owe our guests an apology.

HAROLD — Oh, no, he doesn't. Come on, Gilbert. (*He takes his arm, Gilbert pulls away. Harold starts for the door.*)

MARGARET — Shall we start now, Gilbert?

GILBERT — I'm sorry, but I'm not going.

MARILYN — But why not, dear?

GILBERT — Do I have to explain my reasons? I have no right to go. (*To Harold*) I've fallen behind the procession, that's all. (*Crossing to Bertram*) I was a good little wagon, but I've done broke down! I'm as poor as Burton, is that clear? I'm broke, absolutely broke. (*To Marilyn*) Do you understand that?

MARILYN — Yes, of course, but I think it's a silly way to be.

GILBERT — Oh, my God! So do I, but we've come to it, and now that we have I know just what to expect from my friends.

Harold is inclined to resent this, but his is rather a pallid resentment, and Gilbert is ready to meet it. He knows the Winston type — the fellow whose specialty it is to get up parties and then be called to the telephone when the check is due. "You're just a bunch of spongers, that's all!" he shouts at them in his wrath; "and decent people shouldn't tolerate you! In fact, decent people don't. It's only those that have left the decent life that associate with your kind. And now I want you all to get out of my house!"

Naturally they are shocked; quite put out, in fact. But they go — and take two bottles of "hootch" with them. Marilyn is furious at the insult Gilbert has offered their friends — her friends. "I won't tolerate such humiliation," she shouts at her excited young husband. "Why I'll never be able to look at those people again."

GILBERT — I never want you to.

MARILYN — *You* don't want me to? What have you to say about what I shall and shall not do? I didn't get married to be your slave. Oh, I'm ashamed of you; why you actually told them to get out as if—as if—well, I'm going to get out, too. . . . If you had any consideration for my feelings you couldn't say such terrible things to people I like, even if you have turned against them. . . . I know why you wouldn't go out tonight, you're jealous because I was out dancing with Harold Winston again. And you can afford to be jealous of him, because he at least is a gentleman. Well, I'm going—do you hear me? I'm going! I'm leaving you forever, do you realize that? I'll send for my things tomorrow, but I never want to see you again, and I'll never, never, come back!

GILBERT — All right! That's right in keeping with the whole idea! I put them out because I discovered what loyal friends they were, and now that I'm broke you leave me flat. Fine! That's twentieth century devotion! Well, go on, then! Beat it! See if I care! But before you go, I want you to know that you've been just as much of a leech as they ever were.

MARILYN — (*startled by his sudden attack*). Gilbert!

GILBERT — Ever since you married me you've accepted my support, I've paid for your living, your clothes, your luxuries. I've even furnished a dancing partner for you, and what have you ever done? Nothing!

MARILYN — Gilbert, are you going to scold me?

GILBERT — No, I'm just going to give you hell!

And, in fact, he does. As a wife she has been many things she should have been and a lot no helpful wife would have been. For one thing she's that most trying of all wifely types, "the vamping wife." A man can get away from a "nagging wife," but with a vamp he hasn't a chance. And she has literally "baby deared" him into a mess he'll never be able to get out of!

GILBERT — You believed in a woman being proud of her home. You were always going to cook my meals for me. Why, we haven't had a meal in here in months, and I haven't had any more indigestion. But I was willing to drink your terrible coffee, and eat your burnt biscuits, just to please you.

MARILYN — But Gilbert —

GILBERT — We were going to sit in our vegetable garden and watch little Gilbert pick radishes. We'd have a little Marilyn also romping around, just to make our home complete. Why we even contemplated twins. (*He rises and moves across the room*) We were going to sit before the fireplace and read our future in the dying embers. Those embers have been dead for a long time, and we have no future together now. I've not only lived beyond my means, but I've stolen money to do it with.

MARILYN — (*jumping to her feet*). Gilbert! No!

GILBERT — That's why Mr. Stapleton was here tonight, to call me a thief! And now that I've told you what's on my mind you can go whenever you're ready. I deserve to lose everything, anyway. (*He breaks down, sinks down on the divan and buries his head in the pillows.*)

MARILYN — (*after a pause she moves over and stands over him*). Gilbert, I — (*The door opens, and Smith, a detective enters.*)

SMITH — Mr. Sterling?

GILBERT — *Yes?*

SMITH — (*opening his coat and displaying his police badge*). May I have a word with you?

MARILYN — (*rushing to Smith, and crying*). Oh, please, please don't take him away! He hasn't done anything wrong. I know he hasn't! We can pay every cent of the loss! We can borrow from mother! We can sell the house! We can sell the car! We can sell everything! (*She turns and runs into Gilbert's arms, sobbing.*)

GILBERT — (*trying to comfort her*). There, there dear, don't cry. Let's be a couple of good losers. (*She is still sobbing, he kisses her, turns, and walks up to Smith*) Come on, I'll go with you.

SMITH — You? I've got a summons here for Mrs. Sterling, she's been exceeding the speed limit again. (*Marilyn stops sobbing, looks up with an amazed expression, and sits abruptly on the divan behind her. Gilbert looks at Marilyn. The curtain falls as Smith continues speaking*) The chief told me to tell you that if she doesn't cut out this fast driving he'll see that she not only gets a fine, but a few days in jail —

The curtain falls

ACT III

A month later the Sterlings are living in the same West Forty-Eighth Street apartment building which houses the Burtons. "It is typical of apartments of that class, the wallpaper is old and streaked and the furniture is of cheap golden oak."

Marilyn is doing her own work, and is at the moment taking delight in a freshly baked loaf of home-made bread Mrs. Burton has brought in. It has been rather a trying experience for Marilyn, losing everything and moving from her dear little suburban home into a stuffy "walk-up" apartment in New York — particularly as she now feels very keenly her own responsibility in the matter. She loves Gilbert more than anything else in the world, she admits to Mrs. Burton, but "Gee, I'm a punk wife!"

"Was" a punk wife would probably be better, for Marilyn has changed the last month. She is still "vamping" successfully, but she is mixing housework and homemaking with it, and Gilbert has recovered some of the spirit he had in the days of the honeymoon.

He comes in now, lugging a long, low, rakish and heavy box that is later to be revealed as a surprise for Marilyn. Finding Burton present he puts his present aside for the moment. Gilbert has been spending the day, as usual, looking for a "real" job. They are pretty scarce, he finds, but he is young and hopeful.

BURTON — I suppose you got enough out of the house to hold you over for a while?

GILBERT — (*crossing to him*). No, I didn't.

BURTON — Too bad.

GILBERT — (*sitting on the trunk beside Burton*). I didn't even get enough to pay Mr. Stapleton in full.

BURTON — You know, I don't think that fellow is giving you a square deal. Why he's just grinding you down.

GILBERT — No he isn't. Why he's giving me a chance to make good. Gosh, I still owe him a thousand dollars, and all I can send him is a measly ten dollars a week.

BURTON — And you're only getting thirty-five?

GILBERT — That's not the idea. He's giving me a chance to pull myself out of a hole that I got myself into, and don't you forget, there are a lot of poor fellows in jail right now whose intentions were just as good as mine.

BURTON — You don't have to worry about jail, and you don't have to pay him another nickel until you're in a position to. When he accepted your first money he condoned the whole business, and he can't prosecute you now without getting in trouble himself.

GILBERT — I know that. But my conscience can. It's a matter of honor with me. Why I can never hold up my head again until this thing is paid, and I wanted to do it tomorrow, because I promised I'd pay it in thirty days.

But there isn't much chance of his being able to do that — unless he can sell the car. Yes, the "old boat" still remains anchored to him, though he has advertised it every day, made the rounds of all the dealers, and answered all the inquiries for cars. "I seem to be the only sucker left in the world," Gilbert concludes. Of course he has had offers, but he can't afford to sell for less than the thousand dollars he needs to square his account with Stapleton. Meantime he cannot even afford a garage, and the car has been parked in front of the building ever since they moved in. But, there is hope! Gilbert has sent for Donroy, the best little automobile salesman in the business, and Burton is sure everything is coming out all right.

BURTON — Say, if you'll just make up your mind that your troubles are all over, and really think it, there's nothing to it. Think it when you get up in the morning, and all day long just keep saying to yourself, "Well — everything's going to be all right." Can you say that?

GILBERT — I feel terrible, but I've got to laugh at you.

BURTON — Is that so? Well, never mind laughing at me, go on, just say it: "Everything's going to be all right."

GILBERT — No, that's a lot of bunk.

BURTON — It's not a lot of bunk. Will you say it?

GILBERT — Oh, very well. Everything is going to be — (*There is a knock on the door*) Come in.

BURTON — (*crosses to the door and opens it. Tom,*

the janitor, stands in the hallway). Ah, the janitor. Hello, Tom.

TOM — Mr. Burton. (*Sees Sterling sitting on the trunk and crosses to him*) Say, excuse me, Mr. Sterling, but a policeman downstairs just tells me that the law allows half an hour for parking. He allows a couple of hours, but he says your machine has been standing there a couple of weeks. He threatens to pinch you and see that you pay a heavy fine.

GILBERT — (*rising from the trunk*). Everything is going to be all right!

BURTON — Where's the cop now, Tom?

TOM — Downstairs at the door. I told him Mr. Sterling wasn't at home. (*Turning to Gilbert*) But later on you'd better take your machine around to a garage, for he's liable to come up here and —

GILBERT — All right, Tom, thanks. Everything is going to be *all right.*

Gilbert thinks some of getting Tom to help him with Marilyn's present, which, it now appears, is a window box to sort of take the place of the garden she misses so much. When Tom smilingly admits that he loves to do any kind of little odd job, just to pick up extra money, Gilbert decides to put in the box himself.

Everything is going to be all right! But it has a slow way of working around that way. Even Donroy fails them. He is no longer in the automobile business, but is selling suburban real estate. Then Gilbert thinks perhaps he might sell the car back to Burton, seeing that that thrifty neighbor has confessed to having saved a thousand dollars since he has returned to the simple life. But Burton only laughs at the suggestion. He has the thousand, it is true, but he would like to see anyone get it away from him.

Something, however, will have to be done. Tom, the janitor, is back to report that the policeman is again demanding that the car be moved. It can't stand in the street forever.

GILBERT — Tom, I'm trying my best to do something about it. Do you know anyone who wants to buy a machine?

TOM — Well, I might, if the price is right.

GILBERT — Well, I'll tell you —

MARILYN — (*moving over towards Gilbert*). A thousand dollars.

GILBERT — Yes, if I can have cash.

DONROY — (*crossing to Tom*). Wait a minute, Sterling, you can get more than that. (*To Tom*) You say you know some one who might buy it.

TOM — Yes, I think so.

DONROY — Then I'll tell you what I'll do. I want to help Mr. Sterling, and selling cars is my middle name. Now this machine isn't worth more than a thousand dollars, but I'll get fifteen hundred for Sterling, and a commission for you. You tell me where this bird lives, I'll go and see him myself. Who is he?

TOM — Me.

GILBERT — What a fine help you turned out to be.

BURTON — (*coming to Tom*). Tom, are you really thinking of buying a car?

TOM — Yes, Mr. Burton, I've been thinking of it for some time. (*To Gilbert*) I've examined your car, Mr. Sterling, and it looks all right to me. (*Over his shoulder to Donroy*) And I know something about machines. (*To Gilbert*) How much?

MARILYN — A thousand dollars.

GILBERT — Yes, that's right. If I can have the cash tonight.

TOM — Just a minute. (*He goes out into the hall and calls downstairs*) Mary! Oh, Mary!

MARILYN — What do you want with her?

TOM — My check book.

So Tom buys the car, in spite of Gilbert's frank warning that he should not, when he sees the janitor really is in earnest. "I want to sell it, Lord knows, but I hate to see you get in wrong. Look at Burton, he owned the car before I did, and it almost sunk him! I bought it, and it rode me out of a nice little home into all this mess! Forget it, Tom, I'm tipping you right. Every man who can afford it should own an automobile, but not a couple of young fellows like us, just trying to succeed. See what I mean?"

Sure Tom sees. But it happens he *can* afford it. He is janitor for twenty buildings and he gets forty dollars a month from each of them. With a car devoted to the business he may add a few more. "Tom, are you really buying this car for yourself?" Burton demands. "Certainly, Mr. Burton. You see, my wife has one of her own!"

And when Mary, his wife, comes with the check book she is wheeling *her* car — with a baby boy in it!

With Tom's check for a thousand dollars in hand Gilbert is ready to meet the Stapleton note the following day, but as it happens he is not able to keep it even that long. While they are getting their supper, Gilbert all dressed up in a kitchen apron ready to help, there is a knock at the door and Mr. Stapleton himself enters. He has come to do a little more investigating, and what he finds this time pleases him, although his preliminary remarks do not intimate as much.

STAPLETON — Well, tomorrow is the first of the month.

GILBERT — Yes sir, and I have the money for you, that is, if you care to accept this check. If not, I'll bring you the cash in the morning. (*Hands him the check.*)

STAPLETON — (*looking at the check*). For the car?

GILBERT — Yes sir.

STAPLETON — I suppose you think I've been pretty hard on you?

GILBERT — Well, it wasn't very easy, but I'm glad to be able to square our account. And now that I have, I want to tell you again that I never really intended to misuse your money. I want you to believe that.

STAPLETON — Sterling, I couldn't think any more of a son than I thought of you, but you had to find bottom. You had to face the consequences of your own mistakes. That's where most men fall down. They can't come through and meet the test. When you sold your home to pay me some money on account, I said to myself, well, it's hard on him — but he needs the lesson more than I do the money. But, I want to tell you that that little ten dollars a week you sent me was the biggest money I ever got. (*He pauses*) Well, how's Mrs. Sterling?

GILBERT — She's very well, thanks.

STAPLETON — I suppose she's unhappy here?

GILBERT — No, indeed. Why she's a regular little woman. That's one thing I've found out in all this mess. She cares more for me than all the luxuries we ever had.

STAPLETON — Well, that helps a man through trouble, doesn't it?

GILBERT — You bet it does.

STAPLETON — Yes *sir!*

GILBERT — Yes *sir!*

STAPLETON — You know, when my wife and I were your ages, we lived in a little room over a junk shop. Now, they say that my house is the finest on the island. But I'd trade it all for that little room, if I could go back there and find my wife waiting for me.

GILBERT — (*after a pause*). I'm sorry.

STAPLETON — That's all right. That's all right. (*After a pause*) Well, you're broke I suppose?

GILBERT — Yes *sir*.

STAPLETON — Sterling, I'm going to help you to a start. (*Holds out the check to him*) You can owe me this.

GILBERT — No, thank you, sir. I want to wipe the slate clean. (*He takes the check*) I'll endorse it. (*He endorses the check and hands it back to Stapleton.*)

STAPLETON — (*putting the check in his pocket*). Well, I'll expect you at the office in the morning.

GILBERT — Mr. Stapleton, you don't mean —

STAPLETON — I think you're still the man for that job.

For a moment Gilbert is too stunned to realize his sudden fortune. And then he is too choked with emotion to voice his thanks. There are tears in his eyes as he puts out his hand and gives his forgiving employer a mighty grip. To relieve the boy's embarrassment the older man discreetly withdraws and the next minute Marilyn has burst through the kitchen door radiantly happy.

MARILYN — Oh Gilbert, isn't it wonderful? I heard every word. Now, maybe we can buy one of those nice little bungalows from Mr. Donroy, and maybe a little car —

GILBERT — (*interrupting*). No *sir,* no car!

MARILYN — But dear, I mean a car like Mary has.

GILBERT — A car like Mary has?

MARILYN — And you'll have to buy me that, whether you want to or not.

GILBERT — (*taking her in his arms*). Everything is going to be *all right!*

The curtain falls

"THE HERO"

A Tragi-Comedy in Three Acts

BY GILBERT EMERY

THE playgoing public, as such, did not approve of "The Hero." At least it was not a popular success. But those who did approve of it were so enthusiastic in their approval, and their enthusiasm was, to us, so thoroughly justified, that we could not conscientiously (for reasons that are more fully set forth in the introduction to this volume) substitute for it a less worthy drama with a greater popular success and a longer run to its credit.

"The Hero," whose author, Gilbert Emery, is better known to the readers of short stories under his own name, Emery Pottle, was first tried at a series of special matinee performances in the spring of 1921. It gave such promise at the time that it was immediately withdrawn by its producer, Sam H. Harris, and held for revival as a feature of the regular season in the fall.

On September 5, 1921, it was revived at the Belmont Theater, Richard Bennett succeeding Grant Mitchell in the rôle of Andrew. It ran for eighty performances and was then withdrawn, presumably until, as the Great War recedes farther into the background, the attitude of the people toward its heroes in uniform is ruled a little more by common sense and a little less by sentiment.

"The Hero" tells the story of two brothers — one a fighting hero, but a moral rotter, the other a plodding ne'er-do-well who, with unconscious heroism, meets the everyday problems thrust upon him and solves them to the best of his limited ability.

In the dining room of a "small, rented, jerry-built

house" in a small town near New York live Andrew Lane, his wife Hester, and his six-year-old son, Andy. Living with them are Andrew's mother, Sarah Lane, and Marthe, a Belgian refugee whom the Lanes took in, early in the war, in an effort to do their bit in alleviating the sufferings entailed by the struggle. Hester Lane, the most sentimentally patriotic of the Lanes, is largely responsible for the introduction of Marthe into the household. Andrew is eager to do his part, but he finds his meager salary as an insurance solicitor insufficient to meet the mounting expenses of his home, and he is, therefore, somewhat less enthusiastic about the arrangement.

In the opening scenes of the play we learn from the mother, a querulous, whining, pessimistic old lady of sixty, that her youngest son, Oswald, is a soldier in France, and we suspect from her spirited defense of him that he was not only a wild boy in his youth, but that he had run away from home a dozen years before to escape the consequences of the more serious of his escapades.

Hester Lane is in the village, doing the day's marketing. On her return, excited by news that she has heard, she maneuvers Marthe and little Andy out of the house that she may the more freely tell her mother-in-law what she has heard.

HESTER — (*her eyes shining with excitement*). Mother! I've got something to tell you. While I was out I met Hilda Pierce at the library. She's just back from France. You remember her? She went with the Red Cross. Oh, she had such a wonderful experience!

SARAH — Women better stay to home where they belong. If the men want to fight — let 'em.

HESTER — Hilda was in a sort of group — I don't know — that visited hospitals and things — wrote letters for the men — and talked to them.

SARAH — I guess she talked to 'em, all right.
HESTER — Mother — she saw — Oswald!
SARAH — (*in agitation*). Oswal'! *Tell* it — can't you? Can't you talk? (*In sudden fear*) He ain't — dead — is he?
HESTER — (*patting her hand soothingly*). No — he isn't dead. Or, at least, I don't think so. It was in a hospital — I can't remember the place — and this man was wounded — it was towards the end of the war it happened. Hilda got acquainted with this man. His name was Lane. Then — one day it all came out that he was Andrew's brother.
SARAH — (*with almost a sob*). Oh, my Lord! Was he real sick, did she say?
HESTER — His leg was bad, but the doctors said he'd get well. He didn't know anything about Andrew being married to me, or you being with us, or anything. Hilda was going to write a letter to you for him, but before she got to it they moved him off to another hospital — somewhere — and she never saw him again.
SARAH — (*anxiously*). And she don't know where he is now?
HESTER — No. But, mother, he was with the French Army, not with ours. In a thing they call the "Foreign Legion." And he was all decorated. He'd been perfectly splendid. Just a regular hero! Oh, mother, I think it's just fine — after everything — that — that —
SARAH — (*abruptly and suspiciously*). Ever'thing? What'd Andrew ever tell you about Oswal' I'd like to know?
HESTER — Why — nothing so very much, except that he was — well, pretty wild when he was a boy, and ran away and all that. Why?
SARAH — Nothin'! That's why. An' if you ever hear anything real bad about my Oswal' 'tain't true! An' don't you believe it is. He warn't sech a good son as Andrew, but he warn't bad. He warn't bad, I tell ye!

HESTER — Andrew never said he was.

SARAH — How'd she say he looked?

HESTER — Hilda said he was handsome. Handsome, in spite of being sick. Oh, I'd have given — I don't know what, for her experience.

SARAH — I guess Oswald's about as good-lookin' as the Lord intends men folks should be — though that ain't nothin' for a man to boast of. She said he warn't wounded — bad?

HESTER — No. His foot or his leg, I think.

SARAH — Oh dear — if I could only see 'im. Hester, you ain't suffered. You ain't suffered. I tell you women *has* to suffer. Then they *know*.

HESTER — (*not bitterly, but regretfully*). Oh, it's hard enough, this is, when you're never sure from one week's end to another where the money's comin' from to pay the bills. It seems to me that lately, everywhere I go, everything I do, I just find pretty things thrown in my face — only *I* can't have them. It isn't that it's always *pretty* things, though I do like what's nice, but *interesting* things. Things to give women a chance to look outside their own little dooryards — I don't know — to *be* something. Something that counts more in the world — I can't express it, and I don't suppose you'd understand. But it's always been like that — just scraping along, mamma and I, in that boarding house in Brooklyn.

SARAH — (*who has listened with sniffs and snorts of disdain*). Well, Hester Lane! Of all the speeches I ever heard! *Pretty* things! *Interesting* things! I never! I dunno what women's comin' to nowadays! Votin'! I s'pose you'll want ter be votin' too — an' dancin'! Wimmin's old 's I be, hoppin' 'round like monkeys on a hot stove lid, and a smokin' of them nasty cigarettes! Their legs a showin' at one end and their backs and bosoms at t'other. You, a married woman with a child and 's good a husband 's a girl should want, talkin' like that! I'm ashamed of you!—Hester—a *chance!* *Chance,* fiddlesticks!

HESTER — (*out of patience*). You don't understand! I can't tell you! I can't ever tell you. You always scold me like this.

SARAH — Next thing you'll want to get a divorce, I s'pose — like all the rest of 'em.

HESTER — Divorce? You don't think I'm going to run away, do you?

SARAH — (*horrifiedly*). Hester — for the Lord's sake! You ain't thinkin' of runnin' away?

No, Hester isn't thinking of running away, but every woman longs for a chance to be somebody. A ring at the front doorbell follows the elder Mrs. Lane's disappearance into the kitchen with the announced intention of starting the evening meal. A moment later Hester admits " a young man about twenty-eight, of more than ordinary good looks somewhat marred by dissipation, rough living and vagabond wanderings. Despite his battered past he has kept a certain appealing young charm, a combination of boyishness, impudence, high spirits, recklessness, virility and moral weakness. The sort of man likely to be rashly loved and rashly forgiven by most women, many men, children and dogs. He is dressed very shabbily in cheap garments of assorted colors and qualities. In his buttonhole are tiny ribbons indicative of military decorations. He is slightly lame and carries a stick. On a lead he has a wretched little yellow female dog."

The stranger is looking for Andrew Lane. He knew Andrew, he reports, when they were boys together in the same " hick " town. He knew " Mother Lane," too, but he hasn't time at the moment to stay and meet her. He guesses he'll be pushing on. Perhaps he will meet Andrew at the station. What name? Oh, just tell Andrew that Little Willie called — Little Willie Smart.

. . . He has gone. Andrew's mother can't remember any Smarts in Fisherville, when Hester tells her of the strange young man's call. He's a burglar, that's mother's opinion!

But the mystery is soon cleared. Andrew telephones from the station that he has found the long lost Oswald and is bringing him home, an announcement that all but throws Mrs. Lane into a state of nerves.

SARAH — (*hysterically*). My boy! Oswal'! Comin' home! Are you sure? (*Hester nods assurance*) Oh, my Lord! He's comin' home! (*Hustling about*) Well, he'll want his supper! We better git the table set right off. . . What'd I tell you this mornin' — when I dropped that fork and it stuck right up in the floor? Visitor comin'! Is they any sour milk in the house? If they is I'll mix up a pancake batter for supper. Oswal' allus loved pancakes. Hester — don't stand there 's if you was moonstruck! Do somethin'! My land! My land! My land! (*Sarah rushes off into kitchen.*)

. . . .

SARAH — (*rushing in from kitchen*). Where's he goin' ter sleep I'd like ter know?

HESTER — Oh, dear! Well — he'll have to have Marthe's bed — that's all. He's been a soldier and deserves the best we can do. And Marthe will have to sleep on that cot in the attic.

SARAH — And plenty good enough fer her, *I* say. I ain't goin' ter have her tryin' none of her monkey shines on my Oswal'!

A moment later Andrew and Oswald arrive. "Oswald still has the dog on the lead and is carrying a battered old suitcase. Andrew Lane is a man about forty. Growing fattish and baldish. Dressed in worn, but very neat clothes and with a face that shows unmistakably his simplicity of nature, his indefatigable good humor, his affectionate heart, his lack of mental capacity to carry him farther than he is today—a faithful, honest insurance clerk—and his reliability as a husband, son and a citizen. His fixed belief that everything is going to turn out all right helps him to face cheerfully the financial worries from which he has never in his life had a respite. He has an irritating trick of snapping his fingers as he talks, and this is particularly distasteful to Hester. He carries in his hands two paper bags, tied up as though from the grocer's."

The reintroduction of " Willie Smart " is accompanied by considerable excitement. Now he is accepting, with good-natured tolerance and some little show of interest, his mother's embrace, and she is sobbing delightedly on his shoulder. Andrew seeks to shoulder his way into the greeting.

ANDREW — Well, Ma, what do you think of what the cat dragged in? . . . Hey, there, old son — this is your sister, Hester — guess she'll give you a kiss, too. Go to it, bo!

OSWALD — (*hesitates*). I never had a sister.

ANDREW — (*laughing*). He's bashful!

OSWALD — (*with his most disarming smile, looks straight into Hester's eyes, then goes to her and kisses her on the lips*). Gee — I'm glad it's you!

HESTER — (*a little confused*). And I never had a brother. Oh, why didn't you tell me it was you just now? I almost guessed it — I —

OSWALD — Well — what do you know about that? Say, sister, we've got to make up for lost time.

ANDREW — No time like the present.

OSWALD — I wanted to see Andy first. I didn't know whether he'd want a poor nut like me to come in here and muss up his front parlor.

ANDREW — Aw, shut up! Ain't he the card? Comes walking right up to me when I got out of the train, he did — just landed this morning, he did! And he says, "Hello, And!" just like —

Gradually as the excitement simmers, Oswald is made to feel as much at home as a returned prodigal should. Andy, he thinks, has got things pretty soft — with a home and a wife and a kid. They manage to trail along, all right, Andy assures him.

They tell him about Marthe, and how she came to live with them, the second year of the war. She's a good girl, Andrew agrees, and an orphan. "Folks killed in the war right in front of her. She kinda helps Hester. She'll go away pretty soon, I guess. Studyin' to be a stenographer —"

HESTER — I wanted to do something. Andrew thought we couldn't. We — oh — it seemed so dreadful not to help poor little Belgium! It wasn't much — but it was our little bit. I — I wanted to do such a lot — you understand? Like you. Oh, we've heard — we've heard just today about *you!*

. . . .

OSWALD — (*flattered*). Me? Aw — who's been handin' you the bunk about me? Don't you —

HESTER — You were *splendid!* We know — and you were wounded!

ANDREW — What'd you think he was — a rockin' chair soldier?

HESTER — (*her eyes shining with excitement. Turns to Andrew*). Andrew — he was just wonderful! Why, Hilda Pierce is back from France, and she says — (*Looking at Oswald who is facing them*) And just look at the ribbons in his buttonhole!

ANDREW — (*laughing boisterously*). Thought they was somethin' some girl give him. (*Sarah Lane enters from the kitchen and starts for the sideboard just in time to hear the last of this statement.*)

SARAH — Mercy, Oswal'! You ain't *married*, are you?

OSWALD — (*grinning*). Sure Ma. Two twins right outside in the limousine. I call 'em Clemenceau an' Lloyd George for short. Want to see 'em?

Marthe and little Andy are back from their walk. Oswald takes immediately to the little boy, and little Andy is greatly impressed with his new-found uncle. They are pals in no time.

The brothers are a little embarrassed when they are left alone. "Each is looking at the other, and old thoughts, old memories are surging through their minds. Oswald seems rather self-conscious." But gradually they work around to the things that each knows must be talked over sooner or later.

ANDREW — When pa died — you knew about his dyin' — didn't you, Os?

OSWALD — Um-hum.

ANDREW — Ma come here to live with us. Pa didn't leave a red cent. When everything was settled and the debts paid, there wasn't a darn thing but just a little furniture ma hung on to.

OSWALD — (*with a little embarrassment*). I was a good deal of a darn fool in those days, Andy. I dunno why I ever got into that mix-up.

ANDREW — (*awkwardly*). I s'pose most every fellow wonders that — when it's over. I don't know — I'm no better than anybody else — don't pretend to be. Only I never had the money — had to work too hard to raise much cain. And now—with Hess and the kid—I—

OSWALD — (*sincerely*). Well, you can mark it right down in your diary that little ol' Os is going to play straight from now on. Honest, I am, And!

ANDREW — I'm glad to hear it, Os. We're right with you.

OSWALD — (*rising, shiftily*). Say — was pa — ? When he found out — ?

ANDREW — (*frankly but kindly*). It pretty near killed him. I guess it *did*, anyway. You see — well — the money part of it was awful tough — but when it come out about Millie — he — well, I guess you know how he'd feel. Os — she's *on the street* now, in Rochester, they say.

OSWALD — Damn it! I'm sorry — but everything wasn't my fault. If dad'd ever treated me like — oh well — what's the use?

ANDREW — Boy — I don't want you should ever say anything — too hard against the old man. He come right acrost when it was up to him. And so did ma. And nobody ever knew the worst of it, but old Peters in the bank and us. Folks didn't even know about Millie.

OSWALD — Say, Andy — does *she* know?

ANDREW — Hess?

OSWALD — Um-hum.

ANDREW — No. I never told Hester a word — beyond — well, that you was a pretty frisky young feller and run away from home. Pa and I — you know that part. We worked and paid back the money on that check you — and the bank let it drop. It came hard for us, Os, but if you've learned your lesson — why —

OSWALD — Much 'bliged — Andy.

ANDREW — That's all right. And Os, I appreciate your wanting to see me first before you told Hess who you were. I don't want to pick open any old sores, boy, 'specially tonight, when you've just come home to us. An' I just wan' to tell you that what's done 's — done. Nothin's gained by harping on old mistakes. You're back and I guess you've about wiped out all that tomfoolishness — or worse — by what you've done over there in the war. I guess they didn't give you those ribbons in your buttonhole for looking at the view.

But now, the old war's over and everybody's glad of it. Boy, I want you should make my home your home till you get a start, till you get a job; gol darn it, till you get a little home and a wifie of your own. See? (*He sings in a kidding way*)

"With his baby on his knee, he's as happy as
can be
For there's no place like Home Sweet Home."

OSWALD — You're damn kindly, Andy. I — I appreciate how you all have — treated me. Far's the war's concerned, as the Irishman says, "'Twas a hell of a war, but 'twas the only war we had!"

Soon the preparations for supper are in full blast, with everybody taking a hand and everybody happy. During the excitement Andrew manages to have a few words with Hester, to tell her, first, that Oswald likes her a lot, and to suggest, guardedly, that now that he is to live with them perhaps it will be just as well if they hint to Marthe that she had better be thinking of finding another home — as soon as she can get a job. Of course, there will be the added cost of taking care of Oswald and all, and—But Hester does not agree. Marthe can't be put out that way, nor will she risk hurting the girl's feelings by any such suggestion. In time she will find a place, but for the present things must go on as they are.

Oswald's meeting with Marthe is quite informal. His appraisal of the girl being favorable, as she busies herself setting the table, he assumes his natural "kidding" way with her and ends by trying to kiss her, to which the girl replies by striking at him. "Aw — say, Martha!" he protests. "Hit a poor soldier? Why, say, I bin fightin' for your country. Got wounded up there —see that lame foot? *Vous êtes* naughty girl!"

"She looks him piteously in the face, overcome by an emotion she cannot rightly interpret. She speaks in a low tone as it were almost a sacrament."

"It is *I*, who kiss *you* — for my country!" she says, as she kisses him upon the forehead. Then, surprised at herself, she bolts into the kitchen. "You're a funny kid," is Oswald's comment, as he gazes amusedly after her.

Hester takes up the work of completing the table setting — and also that of getting acquainted with Oswald. His manner toward her is a little more restrained, but he is still in a lightly flirtatious mood. She tells him how glad everyone is that he has come home, how his mother cried and cried —

OSWALD — I don't suppose it makes much difference to *you*, my coming back, does it?

HESTER — Do you want me to say I'm sorry you came?

OSWALD — (*ingratiatingly*). You're awful good to — to your little brother.

HESTER — You're the first *hero* we've ever had.

OSWALD — Aw — cut that hero stuff out — Hester.

HESTER — I can hardly wait for you to tell me about your experiences in the war. They've laughed at me so here — because I cared about the war so — oh! I did care! Awfully! Like you!

OSWALD — (*amused*). Like me?

HESTER — But you *must* have, if you went there.

OSWALD — Oh! (*With an amused little whistle of two notes.*)

HESTER — And now you're coming back — one of us — from the war! It makes it more — *ours*, don't you see? Gives *us* a share in it.

OSWALD — (*admiringly*). Say, you're a regular little patriot, eh? Hip-hip stuff! (*Maliciously*) Brother Andy didn't go to war, did he?

HESTER — No. He couldn't — he — you see, with us women and baby and —

OSWALD — Did he want to go?

HESTER — How could he? If it hadn't been for baby, *I'd* have gone! I'd have loved going! And doing anything! Washing dishes! Scrubbing floors! Washing the boys' clothes! Anybody who's been there is just wonderful to me!

OSWALD — (*with satisfaction*). Oh!

HESTER — I suppose you think I'm — awfully foolish — like everybody else does.

OSWALD — Who does?

HESTER — Oh — I don't know. Do *you?*

OSWALD — (*leaning over to her*). You want to know what I think? Well I think you're just about the sweetest little bit of —

HESTER — (*breaks in, blushing with embarrassment and pleasure*). And I think you're just the biggest little jollier that —

They are standing very close to each other when Andrew's return interrupts the scene. As Hester leaves the room she flings back a tantalizing smile at Oswald. "Willie Smart," she calls, teasingly.

"Willie Smart," echoes Andrew. "Ha — you can't fool that little girl, Os!"

"Oh, no!" answers Cswald. "I guess I'm in the right pew here, all right, all right."

ACT II

In the sitting room of the Lane home. "The furniture and ornaments are a mixture of Mrs. Lane's 'front parlor set,' transported hither from western New York State after her husband's death — black walnut and green overstuffed pieces of atrocious appearance and less comfort — and some of the relics of 1890 from Hester's girlhood home, a Brooklyn boarding house."

It is a December evening and the family is absent at the church attending a meeting of the brethren at which

Oswald, home three months now, modestly relates some of his reminiscences of the war and thus helps to increase the contributions to the church fund. Andrew is treasurer of the church.

The friendship between Marthe and Oswald has evidently made considerable headway during the past three months, and as he comes in now, having eluded the others, she greets him effusively and with a passionate intensity that indicates her dependence upon him.

"Oswald is dressed in his poilu uniform — worn, ill-fitting, blue. He wears it jauntily and has put on his medals — the French croix-de-guerre with palms, the Medaille Militaire. On his left shoulder is the red cord, the fouragere, granted to Legionaires. There are four gold service stripes on his arm."

MARTHE — Let me look at you! Oh — you are so beautiful in your uniform, my soldier! My hero!

OSWALD — Feels kinda good to get into the old duds again, Marty. You know, kid, I get kinda fed up sometimes with — with things here. All these damn rich — a fellow like me — what show's he got? They want to make him work for 'em — for the damn capitalists, that's what. 'Tain't fair! I got 's good a right to be rich — better, by God, 'n' this old uniform's the proof of it! Good 's those greasy hogs! Divide up property, Martha, share and share alike, I say!

MARTHE — (*passionately*). Oswald — let us go away! Take me away from here. I — I — hate it! Take me to — I don't care where, I'll work for you — I'll —

OSWALD — Sure, kitten, sure — gimme time — gimme time!

MARTHE — Your brother does not want me to stay here any longer.

OSWALD — Why don't he? How do you know?

MARTHE — Your mother, too. She 'ates me! She is

afraid that I should make you with love for me! I know! I see!

OSWALD — Ma! Oh — don't let ma get your goat, Marty! If ma ever felt real good about anything in the world she'd think she was sick and take Peruna. But what's the dope about Andy? I mean — what'd you mean about him? Wantin' you to go? Has — has he got on to anything do you think?

MARTHE — Oh, Oswald — cannot we tell them now? I do not like this always 'iding and concealing. Let us tell them. Then we go and —

OSWALD — What about Andy? Get down to brass tacks. Has he said —?

MARTHE — No. But I know. I feel. I see him *look* — *look* — if we speak or sit together. W'y does he do this?

OSWALD — (*somewhat relieved*). You keep your shirt on, Marty. Old And hasn't got anything on you — nor on me. He couldn't see the hole in a doughnut — not if you took it out and give it to him. But, if you feel like this about it — why don't you beat it?

MARTHE — You mean — go away?

OSWALD — Um-hum.

MARTHE — You know w'y I stay here. For you!

OSWALD — (*patting her shoulder*). Yah! Sure. I get you. We're all right. But now, kid, about this tellin' 'em — why naturally I'm all for it. But it's like this. I ain't just found out what I want to do yet. I ain't going to get all tied up in bow knots with some darn thing that — well, that I can't show my ability at and make good money, too. And you ain't got that stenographer job yet, see? We'd want to make our getaway from here if we told. No. You just trust your Uncle Oswald a little longer, girlie, and by golly you'll wear diamonds yet.

Marthe would like to believe in Oswald. She would,

if she could, control her awakening jealousy of him and his interest in the others — in little Andy, for one, and yes — his interest in Hester, too. She has noticed that! Hester would love him if she dared, Marthe screams accusingly, and he knows it, which puts Oswald in a rage. But though she is intimidated by his threatening manner, and fearful that she may lose him to another, Marthe persists hysterically in demanding that he declare his love for her and his determination to protect her. Finally the breaking point comes and she pathetically confesses her condition.

MARTHE — You see — I must go.

OSWALD — Stop crying, kid. I gotta think. You lemme think. (*She sobs aloud*) Sure, we'll go away — but you gotta lemme fix things — *Don't you tell anybody!* You hear? (*The outer door slams*) Oh, Christ! Here they come! Stop crying!

Oswald succeeds in pushing the unhappy Marthe out of the room before the family, returning from the church meeting in high spirits, troops in. They are full of congratulations for the hero of the evening, and proud of the fact that his talk helped to boost the collections to five hundred dollars, which Andrew, as treasurer, has brought home with him.

SARAH — You done reel well, Oswald! Land alive! What a time of it you had over there with them creechers!

ANDREW — Craters, Ma!

SARAH — Ten days he said he was in one —

ANDREW — Ten hours, Ma!

SARAH — And nothin' ter eat or drink but scrapple!

HESTER — Shrapnel!

SARAH — It don't signify! Your pa was a good talker, too. At prayer meetin' and down to the grange. I'm glad you done so good Oswal', jest to show folks in this town that there's other folks as good as they are and some better. The Laneses kin hold their heads up with any of 'em.

ANDREW — (*counting the church collection at the desk*). That's right, Ma.

. . . .

HESTER — I can't get it out of my head. All the cold, and mud — and suffering — and disease — and the wounded — and the dying —

ANDREW — And the dead!

HESTER — Oswald — you really advanced right over the piled-up bodies of your comrades, as they lay there —dead and dying, in the trenches?

OSWALD — Um-hum.

HESTER — Oh! How could you?

ANDREW — Had to be done, dearie.

HESTER — Why, we don't realize over here what you boys went through! (*Looking at Andrew*) There isn't anything in the whole world too good for you — not *anything!* Oh! Those awful battles — I can just understand how you felt!

OSWALD — So could Fritz!

SARAH — Land, Andrew! How can you laff? I do' wan' to think of it even! Gives me the nawshy!

The chatter in the sitting room has awakened little Andy, and he has romped away from Marthe. Only his Uncle Oswald can do anything with him in the crisis, but he goes back to bed willingly enough once he is properly escorted by his favorite soldier, which gives Andrew a chance proudly to inform the family that his boss was at the night's meeting and that he took quite a fancy to Os. The boss is going to offer Os a job as an insurance man, in fact. And Andrew thinks Os ought to take it. He has been rather careless turning down jobs, Os has, considering the cost of living and everything.

The women folks are not so sure. Of course, they want Oswald to go to work as soon as he is able, but they would hate awfully to see him overdo before he is strong and well. Hester, too, would hate to see him go — the house has been so much brighter since he has been there. If anybody has to go, mother can't see why it shouldn't be Marthe. And Marthe, according to Hester, is going. As for Oswald —

HESTER — Oswald's trying. I know he's trying to get something to do.

ANDREW — Sure. I don't say he isn't — but — darn it all, if I was a rich man I'd let him set here till he got good and ready. I bought him a new suit yesterday, too.

HESTER — You did?

ANDREW — You know, Hess, we've got little Andy to think of. That money we're puttin' by for his college education don't grow very fast.

HESTER — (*discouraged*). Oh, dear! Nothing seems right in this world.

ANDREW — (*cautiously*). What I was going to say was — Hess — that if you could sort of — you know — to Os. He likes you, and if you could maybe suggest that —? This is a good offer of the boss's —

HESTER — I know Oswald will take it.

ANDREW — Yes. I guess he will. Hess — About — Mattie's going—(*Confidentially*) There ain't any— *special* reason for it — is there?

HESTER — Special? Reason? What do you mean?

ANDREW — Oh — I don't know — but —

HESTER — But what?

ANDREW — Well — Os — you know, he's always — sort of — joshin' everybody — and — well, I didn't know but maybe he'd be gettin' fresh with Mattie — maybe —

HESTER — Why, Andrew Lane

ANDREW — I don't suppose —

HESTER — I don't know how you can even think of such a thing!

ANDREW — Well — when two young people get together —

HESTER — I don't believe a word of it!

Hester's jealousy "is so evident that anybody but Andrew would see it." He, however, is content to let the matter drop, which is more than Hester is willing to do. She starts back for the stairs as though she would rush up immediately and demand a denial from Oswald on the instant — a denial that he ever thought now, or ever had thought of Marthe in that way. She meets the young man coming down and is momentarily flustered. But she manages to effect a hurried escape without attracting further attention.

It is his mother's suggestion that Oswald had better sleep downstairs that night on the living room couch. Pressed for a reason, she answers:

SARAH — I'd feel safer 'bout that money. Them burglars kin git anywhere. Church money, and give for them little babies, too.

OSWALD — All right, Ma.

SARAH — Oswal' — that Mr. Thornton has told Andrew he'd give you a good job — sellin' insurance. I want you should go right down to the city tomorrow and

OSWALD — Me? Sell insurance? Nix!

SARAH — You can't go on livin' on Andrew's shoulders. Andrew says he thinks you ain't tried as hard as you might to git somethin' to do. He says —

OSWALD — Oh! He throws that up to me, does he? 'Course I can go and fight so's he can live at home on Easy Street! Damn slacker! That's what they call "Keep the world safe for democracy!" Well, you can tell him from me I ain't going to trouble him much longer!

SARAH — What you goin' ter do? (*Anxiously*) You ain't goin' off again, traipsin' 'round the world, be you?

OSWALD — I got plans.

SARAH — Oswal' — you take this job. Everything'll be all right then. (*Wheedlingly*) I want you should git to earnin'. I guess I ain't any too welcome in this house. Ossie — you take it, and we'll git a little place to ourselves. Me and you. And I guess if you wanted to, you could git that Pierce gal — from the flirty way she acted tonight, carryin' on so about you — (*Picking at his sleeve*) Ravelin' on your sleeve! Sign o' money!

OSWALD — Money? Oh, well — I'll see — don't you fret, Ma —

SARAH — (*piteously*). Don't seem's if I could bear to have you run off agin. I ain't one to tell my feelin's, but this being away of yourn has jest about killed me — 'f you should start off now — (*A sudden thought and she looks at him anxiously*) Oswald — you ben a good boy — ain't you, since you been home? You ain't done nothin' wrong, have you?

OSWALD — Oh! Between you — you and Andy — you'd drive a fellow right into Sing Sing! Harp! Harp! Harp! Every chance you get! Over a mistake I made once. Can't you let it drop? Can't lemme forget? Oh — I'm sick to death of the whole show! I wish I'd never come home!

SARAH — 'F you had any respect for my feelin's you wouldn't talk like that. Pretty way for a boy to talk, after all your pa and I and Andy have done for you. you?

OSWALD — Go on! Rub it in! Rub salt on the sores! You're having fun, ain't you?

SARAH — I'd cut my hand off fer you Ossie, and well you know it, 'f I thought it'd do you any good.

OSWALD — Oh, well — I know it, Ma — I — I'm all

tired out tonight. I'm worried — about things. We'll talk it over tomorrow. It'll all be all right.

. . . .

SARAH — I'm goin' to bed. I'm about beat out. (*As she gathers up her patent medicine*) I hope we'll all be alive in the mornin'.

OSWALD — You don't ever worry or anything, do you, Ma?

SARAH — Land! What a day we've had of it! And me gittin' up and goin' to old Mrs. Trumble's funeral tomorrer mornin'. I like to forget it. Andy, I see that oldest Trumble boy on the street the other day. You know, that lean, pimply-faced one. To my mind, he ain't no better'n a loon. I says, "How's yer ma?" I says. And he says, "She's been practically unconscious for two days and she ain't et nothin' fer a week, and her tongue's black's the bottom of a kittle; an' — " he says, "you can't tell me them 're good signs!" Good signs! — she was deader'n a door nail inside twenty-four hours! 'Night!

It isn't a pleasant chat Andrew and Oswald have as soon as their mother has retired. Oswald is ugly. So, they want to throw him out, do they? No, Andrew tries to assure him, they are just a little bit in hopes he will find a job soon, so that he can be earning his own living.

OSWALD — . . . Why don't you come right out and say what you mean — that you don't want me here? You're like all the rest of 'em — fight for 'em — get wounded for 'em — croak for 'em, by God! Save their old country for 'em, by God, and then have 'em tell you to go to hell! No sir! Not any in mine!

ANDREW — Say — what's the matter with you, anyhow? What's the great idea? You talk like one of these here Bolsheviks. For the Lord's sake, Os — keep off that stuff! 'Twon't do you or anybody else any good.

OSWALD — It would make a man a Bolshevik just to listen to them rotten riddles of yours. I don't see how Hester stands it.

ANDREW — You needn't worry about Hess.

OSWALD — (*with an open sneer*). No — nor you.

ANDREW — (*regaining his good nature with an effort*). Well — don't let's get to arguing, Os, Sunday night and all. I shouldn't wonder if what you've done over there has kinda tired you out and put you on the blink, physically. And you've kinda lost your pep. That's what the doctors say about a lot of the boys. All I wanted to say was — that we all — love havin' you here with us, but seein' as how Morgan forgot to — (*With an attempt to make a sorry joke*) to take me into partnership with him last week —

OSWALD — (*ironically*). Ha — ha!

Of course, Andrew continues, with Marthe gone, things will be a little easier — So they are driving out Marthe, too, are they? Oswald's solicitude sounds suspicious to Andrew. "There ain't anything — funny — between you and Mattie — is there?" he inquires anxiously. "No, there ain't!" Oswald replies, furiously. " . . . Is there any other damn thing you can throw up to me? You've done pretty well so far. Piker! Bolshevik! Yellow dog! And now — "

Hester is coming down the stairs. She has heard a part of the row for all Andrew's efforts to prevent it, but neither of the boys will satisfy her curiosity as to what it is all about.

Andrew, it now transpires, has an early morning engagement in a neighboring town, necessitating his taking a night train over. He expects to be back the first thing in the morning — but if he isn't he wants Hester to be sure and take the church money around to the bank and deposit it. It's too much to have lyin' around loose.

Now he has gone and Hester and Oswald find themselves alone. The silences are a little embarrassing, they find, and conversation a bit difficult, though Hester holds it pretty consistently to a demand to know what had passed between Andrew and Oswald before she interrupted them. But she gets little satisfaction from Oswald.

Learning that he is planning to sleep on the couch, she insists upon fussing about his being cold, which further irritates him. He'll be all right with his overcoat. He's slept in worse places — the thought of which reduces Hester to sympathetic tears. She, too, is cold and hungry for comfort. He lights the gas log in the grate and sits before it as she tells him what a difference his being in the house has made to her — to all of them, in fact.

But, he is going away —

It is the first she has heard of it! Now she knows what the quarrel with Andrew had meant! She will never, never forgive Andrew! But Oswald manages to quiet her. She is nervous and excited and tired — and she had better go to bed, he tells her. Still she lingers — long enough to mend a rip in his coat sleeve, and to quiz him, subtly, about the women in France who were especially nice to him — after he got out of the hospital. "Oh — women?" admits Oswald, when she forces him finally to answer: "Oh, they's women enough everywhere. Too many of 'em! Say, it's getting warm here."

HESTER — Isn't it nice — being here — so warm, and comfy? Do you know it is the first time we have been really alone? Tell me more about the war. I love to hear about it and you boys that have really done things — won't ever talk. . . .

OSWALD — (*stretching himself out at ease on the couch, after a silence*). So warm — and comfy. Sometimes, over there, when I'd maybe be settin' up to my waist in ice water and just cussin' out the whole damn show — I'd think of places, warm — and comfy. I'd never had 'em. But I'd seen 'em and heard about 'em —like this. I'm a poor lot, Hester, I guess. I've hoboed it, and dead-beat it all over the damned place, ever since I was a kid of sixteen. I've seen the worst of everything — women and men — and God's made some birds, I'll say. I've gone down the line with 'em. Greasers in Mexico, Chinks in Shanghai, Wops in Naples, Niggers in Port Said — oh, God, I do know everything. Every damn thing! If they'd been a kid like you waitin' for me — maybe — Then comes the war. I goes in along with a guy named Bill that I picked up over in Chili — a Swede. We gets in the Foreign Legion. God! What a swell bunch! Gee! Old Bill was a card. He got his all right. Falls down in the attack right by me. "Come on, Bill!" I says, "to hell with 'em!" "I got mine!" he says, and he had. I couldn't stop to do anything. I never saw Bill again. They gimme that junk — (*Pointing to the medals on his coat.*)

HESTER — War cross and two palms!

OSWALD — — for what I done that day.

HESTER — Taking that dreadful machine gun!

OSWALD — And bringin' six Fritzies back by the tails — and the next day, I gets mine. (*Resentfully*) Only I don't die — bum foot. (*He raises the built-up shoe and lets it down with a thud.*)

"Hester slips down to the couch and as she sits there she lays her cheek against his left arm. Oswald regards her, half in pity and half in amusement; he seems to be working out some plan in his mind. He frowns. His eyes wander to the secretary, speculatively."

HESTER — All you've seen and done. And all I haven't. It doesn't seem fair, somehow.

OSWALD — You mean you're fed up, sis?

HESTER — I can't explain — you wouldn't understand. Something's wrong, somewhere. Life is wrong, I guess. (*Bitterly*) Oh—what does it all matter?

OSWALD — (*trying her out*). Suppose — just for instance — suppose I told you that I was fed up — you understand what I mean — and wanted some place, warm — and comfy as you say, and somebody who'd help make it so. Somebody who'd want me there. Somebody — who'd understand me, and stick to me — through hell. My kind o' girl. Every fellow's got his kind, you know. Suppose I said I'd been homesick for her, just plain nutty — till I got right where I'd got to have her by me — for keeps. *Had* to! Dotty about her. Suppose I said all that, Hester? What would *you* say, sis? (*So great is Hester's emotion that she cannot reply. Oswald eyes her with a certain amusement, a certain contempt*) You'll know — when I'm gone.

HESTER — Oswald! Don't go —

OSWALD — (*in a cold, matter-of-fact voice*). No. I ain't your kind, sis — do you get me? Gee! It's 'most eleven o'clock. What do you know about that? You're all tired out. All in. You'll feel better in the morning. . . . Hess — lemme give you a tip. You stick to your kid — *he's* hero enough for you.

"Hester, utterly at sea, hesitates miserably, seeing her poor little dream shattered to bits. At last she rises and without a backward glance drags herself hopelessly out of the room and upstairs. Oswald coolly watches her go, a little smile of contempt on his face. As she disappears he laughs shortly."

Now he prepares to sleep on the couch. The prospect isn't particularly pleasing to him. Suddenly he remembers a cablegram that came for him earlier in the day. It offered him a job in Paris, so he told Marthe. He re-reads it and with a determined "You bet ye I will!" thrusts it into his pocket and goes quickly to the secretary.

He starts to write an answer to the cablegram, but hesitates before it is finished. His eye falls on the drawer in which he has seen Andrew put the church money. Evidently he is trying to decide whether or not he should take it. The temptation is strong, but he fights it off. He goes back to the couch — but again his thought is drawn to the desk and the money. Suddenly he makes up his mind and goes swiftly back to the desk. Finding the key, he unlocks the drawer, takes out the bag of money and stuffs it into his overcoat pocket. He is just turning away when a gasp of anguish back of him causes him to turn quickly. In the archway leading to the stairs stands Hester. She is in her nightdress, with a wrapper thrown over it. Across her arm she carries a blanket she is bringing to him. She has seen him steal the money.

"The two stare at each other for a moment of silence. Marthe runs down the stairs and into the room. Her eyes are on Hester with furious accusation. Her gaze travels to Oswald for explanation. With a mutter of rage Oswald rises and pushing between the two women he goes upstairs to his room. Marthe regards Hester with loathing and anger for a moment and then with a little cry of 'Oswald!' she follows him up the stairs. Hester stands petrified with horror and anguish. The blanket falls from her nerveless arm as she looks straight before her."

The curtain falls

ACT III

All night long Hester watches the stairs and the front door, determined that Oswald shall not leave the house with the church funds. Eight o'clock the next morning finds her wrapped in the afghan that was to have covered Oswald, still keeping her vigil at the foot of the stairs. There is a step on the stairs and Hester starts nervously — but it is Marthe who comes down. "Her disordered hair, red eyes, and distraught countenance betray only too well the fact that she, too, has spent a sleepless night filled with tears and anguish. She gives Hester a look of fierce contempt —"

They are both on the verge of nervous hysteria. It takes little to start them covertly sneering and snapping at each other. Marthe is even defiant in her boast that it is she, and not Hester, whom Oswald loves, try as Hester did to take him away from her. Yes, he is her lover! He is going to marry her! Together they will go away, far away! It is necessary that they should go away —

Hester's disgust is heightened by this last revelation of Oswald's perfidy, but Marthe is proud, proud, proud — and prepared to scream the fact at the top of her voice.

MARTHE — You hate me — because I am happy!

HESTER — *You* — happy? Oh! Martha!

MARTHE — Yes — yes — yes!

HESTER — This is a happy house! (*Marthe sobs hysterically*) Stop crying! Stop! (*The physical strength of Hester dominates the girl and makes her stop crying just as though she were a child. Hester speaks to her in a cold, precise voice*) I don't care what he does — or what you do! He can take you wherever he pleases — the sooner, the better. After I've seen him. Do you understand? Listen to me! Are you listening? I want you to tell me everything you know about last night! Don't lie!

MARTHE — (*whimpering*). I hear you talk! And talk! Downstairs. I wait for you to come up. You take off your dress — you go down — to *him*. Oh! Madame! *You shall not take him from me!*

HESTER — Oh — stop that ridiculous stuff! There's no good going on like that. I want to know what you two intend doing with that money.

MARTHE — Money?

HESTER — Who planned it? You or he? He did, I suppose — didn't it mean *anything* to you that you'd had a home here? Kindness — friendship? Care? That you could calmly plot together right under this roof? Knowing what it would mean to us? After having sunk as low as you could with him — you could plan that!

MARTHE — *Mon dieu!* Plan what?

HESTER — That! (*Points towards the secretary*) You knew what he was going to do! That's why you came down. (*Less convincingly*) You have said very wicked things of me this morning. You — you had no right to do so. You ran away from me last night. You wouldn't let me explain. I came down last night to see if he had enough covers on his couch — it was cold — he was going to sleep here on account of the money. It's true! (*Marthe sneers*) When I got to that door — he was — I saw him—*stealing that church money from the drawer!*

MARTHE—No! No! *O mon amour. Tu as fait ça pour moi!*

HESTER — Stop talking French! You wicked girl, I want you to understand one thing clearly. Neither you nor he is going to leave this house till every cent of this money is —

MARTHE — (*on her knees before Hester*). Madame! I swear to you, as God is my witness, I did not know *anything* of this — believe me — not anything! It is for me that he has done this! For me! Madame — he is not bad. No! No — you shall not hurt him! You shall not!

SARAH — (*calling from upstairs*). Hester!

HESTER — (*puzzled*). You didn't *know* — you —

MARTHE — Non! Non! *Non!*

SARAH — (*calling*). Hester! Hester! You there — Hester?

HESTER — Sh —! She's coming. I must get my clothes on. Whatever the truth of this thing is, he mustn't leave this house with that money. *He shan't.* It would be awful for us! For everybody. Can't you see — the war — and little Andy — and everything? *You must not let him go till I get back!* (*She grips Marthe by the arm, pulling her to her feet*) You promise?

MARTHE — Yes! Yes! Yes!

Mother Lane finds them both lookin' like death and destruction, and she can't at all understand whatever has come over everybody in that house lately. Seein 's she's goin' to Mrs. Trumble's funeral that mornin' and is particularly anxious about gettin' there early, so's to see what they've laid the old lady out in, it does seem to Mrs. Lane that some folks might reasonably bestir themselves about breakfast, and the other necessary things that have got to be attended to.

Hester makes a hurried toilette and is back in the living room, waiting anxiously, prayerfully, for Oswald. That young man has been helping little Andy to get dressed upstairs. Now he comes down, in response to the boy's calls. He is calm, and neatly dressed in the new brown suit Andrew bought for him. He still wears something of the smile of a conqueror, or at least the smile of a master of the situation. Hester eyes him furtively, avoiding his more direct gaze. She hesitates just a little about leaving him alone with Andy when she is obliged to go to and from the kitchen. But something assures her that he will not bolt. And Andy must have his breakfast if he is going to get to his kindergarten in time. . . .

Mother Lane takes little Andy to school when she goes to the funeral. Oswald stops them at the door. "Bye — Ma" he says, awkwardly, as he puts his arms about her and kisses her cheek, which greatly surprises the old lady. It isn't like Oswald to treat her as if she was goin' on a journey when she's just goin' to a funeral. While Hester is at the outer door with them, Marthe edges her way in carefully from the dining room as though she had been listening at the door and awaiting a chance to speak to Oswald. But she no more than mentions his name, before he pushes her back into the other room. He has other matters to settle before he can talk with Marthe. And Hester is coming.

HESTER — (*in a low, tense voice*). You've got to give back that money! Right now!

OSWALD — That's what *you* say.

HESTER — (*desperately*). Give it back! (*Oswald gets ready to go*) Give it to me! (*Oswald pays no attention*) Do you mean you won't?

OSWALD — You've guessed it!

HESTER — (*wildly*). You shan't go out of this room with that money!

OSWALD — Who's going to stop me?

HESTER — I will! (*She faces him resolutely.*)

OSWALD — What do you care about it?

HESTER — What do I care? Why — it's terrible! It's awful! It's criminal! We'll be ruined! The disgrace of it to the family! Give it back! Now! This instant!

OSWALD — Well — Andy'll have to pay it.

HESTER — Andy — pay it! Why — we haven't got a penny and you know it.

OSWALD — Oh — he can get it somehow. What's he ever done, anyhow? He didn't go to war, did he? Let him pay then. I'm a soldier. I'm his brother. Let him pay.

HESTER — (*in a fury of anger*). Soldier! You! Andrew pay! Why should he pay for you — and your horrid women? Oh! I know the story of that wretched girl, here, in this very house — right under our eyes. Mine! And your mother's. I got it out of her this morning. How you'd planned to rob us in order to run away and cover up the filthy tracks of your nasty — dirty — ugh! I can't talk of it!

OSWALD — (*insolently*). Go to it, Phœbe Snow! You're doing fine! *You're* all right! *You're* pure! God, but you're pure!—but it's going to cost you money to pay your laundry bill, my little snowflake. But lemme tell you one thing. Your dope on Marty is all wrong. She didn't know anything about the little sum of money I — borrowed, the kid didn't. Not a thing.

HESTER — You expect me to believe that? Do you think I don't know you *have* to take her away! And why?

OSWALD — Do I?

HESTER — It's all plain enough, now. What a fool I was, not —

OSWALD — You were a fool all right. That ain't the half of it, dearie!

HESTER — Oh, you're the wickedest man! You — you *hero!*

OSWALD — (*brutally*). What did you come down here last night for? Afterwards? You think I don't know? You haven't got anything on me, young lady.

HESTER — Oh, you coward! You coward!

OSWALD—Oh, can that stuff! 'T isn't going to help you any. Listen to me.

HESTER — (*distractedly*). Haven't you any pity?

OSWALD — Listen here. You tried to find out last night if there was any other woman. You know why you wanted to know. And then I handed you that "supposing" stuff. Supposing you were the goat? And you were all right. God, you were easy. Fell for it like a hired girl for a policeman. When I first came here I thought you were — well, different from the ordinary run of women. You looked like a good girl — married, with one of the finest kids a woman ever had. And then — little by little I began to see how the wind lay. Just like 'em all, you are. I tested you out last night. Just a regular — well, you know. I'm going to tell you something. I'm going back to France. Back to France, see? To my girl. That's where she is. "My kind o' girl." She wants me and I want her. And I'm going to take this money to do it with. Oh, I know all the sweet things you'd like to say about me. What the hell do I care! You and Andy have got to pay it. That's the price of that little show you tried to pull off last night. Do you get me?

. . . .

HESTER — I don't care *what* happens! *What* you do! I won't let you take that money!

OSWALD — What'll you do? Call the police? And disgrace the family? What about your nice pious friends when they hear the police have arrested the church treasurer's brother? . . . Why — you haven't got the nerve to do it! And *you know it!* That money's going to take me back to France.

HESTER — Oh! Oh! And Marthe! Marthe — what about her? What are you going to do about her? As she is!

OSWALD — (*casually*). Marthe? Oh — nothing. Leave her for you and Andy.

Calmly he takes his overcoat from the chair and puts it on and goes into the hallway for the suitcase he had left there. He hears the pleading of Hester that, for all their sakes, he will not take the money, but it makes not the slightest impression on him. "You weren't thinking of them last night," he sneers. "Cut that sob stuff out. I've got to go. You understand. *Got* to! . . . Think over what I've said, sis. You're up against it. You can't do one damn thing but take your medicine."

Hester sinks helplessly into a chair, beaten. "You coward! You coward!" she mutters, but as a conviction rather than as an epithet. She is pathetically helpless now.

"Say — give my dog to little Andy for me, will you?" calls Oswald cheerily as he leaves. The door slams.

Agitatedly, from the dining room, Marthe rushes in, demanding to know what has happened. For a long time she has been listening and has heard Hester and Oswald talk and talk. But she could not make out clearly what it was they were saying.

He's gone, Hester tells her, gone for good. But Marthe will not believe it. It is only a lie Hester is telling to cover her chagrin because Oswald refused her advances. Even with all the accumulated evidence Hester is able to produce, Marthe still insists it cannot be — Oswald will not go! He will not leave her! There is no other girl in France! But, "If he goes, I go!" she screams. "Good or bad, I go with him! Out of your horrible house — forever!"

She rushes out, nearly bowling over the returning Andrew as she does. He is back from his night's trip and full of conversation. It is about Os he wants to talk mostly. Funny thing, how Os should get it into his head that he was not welcome in that house. "Funny kid, Os," he ruminates; "gittin' into scrapes since the day he was born, and skinnin' out of them by the skin of his teeth. But he ain't bad, Hess — touchy, headstrong; gets an idea into his nut — you know I wouldn't have him think we didn't want him here for a thousand dollars."

Pathetically Hester listens to him. Once or twice she tries to speak, as though she had that moment found the courage to confess and was eager to get her worries off her mind. But when Andrew turns to her and looks steadily into her eyes her courage falters. She looks all tired out, Andrew agrees. She certainly needs a rest. He wishes he could take her on some kind of vacation trip — to Niagara Falls, or somewhere. But they're so darned poor —

The thought of money reminds him of the church funds, and the church funds suggest Oswald. Andrew starts toward the secretary. Suddenly he turns to Hester to ask if she has seen Os. And what had she said to him? And how had he taken it?

Hester can put off the dreadful moment no longer. But as she begins to speak she all but swoons. "I guess I'll go up and lie down!" she mutters weakly. And Andrew guesses she better had. "Andrew — oh, Andrew!" she pleads. "Be good to me!" He doesn't understand — but of course he will be good to her. He will even carry her upstairs right now —

A bell that has been tolling in the distance — Hester thought it was for Mrs. Trumble's funeral — suddenly clangs out a more excited warning. It is the fire bell, and engines and crowds of neighbors are rushing past the house.

"Guess I'll go to that fire when I take that money over to the bank," observes Andrew, turning again to the secretary. Now he has the key and is about to open the drawer in which he had placed the funds when a cry at the window stops him. It is one of the neighbors calling to him to come, to come quick!

He is out of the house with a rush. As the front door swings open the noise of the crowd and the puffing of nearby engines drift in. In the confusion there are to be heard bits of broken sentences, such as "Don't get excited, Lane — " "Your brother — " "Fire — "

"Hester, relieved at anything that could stop the immediate discovery of the theft, has let her head drop helplessly on the desk. Suddenly there is an agonized cry from Andrew out in the hall and there is the sound of a door slamming. Presently Marthe enters. Her face is ghastly and gray with horror. She comes slowly as though in a trance. She gets to the front of the sofa and there she suddenly covers her face with her hands as though to shut out some dreadful sight. Her knees give way and she sinks to the sofa with a little cry, a mute figure of utter desolation."

Brokenly, Marthe tries to tell what has happened, "her tearless grief choking her words." All Hester can make out is that someone is dead — and that the fire was in the kindergarten — With a wild cry for her baby she rushes out of the house. At the end of the sofa Marthe lies crumpled, "like a frightened little child." "I'm so afraid! I want my mother!" she mutters, staggering to her feet. "I — want — my mother!" Sobbingly she disappears into the dining room. . . .

Andrew carries little Andy in, Hester following anxiously. He is wrapped in his Uncle Oswald's overcoat, which is burned in spots and streaked with soot. Andrew puts him in his mother's arms.

LITTLE ANDY — I ain't hurted Mummy — not a bit. Uncle Oswal' come and got me. He found me. The fire got everywheres an' then Uncle Oswal' come. Where's Uncle Oswal'?

HESTER — (*turns her eyes dumbly towards her husband. He bursts into a sob*). Tell me.

ANDREW — He's gone.

HESTER — Tell me —

ANDREW — I do' know. The kindergarten. Andy lit a campfire, he says, and it was all afire in no time. Andy was missin' and Oswald run in and got him. An' then he run back again after another little boy, that's what they say — an' the roof fell in on 'em. Oh, God, it's awful! Burned to death! That's his overcoat there on baby! And he's gone! An' I was here — a-talkin' and a-makin' jokes! It's awful!

ANDREW — I can't bear it, Hess! If Os had only parted friends with me — why I wouldn't a hurt him any more'n I would little Andy. He was just a kid to me — Os was. I couldn't help but forgive him for the things he'd do. He thought I didn't want him here! Why I —

HESTER — Don't! You mustn't, Andrew. You mustn't, Andrew! You mustn't feel that way.

ANDREW — Everybody loved Os! Andy, you, Martha, everybody. But me — he thought I was hard on him — he died — thinkin' —

HESTER — (*gently out of her own deep pain*). Andrew — listen, dear. Don't abuse yourself like that. You were good to him. Wonderful — I — I — oh, Andrew — Andrew, if I'd only been — as good as you!

ANDREW — (*wiping his eyes*). Didn't he say — anything — this morning — when he went — about me?

HESTER — (*shaking her head negatively, and then deciding to tell a white lie to make it easier for this poor little man*). He said, "Tell Andy — I'm sorry — about last night. He's a good old scout."

ANDREW — He said—that? Why—that means everything. You don't know what that means to me, Hess. "Good old scout!" That's like him — just like him. Oh, I knew he was all right. Bless him for that.

HESTER — Andrew! — poor Andrew. (*Pause*) Andrew, God'll forgive our mistakes, won't he? (*Andrew places his arm about her and holds her close*) Andrew — there is something else — something —

ANDREW — "Good old scout!" he said. What is it you say, darling?

HESTER — (*with faltering voice*). Andrew, that money — the collection — the money you —

ANDREW — Yes?

HESTER — I gave it — to Oswald — to put it in the bank.

ANDREW — Now? This morning?

HESTER — Just now.

ANDREW — (*scarcely comprehending*). Then it's gone. It's burned. With him.

HESTER — He took it — to put it in the bank. (*Andrew sighs heavily, but he squares himself to meet the blow.*)

HESTER — He took it — to put it in the bank.

ANDREW — (*sighs heavily, but he squares himself to meet the blow*). Then we'll have to make it up. That's all. We'll have to — make it up —

HESTER — Yes. We'll have to pay it — oh, Andy, if you knew —

ANDREW — 'Tain't your fault, Hester. Don't you worry. Natural enough for you to give it to him to put it in the bank for you. Don't fret, honey — 'bout that.

HESTER — Oh, Andy — Andy! Why didn't I understand?

ANDREW — Sh—! It's all right. (*He sighs heavily*) Seems sometimes 's though everything hits you all in a heap. We'll get out of it somehow. I'm so damn sorry for you, Hess. I know you miss all the nice things other girls have —

HESTER — Andrew! Don't!

ANDREW — Well, it's true — an' I don't blame you. Maybe I can borrow a little money somewhere. And there's that money we've been saving for little Andy's education. (*Hester sighs bitterly*) Yes. It's tough, but it's got to be done.

HESTER — I don't mind, Andrew. I'll help you. Oh, Andy — I'm so sorry! Sorry! I'll always love you, Andy.

ANDREW — Why, of course. There doesn't anything matter much, dear, so long as I got you and the boy. Thank God for that! (*Pause, and the two of them are offering a silent prayer of thanks*) Now I must go and find ma. Poor ma! And then — back there to — him —

HESTER — You are a good man, Andrew. Now I know! A good, *good* man.

ANDREW — Me? I'm just old Andy, I am. But Os — Os was a hero.

The curtain falls

"THE DOVER ROAD"

A Comedy in Three Acts

By A. A. Milne

FOLLOWING his previous season's success, "Mr. Pim Passes By," A. A. Milne, the English playwright, was represented on the New York stage this year by three comedies: "The Dover Road," "The Great Broxopp," and "The Truth About Blayds." Of the three, "The Dover Road" was the biggest popular success. "The Truth About Blayds" was not far behind it in public esteem, however, and even "The Great Broxopp," though listed as a quasi-failure, was favorably received by a majority of the reviewers.

"The Dover Road," produced at the Bijou Theatre, December 23, ran the season out. It is a charming light comedy, touched with polite farce in a few of its mildly extravagant situations. The three acts are played in the reception room of a certain Mr. Latimer, an amiable eccentric living a little way off the road to Dover, which is the road eloping couples from London take on their way to Paris or the south of France.

"What Mr. Latimer prefers to call the reception room of his house is really the hall," Mr. Milne explains. "You come straight into it through the heavy oak front door. But this door is so well built, so well protected by a thick purple curtain, and the room is so well warmed by central heating, that none of the usual disadvantages of a hall on a November night attach to it. Just now, of course, all the curtains are drawn, so that the whole of this side of the hall is purple hung. Over the whole room there is something of an Arabian-night-adventure air; Dulac might have had a hand in the designing of it. In the daytime, perhaps, it is an ordinary hall, furnished a trifle freakishly, but in the nighttime one wonders what is going to happen next."

As the play opens Dominic, "tall, stout and grave, the major-domo of the house in a butler's old-fashioned evening dress" comes in. He is there to see that all is in readiness for the ensuing adventure. Shortly he is followed by "the staff," consisting of two footmen and two chambermaids. They, also, are a little freakishly dressed. They stand in line to receive Mr. Dominic's instructions and to make their reports. From them, we learn that the blue room in the east wing and the white room in the west wing are in readiness for expected guests and that "the procedure will be as before."

The bell rings. The heavy curtains are drawn from in front of the big oak door and the door is opened. Following the surprised queries of a young man on the other side, who fears he has mistaken a private residence for a hotel, Leonard and Anne are ushered into the room. Leonard, as Mr. Milne sees him, "is a big, well-made man of thirty-five, dark, with a little black toothbrush mustache." Anne is "young, tall, pretty, cool and self-confident in the ordinary way, but a little upset by the happenings of the night."

Leonard is still mystified and considerably put out. The chauffeur had assured him that this was "an hotel." Evidently it is not. He will call Saunders, the chauffeur, and they will continue their journey. Dominic assures him, however, that it is "a sort of hotel," and that Saunders has gone. It may be only to the garage. If his lordship and her ladyship will come in he will do his best to make them comfortable. Whereupon he shuts and bolts the door and Anne and Leonard find themselves locked in.

Evidently they were expected. But by whom? Apparently they are known — at least Leonard's rank is known. But how? It is quite mystifying. Leonard doesn't like it. Calmly enough Dominic continues his efforts to at least make them feel at home. Supper, he informs them, will be served in five minutes.

Whatever the explanation they decide that probably whoever owns the house will be willing to put them up for the night and in the morning they will continue on to Dover. Their reception is a little strange, but certainly no one could have known that they were coming. If it had not been for the accident that had stopped them they would be well on their way to Calais by this time. However, the only sensible thing to do is to make the best of the situation. That is Leonard's decision. But Anne is worried.

ANNE — I told you from the first that it was runaway or nothing with me; there was going to be no intrigue, no lies and pretences and evasions. And somehow it seems less — less sordid, if we begin our new life together in a new country. (*With a little smile*) Perhaps the French for what we are doing is not quite so crude as the English — yes, I know it's absurd of me, but there it is!

A little blunderingly Leonard tries to calm her fears. He reassures her of his devotion, and though everything does somehow seem to have been arranged for their reception in this strange house, he is as puzzled as she. Certainly he has had nothing to do with it! "Well, somebody did," Anne insists.

At which point Mr. Latimer, preceded by the staff, appears on the scene. "He bows with an air. A middle-aged gentleman, dressed rather fantastically as regards his tie and his dinner jacket and the flower in his buttonhole."

LEONARD — Good evening! Er —

LATIMER — You will forgive me for being announced

in my own house, but I find that it saves a good deal of trouble. If I had just come in and said, "I am Mr. Latimer," then *you* would have had to say "And I am — er So-and-So, and this is — er — " Exactly. I mean we can get on so much better without names. But of course —

LEONARD — You will excuse me, sir, but —

LATIMER — (*going happily on*). But, of course, as you were just going to say, we must call each other *something*. (*Thoughtfully*) I think I shall call you Leonard. There is something about you — forgive the liberty — something Leonardish. (*With a very sweet smile to Anne*) I am sure you agree with me.

ANNE — (*smiling*). I am wondering whether this is really happening, or whether I am dreaming it.

LATIMER — (*his back to Leonard*). And Leonard isn't wondering at all; he is just tapping his forehead with a great deal of expression. (*Leonard, who was doing this, stops with some confusion.*)

LEONARD — (*coldly*). I think we have had enough of this, Mr. Latimer. I was giving you the benefit of the doubt. If you are not mad, then I will ask you for some other explanation of all this nonsense.

LATIMER — (*sniffing at the flower in his buttonhole*). An impetuous character, Leonard. It must be so obvious to everybody else in the room that an explanation will be forthcoming. But why not a friendly explanation following a friendly supper?

ANNE — Are we your guests?

LATIMER — Please.

ANNE — Thank you.

LATIMER — But there is still this question of names. Now we agreed about Leonard —

ANNE — (*looking at Latimer fearlessly*). My name is Anne.

LATIMER — Thank you, Miss Anne.

LEONARD — (*awkwardly*). Er — my wife.

LATIMER — Then I am tempted to leave out the "Miss."

Supper is served elaborately. But neither of the guests has much appetite. Leonard is still so fussed he even hesitates about drinking to Mr. Latimer's toast: "To a happy ending!" He finds Mr. Latimer's evasive replies as to where they are, and to whom they owe the honor of having been expected, extremely irritating. But Anne is enjoying herself, and the dinner as well. She is even a little amused at Leonard's discomfiture.

ANNE — I'm liking my supper.

LATIMER — I am so glad. (*As Anne is helped*) I shot this bird myself. (*He looks at it through his glass*) What is it, Dominic?

DOMINIC — *Poulet en casserole* with mushrooms, sir.

LATIMER — I shot the mushrooms — a large help for his lordship, Dominic. (*To Leonard*) Let me introduce your chicken to you, Leonard. One of the Buff-Orpingtons. I dare say you know the family. His mother was a Wyandotte. He was just about to contract an alliance with one of the Rock girls, the Plymouth Rocks, when the accident happened.

They are alone again now, plates and glasses well filled. Leonard, who has been waiting impatiently for the staff to go, pushes back his chair and gets up.

LEONARD — Now look here, Mr. Latimer, this farce has gone on long enough. I do not propose to sit through a whole meal without some further explanation. Either we have that explanation now, or else — Anne, dear — or else we'll be getting on our way.

LATIMER — (*thoughtfully*). Ah, but which is your way?

LEONARD — Dover. My chauffeur seems to have got

off the track a little, but if you can put us on to the Dover Road —

LATIMER — (*to himself*). The Dover Road! The Dover Road! A dangerous road, my friends. And you're traveling in the dark.

LEONARD — Really, Mr. Latimer, that needn't frighten us.

ANNE — (*putting her hand on his arm*). What do you mean?

LATIMER — A strange road, Anne, for *you*. A new, untraveled road.

LEONARD — Nonsense. She's often been this way before. Haven't you, dear?

ANNE — (*shaking her head*). No—but I'm not frightened, Mr. Latimer.

Supper being over, finally, explanations seem to be in order, with Leonard prowling about uneasily, though he finally settles himself in a huge chair that all but rocks over with him.

LATIMER — Let me help you up, Leonard. You have the wrong chair again. It is difficult to be properly indignant in that one. (*He helps him into a sitting position*) That's better. You were saying —

LEONARD — You mean to tell me that you had the audacity to bribe my chauffeur?

LATIMER — No, no, Leonard. What I mean is that you had the foolhardiness to bribe my friend Saunders to be your chauffeur.

LEONARD — Upon my word —

ANNE — Who is Saunders?

LATIMER — Saunders? He's Joseph's brother. Joseph was the gentleman in orange. I don't know if you noticed him. He helped you to fish.

LEONARD — (*out of the chair at last*). How dare you interfere in my concerns in this way, sir?

ANNE — Before you explain who you are, Mr. Latimer, I should like to know *why* you are so interested in us. Who are you?

LATIMER — No more than Mr. Latimer. It is purely an impersonal interest which I take — and I take it just because you are going the Dover Road, my dear, and it is a dangerous road for a young girl to travel.

ANNE — (*very cool, very proud*). I don't think I asked you to be interested in me, Mr. Latimer.

LATIMER — Nobody does, my dear. But I am very interested in all my fellow-travelers. It is my hobby.

Again Leonard grows rebellious. Particularly when he learns that it is Mr. Latimer's intention to keep them practically prisoners in his house and the garden adjoining for several days. Leonard is almost ready to fight at that suggestion, but Mr. Latimer effectively calms him by summoning Dominic and blandly inquiring of that heavy gentleman how the last young man who started trouble is faring at the hospital. "The young gentleman is getting on nicely," Dominic reports; "he was able to take a little bread and milk this morning."

Leonard grows more passive after that, but not less earnest in his protests. Several times he is bold to insist that such treatment is simply monstrous! To which Mr. Latimer is willing, within limits, to agree. It is interfering of him, damnably interfering. But he happens to know more of their story than they suspect. He knows that they are not married; that they are running away, and he assumes that after Eustasia, Leonard's wife, divorces him, they expect to be married and "live happily ever after." They admit it. Anne is even a little defiant in admitting it. She questions the right of Mr. Latimer, a bachelor, living alone within high walls, to jump to the conclusion that once married two people cannot live happily according to the fairy-book promise.

ANNE — (*raising her eyes to his*). I take the risk, Mr. Latimer.

LATIMER — But a big risk — oh, believe me, I am not so much out of the world as you think. Should I have known all about you, should I have brought you here, if I were? I know the world; I know the risks of marriage. Marriage is an art — well, it's a profession in itself. (*Sharply*) And what are you doing? Marrying a man whose only qualification for the profession is that he has tried it once, and made a damned hash of it.

LEONARD — Well, really sir!

LATIMER — Isn't it true?

LEONARD — Well — er — I admit my marriage has not been a happy one, but I venture to say — well, I don't wish to say anything against Eustasia —

LATIMER — Go on. Life is too short for us to be gentlemen all the time.

LEONARD — (*explosively*). Well, then, I say that not even St. Michael and all his angels could have made a success of it. I mean, not even St. Michael.

LATIMER — Yet you chose her.

LEONARD — Er — we — (*He is silent.*)

LATIMER — (*after a pause*). Miss Anne, I am not being moral. You see, I am a very rich man, and we know on good authority that it is difficult for a very rich man to be a very good man. But being a very rich man, I try to spend my money so that it makes somebody else happy besides myself. It's the only happy way of spending money, isn't it? And it's my hobby to prevent people — to try if I can prevent people — making unhappy marriages — it's wonderful what power money gives you. Nobody realizes it, because nobody ever spends it save in the obvious ways. You may say that I should have prevented Leonard from marrying Eustasia in the first place. I have done that sometimes. I have asked two young people here — oh, properly chaperoned — and guests, not prisoners as you are — two young people who thought that they were in love, and I have tried to show each to the other in the most unromantic light. I have let the girl see her lover when he was angry, when he was sulky, when he had lost his sense of humor. I have shown the girl to the man when she had forgotten her dignity, when she was greedy, ill-tempered. Sometimes the engagement has been broken off. Sometimes they have married and — lived happily ever after — or, from the letters I get, seem to be in the way of it. But mostly it is my hobby to concentrate on those second marriages into which people plunge — with no parents now to restrain them — so much more hastily even than they plunge into their first adventure. Yet how much more carefully they should be considered, seeing that one at least of the parties has already proved his utter ignorance of the art of marriage? . . . And so, my dear friends, when I hear — and a rich man has many means of hearing — when I hear that two people are taking the Dover Road, as you were taking it tonight, I venture to stop them, and say — in the words of the fairy-book, "Are you *sure* you are going to live happy ever afterwards?"

LEONARD — (*after a pause*). Your intentions may be good, but I can only repeat that your interference is utterly unwarranted. And you are entirely mistaken as to the power and authority which your money gives you.

LATIMER—Authority, none. But power? (*He laughs*) Why, my dear Leonard, if I offered you a hundred thousand pounds to go back to your wife to-night, this lady would never see you again.

LEONARD — Well, of all the damnable things to say —

LATIMER — How damnable the truth is! Think it over tonight, Leonard. You are a poor man for your position — think of all the things you could do with a hundred thousand pounds. Turn it over in your mind

—and then over and over again. A hundred thousand pounds! (*For a moment it almost seems as if Leonard is beginning to turn it, but Anne interrupts.*)

ANNE — (*scornfully*). Is this part of the treatment? Am I being shown my lover when he is mercenary?

LATIMER — (*with a laugh*). Oh, no! If that were part of my treatment, there would be no marriages at all. Oh, no, it isn't a genuine offer. (*To Leonard*) It's off, Leonard. You needn't think it out any more. (*Leonard wakes up suddenly, a poor man*) Besides, you misunderstand me. I don't want to separate you by force — I have no right to.

ANNE — But how modest suddenly!

LATIMER — (*with a bow and smile*). Madame, I admire your spirit.

ANNE — Leonard, I am receiving the attention of another man. Beware of jealousy. All part of the treatment, Mr. Latimer?

LATIMER — You're splendid. (*Seriously*) But I meant what I said just now. I am not preventing you from going the Dover Road, I am only asking you to wait a few days and see how you get on. It may be that you two are the perfect soul-mates; that your union has already been decreed in heaven and will be watched over by the angels. If so, nobody will rejoice in your happiness more than I. I shall not say, "You have no right to be happy together. Leonard must remain with his lawfully-wedded Eustasia." Believe me, I do not waste my money, my time, my breath in upholding the sanctity of an unhappy marriage. I was brought up in the sanctity of an unhappy marriage; even as a child I knew all about it. (*Less seriously*) But, oh, my dear Anne, let us have a little common sense before we adventure marriage with a man who is always making a mess of it. We know what Leonard is — how perfectly hopeless as a huband.

ANNE — I don't think it is quite fair.

LATIMER — Well, as far as we can tell. You've never made a happy marriage yet, have you, Leonard?

LEONARD — (*sulkily*). I don't want to say anything against Eustasia —

LATIMER — Good God, man, aren't you shouting it all the time? Why else are you here? But don't try to pretend that it's all Eustasia's fault.

LEONARD — (*doubtfully*). Well —

LATIMER — Or that it will be all Anne's fault *next* year.

LEONARD — What do you mean, next year?

LATIMER — I beg your pardon. I should have said the year after next. (*There is a little silence.*)

ANNE — (*getting up*). I think I will go to bed. How long do you want us to wait, Mr. Latimer?

LATIMER — Can you spare a week? You, with so many years in front of you.

ANNE — I have a father. I left him a note to say what I was doing. We don't see much of each other, but I thought it polite. Does that interfere with your plans at all?

LATIMER — (*smiling*). Not at all. There was a little mistake about the delivery of that note. Your father is under the impression that you are staying with friends — in Kent. A great power — money.

ANNE — I congratulate you on the perfection of your methods. Good-night, Mr. Latimer.

She takes his hand, "without prejudice," she assures him, and retires to the east wing accompanied by the maid. Resigned to the situation, though he still insists it is outrageous, Leonard is induced to take a drink and a cigar — and soon he is on his way — to the west wing, accompanied by two footmen.

Mr. Latimer is smiling over a magazine article as the curtain falls.

ACT II

The scene is the same. Time, next morning. "Eustasia, Leonard's wife," reports Mr. Milne, "who should be sitting patiently at home wondering when he will return, is having breakfast with a long-legged, attractive young man called Nicholas. She is what people who talk like that call a nice little thing; near enough to thirty to wish it were twenty. At present she is making a good deal of a fuss over this dear boy, Nicholas. Breakfast is practically over. Nicholas, in fact, is wiping his mouth."

Eustasia is sure Nicholas has not eaten enough breakfast. He could eat more if he only would. But if he won't, "then he shall sit in a more comfy chair while he smokes his nasty, horrid pipe, which he loves so much better than his Eustasia." Of course, Nicholas protests that he doesn't love his pipe more than he does his Eustasia, and kisses Eustasia dutifully upon the cheek to prove it. Nicholas may be a little bored with his Eustasia, but he is at gallant pains to conceal that fact from her. He has found the probationary week they have spent with Mr. Latimer a bit trying, but he is much too much of a gentleman to confess it. Oh, much too much.

NICHOLAS — Er — Eustasia.

EUSTASIA — Yes, darling.

NICHOLAS — We've been here a week.

EUSTASIA — Yes, darling. A wonderful, wonderful week. And now today we leave this dear house where we have been so happy together, and go out into the world together —

NICHOLAS — (*who has not been listening to her*). A week. Except for the first day, we have had all our meals alone together.

EUSTASIA — (*sentimentally*). Alone, Nicholas.

NICHOLAS — Four meals a day. That's twenty-four meals.

EUSTASIA — Twenty-four!

NICHOLAS — And at every one of those meals you have asked me at least four times to have something more; when I had already said that I didn't want anything more; or, in other words, you have forced me to say "No, thank you, Eustasia," ninety-six times when there was absolutely no need for it.

EUSTASIA — (*hurt*). Nicholas!

NICHOLAS — (*inexorably*). We are both young. I am twenty-six, you are —

EUSTASIA — (*quickly*). Twenty-five.

NICHOLAS — (*looking at her quickly, and then away again*). You are twenty-five. If all goes well we may look to have fifty years more together. Say, two thousand five hundred weeks. Multiply that by a hundred and we see that in the course of our joint lives, you will, at the present rate, force me to say, "No, thank you, Eustasia," two hundred and fifty thousand times more than is necessary. (*He relights his pipe.*)

EUSTASIA — (*pathetically*). Nicholas! (*She applies her handkerchief.*)

NICHOLAS — I wondered if we couldn't come to some arrangement about it, that's all.

Which convinces Eustasia that Nicholas is cruel, and it takes considerable tactful lovemaking to assure her that he has no intention of being so. Of course, Eustasia admits, she loves Nicholas. That is why she is so eager to see that he is well fed and well taken care of. She had perfectly adored taking care of him when he had that horrid cold the first day they were there, after they had lost their luggage and everything. Leonard was never ill.

Nicholas doesn't care for the reference to Leonard. He had much rather not think of Eustasia's husband. He had taken her away from Leonard, and here they were. And they would go on. No matter what happened they would go on. By the time Mr. Latimer happens in suddenly Eustasia has been finally comforted and is almost herself again. They exchange cheerful good-mornings.

LATIMER — So you are leaving me this morning and going on your way?

NICHOLAS — (*without enthusiasm*). Yes.

EUSTASIA — But we shall never forget this week, dear Mr. Latimer.

LATIMER — You have forgiven me for asking you to wait a little so as to make sure?

EUSTASIA — Oh, but you were so right! I was just saying so to Nicholas. Wasn't I, Nicholas?

NICHOLAS — Yes. About a minute ago. About two minutes ago.

LATIMER — And so now you are sure of yourselves?

EUSTASIA — Oh, so sure, so very sure. Aren't we, Nicholas?

NICHOLAS — Absolutely sure.

LATIMER — That's right. (*Looking at his watch*) Well, I don't want to hurry you, but if you have any little things to do, the car will be here in half an hour, and —

EUSTASIA — Half an hour? Oh, I must fly. (*She begins.*)

NICHOLAS — (*not moving*). Yes, we must fly.

LATIMER — (*going to the door with Eustasia*). By the way, you will be interested to hear that I had two other visitors last night.

EUSTASIA — (*stopping excitedly*). Mr. Latimer! You don't mean another — couple?

LATIMER — Yes, another romantic couple.

EUSTASIA — Oh, if I could but see them before we go! Just for a moment! Just to reconcile them to this week of probation! To tell them what a wonderful week it can be!

LATIMER — (*very gravely*). You shall. I promise you that you shall.

Eustasia and Nicholas are off to pack for their journey when Dominic comes to make his morning report. His lordship, (meaning Leonard) is a little depressed, according to Dominic. There had been some misunderstanding about the luggage and Leonard had no fresh linen, nor any shaving kit. It really was quite sad. Of course Dominic had offered to furnish what he could and Joseph had even offered to lend his lordship a comb, which was very good of Joseph, seeing the comb was a birthday gift. But his lordship had reluctantly decided not to avail himself of the offer.

Anne is quite cheerful when she comes down to breakfast. She has slept well and is refreshed.

LATIMER — You are ready for breakfast?

ANNE — Quite ready, Mr. Latimer. But what about Leonard?

LATIMER — Leonard?

ANNE — I made sure that I was to have a practice breakfast with Leonard this morning. I have been thinking of a few things to say up in my room.

LATIMER — (*smiling*). Say them to me instead.

ANNE — They are very wifely. (*She sits down.*)

LATIMER — But think what good practice.

ANNE — (*smiling*). Very well. (*At the cups*) Tea or coffee, darling?

LATIMER — Oh, no, that will never do. You know by now that *I* always have coffee — half milk and three lumps of sugar.

ANNE — Of course. How silly of me! (*She pours out the coffee.*)

LATIMER — (*taking the covers off the dishes*). Omelette — fish — kidney and bacon?

ANNE — Now *you're* forgetting.

LATIMER — (*putting back the covers*). No, I'm remembering. Toast and marmalade — isn't that right?

ANNE — Quite right, dear.

LATIMER — (*to himself*). I knew she would like marmalade. No wonder that Leonard ran away with her. (*He puts the toast and marmalade close to her.*)

ANNE — Your coffee, darling.

LATIMER — Thank you, my love. "My love" is very connubial, I think.

ANNE — Delightfully so. Do go on.

LATIMER — Er — I am sorry to see in the paper this morning — which I glanced at, my precious, before you came down — How do you like "my precious"?

ANNE — Wonderfully life-like. Are you sure you haven't been married before?

LATIMER — Only once. Eustasia. You had not forgotten Eustasia?

ANNE — I am afraid I had. In fact, I had forgotten for the moment that you were being Leonard.

LATIMER — (*bowing*). Thank you. I could wish no better compliment.

ANNE — (*laughing, in spite of herself*). Oh, you're too absurd!

LATIMER — (*in Leonard's manner*). Of course, I don't wish to say anything against Eustasia —

ANNE — My dear Leonard, I — I really think we might leave your first wife out of it.

LATIMER — Yes, you want to get that off pat. You'll have to say that a good deal, I expect. Well, to resume. I am sorry to see in the paper this morning that Beelzebub, upon whom I laid my shirt for the two-thirty race at Newmarket yesterday — and incidentally your shirt, too, darling — came in last, some five minutes after the others had finished the course. Tut, tut, how annoying!

ANNE — Oh, my poor darling!

LATIMER — The word "poor" is well chosen. We are ruined.

ANNE — At least, let me share your ruin with you.

LATIMER — No, we are not ruined. Pass the toast. I can always refuse to pay my gambling debts.

ANNE — Oh, my love, I thought you were a man of honor!

LATIMER — So I am. Then I shall write my autobiography instead.

ANNE — You know what I *want* you to do, Leonard?

LATIMER — No. I have forgotten.

ANNE — (*seriously*). I should like to see you in the House of Lords, taking your rightful place as a leader of men, making great speeches.

LATIMER — My dear Anne, I may be a peer, but I am not a dashed politician.

ANNE — (*wistfully*). I wish you were, Leonard.

LATIMER — (*himself*). I will be anything you like, Anne. (*Latimer leans towards her, half-serious, half-mocking.*)

ANNE — (*with a little laugh*). How absurd you are! Some more coffee?

LATIMER — (*passing his cup*). To which I answer "A little more milk." Do you realize that this goes on for fifty years?

ANNE — Well, and why not?

LATIMER — Fifty years, a solemn thought. But do not let it mar our pleasure in the meal that we are having together now. Let us continue to talk gaily together.

And they do. They tell each other of the dreams each is supposed to have had. Anne's dream was of her experiences in running away with Leonard and of their being stopped by a strange man living in a mysterious house. It was only a dream, she is sure of that, and now that she is awake, she and Leonard will be allowed to go on as they planned.

LATIMER — There's no accounting for dreams. I had an absurd one, too, last night.

ANNE — What was it?

LATIMER — A lonely house. Father and daughter living together. Father, old, selfish, absorbed in his work. Daughter, left to herself; her only companions, books; knowing nothing of the world. A man comes into her life; the first. He makes much of her. It is a new experience for the daughter. She is grateful to him, so grateful; so very proud that she means anything to him. He tells her when it is too late that he is married; talks of an impossible wife; tells her that she is his real mate. Let her come with him and see something of the world which she has never known. She comes — dear me, what silly things one dreams!

ANNE — Absurd things. When can we have the car?

LATIMER — The car?

ANNE — Leonard's car.

LATIMER — You wish to continue the adventure?

ANNE — Why not?

LATIMER — Dear, dear! What a pity! (*Looking at his watch*) In twenty-five minutes?

ANNE — That will do nicely, thank you.

LATIMER — We must let Leonard have a little breakfast first, if he is to cross the channel today. (*He gets up*) In twenty-five minutes, then.

ANNE — (*half holding out her hand*). I shall see you again?

LATIMER — (*bending and kissing it*). If only to wish you God-speed.

Anne is in the garden when Leonard comes down. "He is in a dirty, rather disreputable, once white, bath-gown. His hair is unbrushed, his cheeks, the cheeks of a dark man — unshaved and blue. He has a horrible pair of bedroom slippers on his feet, above which not only his socks, but almost a hint of pantaloons may be seen on the way to the dressing gown."

Leonard is quite miserable. He has caught a terrible

cold in the damnedest, draughtiest room he ever had tried to sleep in, and to top everything else, the loss of the luggage and all, Joseph had accidentally dropped his only available suit of clothes in the bathtub. It is Leonard's private opinion that Joseph ought to be shot. Mr. Latimer is quite distressed at the news, or says he is. Of course he will do everything he can, but —

Anne has finished her walk in the garden. She is a little startled at Leonard's appearance, and plainly worried about his cold — it is the first cold Leonard has ever had and he makes rather a show of trying to sneeze naturally. He manages, however, to eat a very good breakfast — a disgustingly hearty breakfast, it seems to Anne, who never takes more than toast and marmalade. But finally he appears to have finished and has extracted from his mouth the last of the fishbones that have been worrying him.

Then Anne, with studied patience, seeks to turn his mind back to their present problem. The car will be there, she tells him, in a quarter of an hour and he has, she judges, quite a lot to do if he is to be ready for it.

LEONARD — B-but I can't possibly go like this.

ANNE — No, that's what I say.

LEONARD — I mean I haven't got any luggage for one thing — and with a cold like this, I'm not at all sure —

ANNE — You've lost your luggage?

LEONARD — Apparently it was left behind by —

ANNE — (*with anger*). You let yourself be tricked and humiliated by this Mr. Latimer, you let *me* be humiliated, and then when I say that whatever happens I *won't* be humiliated, you — you lose your luggage!

LEONARD — *I* didn't lose it. It just happens to *be* lost.

ANNE — And you catch a cold!

LEONARD — *I* didn't catch it. It caught *me*.

ANNE — The — the humiliation of it! And what do you propose to do now?

LEONARD — As soon as my luggage turns up and I am well enough to travel —

ANNE — Meanwhile, you accept this man's hospitality —

LEONARD — Under protest. (*Helping himself from the dish*) I shall keep a careful account of everything that we have here —

ANNE — Well, that's your third kidney; you'd better make a note of it.

LEONARD — (*with dignity*). As it happens, I was helping myself to a little more bacon — as I say, I shall keep a careful account, and send him a check for our board and lodging as soon as we have left his roof.

ANNE — Oh! — I had some coffee and one slice of toast and a little marmalade, about a spoonful. And a cup of tea and two thin slices of bread and butter upstairs. Oh, and I've had two baths. They're extra, aren't they? A hot one last night and a cold one this morning. I think that's all, except supper last night, and you wouldn't let me finish that, so I expect there'll be a reduction. You want a notebook with one of those little pencils in it.

LEONARD — (*reproachfully*). I say, Anne, look here —

ANNE — Do go on with your breakfast.

LEONARD — You're being awfully unfair. How can we possibly go now? Why, I haven't even got a pair of trousers to put on.

ANNE — You're not going to say you've lost those, too!

LEONARD—(*sulkily*). It's not my fault. That fellow — whatsisname —

ANNE — (*wonderingly*). What made you even think that you could take anybody to the south of France? Without any practice at all? If you had been taking an aunt to Hammersmith — well, you might have lost a bus or two — and your hat might have blown off — and you would probably have found yourself at Hampstead the first two or three times — and your aunt would have stood up the whole way — but still, you might have got there eventually. I mean, it would be worth trying — if your aunt was very anxious to get to Hammersmith. But the south of France! My dear Leonard! It's so audacious of you!

Now Mr. Latimer arrives with his own shaving things for Leonard to use. Mr. Latimer thinks it would probably be better for Leonard to shave in the reception room — there are plenty of mirrors about — rather than risk standing in another draught in his sleeping room. Leonard doesn't think much of the idea, but perhaps it would be safer. And, they leave him to complete his toilet. He is hard at it when Eustasia's Nicholas appears.

Nicholas is sympathetic, but Leonard is irritable and they do not get along very well together until they discover that they have much in common. They are fellow sufferers in this conspirator's house.

NICHOLAS — You haven't tumbled to it, yet?

LEONARD — (*not understanding*). Tumbled to what?

NICHOLAS — The fact that a week ago there were reasons why it was necessary for *me* to shave in the hall.

LEONARD — You! — you don't mean —

NICHOLAS — Yes, I do.

LEONARD — You lost your luggage?

NICHOLAS — Yes.

LEONARD — You woke up with a cold?

NICHOLAS — Yes — horrid, sneezing when you're all covered with soap.

LEONARD — (*excitedly*). I say, that fellow — whatsisname — didn't drop your clothes in the bath?

NICHOLAS—Oh, rather—damned smart chap, Latimer!

LEONARD — Damned scoundrel!

NICHOLAS — Oh, no. He's quite right. One learns a lot down here.

LEONARD — I shall leave this house at once — as soon as I have shaved.

NICHOLAS — You still want to? (*Leonard looks at him in surprise*) Oh, well, you haven't been here long enough, I suppose.

LEONARD — What do you mean? Don't *you* want to any more?

NICHOLAS — Latimer's quite right, you know. One learns a lot down here.

LEONARD — (*shaving*). What about the lady?

NICHOLAS — That's the devil of it.

LEONARD — My dear fellow, as a man of honor, you're bound to go on.

NICHOLAS — As a man of honor, ought I even to have started?

LEONARD — (*in the midst of lathering himself a second time*). Curious creatures, women.

NICHOLAS — Amazing.

LEONARD — It's a life's work in itself trying to understand 'em. And then you're no further.

NICHOLAS — A week told *me* all I wanted to know.

LEONARD — They're so unexpected.

NICHOLAS — So unreasonable.

LEONARD — What was it the poet said about them?

NICHOLAS — What didn't he say?

LEONARD — No. *You* know the one I mean. How does it begin? — "O woman, in our hours of ease — "

NICHOLAS — " Uncertain, coy and hard to please."

LEONARD — That's it. Well, I grant you *that* —

NICHOLAS — Grant it me! I should think you do! They *throw* it at you with both hands.

LEONARD — But in the next two lines he misses the point altogether. When — what is it? " When pain and anguish wring the brow — "

NICHOLAS — (*with feeling*). " A ministering angel, thou."

LEONARD — Yes, and it's a lie. It's simply a lie.

NICHOLAS — My dear fellow, it's the truest thing anybody ever said. Only — only one gets too much of it.

LEONARD — True? Nonsense.

NICHOLAS — Evidently you don't know anything about women.

LEONARD — (*indignantly*). *I?* — not know anything about women?

NICHOLAS — Well, you said yourself just now that you didn't.

LEONARD — I never said — what I said —

NICHOLAS — If you did not know anything about 'em you'd know that there's nothing they like more than doing the ministering angel business.

LEONARD — Ministering angel?

NICHOLAS—"Won't you have a little more of this, and won't you have a little more of that, and how is the poor cold today, and — "

LEONARD — You really think that women talk like that?

NICHOLAS — How else do you think they talk?

LEONARD — My dear fellow! Why, I mean, just take my own case as an example. Here am I, with a very nasty cold, the first I've ever had in my life. I sit down to a bit of breakfast — not wanting it particularly, but feeling that, for the sake of my health, I ought to try and eat something. And what happens.

LATIMER — (*entering unobserved and trying to guess the answer*). You eat too much.

LEONARD — (*turning around angrily*). Ah, so it's you! You have come just in time, Mr. Latimer. I propose to leave your house at once.

LATIMER — (*surprised*). Not like that? Not with a little bit of soap just behind the ear? (*Leonard hastily wipes it*) The other ear. (*Leonard wipes that one*) That's right.

LEONARD — At once, sir.

NICHOLAS — You'd better come with us. We're just going.

LEONARD — Thank you.

LATIMER — Four of you. A nice little party.

LEONARD — (*as Anne enters*). Anne, my dear, we are leaving the house at once. Are you ready?

ANNE — (*looking from one to the other in surprise*). But I've just taken my hat off. Besides, you can't go like that? (*Leonard hastily wipes his ear again.*)

LATIMER — No, no. She means the costume this time.

LEONARD—Mr. Latimer, I insist on having my clothes restored to me.

LATIMER — Wet or dry, you shall have them.

ANNE—But—

EUSTASIA — (*from outside*). Nich—o—las!

NICHOLAS — (*gloomily*). Hello!

EUSTASIA — Where — are — you?

NICHOLAS — Here!

EUSTASIA — (*entering*). Are you ready, darling? (*She stops on seeing them all and looks from one to the other. She sees her husband*) *Leonard!*

NICHOLAS — (*understanding*). Leonard!

LEONARD — Eustasia!

ANNE — Eustasia!

"They stare at each other open-mouthed — all but Mr. Latimer. His eyes on the ceiling, whistling a little tune to himself, Mr. Latimer walks — almost, you might say, dances — up and down, up and down behind them. 'I did this!' he is saying to himself, 'I did it!'"

ACT III

"We are just where we were," explains the author, "except that Mr. Latimer has stopped his dance and is regarding his visitors benevolently. Their mouths are now closed, but they have not said anything yet."

Anne is the first to recover her wits. Someone, she thinks, might at least introduce her to Leonard's wife. Goodness knows Leonard will never think of it.

So Mr. Latimer gracefully accepts the assignment and the introductions are formally made and formally acknowledged — all except Leonard's introduction to Nicholas. It is Nicholas' opinion that he and Leonard have met; that, in fact, they are already quite old friends.

LEONARD — I repudiate the friendship. We met — under false pretenses. I — I — well, upon my word, I don't know *what* to say.

NICHOLAS — Then don't say it, old boy. Here we all are, and we've got to make the best of it.

LEONARD — I — I — a — tish — oo!

EUSTASIA — (*alarmed*). Leonard, you have a cold?

NICHOLAS — A very nasty cold.

ANNE — (*coldly*). It will be better when he has finished his breakfast.

LEONARD — (*hurt*). I *have* finished my breakfast. A long time ago.

ANNE — I beg your pardon. (*She indicates the towel around his neck*) I misunderstood.

LEONARD — (*pulling it away*). I've been shaving.

EUSTASIA — But, Leonard, dear, I don't understand. I've never known you ill before.

LEONARD — I never have been ill before. But I am ill now. Very ill. And nobody minds. Nobody minds at all. This fellow Latimer invaygles me here —

LATIMER — Inveegles.

LEONARD — I shall pronounce it how I like. It is quite time I asserted myself. I have been too patient. You invaygle me here and purposely give me a cold. You (*Pointing accusingly to Anne*) are entirely unmoved by my sufferings, instead of which you make fun of the very simple breakfast which I had forced myself to eat. You (*To Nicholas*) run away with my wife, at a time when I am ill and unable to protect her, and you (*To Eustasia*) — well, all I can say is that you surprise me, Eustasia, you surprise me. I didn't think you had it in you.

LATIMER — A masterly summing up of the case. Well, I hope you're all ashamed of yourselves.

EUSTASIA — But, Leonard, how rash of you to *think* of running away with a cold like this. (*She goes up and comforts him*) You must take care of yourself — Eustasia will take care of you, and get you well. Poor boy! He had a nasty, nasty cold, and nobody looked after him. Mr. Latimer, I shall want some mustard, and hot water and eucalyptus —

LEONARD — (*to Anne*). There you are! As soon as somebody who really understands illness comes on the scene, you see what happens. Mustard, eucalyptus — she has it all at her fingers' ends.

DOMINIC — (*entering*). Yes, sir?

LATIMER — A small mustard and water for his lordship.

EUSTASIA — It's to put his feet in, not to drink.

LATIMER — A large mustard and water.

Eustasia soon has Leonard nice and comfy, and Leonard revels in the attentions that once were such a bore to him. Anne and Mr. Latimer look on amusedly, Nicholas sympathetically. Leonard resents both attitudes, but there isn't much he can do about either.

With Leonard safely put away from the draughts back of a screen, and Anne gone to her room to pack, Nicholas steals a chance to consult Mr. Latimer personally, as it were. Wouldn't it be better for him (Nicholas) as a man of honor, to — er — withdraw? Nicholas inquires. Of course, he is just as devoted to Eustasia as ever, but, under the circumstances, and in view of the still existing devotion between Eustasia and Leonard — wouldn't it be better if he quietly disappeared?

Before Mr. Latimer can answer Anne reappears. She had gone to pack and intended leaving at once — but, there is a reason why she has now decided to remain, if Mr. Latimer doesn't mind. Mind? Mr. Latimer is quite delighted.

So Anne is drawn in to give her advice to Nicholas and she promptly decides against his going. He must not go, in fact. She, Anne, wants him to stay, which so pleases Nicholas that he decides straightway to stay. In fact, when Mr. Latimer finally collects them into a sort of family conference they all decide to stay, for the present, at least. Eustasia feels she must stay to look after Leonard. Anne must stay — well, because of something that is not yet quite clear. Nicholas must stay because Anne has asked him to so pointedly, and Leonard — well, at the moment Dominic and the staff are advancing with an assortment of mustard baths, plasters, eucalyptus, etc. which promise to keep Leonard busy for some days. On this scene of accepted circumstances the curtain is lowered to indicate a passage of time.

Three days later Anne calls Nicholas into the garden, and Nicholas responds with alacrity. They have been rather pleasant, these last three days. If Anne hasn't actually flirted with Nicholas, she at least has been very nice to him, and his heart has been deeply affected, if not actually touched. Now it transpires that there was, as you might say, reason in Anne's seeming madness. She must borrow one pound two and sixpence to pay her way home! And there is no one to whom she feels that she can appeal except Nicholas. He is such a kind, understanding, brotherly sort.

ANNE — (*ashamed*). You see, I — I only have three and fourpence ha'penny. And it costs one pound five and tenpence to get home. (*Indignantly*) Oh, it's a shame the way men always pay for us, and then when we really want money we haven't got any. But I will pay you back on Sunday. I have some money at home; I meant to have brought it.

NICHOLAS — But — but why do you suddenly —

ANNE — Suddenly? I've been wanting it ever since that first morning. I went upstairs to get my hat, meaning to walk straight out of the house — and then I looked in my purse and found — (*Pathetically*) three and fourpence ha'penny. What was I to do?

NICHOLAS—Anyone would have lent you anything.

ANNE — (*coldly*). Leonard, for instance?

NICHOLAS — (*thoughtfully*). Well — no — no. You couldn't very well have touched Leonard. But Latimer—

ANNE — (*scornfully*). Mr. Latimer! The man who had brought us here, locked us up here, and started playing Providence to us — I was to go on my knees to *him* and say "Please, dear Mr. Latimer, would you lend me one pound two and sixpence, so that I may run away from your horrid house." Really!

NICHOLAS — Well, you seem to have been pretty friendly with him these three days.

ANNE — Naturally I am polite to a man when I am staying in his house. That's a different thing.

NICHOLAS — As a matter-of-fact, Latimer has been jolly decent. Anyway, he has saved us both from making silly asses of ourselves.

ANNE — (*scornfully*). And you think I am grateful to him for that? Doesn't any man understand *any* woman?

NICHOLAS — (*annoyed*). Are you suggesting that I don't understand women?

ANNE — I'm suggesting that you should lend me one pound two shillings and sixpence.

NICHOLAS — (*sulkily, feeling in his pockets*). Of course, if you're in such a confounded hurry to get away from here — do you mind all silver?

ANNE — Not at all.

So the loan is effected, though with a further show of reluctance on Nicholas' part. It is disappointing to find the lady you thought was falling in love with you was only paving the way for a loan! However, that's that, and Nicholas is a pretty fair sport.

Now we have Leonard and Eustasia. Leonard is quite fit again, but Eustasia is not taking any chances. His temperature is up again today and he must be careful. She thinks, perhaps, after he is nice and comfy again she will sit and talk with him, quietly. Or read to him? Which would Leonard prefer? Leonard isn't quite sure, but he believes he would prefer the reading. So Eustasia gets her book and proceeds " in her reading-aloud voice " with a chapter on " the sandy deserts of Arabia and Africa."

" It's very nicely written," Eustasia agrees, after reading for several minutes (*She is obliged to stop occasionally to be sure that Leonard is still awake*), "but I don't think it is very exciting. I don't think Mr. Latimer has a very good taste in books. I asked him to recommend me something really interesting to read aloud, and he said the two most interesting books he knew were Carlyle's *French Revolution* and — and (*Looking at cover*) Gibbon's *Roman Empire!* Fancy! There are four volumes of it and six hundred pages in a volume. We're at page nineteen now."

Nicholas interrupts them. He is still inclined to be patronizingly sympathetic. It was Carlyle that Eustasia read to him. And he found it topping. Leonard should try that — when he has finished Gibbon's. . . .

Now Eustasia has gone to dress and Nicholas and Leonard are alone.

NICHOLAS — (*after a pause*). Curious creatures, women.

LEONARD — Amazing.

NICHOLAS — They're so unexpected.

LEONARD — So unreasonable.

NICHOLAS — Yes —

LEONARD — (*suddenly*). I *hate* England at this time of year.

NICHOLAS — So do I.

LEONARD — Do you go south as a rule?

NICHOLAS — As a rule.

LEONARD — Monte?

NICHOLAS — Sometimes. I half thought of Nice this year.

LEONARD — Not bad. I think I prefer Cannes myself.

NICHOLAS — There's not much in it.

LEONARD — No — (*After a pause*) Between ourselves, you know — quite between ourselves — I'm about fed up with women.

NICHOLAS — Absolutely.

LEONARD — You are, too?

NICHOLAS — Rather, I should think so.

LEONARD — They're so dashed unreasonable.

NICHOLAS — So unexpected.

LEONARD — (*suddenly*). Had you booked your rooms?

NICHOLAS — At Nice? Yes.

LEONARD — So had I.

NICHOLAS — At Cannes?

LEONARD — Yes — I say, what about it?

NICHOLAS — Do you mean — (*He waves a hand at the door.*)

LEONARD — Yes.

NICHOLAS — Evaporating?

LEONARD — Yes. Quite quietly, you know.

NICHOLAS — Without ostentation?

LEONARD — That's it.

NICHOLAS — It's rather a scheme. And then we shouldn't waste the rooms. At least, only one set of them. I'll tell you what. I'll toss you whether we go to Nice or Cannes.

LEONARD — Right. (*He takes out a coin and tosses.*)

NICHOLAS — Tails —

LEONARD — (*uncovering the coin*). Heads! Do you mind coming to Cannes?

NICHOLAS — Just as soon, really. When shall we go? Tomorrow?

LEONARD — Mightn't get a chance tomorrow. Why not tonight? It seems a pity to waste the opportunity.

NICHLAS — You mean while Eustasia's dressing?

LEONARD — Yes. Sleep the night at Dover and cross tomorrow morning.

Nicholas doubts that they can bring it off. Eustasia is bound to be after them like a bird. She's not one to be put off when she has got somebody ill to look after.

So they call Mr. Latimer in as a sort of advisory counsel. He agrees that their plan is a good one, but — Suddenly Mr. Latimer has an inspiration. It might be arranged if they could find someone else who would agree to be ill and thus keep Eustasia occupied! Perhaps Dominic would help them out! But Dominic politely declines. He even refuses to be bribed. So there is nothing else to do — Mr. Latimer must sacrifice himself. He is somewhat influenced in this decision by the thought that if Eustasia goes Anne will go, too, and he doesn't want Anne to go. So he agrees to have something — a sprained ankle, perhaps. He might try something stomachic, as Dominic suggests, but that would interfere more or less seriously with his customary habits at meal time. So he compromises on neuralgia, and is stretched his full length on the couch, moaning audibly when — Anne enters. He had expected Eustasia.

Anna has her hat on and carries her bag. She is at the door before she hears Mr. Latimer's signals of distress. Then she comes promptly back to investigate. She is quite distressed, naturally. She knows something about neuralgia, too. Her father had suffered at times, and she had often helped him by rubbing his head. Perhaps —

Mr. Latimer is sure that is the very treatment necessary. So Anne takes off her gloves and gently passes the tips of her fingers over Mr. Latimer's forehead. He finds the treatment most efficacious.

LATIMER — Why do you wear a hat on your chin? (*She laughs*) Why do you wear a hat, Anne?

ANNE — I was going away.

LATIMER — Without saying good-bye?

ANNE — (*ashamed*). I — I think so.

LATIMER — Everybody is going away.

ANNE — Who?

LATIMER—Nicholas—and Leonard.

ANNE — Nicholas? Oh! And I owe him one pound two and sixpence (*She has drawn her hands away in her surprise.*)

LATIMER — (*groaning*). Ough!

ANNE — What is it?

LATIMER — (*touching his forehead*). A sudden twinge. (*She goes on with the treatment*) Ah! How different!

ANNE — Can you give me his address? I must send him the money.

LATIMER — Why is Nicholas going away?

ANNE — I don't know. (*With a little smile*) Unless because he thought he was falling in love with me.

LATIMER — I expect he was.

ANNE — In three days?

LATIMER — It can be done in three hours, Anne.

They are silent for a moment, and then a slight stirring back of them causes Anne to turn halfway round. It is Leonard and Nicholas quietly creeping out the front door.

ANNE — What was it? Was it —

LATIMER — An episode in your life. Over, buried, forgotten —

ANNE — (*softly*). Thank you. (*Suddenly with emotion*) Oh, I do thank you!

LATIMER — I have forgotten what you are thanking me for.

DOMINIC — (*comes in, and stops suddenly on seeing them*). Oh, I beg your pardon, sir. (*Anne looks round suddenly.*)

LATIMER — Go on, Anne. (*Happily*) I am having neuralgia, Dominic.

DOMINIC — Yes, sir. A stubborn complaint, as I have heard, sir.

LATIMER — Miss Anne is making me well — what did you want, Dominic?

DOMINIC — Her ladyship says will you please excuse her if she is not at dinner tonight?

LATIMER — (*to Anne*). Shall we excuse her if she is not at dinner tonight? (*Anne's eyes say that she thinks they might.*)

DOMINIC — The fact is, sir, that Joseph is taken ill suddenly, and —

LATIMER — (*to himself*). I never thought of Joseph!

ANNE — Oh, poor Joseph! What is it?

DOMINIC — A trifling affection of the throat, but necessitating careful attention, her ladyship says.

LATIMER — Please tell her ladyship how very much I thank her for looking after Joseph — and tell Joseph how very sorry I am for him.

DOMINIC — Yes, sir.

LATIMER — You can't go now, Anne. You will have to stay and chaperon Eustasia and me. (*She laughs*) Take your hat off just to show that you are staying. (*She begins*) Joseph's illness will probably be a lingering one, and you can't keep your hat on all the time. (*She takes it off.*)

ANNE — You are making me your prisoner again?

LATIMER — I can't let you go.

ANNE — (*softly*). I am not sure that I want to go.

LATIMER — (*timidly*). Could you possibly pretend that I didn't hear that the first time, and — and just say it again?

ANNE — (*shyly*). I am not sure that I want to go.

LATIMER — (*happily*). She did say it. (*They are silent, thinking their own happy thoughts. Suddenly the bell rings.*)

LATIMER — (*sitting up with a start*). Good Lord!

ANNE — What is it?

LATIMER — Another couple arriving. I'd absolutely forgotten.

ANNE — Oh! (*Dominic comes in.*)

LATIMER — (*entreatingly*). Dominic —!

DOMINIC — I quite understand, sir. (*He opens the door. Latimer and Anne wait anxiously.*)

A VOICE OUTSIDE — Oh — er — is this an hotel? My chauffeur said — we've had an accident —

DOMINIC — He was quite correct, sir. This is a sort of hotel. But it's closed just now, sir — (*He glances round at Latimer and Anne, and then back again*) pending a change in the management.

"He shuts and bolts the door, then draws the curtains. There is an air of finality about it."

The curtain falls

"AMBUSH"

A Drama in Three Acts

By Arthur Richman

SOME one asked Arthur Richman, following the Theater Guild's production of "Ambush," where such a family and home as he has written this play around could be found. "In Jersey City," he answered, from which statement grew the story that he had actually taken the experiences of a Jersey City family as the basis of his drama. Being a probable story it was difficult to stop it spreading.

Mr. Richman was later at some pains to explain, however, that he merely meant to say that he had seen in Jersey City and a dozen other suburban centers such homes and characters as he visualized for his own guidance during the writing of "Ambush." The story, if not typical, is at least possible in practically any environment, though it belongs more particularly to the bigger cities. Where poverty and temptation flourish, there drama is also abundantly fruitful.

"Ambush" was one of the early-season productions of the Theater Guild, being produced at the Garrick, October 10, 1921. It was played there until November 26, and then transferred to the Belmont, where it continued for several weeks.

This particular section of life concerns the Nichols family — Walter, Harriet, his wife, and Margaret, his daughter. Walter Nichols "is forty-five, but looks older. He is of medium height and slim, but his face is thickly lined and his hair is beginning to turn gray. He looks the typical clerk. There is something gentle, almost benevolent, about Walter. Life for him has been a continual struggle, but it has bred in him no bitterness. He is quiet, well-mannered, very considerate, a little too deferential; and while others have passed him in the race for financial success he has watched them with no envy. His own aim has been to keep his character untarnished and to see his wife and daughter shape their lives in accordance with the accepted conventional code."

Harriet Nichols, on the other hand, a few years younger than her husband, "is a woman accustomed to doing her own housework and shows the effects of it. She has performed her duties faithfully but grudgingly, and year by year little bitternesses have piled up in her heart, corroding the illusions that once dwelt there. If she had a sense of humor it has mostly disappeared; what remains is a dull cynicism. Her condition differs from her husband's as the condition of a person who has no inner resources will always differ from the condition of one who has. She has seen glimmers of her husband's personality without ever comprehending what she saw. . . . As a matter-of-fact, the natural dignity of his character and the innate refinement of his speech and manner have bred in her a vague respect for his feelings, mixed with resentment for his aloofness."

The Nichols are living not in, but near, Jersey City. Their home is extremely modest and a little shabby, but neatly kept. In the living room, which serves also as the dining room, the evening meal has just been finished and Harriet Nichols is clearing away the dishes, while Walter lingers over his coffee. Upstairs the daughter, Margaret, is dressing. She is going automobiling with a Mr. Kraigne, who lives over Morristown way. Mrs. Nichols supplies these details with a suggestion in her tone that she is a little proud of Margaret's friends. She is explaining to Harry Gleason, who has called to see Margaret, why he will have to wait for her to come down.

This is the first time young Mr. Gleason has called in two or three weeks, which suggests to Walter that he and Margaret may have quarreled. It is evident that they have, though Gleason would put it another way. He smiles, for instance, when Walter tells him that not only is Margaret still working in New York, but doing very well. "You seem surprised; did you expect Margaret to lose her position?" demands Walter. "Not lose it," replies Harry. "But when people outgrow their friends they sometimes feel too big for their jobs, too."

As a matter of fact it is Harry Gleason's private opinion that Margaret has quit being his girl because she had rather go around with men who can spend more money on her, and his pride is severely bruised. It makes him look foolish. The way it used to be he and Margaret were seen together a lot. Now, when people ask him where she is he doesn't know what to say.

Margaret comes down a moment later. "She is twenty and very pretty. Her clothes are inexpensive, but in the prevailing fashion. She is more her mother's daughter than her father's. She resents the fate that compels her to live in a middle-class environment and she keeps before her the picture of a more luxurious life to come. Her manner and voice are sweet and gentle; it is only at certain moments that either takes on any hardness."

Her attitude toward her caller is intimate, but not cordial. She knows what is in his mind even before he releases it. He has come, first, to protest that she isn't treating him right, and, second, to ask her if she wouldn't like to go to the movies, or something. They go out on the porch to finish their argument.

What Harry has said about Margaret's seeming to prefer the society of rich people recently worries Walter. He, too, has noticed that his daughter's ideas are changing. And tonight, after he has turned his weekly pay envelope over to his wife, and listened patiently to her regret that it is not more, and offered his set argument that while they are not so well off as some they are much better off than others; and after he has listened to her enthusiastic report of how well their friends, the Jennisons, are doing, permitting them to have a new automobile and other luxuries, and suffered the familiar observation that caring about character and principles never got a man anywhere—after his customary evening interlude has been taken care of Walter takes it upon himself to speak to Harriet about their daughter.

WALTER — I'm worried about Margaret.

HARRIET — What's the matter with Margaret?

WALTER — Some things Harry said that you didn't hear — they're partly true.

HARRIET — What did he say?

WALTER — He feels that Margaret cares to know only people of wealth. That's what I understand him to mean.

HARRIET — Why do you take stock in what *he* says? He likes Margaret and he hates having her go with anybody else.

WALTER — I seemed to notice the same thing in her, myself.

HARRIET — That she only cares about people with money? I guess three-quarters of the world is like that.

. . . .

HARRY — (*as he and Margaret come in*). Well, I haven't got one.

MARGARET — (*smiling*). No, Harry, I know you haven't.

HARRY — If you're going to change your friends on account of money and automobiles, it's your own business.

MARGARET — Harry, you talk like a fool!

HARRY — I may *talk* like one, but that don't mean that I *am* one.

MARGARET — If it comes to that, I've a right to choose my friends wherever I feel like it. It's nothing against a man to be rich.

HARRY — All right. I thought I'd save you some trouble, that's all. Some o' the people around here are beginning to talk.

MARGARET — Let them talk, what do I care?

HARRY — Oh, I know. It's none o' my business. And if I didn't think so much of your mother and father, I wouldn't say anything about it.

WALTER — Harry, I'm surprised that you should take this tone to Margaret.

MARGARET — He's mad because I won't go out with him. (*To Harry*) Well, I won't. Not only tonight, but I won't go out with you any other night either. You don't need to come around here and you don't need to call me up.

HARRY — You needn't take it like that. Maybe I got too fresh. I apologize. (*She makes an impatient gesture*) I can't do any more than that.

MARGARET — (*takes gloves from sewing table*). Better hurry if you're going to play fool — your friends'll be waiting for you.

To this suggestion Harry makes no reply. He jams his hat down on his head and flounces angrily out of the house. Walter is sorry. They used to be such good friends, Margaret and Harry! It is hard for Margaret to believe. When she sees him now she can't understand how she ever stood him. He's a common little sneak. That's what he is. What business is it of his, or anybody's, whom she goes with — or where?

It matters a good deal to Margaret's father. He is even interested in knowing where she is going tonight, how many there are to be in the party, and what time she expects to get home —

MARGARET — (*angrily*). For heaven's sake, stop asking questions!! (*Walter starts to speak*) I know what you're going to say — it's only your love for me. But I'm nearly twenty, Dad, and for two years I've been working in New York. I think I'm entitled to do as I please, *once* in a while!

WALTER — (*gently*). I meant nothing by my questions. It's natural that I should want to know what you do and who your friends are. Your mother feels the same way about it, I'm sure.

HARRIET — No, I don't. Leastways, I don't ask questions.

WALTER — There's only one thing, Margaret. When you stay out late I worry. (*Margaret starts to speak*) I can't help it — I'm made like that. Last Tuesday —

MARGARET — Have I got to hear about *that* again?

WALTER — I am merely asking you, dear, please not to stay out too late again. You were late at the office twice last week — you told me so yourself — and that's a mistake. Now, am I forgiven?

Walter is forgiven, but not with much enthusiasm. He is rather a trial to his family. He is always making mountains out of the most insignificant molehills. Hardly has he finished explaining his attitude about the proposed automobile ride than he notices a handsome bracelet Margaret is wearing and is in trouble again. It's nothing, Margaret assures him. Nothing but imitation jewelry. She bought it for herself and it is so silly of him to object to her wearing it. What if it is imitation? What does it matter what people think?

But Walter is determined to carry his point and demands that the bracelet be left at home and that it be returned to the store from which it was purchased the following day. Pretending to be what you are not is vulgar, insists Walter. Then everybody is vulgar, replies his wife. But, though both his wife and his daughter are against him, he carries the day and retains the bracelet, not without seriously straining Margaret's patience, however. She knows he means well, and she knows that it is natural for a father to want everyone to honor and respect his daughter — but she is pretty mad, just the same. Even when Walter reminds her of the ten thousand dollars in bonds that he is saving for her as a marriage gift, sacrificing everything to keep the sum intact from the day his brother had left it to him, she is no more than perfunctorily forgiving. But she makes the best of an unpleasant situation.

And then the Jennisons come. Seymour Jennison "is the same age as Walter, an aggressive, opinionated, loud-talking man of the salesman type. His wife, short and stout, is far more wholesome, but has been trained to 'back up' her husband in all he says and does. His method is to appeal to her for corroboration whenever he finds it expedient and she never fails him. Although he does not know it, some of his bizarre methods cause her real agony."

Seymour used to be a jewelry salesman, but at the moment he is a promoter. Magnificus Oil, he is willing to inform the world, is not only about to make his fortune, but the fortunes of many other fine, far-seeing, courageous men. It has, we assume, already helped Seymour in the purchase of a handsome six-cylinder car — and a liveried chauffeur.

SEYMOUR — (*chewing off end of a cigar as he goes on talking*). Some people call it "luck" the way I got into this thing But it ain't luck — it's grasping an opportunity. I saw from the prospectus that the property they owned was one o' the most valuable oil producing properties in the country. Remember, Julia, how I came home and said so? (*Mrs. Jennison nods*) And I knew that with intelligent direction the output could be increased and increased and increased until — it's tremendous — tremendous! In heaven's name, Walter Nichols, why don't you take a chance?

WALTER — (*slowly, ill at ease*). I'm a conservative, Seymour.

SEYMOUR — Pah!

WALTER — Besides, what have I got to take chances with? Even if I wanted to, I mean.

SEYMOUR — Enough for a starter. What did *I* have? Only Julia's money and there wasn't much of that. But Julia had courage. (*In his enthusiasm he leans over and slaps his wife's back. She winces, but says nothing*) Courage! That's what is needed in modern life. Look at the successful men we know. Look at your boss, L. A. Preston. Where would he be if he didn't have courage? Or the fellow Margaret works for — what's his name? Good heavens! You're not going to spend your whole life like *this*, are you?

WALTER — What's the matter with *this?*

SEYMOUR — What's the matter with it? Why it's awful.

WALTER — (*warmly*). It's been good enough for *you* these last fifteen years.

SEYMOUR — (*sings*). "It may be for years. But it wont't be forever." (*Laughs*) No, *sir!* That's the point, *I* wasn't satisfied, I said. Here's a chance — the chance of my lifetime, perhaps. Opportunity comes once to every man, and my judgment tells me Magnificus Oil can't go wrong." So what did I do? I took Julia's money and invested it!

And that is exactly what Walter should do. He should invest in Magnificus Oil. He owes it to Harriet. He owes it to Margaret. He owes it to himself to have some ambition. Walter insists that he is ambitious, but his ambitions are of a different kind. He doesn't believe in speculations and, besides, he doesn't enjoy being put in a bad light before his women folk. And it only makes them more resentful to hear—

Seymour is inclined to laugh at this argument, but a new idea strikes him. He thinks he will buy the house

Walter is living in. There is almost sure to be a rise in property values in that neighborhood, and he might as well be in on it. Of course, Seymour himself expects to move over to Riverside Drive as soon as Mrs. Jennison can find an apartment to suit them. But he will still be interested in the old neighborhood —

Alan Kraigne has called for Margaret. He is a "good looking, well dressed youth of twenty-four, breezy and likable, with easy manners and a cheerful disposition." Everybody is pleased to meet Mr. Kraigne, including the Jennisons. Seymour thinks perhaps they will drive over to Morristown Sunday and look up the Kraigne estate.

WALTER — I've seen you before, Mr. Kraigne.

ALAN — Really; where?

WALTER — I work at Preston's. I've seen you in Mr. Preston's office.

ALAN — I've been there on business. (*Laughs*) They trust me to carry messages. I don't recall —

WALTER — You wouldn't be likely to remember me. (*Playing with Margaret's gloves*) I'm one of the clerks. But I know your father — he usually stops and chats with me when he's in the office. I've been there seventeen years.

Margaret and young Kraigne are gone now, and Walter and Harriet are alone. It is time for a summing up of the events of the evening.

WALTER — You think me a pretty queer fish, don't you, Harriet?

HARRIET — When you've been living with a person for twenty-five years, you don't think much about 'em one way or the other.

WALTER — But there are times when you're puzzled about me? When you can't understand my reason for feeling as I do about things?

HARRIET — You're awfully old fashioned.

WALTER — I thought you felt something of that sort. (*Thoughtfully*) When I was a young fellow I used to flatter myself that I had ideals.

HARRIET — We all have queer ideas when we're young.

WALTER — (*laughs*). You're not very complimentary — (*Seriously*) As we grow older, we gradually compromise with our ideals.

HARRIET — (*who has not heard*). What?

WALTER — The trouble with me is that I can't shake off the ideas I used to have.

HARRIET — That's what I said — you're old fashioned

WALTER — I don't think it's that. It isn't as though I took my ideas from my parents, and I'm certainly not narrow in my religious beliefs. What I hate is coarseness, anything that cheapens one. When I saw that bracelet on Margaret tonight, do you know the first thought that flashed through my mind?

HARRIET — To make her take it off, I suppose.

WALTER — I'm ashamed of it. But for just a second I wondered if some man had given it to her.

HARRIET — Well, none did. Margaret talked to me about it the other day — But I think it's a shame your not letting her wear it.

WALTER — Why?

HARRIET — You're pushing the girl too far. She's young and she's pretty, if I do say it, and girls nowadays believe in making the most out of their looks. It's natural for her to feel out of place if she's the only girl in a crowd who hasn't got nice things.

WALTER — That's it — that's the danger of her associating with people who can afford the things *she* can't. I guess I'm an old fool. If it gives her pleasure, let her wear it. I'll give it back to her in the morning.

HARRIET — That's more sensible.

WALTER — I'm going to turn over a new leaf. I'm going to give up being what you call old fashioned —

I call it "compromising with one's principles." I've noticed that your ways get along a lot better with Margaret than mine do, so I'm going to pattern myself after you. Way down in your heart you have the same feelings about things as I have — Margaret's welfare means as much to you as to me.

HARRIET — I'm glad you realize it.

Walter's reform does not include an agreement to invest Margaret's $10,000 in Magnificus Oil, however. And even though Harriet urges him, and Seymour Jennison returns and tries to browbeat him into an agreement to buy the oil stock, he will not be moved. Everybody is going into it and everybody is going to be rich — but Walter is content. It is while he is showing Seymour his bonds and explaining that he had rather have four and a half per cent. interest on them and be sure of getting it than he would to have a whole lot of speculative stock and not be sure of it that Seymour catches sight of the bracelet Walter had taken away from Margaret earlier in the evening.

SEYMOUR — Damned if I understand you. Walter. And I'm afraid *you* don't understand your family. (*Walter looks up sharply*) Women are funny about some things — they don't like a man to be too cautious. And nowadays — people ain't so plain and simple as you'd have them. Here, let me ask you something. Why isn't Margaret wearing this bracelet?

WALTER — Oh, I had some idea that she oughtn't. But I just told Harriet —

SEYMOUR — I knew it! She *wants* to wear it, don't she? (*Before Walter can reply*). 'Course she does. Going out with a feller like Kraigne she wants to look as well as she can. And you won't let her! Do you suppose she understands your reasons? I don't know what they are myself. Or, say she does. Does she think they're right? (*Looks at bracelet.*)

WALTER — (*with an embarrassed laugh*). Don't look at it, Seymour, it's too ridiculous.

SEYMOUR — (*examining it under the light*). What's ridiculous about it?

WALTER — Of course you know what it's worth.

SEYMOUR — I can't guarantee to come nearer than two or three hundred, but the stones are very fine quality.

WALTER — (*slowly, turning pale*). Very — fine — quality?

SEYMOUR — The stones. And the setting is a peach. It's a new piece, isn't it?

WALTER — You're sure it's very good?

SEYMOUR — Of course — I know jewelry. But you must know what it's worth, if you bought it. (*Returns bracelet to Walter.*)

WALTER — (*quickly*). Of course. (*Replaces the bracelet, mechanically locking the box*) Seymour!

SEYMOUR — What?

WALTER — Will you do me a favor? Don't mention the bracelet to Harriet or Margaret. You see, it only reminds them and causes trouble.

SEYMOUR—(*dryly*). It ought to.

WALTER — You won't mention it? (*Harriet comes in with lemonade and glasses on tray. Mrs. Jennison precedes her.*)

HARRIET — Let's go out on the porch — it's cooler.

SEYMOUR — You bet! (*Starts for the door.*)

WALTER — (*pleadingly*). Seymour!

SEYMOUR — Don't be afraid, I won't mention it.

Seymour follows the lemonade to the porch. Walter stands at the table a moment, staring blankly, helplessly at the bracelet. He starts for the door as the curtain falls.

ACT II

It is eleven o'clock the following morning. Margaret has not yet come in. Walter, trying to read the Sunday paper, is pale and nervous, his face gaunt with the look of a man who has not slept. He starts at every sound from the street.

Harriet, too, is worried about Walter's mussing up the room with his Sunday papers. So far as Margaret is concerned she is convinced she is all right. Probably she motored with Mr. Kraigne to Orange and spent the night with his girl cousin. She has often spoken of her. Perhaps she has tried to telephone this morning and couldn't get the house or something. The service is often as bad as that.

Walter insists that they should at least try to find out what has happened. There might have been an accident. He could call the Kraigne home and ask, casually, about young Alan. But Harriet insists he shall do nothing of the kind. Any 'phoning would be bound to look bad — as if he thought Alan and Margaret — even the thought of such a suspicion is horrible. Walter refuses to let his wife finish the sentence.

HARRIET — When she comes I suppose you'll lose your temper?

WALTER — No — no.

HARRIET — Well, don't. Margaret's angry yet about the bracelet — I know the way she takes things — and there's no use in you two quarreling.

WALTER — (*trying to speak lightly*). How long ago did Margaret buy the bracelet?

HARRIET — (*without looking at him*). Two or three days ago. Thursday, I think.

WALTER — You weren't with her when she bought it?

HARRIET — You know I wasn't in New York last week.

WALTER — What was the first intimation you had of it?

HARRIET — What's the sense of all this fuss?

WALTER — I was just wondering. Can you remember?

HARRIET — (*impatiently*). Yes, I remember very well — one day — Tuesday or Wednesday — she told me she'd seen an imitation bracelet she'd like to have and that she'd saved enough money to buy it. I haven't got the same ideas about things that you have and I know how young girls feel about having pretty things, so I told her to go ahead. On Thursday she showed it to me, and that's all there is to it. (*Walter goes to her. With a faint smile, he kisses her cheek*) (*Surprised*) What's *that* for?

WALTER — You're a good woman, Harriet.

HARRIET — It's a funny time to tell me, now I'm forty-two years old.

It is Harriet's idea that they should get ready, if they are going automobiling with the Jennisons, but Walter cannot think of leaving the house with Margaret away. He is surprised that Harriet can. As soon as Margaret comes he hopes to go upstairs and lie down. He feels pretty ragged. But he can't get Margaret out of his mind. Is it a good thing — does Harriet think it is a good thing — for her to go with young Kraigne? And men of his type?

If she is to marry well, Harriet insists, she's got to get out and meet people. She would never be satisfied to live as her father and mother do, or as their friends live. But — Walter is persistent — do men like Mr. Kraigne ever want to marry girls of Margaret's station? Of course it has happened, but is it common? And has Margaret ever intimated that Alan Kraigne really does want to marry her?

Harriet doesn't answer directly "There's one thing certain," she half shouts; "nobody'll want to marry her if you spoil her disposition every time she goes out!"

And then the Jennisons come with their car — and chauffeur. Little Mrs. Jennison wears an old coat and veil, but Seymour is resplendent in a new outfit of the latest motor apparel. "Everybody ready?" Everybody isn't, quite. Walter isn't going. Doesn't feel well. Of course, what Walter needs is fresh air, bawls Seymour, but if he'd rather stick at home perhaps Harriet better give him a dose of soothing syrup and let it go at that. Perhaps Margaret would like to go?

They explain that Margaret spent the night at the home of a friend. They are just about to leave, with a parting shot or two at Walter, when Margaret comes quietly up the porch and into the room. Involuntarily Walter springs to meet her, but recovers control of himself. Harriet, her face tense with irritation diplomatically sends the others on to the car that the family may be alone. With the Jennisons gone she turns angrily upon her daughter.

HARRIET — You ought to be ashamed of yourself!

MARGARET — (*on her dignity*). Well, *I'll* say that is a nice reception.

HARRIET — Where have you been?

MARGARET — (*lightly*). At the Lydall's.

HARRIET — Who?

MARGARET — Louise Lydall is Alan's cousin — I've told you about her. We went there last evening and she persuaded me to spend the night.

HARRIET — Why didn't you telephone? Your father and me up half the night, worrying!

MARGARET — You don't look very bad. I didn't telephone because I couldn't get the number. I called and called, but there was no answer.

HARRIET — I thought that was it. (*Starts for the door.*)

MARGARET — Isn't father going with you?

HARRIET — I don't think so. (WALTER *shakes his head.*)

MARGARET — (*suddenly, as Harriet is at the door*). Oh, mother —

HARRIET — What? (*She crosses swiftly and whispers to her mother. Harriet is seen to whisper in reply, then she speaks in her natural tone*) I don't blame you.

MARGARET — (*earnestly*). Remember — I mean it!

HARRIET — (*to Walter*). Margaret's afraid you're going to make a fuss after I go. (*Walter is silent.*)

MARGARET — Are you? 'Cause if you are, I'll go out again.

WALTER — Margaret dear, you musn't talk like that.

MARGARET — Besides, Alan's coming for me in the afternoon and we're going out for dinner. I don't want to look all nervous and unhappy.

WALTER—(*involuntarily*). You're going out again!

MARGARET — (*ugly*). You see! Now, listen to me! If you've got any questions to ask, ask them now, because I intend to get some rest.

WALTER — You were with Mr. Kraigne's cousin who lives in Orange?

HARRIET — I thought that's where she was.

MARGARET — What about it? She insisted on my staying there and I had every intention of phoning and telling you so. Well, I couldn't — it wasn't my fault. Alan had already gone and there was no way for me to get home.

WALTER — All right, dear, all right!

MARGARET — Anything more?

HARRIET — The poor girl did everything she could.

There can be no rest for Walter, however, until he has had a talk with Margaret; until he knows that the gathering suspicions that assail him have no foundation in fact. He is gentle when he calls her, gentle when he insists that she shall come down, even though she is inclined to be defiant and refuses to answer so much as a single question.

In the end he does know. He knows that Margaret frankly hates her home; that to her the only thing that makes it bearable is the fact that she can get away from time to time and know something of a brighter life.

He knows, too, that she had lied about the bracelet before and that she is lying to him again now, as she insists the first story was true; that the bracelet is an imitation and that she bought it out of her own savings.

WALTER — I know better, dear. The diamonds are real.

MARGARET — Well, what if they are? Diamonds of poor quality are almost as cheap as imitations.

WALTER — You couldn't have possibly paid for it. (*A pause, Margaret, pale and tense, is like an animal driven into a corner, ready to fight.*)

MARGARET — Now remember; if you drive me too far, I'll leave this house and never come back!

WALTER — I'm not trying to hurt you — oh darling, can't you see I'm trying to help you? (*She starts for the stairs*) There's no use in your running away — I'll follow you and wait. (*She is undecided*) I must understand this, because, if I don't, I'll never have another peaceful hour. I only want it settled now — between us — so your mother needn't know.

MARGARET — (*quickly*). You don't want mother to know about it?

WALTER — Not if we can possibly help it. It would hurt her too much. Now dear.

MARGARET — If you must know, it was given to me.

WALTER — Why didn't you say so from the start.

MARGARET — You'd have made me give it back. I wanted to keep it.

WALTER — You preferred to deceive me about it, and to deceive your mother.

MARGARET — I deceived you both. What about it?

WALTER — Who gave it to you? (*No answer*) Mr. Kraigne?

MARGARET — Maybe.

WALTER — (*exasperated*). Was it Mr. Kraigne?

MARGARET — Yes, it was Alan. (*Now she has answered, his voice loses all asperity.*)

WALTER — Men don't make gifts like that unless they are very fond of a girl.

MARGARET — What do you know about such men? They're not like you and your friends. (*Archly*) As a matter of fact, though, Alan does like me.

WALTER — It's more than that!

MARGARET — (*trying to be angry, but actually frightened*). What do you mean by that?

WALTER — (*looks at her closely. She drops her eyes. He backs away — she bursts into tears*). Dearest — (*For an instant he cannot go on*) Oh, my little girl, all I want in the world is to see you happy. Whatever has happened, I will never blame you — never. Trust me. If you have made some mistakes — nobody need ever know. Just you and I, darling — no one else. Why, I'll surround you with tenderness and love —

MARGARET — I'm not good enough to touch you!

Walter's fear now becomes a certainty. "He looks before him with dull eyes and open mouth." There is a moment of silence, broken by the girl's sobs. Then Walter resumes his comforting. He is not the kind of a father who would turn his girl out of the house. He is going to love her and make her forget. She is still but a child. And, Margaret, gaining comfort from her father's sympathy, declares that she will have nothing more to do with Alan; that she will 'phone him not to call for her that afternoon. Which she does, though she is unable to get Alan. He has not yet been home. So she leaves a message for him not to come.

MARGARET — If he comes here, we musn't see him, father — not you, either — (*She sobs.*)

WALTER — (*tenderly*). Do you love him, dear?

MARGARET — Do you think, if I didn't — ?

WALTER — No! No! I understand. He made love to you, he made you believe — Did he promise to marry you?

MARGARET — He loved me, Father, and he promised to marry me and *I* love *him*.

WALTER — Of course, dear — what a fool I was not to understand. (*Furiously*) These men, with plenty of money and no conscience, dangle their gifts and their promises before a girl's eyes —

MARGARET — He would marry me, only — only his people won't let him.

WALTER — He has told you that?

MARGARET — His father would disinherit him if he did.

WALTER — The beasts! The beasts! (*After a moment*) Tell me about it, can't you — won't you?

MARGARET — It began a month ago. He told me he loved me.

WALTER — And did you care for him?

MARGARET — Oh, so much, Father! He told me that some day we would be married. You can imagine how I felt. He's the only man I ever loved, Father.

WALTER—Did you ask *when* you would be married?

MARGARET — He said it would happen before the winter. And then — (*She broke down, burying her face in her hands*) I knew I was doing wrong! I knew it! But he said he would marry me and that as long as we were going to be married, it was all right.

WALTER — He said nothing then of his parents' opposition?

MARGARET — A week later. (*Thinks hard*) Yes, it was a week. It nearly killed me. (*A pause.*)

WALTER — (*puzzled*). Even after he told you, you continued to meet him?

MARGARET — (*in a hard tone*). Why not? Nothing mattered any more.

WALTER — You musn't say that! You musn't believe it!

MARGARET — My life is ruined. I don't care now *what* happens to me.

WALTER — No, Margaret. Everything can be all right — it depends on the future.

MARGARET — Do you really believe it can, daddy? Say you believe it —

WALTER — (*encouragingly*). Of course I believe it, dear. You're a good girl at heart.

MARGARET — You'll trust me?

WALTER — Always! (*Holds her tightly*) They've lied to you and made you unhappy. All I've ever wanted was to make you happy. But it's going to be all right dear. If he loves you enough he will break down every obstacle and claim you; if he doesn't, you must bury your love for him deep down in your heart and little by little time will lay the dust on it. (*Margaret raises her head.*)

MARGARET — You must never mention all this again — never!

WALTER — After today not a word will be said. It's our secret. Your mother will never suspect — You'll see.

MARGARET — I couldn't stand it!

Sobbingly she starts for the stairs. Walter's arms are around her protectingly. "With infinite tenderness he takes her in his arms and kisses her . . . Still weeping she rushes from him and hurries up the stairs."

Walter, speaking softly, that Margaret may not hear him, goes to the telephone and calls the Kraigne number in Morristown. He is talking to Howard Kraigne, Alan's father, as the curtain falls to indicate a lapse of time.

. . . .

Howard Kraigne "is a man of fifty-five, tall, good-looking, quiet, dignified." He has come to Mr. Nichols' house, as the latter had requested over the phone, without telling anyone. He could not have told Alan, he explains, because he has not seen his son since dinner time the previous day. Briefly Walter explains the situation to him.

KRAIGNE — I thought it was something like that. How old is your daughter?

WALTER — Nineteen.

KRAIGNE — What sort of a girl is she?

WALTER — "What sort —?"

KRAIGNE — Is she lively, or is she the quiet domesticated type?

WALTER—(*in difficulties*). What happened came as a great shock.

KRAIGNE — Your wife is living?

WALTER — She is out at present.

KRAIGNE — What I am trying to find out is this: Is your daughter a girl who knows something of life and so may be presumed to know what she is doing, or is she —?

WALTER — I will let you judge for yourself, later. I thought it best for you and me to talk before I call her.

KRAIGNE — By all means. You will find me very easy to reason with. There has been some sort of an affair, I take it, between your daughter and Alan? (*Walter wincing drops his head*). Have you met my son?

WALTER — Last night when he called for Margaret.

KRAIGNE — How did he impress you?

WALTER — Very well, at the time.

KRAIGNE — You see, I believe in looking at a question from every side.

WALTER — I only spoke to him for a moment.

KRAIGNE — Then you didn't know, at that time, what you know now? (*Walter shakes his head*) My son has virtues and vices like most young men brought up as he has been. You see, *I* began life very poor—when I married I was already doing well. My son was brought up with plenty of money, but no traditions regarding the way it should be spent; pleasure is what he has always sought. But he's no worse than other young men in such circumstances — better than most, in fact. (*With conviction*) There's one thing about him — he's honest and truthful and hates deception of any kind. I make a point of that. (*Briskly*) How did you learn what you did?

Walter tells him of the discovery of the bracelet and the confession that followed, when Margaret returned home alone after having spent the night with Alan's cousin, Miss Lydall, in Orange. But, interposes, Mr. Kraigne, rather pointedly, Margaret could not have spent the night at Miss Lydall's because the Lydalls were at the Kraigne home early that morning and complained of not having seen Alan for weeks.

The inference is obvious, and the fact that Margaret has lied to him again is another blow to the trembling Walter. Yet he still defends her. She had tried to spare him, he explains to Kraigne.

WALTER — She isn't to blame! The cause of it was that your son, under the promise of marriage, won my girl's affections —

KRAIGNE — It was foolish of her to *yield*.

WALTER — She is a child.

KRAIGNE — Nineteen is not so young as it used to be.

WALTER — It is still very young.

KRAIGNE — Even at nineteen women have certain restraints. (*Walter is puzzled*) I don't know any better term of it — it's only in the last ten or twelve years that I've had the leisure for reading and study. What I mean is that good women have certain instincts which, so to speak, protect their modesty.

WALTER — And you mean that Margaret —

KRAIGNE — I am generalizing — I merely want to point out that, in love affairs quite as much as in business, it takes two to make a bargain. Alan, you say, promised to marry her?

WALTER — Yes.

KRAIGNE — In that case your daughter made a grave error in judgment. To accord a man the privilege of marriage without having the deal consummated is like giving a man the benefit of a contract and waiving his consideration. (*Warmly*) Nevertheless, that would not excuse my son.

WALTER — I'm glad you take that view of it.

KRAIGNE — I won't have him lie or do dishonest things! If he promised to marry your daughter he must explain his change of mind.

WALTER — He said his parents would disinherit him if he married her.

KRAIGNE — What! (*He exhibits his first sign of excitement but recovers himself immediately.*)

WALTER — Yes!

KRAIGNE — I dare say his mother would disapprove. (*Grimly*) But disinheriting could only be done by *me.*

WALTER — You knew nothing of all this?

KRAIGNE — Certainly not. You're an intelligent man — and educated. More educated than I, for instance, and yet you accept the easiest and most obvious explanations of all the things you see. Don't you know, Nichols, that when a girl is — when she yields — it might be for anyone of a dozen reasons? Sometimes the girl is deceived, but not always. And sometimes the reasons are positively trivial — boredom, love of excitement, curiosity — (*Walter burns*) Oh, yes, my dear Nichols, that's perfectly true — and it's also true that women nowadays are restless — and in a material sense — ambitious. When such women yield it's because they see a chance to advance themselves.

WALTER — (*horrified*). Advance themselves!!!!!

KRAIGNE — In a material sense. Again I apologize if I hurt you, but I take it you are not in a position to offer your women-folk luxuries? Has it never seemed to you that they resent this fact—?

WALTER—(*defensively*). I suppose it's human nature.

KRAIGNE—Of course it is. It's human nature. But it isn't always money that attracts them. As often as not a girl sees in her intimate relationship with a man her only opportunity to associate with people in what is called "a higher social sphere" than her own.

WALTER—I'm sure—

KRAIGNE—I don't say this is true of your daughter—I have no opinion on the subject—(*Shakes his head reflectively*) Such women are usually disappointed. They meet the men-folk all right enough, but until the women-folk accept them they're still derelicts. (*Draws a long breath, laughs*) Good heavens, how far afield we are!

WALTER—(*politely*). It's very interesting, sir.

KRAIGNE—(*dryly*). Yes, I've noticed that the sex problem interests everybody. (*Walter looks up anxiously*) I didn't mean to be frivolous. I beg your pardon. (*Sympathetically*) I know how you feel. I don't pretend I can put myself in your place, for I'm a pretty callous person, but I recognize your grief and I respect it. More than that, my dear Nichols, I shall do all in my power to dispel it. If my son gained your daughter's confidence through promise of marriage, I shall demand that he keep his word.

Walter finds it hard to believe that he hears aright, and is greatly relieved. Of course, Kraigne qualifies, they will have to be satisfied that the young people want to marry. It would do no good to force them into a marriage that neither wants. But Walter is sure that that condition will be easily met. They are very much in love with each other.

WALTER—There'll be no trouble about *that*. Margaret told me your son is very much in love with her, and as for Margaret —

KRAIGNE — (*rises, smiling*). Looks as if we'd done a good piece of business today, doesn't it?

WALTER — I can't tell you how much I appreciate your stand in this matter, sir. My wife and daughter are all I have in the world — (*Kraigne, still smiling, shakes his head*) Why do you shake your head, sir?

KRAIGNE — Because they're not all you have, Nichols. You have another possession that's a beautiful thing in itself, but that's capable of being a pretty heavy burden. (*Walter is puzzled*) Pride, my dear Nichols, pride. The tenderest spot of your whole carcass is your self-respect. When anything wounds *that*, you suffer the agonies of the damned.

WALTER — So you've noticed that?

KRAIGNE — Noticed it!! It's one of the first things I look for in a man — if he's got it he's a gentleman, but it doesn't help him to make money.

There are steps on the porch. Alan Kraigne has arrived to take Margaret to dinner. Hurriedly Walter whispers to Alan's father that Margaret must not know that Alan is there, intimating that they should muffle their voices. When the boy enters the room he starts with surprise at sight of his father, but quickly recovers himself. Now they have told him of the chat they have been having. At the first sound of Alan's voice, however, Margaret is at the head of the stairs and on her way down. She is mystified at finding the elder Kraigne there, and the efforts of Walter to reassure her that though it may be a difficult moment for her, it is all for the best, in no way allays her fears.

MARGARET — I don't understand at all, I'd like to talk to Alan alone for a moment.

KRAIGNE — I'd rather you didn't. (*As Alan starts to*

join her, he cries sternly) Alan! (*Alan stops and Kraigne's voice loses its severity*) I want you young people to understand that I am your friend. (*Briskly*) I am told — it's a devilish hard thing to say, but I am told there has been something of — ah, an intimate nature between you. (*Margaret instinctively turns away, Alan goes to his father.*)

ALAN — (*pleadingly*). Dad—?

KRAIGNE — That much we will take for granted, if you don't object. Now! Did you and Miss Nichols ever discuss marriage? Don't be afraid to speak — I'm prepared to be your friend. Did you ask Miss Nichols to marry you?

ALAN — Look here, Dad, don't you think —

KRAIGNE — Answer me, sir!

ALAN — I'm very fond of Margaret —

KRAIGNE — I didn't ask that.

ALAN — And if there were any good reason why I should marry her —

MARGARET — I won't stand it! Get out of here, both of you! Father, tell them to get out!

WALTER — But, Margaret —

MARGARET — (*hysterically*). Tell them to get out, I say! I wouldn't marry him now if he went down on his knees and asked me to! (*To Alan*) Don't answer any more questions. (*To Walter*) I tell you I won't marry him! I never want to see him again. Do you suppose I'd marry a man who's forced on me? (*To Alan*) If you don't want to drive me crazy, get out!

Embarrassedly, the Kraignes leave, and with a sweep of hysterical anger Margaret turns on her father. "I hope you're satisfied now, you fool!" she shouts. "Why can't you let me handle my own affairs? Why do you have to butt in and make a mess of everything? Don't tell me again you did it for the best, whatever you do!"

Still Walter's attitude is one of patient groping for

the truth. He thought they loved each other, she and Alan, he explains, and that what he did was best. And she did quite right in refusing to marry Alan after the way he acted. . . . Mr. Kraigne had said there never had been any talk of disinheriting his son. He (Kraigne) knew nothing about the whole affair.

Now Margaret is weeping hysterically. Alan had lied to her. She knew that as soon as she saw how kind his father was. What is to become of her now? "It's all as I told you before they came," replies Walter. "The idea that a girl's life is wrecked because she makes a single mistake is ridiculous! . . . Your mother will be home soon. Thank God, she didn't come while they were here!" But as she starts for the stairs he calls to her.

What did Mr. Alan mean by saying: "If there were any good reason why I should marry her?" Can it be there had been anyone else—

Furiously the girl turns upon him. That is the last straw! He has gone too far this time and he'll be sorry for it! Vainly he tries to explain that he did not mean that, but she will not listen. "Damn you! Damn you!" she shouts, and as he tries to take her hand she strikes him soundly in the face and rushes up the stairs. Before he can follow, Harriet and the Jennisons return.

They are excited about the success of their picnic, and Seymour is bursting with a new enthusiasm about the oil stock. Harriet and he have agreed that Walter *must* invest his bond money. "It can't go wrong," he rattles on: "I know all about it, every blessed turn and twist of the business, and if I say it's all right, it is. Harriet is not so young any more and Margaret is at a marriageable age. You owe it to both of them to get a move on."

But Walter refuses to discuss the matter, much to his wife's disgust. She senses that something has happened and as soon as the Jennisons are gone she demands an explanation.

HARRIET — What's happened between you and Margaret?

WALTER — Why, nothing.

HARRIET — I went up to put my hat away and I heard her crying. She acts like you — she says it's nothing, too.

WALTER — Well, it's true.

HARRIET — It is not. You've been asking her questions again.

WALTER — Only about last night — she explained it all perfectly. And I've done what I told you I would — she's to keep the bracelet.

HARRIET — The minute I leave this house, something goes wrong.

WALTER — And there's one other thing — Margaret agrees with me about men like Mr. Kraigne and she's not going to see him any more.

HARRIET — I don't see why. Anyhow you said something to Margaret that's made her terribly mad and we've got to decide how to keep her home.

WALTER — Keep her home!

HARRIET — (*irritably*). Don't stand there repeating everything I say. I tell you Margaret is going to leave us if we don't do something to prevent it. Girls aren't as easily satisfied nowadays as they used to be. They want nice clothes and pleasures that cost money —

WALTER — We can't afford them.

HARRIET — Maybe we can. You see what Seymour Jennison's done. Why can't you do the same thing? If you weren't so obstinate and heartless — yes, heartless — you have no consideration for Margaret and me. Just because *you're* satisfied, you think *we* are.

WALTER — All we have is Margaret's money.

HARRIET — It isn't Margaret's — you've just been saving it for her. And even if it was, could you find any better use for it than to spend it and keep her with us?

Margaret comes down the stairs. She is dressed for the street, has her hat on and carries a small bag.

WALTER — Margaret!

MARGARET — (*dully*). I can't stand it here any more.

WALTER — Dearest, you mustn't go. Mother and I have just made some plans — listen, dear; we both believe that Mr. Jennison's scheme is a good one and I'm going to sell the securities we've been holding and invest the money in it. All but a few hundred dollars. Those few hundred I'll keep out and you can buy anything you want with it.

MARGARET — (*chokingly*). Father! (*He gently takes the bag from her hand, laying it on the chair near the stairs.*)

WALTER — There; that will be all right?

MARGARET — Father, I don't deserve your kindness! I'm a wicked girl! (*He shakes his head*) Yes, I am. But I'll never do anything to hurt you again! Just forgive me this time, Daddy, and I'll never be wicked again; I'll do anything I can to deserve your love!

WALTER — (*overcome*). My darling!

HARRIET — (*to Walter*). Why don't you go over to Seymour's and tell him what you're going to do?

WALTER — I will! I will!

HARRIET — (*to Margaret*). Take off your hat, and take that upstairs again.

"Silently Margaret takes up the bag and starts for the stairs. Walter is at the half-opened door."

"You and her," his wife calls after him, disgust in her tone. "Neither of you ever listen to *me*. And the Lord knows I'm the only one of the three that's got any sense!"

The curtain falls

ACT III

It is winter, six months later. Walter, bundled up for cold weather, is just back from the city. He has aged noticeably in the last six months. "Not only have his looks changed, but he has lost some of his self-control and most of his confidence. But he is still brave and has much of his old-time dignity of manner."

Margaret, coming down from upstairs, finds him hanging up his things. She, too, has changed, but in a different way. "She has never looked happier or better. The suit she wears is of finer material than those in which she previously has appeared."

Their attitude toward each other is now friendly and considerate. Margaret has been home an hour from her work and is ready to go out to dinner. A Mr. Lithridge is coming out to take her to dinner. As she finishes polishing her nails with a buffer she sounds her father on the idea of her giving up her work. She has been seriously considering the move. There isn't much sense in her working if she doesn't have to. It is easier for a girl to get along if she doesn't work. People have a different opinion of her — especially the people she meets. George's friends, for instance. George Lithridge is her employer. And now that the oil stock is going to make her father a lot of money, she doesn't see why she shouldn't get some benefit from it.

Walter isn't very enthusiastic over the idea. The stock market has been showing signs of weakness lately, even if Seymour Jennison has said Magnificus Oil is in for a big rise.

But Margaret still insists giving up work would be a good thing. Mr. Lithridge has suggested it, too. What has he to do with it? Well, he is an awfully good friend of Margaret's, and, naturally, he is interested in her. Perhaps, suggests Walter, Mr. Lithridge has some thought of asking her to marry him. Margaret isn't sure, but stranger things have happened. He would probably feel a lot more inclined to propose if he could introduce her as a girl who lived at home, rather than as one of his employees.

Walter is inclined to think she should wait — a month or two, at least. Things may look better by February, or March. Then, of course, if Mr. Lithridge did say anything, they would tell him — everything. At which suggestion Margaret flies up angrily. She will manage her own affairs this time! . . .

The truth of the matter is that Walter has lost his job. He tells Harriet the sad news as soon as Margaret is out of the room. He had not been doing his work very well lately. He had been worrying a good deal about the stock market and had made one or two mistakes on the books. They had warned him — and then, finally, they had told him he would have to go — after seventeen years' service! There isn't any sentiment to speak of in business. Under the circumstances he thinks Harriet had better encourage Margaret to hold on to her job, for a little while, anyway. . . .

The Jennisons burst suddenly in upon them. Seymour is in a towering rage. Magnificus Oil "has gone to hell!" They are a lot of robbers, that's what they are, those oil people. They've stolen his money and they've stolen Walter's!

A low moan breaks from Harriet. Walter tries to quiet her, but it is of no use. Robbers? Seymour Jennison is the robber! Coming around there telling people how much money they were going to make in his rotten company!

Seymour is sorry, but — it's hard on both of them. He, for instance, will now have to depend on what he can scrape together from his assets. He still owns a few houses — including the one Walter is living in. And this happens to be rent day. That money will come in handy.

But Walter hasn't enough to pay the rent! Seymour will have to wait. But Seymour can't wait. He can get tenants at twice the rent the Nichols are paying! And if they can't keep the house he will have to rent it to some one else.

Mrs. Jennison is the only one who seems to have any sympathy for Walter. She sends Seymour on ahead that she may talk freely. "Always colorless in his presence she now shows a stronger personality than one would guess she possesses. She becomes tender, sympathetic, intelligent."

MRS. JENNISON — I'm awfully sorry things happened like this, Walter. I wanted to tell you not to go in with Seymour, but I was afraid it would be disloyal.

WALTER — Not to go in! Did you know anything about it?

MRS. JENNISON — Not a thing. It's only this: some people seem kind of marked to go through life without success — have you ever noticed that? I'm afraid Seymour's that kind.

WALTER — (*surprised, but polite*). I hope not.

MRS. JENNISON — This sounds as if I was finding fault, but I'm not. Seymour means so well and I understand and love him.

WALTER — Of course you do.

MRS. JENNISON — But sometimes — were you ever very tired, Walter, and knew that you had to keep going? So tired that just to hold your head up hurt the back of your neck? That's how I am. I want to rest — just to stop everything and rest a long, long time. (*As he is about to speak*) Oh, I'm not tired of keeping house and marketing and mending socks — I'm tired of having to be ambitious. I knew you were too — that's why I stopped to talk to you. I thought it might help you to know I understood, and I thought it might help *me* if you understood.

WALTER — How did you know it was that way with me?

MRS. JENNISON — I saw it in lots of things. I used to notice how contented you were to let things slide along and the pride you took in simply being decent.

WALTER — You saw *that* too?

MRS. JENNISON — I'm like that. At least I used to be. But I got so tired of having Seymour tell me I was old fashioned that I learned to hide it.

WALTER — (*with fresh enthusiasm*). There's something fine about having principles, Julia.

MRS. JENNISON — If you can keep them, Walter. (*She says this with great conviction and he does not say what he is about to. Instead, he slowly closes his mouth.*)

WALTER — (*after a moment*). It's hard, sometimes.

MRS. JENNISON — It's a curse to be born like this — we take things so hard that other people brush aside, because sometimes you *can't* keep them. Sometimes Fate seems to close in on you from every side — to get you into an ambush — and you've got to give up. Don't tell Seymour about this conversation, he'd think I was crazy. (*There is a trace of bitterness in her next speech*) You know what's going to happen now? I'll find Seymour with a lot of papers in front of him covered with figures and he'll tell me about the millions of dollars he's going to make in some new scheme or other. He won't tell me about it because he wants my advice — he'll talk in order to convince *himself*. And he'll be convinced.

WALTER — An ambush!

MRS. JENNISON — Isn't that what it is? The other forces — the things we're fighting against — come in on you like this, and this, until there's no way to turn.

Margaret comes downstairs, her toilette completed. On her arm she carries a fur coat. Mrs. Jennison tells her what has happened. She must be kind to her father in this crisis. But Margaret is not the demonstrative kind. The smash doesn't mean much to her. She is going out to dinner with George Lithridge. . . .

George "is a good-looking, easy mannered, cheerful man of forty. He is seldom without a smile." He greets the family cheerily, and is in a hurry to be on his way, seeing that he has a table engaged —

But Margaret holds him, after an animated, whispered conversation with her mother. There is something she wants to talk with him about, if he doesn't mind coming into the pantry for a minute. George doesn't mind. He might steal a cookie to tide him over.

HARRIET — Margaret is awful unhappy.

WALTER — About the m-money?

HARRIET — She counted on it so much.

WALTER — If there were only something I could do!

HARRIET — (*watching him narrowly as she speaks*). She believes Mr. Lithridge might help you.

WALTER — Help me! You don't mean he'd lend me money? I wouldn't take it.

HARRIET — (*dryly*) Beggars can't be choosers. Margaret's a good girl to think about it. But it isn't lend ing you money so much as it's a job. She just told me that maybe he'd offer you something in *his* place.

WALTER — In his business?

HARRIET — Yes.

WALTER — How does he know of our misfortune?

HARRIET — He doesn't. (*Glances at kitchen door*) Maybe he does now. Margaret was going to tell him.

WALTER — (*embarrassed*). But that's so — so much like asking for help.

HARRIET — (*impatiently*). Did anything decent ever happen to you that you didn't find something the matter with it?

They are interrupted by the doorbell. Harry Gleason is calling. "His hair is dishevelled and it is easy to see that he has been drinking." Walter tries to get him to leave. But Harry has something to say and he has come to say it. Even the return of Margaret and Lithridge does not stop him. He is insolently cheerful in greeting George.

MARGARET — (*in a voice that combines scorn and hate*). He's drunk.

HARRY — (*angrily*). I am not drunk. And don't think I'm going right away either, 'cause I'm not.

GEORGE — Evidently a relation.

MARGARET — No, he's not. (*To Harry*) Stay if you want to, but don't interfere. (*To Walter*) Father, George and I have been talking over a certain matter and George has something to say to you.

GEORGE — Mr. Nichols, your wife and daughter tell me you've had a hard knock in the market.

WALTER — (*embarrassed*). I have — rather.

GEORGE — So've I. Only, I guess I can stand it better than some people. They also tell me you've lost a job held for a long time.

WALTER — Seventeen years.

GEORGE — Just so! Now, I've got a pretty good-sized business in New York. Don't think I'm boasting — believe me, I've got nothin' to boast *about*. The business was left to me — it ain't my fault that it is big. But most of the clerks are getting old and little by little they're being retired. I don't retire 'em — I've got people to look after all that. All I do is read letters and sign checks and say " yes " whenever anybody asks me a question. (*Laughs*) What would you say to taking a job as clerk in my business? Mrs. Nichols just told me how much you used to get and I'll see to it that you get twenty dollars a week more.

WALTER — Mr. Lithridge, this is more than I'd hoped for —

GEORGE — Think it over — there's no hurry. Margie

can ring me up in the morning, if you like, and tell me what you've decided on.

Margaret waits a moment after Lithridge has gone to the car. She wants to know what her father is going to do about the offer of a job. He is going to accept, of course, Walter admits. It is a splendid offer.

MARGARET — That's sensible. And here, Father — here is enough money to pay the rent for the house. (*Shoves him some bills.*)

WALTER — No! No! I can't take it.

MARGARET — Don't be foolish. It's a loan and George has such heaps of money it doesn't make any difference to him.

WALTER — I can't take it.

MARGARET — (*irritably*). I'll leave it here. You can do as you please. (*Lays money on the desk.*)

HARRY — Well, I'll be damned. (*They look at him.*)

WALTER — You ought to be ashamed of yourself, coming here in this condition.

HARRY — (*ugly*). Say, is that so? Well, I know what I'm doing, don't you fear. Why do you suppose that fellow is doing all this? (*Margaret is about to protest*) Do you suppose there is nothing more between them than friendship?

WALTER — You're in no fit condition —

HARRY — Ain't I? Well, I'll leave it to anybody. Here's a married man coming to see Margaret, lending her father money, giving him a job —

WALTER — A married man!

MARGARET — Can't you see he's drunk?

HARRY — (*cried loudly*). Oh, I know him! The first job I ever had I used to see him. He's got a wife and two or three kids. Find out for yourself.

WALTER — (*falteringly — to Margaret*). W-what he says isn't true?

MARGARET — (*defiantly*). Well, what if it is?

WALTER — You — you knew it all the time?

MARGARET — I knew he was married before I met him.

WALTER — But only a little while ago you gave me to understand — here, in this v-very room — that you thought he might marry you!

MARGARET — Well, I had to tell you something, didn't I?

WALTER — But — (*Suddenly breaks out*) I can't believe it! I won't!

MARGARET — Can't believe what?

WALTER — After that other time you promised —

MARGARET — Yes, and I meant it.

WALTER — You meant it! Well, then, if you meant it —

MARGARET — (*indicating Harry*). Do we have to talk about this in front of *him?*

WALTER — (*weakly*). I don't understand any of it! All I know is that everything — everything — is going to pieces!

MARGARET — Why wouldn't it, when a man thinks more of fine ideas than he does of supporting his family?

Even with "everything going to pieces" around him Walter tries to find an excuse for Margaret. She is still not to blame. It all started with Alan Kraigne's deceiving her. But Margaret is thoroughly angry now. He might as well know the truth first as last. Alan Kraigne was not to blame. He had never promised to marry her and he was not her first lover. She had belonged to Harry Gleason before that. That's why Harry has been acting as he has.

WALTER — Have you no shame?

MARGARET — (*putting on her coat*). I'm not going to discuss *that*. (*He begs her mutely to remain*) If I wanted to, I could leave here tonight and never come back. Don't you suppose I could live in New York if I wanted to?

WALTER — Not — not if his wife knew about it!

MARGARET — She *does* know. Oh, not who I am — George is too much of a gentleman to let her learn my name. But they haven't lived together for a year. Now listen, I'd rather stay here — it looks better and it'll be easier some day when I want to get married. Besides I'm fond of mother and you. But if I do stay I'll live as I please and I won't have questions and criticisms.

WALTER — Not so loud! We're forgetting your mother.

MARGARET — You see this coat? Well, you may as well know that I've got lots of things upstairs you've never seen. After this I'll wear them.

WALTER — From — Mr. Lithridge?

MARGARET — (*hurt*). You don't suppose I'd accept things from anyone else? What kind of a girl do you think I am? George is so good-natured, he'd wait all night for his dinner if I wanted him to. But now I *must* go. (*Points to desk*) There's the money for the house, if you want to use it. And remember about the job. (*She is about almost at the door, wrapping the coat closely about her when Walter breaks out.*)

WALTER — (*wildly*). I won't have it. I won't! I'll go out there and threaten him. I'll make him understand. (*Walter plunges toward the door.*)

MARGARET — (*calls loudly*). Mother!

WALTER — Margaret! You mustn't let *her* know!

MARGARET — (*calls as before*). Mother! (*Harriet appears*) Father wants to make trouble with George — stop him.

The ambush is closing in. Walter makes one last stand — to keep Harriet from guessing the truth about

Margaret. But Harriet knows — has known all the time. And she will stick by Margaret. If Margaret goes to New York, as she certainly will if Walter doesn't accept Lithridge's help, she'll go with her.

WALTER — Let her go then! She'll continue her shameless life wherever she is — but you won't go!

HARRIET — Don't you know that if she goes it's the very time she'll need me most? No, Walter, the only thing for you to do is to swallow that pride of yours and take the job Mr. Lithridge offers you.

WALTER — Accept help f-from him! I won't! I won't! (*A ring at the bell. Harriet is alarmed*) Maybe she's forgotten something. Now we'll see!

HARRIET — I warn you; I meant what I said. (*He looks at her and sees she is in earnest. Seymour Jennison and his wife enter.*)

SEYMOUR — Julia persuaded me to come and make friends. How about it, Harriet?

HARRIET — Shut the door.

SEYMOUR — We'll let bygones be bygones — that's my nature. (*Offers his hand to Harriet.*)

HARRIET — (*shaking his hand*). All right, Seymour. I'd ask you two to supper, but there isn't enough in the house.

MRS. JENNISON — We've had it, thanks.

SEYMOUR — This is a terrible world. Margaret passed our house a few minutes ago in a limousine with a New York license, and do you know who the chauffeur was? Frank, the boy *I* used to have! (*Collapses in a chair*) Think of it! *He* lives in New York and *I* don't. (*Shakes his head gloomily — then says to Walter*) Have you decided on anything?

HARRIET — Walter's been offered a very good job; we were talking about it when you came in.

SEYMOUR — (*wide-eyed*). That's so? Pretty quick work, isn't it? I've got something too — looks big! If that's so I suppose I can expect my rent before long.

WALTER — (*dully*). Rent?

SEYMOUR — Sure — for the house.

WALTER — (*wavers a moment*). Oh! (*Walter takes a step in that direction, then gulps hard.*)

SEYMOUR — What's the matter, Walter? You ain't sick, are you?

MRS. JENNISON — What is it, Walter?

WALTER — It's nothing — nothing. I — I'm all right now. (*Crosses to desk.*)

SEYMOUR — It's that damn oil company — they're responsible for it all!

WALTER — Here's — here's the money, Seymour — the exact amount —

SEYMOUR — Well! (*Takes the money*) Now tell us about the job, Walter. Is it a good one?

HARRIET — Better than the old one — more money and a chance for advancement. (*At kitchen door*) I've got to attend to supper. Come in the kitchen and I'll tell you more.

SEYMOUR — Coming, Julie?

WALTER — (*raising his head slightly*). They come in on you like this, until there's no way to turn. You and I, Julia — if we'd married, we'd 'a done something of use in the world.

MRS. JENNISON — Hush, Walter. I don't understand you.

WALTER — Everything I stood for — everything I lived for — everything God put me on this earth for — turns out wrong. What can I do now?

MRS. JENNISON — Whatever has happened — you must go on just the same.

WALTER — Why? (*His voice louder*) Why? Why?

The curtain falls

“THE CIRCLE”

A Comedy in Three Acts

By W. Somerset Maugham

THE success of this amusing comedy in New York was unquestionably due in part to the presence in the cast of Mrs. Leslie Carter, returned to the stage from a seven-year retirement in France, and John Drew, who also had been resting for a season or two.

But having satisfied the curiosity of those eager to renew their acquaintance with these popular favorites of another day the play continued to win its way on its merits as good entertainment.

“The Circle” was produced at the Selwyn Theatre, September 12, 1921, and continued there for five months, practically to the capacity of the theatre. Moved to the Fulton, it played an additional four weeks and was then sent around what is known in New York as the “Subway Circuit” previous to starting a road tour that continued until early spring.

In “The Circle” we meet first in the stately drawing room at Aston-Adley, where there are “fine pictures on the walls and Georgian furniture.” “Aston-Adley,” in fact, as Mr. Maugham explains, “has been described, with many illustrations, in ‘Country Life.’ It is not a house, but a place.” Its owner, Arnold Champion-Cheney, M.P., takes great pride in it, “and there is nothing in the room which is not of the period.”

Arnold himself “is a man of about thirty-five, tall and good looking, fair, with a clean-cut, sensitive face. He has a look that is intellectual, but somewhat blood-
At the moment Arnold is considerably upset. Eliza-
less.”

beth, his wife, "a very pretty creature in the early twenties," has insisted upon asking Lady Catherine Champion-Cheney and Lord Porteous down from London for the week-end. It happens that Lady Catherine is Arnold's mother, though he has not seen her for thirty years. When he was five, Lady Catherine, falling in love with Lord Porteous and out of love with Arnold's father, Clive Champion-Cheney, bolted with his lordship, and has lived with him for thirty years practically an exile in Italy. As both Lady Porteous and Arnold's father refused to divorce their respective mates it has been impossible for the elopers to marry. Now, hearing that they were back in England for the first time, Elizabeth, who has a woman's sympathy for Lady Catherine, considered it no more than right that she should be invited to visit her son.

Arnold has agreed to Elizabeth's plans and spent the intervening time praying that all may go well. But now he hears that his father is also about to descend upon them, and the thought of his father and mother and Lord Porteous meeting is almost too much for him. He has sent for Elizabeth to talk the situation over with her, and found her happily preparing for a tennis set with Edward (Teddie) Luton, "an attractive youth in flannels," who is a house guest and a particular friend of Elizabeth's.

ARNOLD — My father will have to be told, Elizabeth.

ELIZABETH — Yes.

ANNA — (*another house guest*). Has he (Arnold's father) ever spoken to you about Lady Kitty?

ELIZABETH — Never.

ARNOLD — I don't think her name has passed his lips since she ran away from this house thirty years ago.

TEDDIE — Oh, they lived here?

ARNOLD — Naturally. There was a house-party, and one evening neither Porteous nor my mother came down to dinner. The rest of them waited. They couldn't make it out. My father sent up to my mother's room, and a note was found on the pincushion.

ELIZABETH — (*with a faint smile*). That's what they did in the Dark Ages.

ARNOLD — I think he took a dislike to this house from that horrible night. He never lived here again, and when I married he handed the place over to me. He just has a cottage now on the estate that he comes to when he feels inclined.

ELIZABETH — It's been very nice for us.

ARNOLD — I owe everything to my father. I don't think he'll ever forgive me for asking these people to come here.

ELIZABETH — I'm going to take all the blame on myself, Arnold.

ARNOLD — (*irritably*). The situation was embarrassing enough, anyhow. I don't know how I ought to treat them.

ELIZABETH — Don't you think that'll settle itself when you see them?

ARNOLD — After all, they're my guests. I shall try and behave like a gentleman.

ELIZABETH — I wouldn't. We haven't got central heating.

ARNOLD — (*taking no notice*). Will she expect me to kiss her?

ELIZABETH — (*with a smile*). Surely.

ARNOLD — It always makes me uncomfortable when people are effusive.

ANNA — But I can't understand why you never saw her before.

ARNOLD — I believe she tried to see me when I was little, but my father thought it better she shouldn't.

ANNA — Yes, but when you were grown up?

ARNOLD — She was always in Italy. I never went to Italy.

ELIZABETH — It seems to me so pathetic that if you saw one another in the street you wouldn't recognize each other.

ARNOLD — Is it my fault?

ELIZABETH — You've promised to be very gentle with her and very kind.

ARNOLD — The mistake was asking Porteous to come too. It looks as though we condoned the whole thing. And how am I to treat him? Am I to shake him by the hand and slap him on the back? He absolutely ruined my father's life.

ELIZABETH — (*smiling*). How much would you give for a nice motor accident that prevented them from coming?

ARNOLD — I let you persuade me against my better judgment, and I've regretted it ever since.

ELIZABETH — I think it's very lucky that Anna and Teddie are here. I don't foresee a very successful party.

ARNOLD — I'm going to do my best. I gave you my promise and I shall keep it. But I can't answer for my father.

ANNA — Here *is* your father.

"Mr. Champion-Cheney is a tall man in the early sixties, spare, with a fine head of gray hair and an intelligent, somewhat ascetic face. . . . He is a man who makes the most of himself. He bears his years jauntily."

It isn't easy to tell the elder Champion-Cheney of Lady Catherine's coming. Elizabeth tries it, but her approach is roundabout. She tells him first of Teddie Luton, who is a manager of a rubber plantation in the Federated Malay States, and has just been demobilized. Finally she summons the requisite courage and blurts out the embarrassing news. Lady Catherine's former husband is a bit startled, but he accepts the situation gracefully. He will, of course, absent himself that they may not be embarrassed. He bears Lady Catherine no particular resentment.

ELIZABETH — No one's ever talked to me about Lady Kitty. It's always been a subject that everyone has avoided. I've never even seen a photograph of her.

CHAMPION-CHENEY — The house was full of them when she left. I think I told the butler to throw them in the dust-bin. She was very much photographed.

ELIZABETH — Won't you tell me what she was like?

C-C.— She was very like you, Elizabeth, only she had dark hair instead of red.

ELIZABETH — Poor dear! it must be quite white now.

C-C.— I dare say. She was a pretty little thing.

ELIZABETH — But she was one of the great beauties of her day. They say she was lovely.

C-C.— She had the most adorable little nose, like yours.

ELIZABETH — D'you like my nose?

C-C.— And she was very dainty, with a beautiful little figure; very light on her feet. She was like a *marquise* in an old French comedy. Yes, she was lovely.

ELIZABETH — And I'm sure she's lovely still.

C-C.— She's no chicken, you know.

ELIZABETH — You can't expect me to look at it as you and Arnold do. When you've loved as she's loved you may grow old, but you grow old beautifully.

C-C.— You're very romantic.

ELIZABETH — If everyone hadn't made such a mystery of it I daresay I shouldn't feel as I do. I know she did a great wrong to you and a great wrong to Arnold. I'm willing to acknowledge that.

C-C.— I'm sure it's very kind of you.

ELIZABETH — But she loved and she dared. Romance is such an illusive thing. You read of it in books, but it's seldom you meet it face to face. I can't help it if it thrills me.

C-C.— I am pitifully aware that the husbands in these cases are not romantic objects.

ELIZABETH — She had the world at her feet. You were rich. She was a figure in society. And she gave up everything for love.

. . . .

C-C.— Are you happy with Arnold?

ELIZABETH — Why shouldn't I be?

C-C.— Why haven't you got any babies?

ELIZABETH — Give us a little time. We've only been married three years.

C-C.— I wonder what Hughie is like now!

ELIZABETH — Lord Porteous?

C-C.— He wore his clothes better than any man in London. You know he'd have been Prime Minister if he'd remained in politics.

ELIZABETH — What was he like then?

C-C.— He was a nice looking fellow. Fine horseman. I suppose there was something very fascinating about him. Yellow hair and blue eyes, you know. He had a very good figure. I liked him. I was his parliamentary secretary. He was Arnold's godfather.

ELIZABETH — I know.

C-C.— I wonder if he ever regrets!

ELIZABETH — I wouldn't.

Clive Champion-Cheney goes back to the cottage, where he is stopping, and Teddie Luton, who has been waiting a chance to offer Elizabeth his "moral support," is glad to find her alone. Their talk is desultory until he becomes a little serious, telling her of his life in the colony. England's all right, but there is something free and fine about living in the colonies, particularly in the F. M. S. "England seems to me full of people doing things they don't want to because other people expect it of them," he explains.

ELIZABETH — What do you do with yourself all the time?

TEDDIE — Oh, one works like blazes. You have to be

a pretty hefty fellow to be a planter. And then there's ripping bathing. You know, it's lovely, with palm trees all along the beach. And there's shooting. And now and then we have a little dance to a gramophone.

ELIZABETH — (*pretending to tease him*). I think you've got a young woman out there, Teddie.

TEDDIE — (*vehemently*). Oh, no! (*She is a little taken aback by the earnestness of his disclaimer. There is a moment's silence, then she recovers herself.*)

ELIZABETH — But you'll have to marry and settle down one of these days, you know.

TEDDIE — I want to, but it's not a thing you can do lightly.

ELIZABETH — I don't know why there more than elsewhere.

TEDDIE — In England if people don't get on they go their own ways and jog along after a fashion. In a place like that you're thrown a great deal on your own resources.

ELIZABETH — Of course.

TEDDIE — Lots of girls come out because they think they're going to have a good time. But if they're empty-headed, then they're just faced with their own emptiness and they're done. If their husbands can afford it they go home and settle down as grass widows.

ELIZABETH — I've met them. They seem to find it a very pleasant occupation.

TEDDIE — It's rotten for their husbands, though.

ELIZABETH — And if their husbands can't afford it?

TEDDIE — Oh, then they tipple.

ELIZABETH — It's not a very alluring prospect.

TEDDIE — But if the woman's the right sort she wouldn't exchange it for any life in the world. When all's said and done it's we who've made the Empire.

ELIZABETH — What sort is the right sort?

TEDDIE — A woman of courage and endurance and sincerity. Of course, it's hopeless unless she's in love with her husband. (*He is looking at her earnestly and she, raising her eyes, gives him a long look. There is silence between them.*)

TEDDIE — My house stands on the side of a hill, and the cocoanut trees wind down to the shore. Azaleas grow in my garden, and camellias, and all sorts of ripping flowers. And in front of me is the winding coast line, and then the blue sea. (*A pause*) Do you know that I'm awfully in love with you?

ELIZABETH — (*gravely*). I wasn't quite sure. I wondered.

TEDDIE — And you? (*She nods slowly*) I've never kissed you.

ELIZABETH — I don't want you to.

The arrival of Arnold interrupts them. He comes to warn them that Lady Catherine and Lord Porteous have arrived, and he suggests that luncheon be served as soon as possible to relieve the situation. "When you don't know what to say you can always eat." Arnold is quite philosophical at times.

"Lady Kitty comes in, followed by Porteous. . . . Lady Kitty is a gay little lady, with dyed red hair and painted cheeks. She is somewhat outrageously dressed. She never forgets that she has been a pretty woman and she still behaves as if she were twenty-five. Lord Porteous is a very bald, elderly gentleman in loose, rather eccentric clothes. He is snappy and gruff. This is not at all the couple that Elizabeth expected, and for a moment she stares at them with round, startled eyes."

The greetings are effusive, so far as Lady Kitty is concerned (although she does promptly mistake Teddie Luton for her long-forgotten son), but Lord Porteous is a grumpy sort with nothing but complaints about the condition of the roads and such things. Anna Shenstone and Luton are introduced and the talk rambles on with Lady Catherine doing most of the rambling.

LADY CATHERINE — Hughie, do you think Arnold takes after me or his father? Of course I think he's the very image of me. Arnold, I think I ought to tell you that I was received into the Catholic church last winter. I'd been thinking about it for years, and the last time we were at Monte Carlo I met such a nice monsignor. I told him what my difficulties were and he was too wonderful. I knew Hughie wouldn't approve, so I kept it a secret. (*To Elizabeth*) Are you interested in religion? I think it's too wonderful. We must have a long talk about it one of these days. (*Pointing to her frock*) Callot?

ELIZABETH — No, Worth.

LADY CATHERINE — I knew it was either Worth or Callot. Of course, it's line that's the important thing. I go to Worth myself, and I always say to him, "Line, my dear Worth, line." What *is* the matter, Hughie?

PORTEOUS — These new teeth of mine are so damned uncomfortable.

LADY CATHERINE — Men are extraordinary. They can't stand the smallest discomfort. Why, a woman's life is uncomfortable from the moment she gets up in the morning till she goes to bed at night. And d'you think it's comfortable to sleep with a mask on your face?

PORTEOUS — They don't seem to hold up properly.

LADY CATHERINE — Well, that's not the fault of your teeth. That's the fault of your gums.

PORTEOUS — Damned rotten dentist. That's what's the matter.

LADY CATHERINE — I thought he was a very nice dentist. He told me *my* teeth would last till I was fifty. He has a Chinese room. It's so interesting; while he scrapes your teeth he tells you all about the dear Empress Dowager. Are you interested in China? I think it's too wonderful. You know they've cut off their pigtails. They were so picturesque.

Suddenly Lady Catherine discovers that she has lost

her lipstick, and is greatly perturbed. She simply can't live without a lipstick. It's so good for the lips, for one thing. And, besides, the men like it. And then, at the French window at back, appears Clive Champion-Cheney "holding in his outstretched hand a little gold case."

C-C.— (*as he comes in*). Has anyone here lost a diminutive utensil, containing, unless I'm mistaken, a favorite preparation for the toilet? (*Arnold and Elizabeth are thunderstruck at his appearance and even Teddie and Anna are taken aback. But Lady Kitty is overjoyed.*)

LADY CATHERINE — My lipstick!

C-C.— I found it in the drive and I ventured to bring it in.

LADY CATHERINE — It's Saint Anthony. I said a little prayer to him when I was hunting in my bag.

PORTEOUS — Saint Anthony be blowed! It's Clive, by God!

LADY CATHERINE — (*startled, her attention suddenly turned from the lipstick*). Clive.

C-C.— You didn't recognize me. It's many years since we met.

LADY CATHERINE — My poor Clive, your hair has gone quite white!

C-C.—I hope you had a pleasant journey down from London. (*He offers his hand.*)

LADY CATHERINE — (*offering him her cheek*). You may kiss me, Clive.

C-C.— You don't mind, Hughie? (*He kisses her.*)

PORTEOUS — (*with a grunt*). Ugh!

C-C.— (*going to him cordially*). And how are you, my dear Hughie?

PORTEOUS — Damned rheumatic, if you want to know. Filthy climate you have in this country.

C-C.— Aren't you going to shake hands with me, Hughie?

PORTEOUS — I have no objection to shaking hands with you.

C-C.—You've aged, my poor Hughie.

PORTEOUS — Someone was asking me how old you were the other day.

C-C.—Were they surprised when you told them?

PORTEOUS — Surprised! They wondered you weren't dead. (*The butler enters.*)

BUTLER — Did you ring, sir?

ARNOLD — No. Oh, yes, I did. It doesn't matter now.

C-C.— (*as the butler is going*). One moment. My dear Elizabeth, I've come to throw myself on your mercy. My servants are busy with their own affairs. There's not a thing for me to eat in my cottage.

ELIZABETH — Oh, but we shall be delighted if you'll lunch with us.

C-C.— It either means that or my immediate death from starvation. You don't mind, Arnold?

ARNOLD — My dear father!

ELIZABETH — (*to the butler*). Mr. Cheney will lunch here.

BUTLER — Very good, ma'am.

C-C.—(*to Lady Catherine*). And what do you think of Arnold?

LADY CATHERINE — I adore him.

C-C.— He's grown, hasn't he? But then you'd expect him to do that in thirty years.

ARNOLD — For God's sake let's go in to lunch, Elizabeth!

The curtain falls

ACT II

The scene is the same. It is afternoon of the second day following. Mrs. Shenstone, Porteous, Lady Kitty and Teddie Luton are playing bridge and not doing very well at it. Porteous is especially put out at Lady

Kitty's game, but she blithely ignores his cutting criticism. "Just because I don't play the same game as you do," she snaps at him, "you think I can't play." "I'm glad you acknowledge it's not the same game as I play," Porteous snaps back. "But why in God's name do you call it bridge?"

Clive Champion-Cheney adds his bit to Porteous' irritation by standing back of the players and commenting on the game. "I agree with Kitty," he agrees. "I hate people who play bridge as though they were at a funeral and knew their feet were getting wet."

The game does not exactly break up in one of those pleasant family rows, but the finish of the rubber finds everybody quite willing to stop. Porteous tries to go on with a game of patience, which is the Englishman's solitaire, but even this is denied him when Lady Kitty insists upon suggesting how it should be done. Finally he rounds on her so savagely that she is threatening tears, and he is forced to follow her into the garden as the official comforter.

Champion-Cheney, Elizabeth and Teddie Luton find themselves alone, and variously impressed with what they have seen. Elizabeth is sympathetic, Teddie a little embarrassed, Champion-Cheney amused, and a little saddened. Yet he knows Lady Kitty is a thorough humbug.

C-C.— My dear, her soul is as thickly rouged as her face. She hasn't an emotion that's sincere. She's tinsel. You think I'm a cruel, cynical old man. Why, when I think of what she was, if I didn't laugh at what she's become, I should cry.

ELIZABETH — How do you know she wouldn't be just the same now if she'd remained your wife? Do you think your influence would have had such a salutary effect on her?

C-C.— (*good-humoredly*). I like you when you're bitter and rather insolent.

ELIZABETH — D'you like me well enough to answer my question.

C-C.— She was only twenty-seven when she went away. She might have become anything. She might have become the woman you expected her to be. There are very few of us who are strong enough to make circumstances serve us. We are the creatures of our environment. She's a silly, worthless woman because she's led a silly, worthless life.

ELIZABETH — (*disturbed*). You're horrible today.

C-C.— I don't say it's I who could have prevented her from becoming this ridiculous caricature of a pretty woman grown old. But life could. Here she would have had the friends to fit her station, and a decent activity, and worthy interests. Ask her what her life has been all these years among divorced women and kept women and the men who consort with them. There is no more lamentable pursuit than a life of pleasure.

ELIZABETH — At all events she loved and she loved greatly. I have only pity and affection for her.

C-C.— And if she loved what d'you think she felt when she saw that she had ruined Hughie? Look at him. He was tight last night after dinner and tight the night before.

ELIZABETH — I know.

C-C.— And she took it as a matter of course. How long do you suppose he's been getting tight every night? Do you think he was like that thirty years ago? Can you imagine that that was a brilliant young man, whom everyone expected to be Prime Minister? Look at him now. A grumpy, sodden old fellow with false teeth.

ELIZABETH — You have false teeth, too.

C-C.— Yes, but damn it all, they fit. She's ruined him and she knows she's ruined him.

Elizabeth is a bit suspicious of Champion-Cheney, she admits when the latter has gone. She thinks it not at all unlikely that he has subtly been warning her to consider seriously the situation into which she is obviously drifting with Teddie. Teddie thinks so, too. But what can they do? Of course they must be perfectly practical about anything they decide upon. He is desperately in love with Elizabeth, Teddie confesses — but still he does not intend that she shall be emotionally swept off her feet.

TEDDIE — You see, I'm not at all romantic and that sort of thing. I'm just a common or garden business man. All this is so dreadfully serious and I think we ought to be sensible.

ELIZABETH — (*with a break in her voice*). You owl!

TEDDIE — No, Elizabeth, don't say things like that to me. I want you to consider all the *pros* and *cons* and my heart's thumping against my chest, and you know I love you, I love you, I love you!

ELIZABETH — (*in a sigh of passion*). Oh, my precious!

TEDDIE — (*impatiently, but with himself, rather than Elizabeth*). Don't be idiotic, Elizabeth. I'm not going to tell you that I can't live without you and a lot of muck like that. You know that you mean everything in the world to me. (*Almost giving it up as a bad job*) Oh, my God!

ELIZABETH — (*her voice faltering*). D'you think there's anything you can say to me that I don't know already?

TEDDIE — (*desperately*). But I haven't said a single thing I wanted to. I'm a business man and I want to put it all in a business way, if you understand what I mean.

ELIZABETH — (*smiling*). I don't believe you're a very good business man.

TEDDIE — (*sharply*). You don't know what you're talking about. I'm a first rate business man, but somehow this is different. (*Hopelessly*) I don't know why it won't go right.

ELIZABETH — What are we going to do about it?

TEDDIE — You see, it's not just because you're awfully pretty that I love you. I'd love you just as much if you were old and ugly. It's you I love, not what you look like. And it's not only love; love be blowed! It's that I *like* you so tremendously. I think you're such a ripping good sort. I just want to be with you. I feel so jolly and happy just to think you're there. I'm so awfully *fond* of you.

ELIZABETH — (*laughing through her tears*). I don't know if this is your idea of introducing a business proposition.

TEDDIE — Damn you, you won't let me.

ELIZABETH — Your said "Damn you!"

TEDDIE — I meant it.

ELIZABETH — Your voice sounded as if you meant it, you perfect duck!

TEDDIE — Really, Elizabeth, you're intolerable.

ELIZABETH — I'm doing nothing.

TEDDIE — Yes, you are, you're putting me off my blow. What I want to say is perfectly simple. I'm a very ordinary business man.

ELIZABETH — You've said that before.

TEDDIE — (*augrily*). Shut up. I haven't got a bob besides what I earn. I've got no position. I'm nothing. You're rich and you're a big pot and you've got everything that anyone can want. It's awful cheek my saying anything to you at all. But after all there's only one thing that really matters in the world, and that's love. I love you. Chuck all this, Elizabeth, and come to me.

ELIZABETH — Are you cross with me?

TEDDIE — Furious.

ELIZABETH — Darling!

TEDDIE — If you don't want me, tell me so at once and let me go out quickly.

ELIZABETH — Teddie, nothing in the world matters anything to me but you. I'll go wherever you take me. I love you.

TEDDIE — (*all to pieces*). Oh, my God!

ELIZABETH — Does it mean as much to you as that? Oh, Teddie!

TEDDIE — (*trying to control himself*). Don't be a fool, Elizabeth.

ELIZABETH — It's you're the fool. You're making me cry.

TEDDIE — You're so damned emotional.

ELIZABETH — Damned emotional, yourself. I'm sure you're a rotten business man.

TEDDIE — I don't care what you think. You've made me so awfully happy. I say, what a lark life's going to be!

They will get away as soon as possible, they agree. Meantime, Teddie feels that it would be dishonorable for him to stay on at the house. He had better go back to London immediately and wait until Elizabeth can join him.

For her part Elizabeth decides that she shall not stoop to the mid-Victorian habit of pinning a note on the pincushion. She will tell Arnold exactly what she intends to do and why. First she will go bathe her eyes, that he may not know she has been crying, and then she will tell him. . . .

Lord Porteous, wandering in from the garden, finds Lady Kitty and Champion-Cheney quite calmly discussing their life together, and the characteristics of their son. Does Arnold favor his mother or his father? The suggested intimacy does not please Lord Porteous, who is still grouchy. If Champion-Cheney had any sense of delicacy Porteous insists, he would have kept away from the house. Yet for the two days they have been there he has been constantly hanging around.

C-C.—My dear Hughie, I don't understand your attitude at all. If I'm willing to let bygones be bygones, why should you object?

PORTEOUS — Damn it all, they're not bygones.

C-C.— After all, I am the injured party.

PORTEOUS — How the devil are you the injured party?

C-C.— Well, you did run away with my wife, didn't you?

LADY CATHERINE — Now, don't let's go into ancient history. I can't see why we shouldn't all be friends.

PORTEOUS — I beg you not to interfere, Kitty.

LADY CATHERINE — I'm very fond of Clive.

PORTEOUS — You never cared two straws for Clive. You only say that to irritate me.

LADY CATHERINE — Not at all. I don't see why he shouldn't come and stay with us.

C-C.— I'd love to. I think Florence in spring-time is delightful. Have you central heating?

PORTEOUS — I never liked you; I don't like you now, and I never shall like you.

C-C.— How very unfortunate! because I liked you, I I like you now, and I shall continue to like you.

LADY CATHERINE — There's something very nice about you, Clive.

PORTEOUS — If you think that, why the devil did you leave him?

LADY CATHERINE — Are you going to reproach me because I loved you? How utterly, utterly, utterly detestable you are!

C-C.—Now, now, don't quarrel with one another.

LADY CATHERINE — It's all his fault. I'm the easiest person in the world to live with. But really he'd try the patience of a saint.

. . . .

C-C.— My poor Kitty, how you've suffered!

PORTEOUS — Really, Kitty, I'm sick of hearing of the sacrifices you made. I suppose you think I sacrificed nothing. I should have been Prime Minister by now if it hadn't been for you.

LADY CATHERINE — Nonsense!

PORTEOUS — What do you mean by that? Everyone said I should be Prime Minister. Shouldn't I have been Prime Minister, Clive?

C-C.— It was certainly the general expectation.

PORTEOUS — I was the most promising young man of my day. I was bound to get a seat in the Cabinet at the next election.

LADY CATHERINE — They'd have found you out just as I've found you out. I'm sick of hearing that I ruined your career. You never had a career to ruin. Prime Minister! You haven't the brain. You haven't the character.

In the heat of her anger Lady Kitty insists that she is through with Lord Porteous forever. If Champion-Cheney will take her back — " In the eyes of the Church I am still your wife," she suggests, tentatively. " The Church is so wise. It knows that in the end a woman always comes back to her first love. Clive, I am willing to return to you."

But Clive is not one to take advantage of her momentary vexation with Hughie. Besides he is quite content with his freedom. " For some years I was notoriously the prey of a secret sorrow," he admits. " But I found so many charming creatures who were anxious to console me that in the end it grew rather fatiguing. Out of regard to my health I ceased to frequent the drawing rooms of Mayfair."

Lady Kitty accepts the rejection of her proposal quite philosophically. " There is only one course open to me now," she sighs, and then to Champion-Cheney's eager " What is that?" she flashes her stunning smile and smartly replies: " To go and dress for dinner."

Elizabeth does not find telling her husband of her intention to leave him as easy as she had hoped it would be. Arnold simply cannot understand. If they have little in common, as she says, isn't the fault hers? Has she ever done anything to interest herself in his two most important interests — politics and home decoration? If, as she says, she does not love him, why did she marry him? No, her story isn't at all convincing. And having made her bed he very much fears she will have to lie on it. Which, to Elizabeth, is extremely foolish. Why should anyone lie on the bed he's made if he doesn't want to? There is always the floor. . . .

ARNOLD — Please don't talk to me as if I were a foolish child. You're my wife and you're going to remain my wife.

ELIZABETH — What sort of a life do you think we should lead? Do you think there'd be any more happiness for you than for me?

ARNOLD — But what is it precisely that you suggest?

ELIZABETH — Well, I want you to let me divorce you.

ARNOLD — (*astounded*). Me? Thank you very much. Are you under the impression that I'm going to sacrifice my career for a whim of yours?

ELIZABETH — How will it do that?

ARNOLD — My seat's wobbly enough as it is. Do you think I'd be able to hold it if I were in a divorce case? Even if it were a put-up job, as most divorce cases are nowadays, it would damn me.

ELIZABETH — It's rather hard on a woman to be divorced.

ARNOLD — (*with sudden suspicion*). What do you mean by that? Are you in love with someone?

ELIZABETH — Yes.

ARNOLD — Who?

ELIZABETH — Teddy Luton. (*Arnold is astonished for a moment and then bursts into a laugh.*)

ARNOLD — My poor child, how can you be so ridiculous? Why, he hasn't a bob. He's a perfectly commonplace young man. It's so absurd I can't even be angry with you.

ELIZABETH — I've fallen desperately in love with him, Arnold.

ARNOLD — Well, you'd better fall desperately out.

ELIZABETH — He wants to marry me.

ARNOLD — I dare say he does. He can go to hell.

ELIZABETH — It's no good talking like that.

ARNOLD — Is he your lover?

ELIZABETH — No, certainly not.

ARNOLD — It shows that he's a mean skunk to take advantage of my hospitality to make love to you.

ELIZABETH — He's never even kissed me.

ARNOLD — I'd try telling that to the horse marines if I were you.

ELIZABETH — It's because I wanted to do nothing shabby that I told you straight out how things were.

ARNOLD — How long have you been thinking of this?

ELIZABETH — I've been in love with Teddie ever since I knew him.

ARNOLD — And you never thought of me at all, I suppose.

ELIZABETH — Oh, yes, I did. I was miserable. But I can't help myself. I wish I loved you, but I don't.

ARNOLD — I recommend you to think very carefully before you do anything foolish.

ELIZABETH — I have thought very carefully

ARNOLD — By God! I don't know why I don't give you a sound hiding. I'm not sure it wouldn't be the best thing to bring you to your senses.

ELIZABETH — Oh, Arnold, don't talk like that.

ARNOLD — How do you expect me to take it? You come to me quite calmly and say: "I've had enough of you. We've been married three years and I think I'd like to marry someone else now. Shall I break up your home? What a bore for you! Do you mind my divorcing you? It'll smash up your career, will it? What a pity!"

Oh, no, my girl, I may be a fool, but I'm not a damned fool.

ELIZABETH — Teddie is leaving here by the first train tomorrow. I warn you that I mean to join him as soon as he can make the necessary arrangements.

. . . .

ARNOLD — Why did you insist on my mother coming here?

ELIZABETH — It seemed to me rather absurd to take up the attitude that I should be contaminated by her when . . .

ARNOLD — (*interrupting*). When you were proposing to do exactly the same thing. Well, now you've seen her, what do you think of her? Do you think it's been a success? Is that the sort of a woman a man would like his mother to be?

ELIZABETH—I've been ashamed. I've been so sorry. It all seemed dreadful and horrible. This morning I happened to notice a rose in the garden. It was all overblown and bedraggled. It looked like a painted old woman. And I remembered that I'd looked at it a day or two ago. It was lovely then, fresh and blooming and fragrant. It may be hideous now, but that doesn't take away from the beauty it had once. That was real!

ARNOLD — Poetry, by God! As if this were the moment for poetry!

Teddie is sent for and answers the summons quite calmly. Did Elizabeth send for him? No, thunders the exasperated Arnold, it was he who had sent — to learn when it would be convenient for Mr. Luton to leave the house.

TEDDIE — I was proposing to go tomorrow morning. But I can very well go at once if you like.

ARNOLD — I do like.

TEDDY—Very well. Is there anything else you wish to say to me?

ARNOLD — Do you think it was a very honorable thing to come down here and make love to my wife?

TEDDIE — No, I don't. I haven't been very happy about it. That's why I wanted to go away.

ARNOLD — Upon my word you're cool.

TEDDIE — I'm afraid it's no good saying I'm sorry and that sort of thing. You know what the situation is.

ARNOLD — Is it true that you want to marry Elizabeth?

TEDDIE — Yes. I should like to marry her as soon as ever I can.

ARNOLD — Have you thought of me at all? Has it struck you that you're destroying my home and breaking up my happiness?

TEDDIE — I don't see how there could be much happiness for you if Elizabeth doesn't care for you.

ARNOLD — Let me tell you that I refuse to have my home broken up by a twopenny halfpenny adventurer who takes advantage of a foolish woman. I refuse to allow myself to be divorced. I can't prevent my wife from going with you if she's determined to make a damned fool of herself, but this I tell you: nothing will induce me to divorce her.

ELIZABETH — Arnold, that would be monstrous.

TEDDIE — We could force you.

ARNOLD — How?

TEDDIE — If we went away together openly you'd have to bring an action.

ARNOLD — Twenty-four hours after you leave this house I shall go down to Brighton with a chorus girl. And neither you nor I will be able to get a divorce. We've had enough divorces in our family. And now get out, get out, get out! (*Teddie looks uncertainly at Elizabeth.*)

ELIZABETH — (*with a little smile*). Don't bother about me. I shall be all right.

ARNOLD — Get out! Get out!

The curtain falls

ACT III

In the living room that evening Clive Champion-Cheney, after having given his son Arnold the benefit of his superior wisdom in the art of handling a difficult situation — particularly a difficult situation in which a woman is concerned — undertakes to apply a sample of his carefully studied diplomacy to the case of Elizabeth and young Luton. He brings out the family album.

C-C.— I thought it might amuse you to see what pretty women looked like five-and-thirty years ago. That was the day of beautiful women.

ELIZABETH — Do you think they were more beautiful then than they are now?

C-C.— Oh, much. Now you see lots of pretty things, but very few beautiful women.

ELIZABETH — (*looking at the album*). Aren't their clothes funny?

C-C.— (*pointing to a photograph*). That's Mrs. Langtry.

ELIZABETH — She has a lovely nose.

C-C.— She was the most wonderful thing you ever saw. Dowagers used to jump on chairs in order to get a good look at her when she came into a drawing-room. I was riding with her once, and we had to have the gates of the livery stable closed when she was getting on her horse because the crowd was so great.

ELIZABETH — And who's that?

C-C.— Lady Lonsdale. That's Lady Dudley.

ELIZABETH — This is an actress, isn't it?

C-C.— It is indeed. Ellen Terry. By George! how I loved that woman!

ELIZABETH — (*with a smile*). Dear Ellen Terry.

C-C.—That's Bobs. I never saw a smarter man in my life. And Oliver Montagu. Henry Manners with his eye-glass.

ELIZABETH — Nice looking, isn't he? And this?

C-C.— That's Mary Anderson. I wish you could have seen her in "A Winter's Tale." Her beauty just took your breath away. . . .

. . . .

ELIZABETH — Oh, what a lovely little thing! Who on earth is that?

C-C.— That?

ELIZABETH — She looks so fragile, like a piece of exquisite china, with all those furs on and her face up against her muff, and the snow falling.

C-C.— Yes, there was quite a rage at that time for being taken in an artificial snowstorm.

ELIZABETH — What a sweet smile, so roguish and frank, and debonair! Oh, I wish I looked like that! Do tell me who it is!

C-C.—Don't you know?

ELIZABETH — No.

C-C.— Why — it's Kitty.

ELIZABETH — Lady Kitty! (*To Lady Kitty*) Oh, my dear, do look! It's too ravishing. (*She takes the album over to her impulsively*) Why didn't you tell me you looked like that? Everybody must have been in love with you.

"Lady Kitty takes the album and looks at it. Then she lets it slip from her hands and covers her face with her hands. She is crying." Elizabeth, unhappy in realizing that she is responsible for Lady Kitty's embarrassment, discreetly drags Champion-Cheney out onto the terrace with her. "Did you do that on purpose?" she demands of him, in a hoarse whisper, as they leave the room.

Lord Porteous is also visibly affected by the sight of Lady Kitty in tears and tries awkwardly to comfort her. "I'm afraid I was very rude to you before dinner, Kitty." he ventures, laying his hand on her shoulder. "It doesn't matter," she replies, taking the comforting hand in hers; "I'm sure I was very exasperating."

Gradually Lady Kitty's spirits are restored. It's hateful to grow old — but it can't be helped. She bravely looks at the picture again. "The fact is," she concludes, "if your bones are good, age doesn't really matter. You'll always be beautiful." A moment later, when Porteous confesses to her that his most recent bursts of ill-temper have been due to the constant hanging around of Champion-Cheney, she is happy. So long as "Hughie" is even a little jealous of her, life is worth living.

They are both greatly cheered by the time Champion-Cheney returns and Porteous is ready to propose another try at bridge, if they can find a fourth. But Teddie Luton has disappeared. He's gone, Champion-Cheney tells them, because he is in love with Elizabeth and she with him. And he thinks Lady Kitty should do all that she can to dissuade Elizabeth from making the same mistake that she has made. Lady Kitty is willing, even eager to do so, and finds a way a moment later to be alone with Elizabeth.

ELIZABETH—I don't expect you to have much sympathy for me. Arnold is your son.

LADY KITTY — So pitifully little.

ELIZABETH — I'm not suited for this sort of existence. Arnold wants me to take what he calls my place in society. Oh, I get so bored with those parties in London. All those middle-aged painted women, in beautiful clothes, lolloping round ball-rooms with rather old young men. And the endless luncheons with their gossip about so-and-so's love affairs.

LADY KITTY — Are you very much in love with Mr. Luton?

ELIZABETH — I love him with all my heart.

LADY KITTY — And he?

ELIZABETH — He's never cared for anyone else but me. He never will.

LADY KITTY — Will Arnold let you divorce him.

ELIZABETH—No, he won't hear of it. He refuses even to divorce me.

LADY KITTY—Why?

ELIZABETH — He thinks a scandal will revive all the old gossip.

LADY KITTY — Oh, my poor child!

ELIZABETH — It can't be helped. I'm quite willing to accept the consequences.

LADY KITTY — You don't know what it is to have a man tied to you only by his honor. When married people don't get on they can separate, but if they're not married it's impossible. It's a tie that only death can sever.

ELIZABETH — If Teddie stopped caring for me I shouldn't want him to stay with me for five minutes.

LADY KITTY — One says that when one's sure of a man's love, but when one isn't any more — oh, it's so different. In those circumstances one's got to keep a man's love. It's the only thing one has.

ELIZABETH — I'm a human being. I can stand on my own feet.

LADY KITTY — Have you any money of your own?

ELIZABETH — None.

LADY KITTY — Then how can you stand on your own feet? You think I'm a silly, frivolous woman, but I've learned something in a bitter school. They can make what laws they like, they can give us the suffrage, but when you come down to bedrock it's the man who pays the piper who calls the tune. Woman will only be the equal of man when she earns her living in the same way that he does.

ELIZABETH — (*smiling*). It sounds rather funny to hear you talk like that.

LADY KITTY — A cook who marries a butler can snap

her fingers in his face because she can earn just as much as he can. But a woman in your position and a woman in mine will always be dependent on the men who keep them.

. . . .

LADY KITTY — Look at me, Elizabeth, and look at Hughie. Do you think it's been a success? If I had my time over again do you think I'd do it over again? Do you think he would?

ELIZABETH — You see, you don't know how much I love Teddie.

LADY KITTY — And do you think I didn't love Hughie? Do you think he didn't love me?

ELIZABETH — I'm sure he did.

LADY KITTY — Oh, of course in the beginning it was heavenly. We felt so brave and adventurous and we were so much in love. The first two years were wonderful. People cut me, you know, but I didn't mind. I thought love was everything. It *is* uncomfortable when you come upon an old friend and go towards her eagerly, so glad to see her, and are met with an icy stare.

ELIZABETH — Do you think friends like that are worth having?

LADY KITTY — Perhaps they're not very sure of themselves. Perhaps they're honestly shocked. It's a test one had better not put one's friends to if one can help it. It's rather bitter to find how few one has.

ELIZABETH — But one has some.

LADY KITTY — Yes, they ask you to come and see them when they're quite certain no one will be there who might object to meeting you. Or else they say to you: "My dear, you know I'm devoted to you, and I wouldn't mind at all, but my girl's growing up — I'm sure you understand; you won't think it unkind of me if I don't ask you to the house?"

. . . .

LADY KITTY — Oh, my dear, what a blessed institution

marriage is — for women, and what fools they are to meddle with it! The Church is so wise to take its stand on the indi — indi —

ELIZABETH — Solu —

LADY KITTY — Bility of marriage. Believe me, it's no joke when you have to rely on yourself to keep a man.

There is also the tragedy of age. Lady Kitty could never afford to grow old. Her hair, prematurely white, must be kept a golden copper shade at any cost. And there were the other women who interested Hughie who were forever trying to get him away from her. Many a night she had tossed sleeplessly knowing or suspecting where Porteous went when he said he was going to play cards at the club. "Of course it wasn't as if there weren't plenty of men only too anxious to console me," she admits. "Men have always been attracted by me, you know." Elizabeth can quite understand that.

LADY KITTY — But I had my self-respect to think of. I felt that whatever Hughie did I would do nothing that I should regret.

ELIZABETH — You must be very glad now.

LADY KITTY — Oh, yes. Notwithstanding all my temptations I've been absolutely faithful to Hughie in spirit.

ELIZABETH — I don't think I quite understand what you mean.

LADY KITTY — Well, there was a poor Italian boy, young Count Castel Giovanni, who was so desperately in love with me that his mother begged me not to be too cruel. She was afraid he would go into a consumption. What could I do? And then, oh, years later, there was Antonio Melita. He said he'd shoot himself unless I — well, you understand, I couldn't let the poor boy shoot himself.

ELIZABETH — D'you think he really would have shot himself?

LADY KITTY — Oh, one never knows, you know. Those Italians are so passionate. He was really rather a lamb. He had such beautiful eyes. (*Elizabeth looks at her for a long time and a certain horror seizes her of this dissolute, painted, old woman.*)

ELIZABETH — (*hoarsely*). Oh, but I think that's — dreadful.

LADY KITTY — Are you shocked? One sacrifices one's life for love and then one finds that love doesn't last. The tragedy of love isn't death or separation. One gets over them. The tragedy of love is indifference.

Now Arnold has come for a sort of last talk with Elizabeth, with Champion-Cheney's advice as to what to do plainly at the back of his head. He is sorry for the attitude he had taken at first and begs Elizabeth to forgive him. If she is quite determined to leave him he will do nothing to prevent her. He would, however, like her to know how much he really has loved her, even though he was absurd enough to think that she would take his great love for granted.

ARNOLD — It wasn't till today when you talked of leaving me that I realized how desperately in love with you I was.

ELIZABETH — After three years?

ARNOLD — I'm so proud of you. I admire you so much. When I see you at a party, so fresh and lovely, and everybody wondering at you, I have a sort of little thrill because you're mine, and afterwards I shall take you home.

ELIZABETH — Oh, Arnold, you're exaggerating.

ARNOLD — I can't imagine this house without you. Life seems on a sudden all empty and meaningless. Oh, Elizabeth, don't you love me at all?

ELIZABETH — It's much better to be honest. No.

ARNOLD — Doesn't my love mean anything to you?

ELIZABETH — I'm very grateful to you. I'm sorry to cause you pain. What would be the good of my staying with you when I should be wretched all the time?

ARNOLD — Do you love that man as much as all that? Does my unhappiness mean nothing to you?

ELIZABETH — Of course it does. It breaks my heart. You see, I never knew I meant so much to you. I'm so touched. And I'm so sorry, Arnold, really sorry. But I can't help myself.

ARNOLD — Poor child, it's cruel of me to torture you.

ELIZABETH — Oh, Arnold, believe me, I have tried to make the best of it. I've tried to love you, but I can't. After all, one either loves or one doesn't. Trying is no help. And now I'm at the end of my tether. I can't help the consequences — I must do what my whole self yearns for.

Very well, then, agrees Arnold, let him do what he can to make the change easy for her. He will make it possible for her to divorce him within, say, six months, and, seeing that Teddie Luton has comparatively little money, he (Arnold) will make her an allowance of two thousand pounds a year. She protests. His sudden burst of generosity is making her perfectly miserable. "But it's the only way I have of showing you how deep and passionate and sincere my love for you is," he insists. Then he embarrassedly kisses her on the forehead and says good night, leaving Elizabeth most unhappy.

Down by the summer house Teddie Luton is waiting to have a talk with Elizabeth before going away. When Lady Kitty and Lord Porteous come in Elizabeth sends Lord Porteous to fetch him. She has suddenly come to realize that life is simply rotten, when it is impossible to be happy oneself without making other people unhappy.

When Teddie comes Elizabeth tells him that she has changed her mind. She can't go away with him. She has decided that she does not love him enough. But he will have none of that kind of an explanation. But he walks boldly over to her, takes her hands and forces her to sit beside him. He is stroking her hands when she draws them away.

ELIZABETH — No, don't do that. Teddie, it wasn't true when I said I didn't love you. Of course, I love you. But Arnold loves me, too. I didn't know how much.

TEDDIE — What has he been saying to you?

ELIZABETH — He's been very good to me, and so kind. I didn't know he could be so kind. He offered to let me divorce him.

TEDDIE — That's very decent of him.

ELIZABETH — But don't you see, it ties my hands. How can I accept such a sacrifice? I should never forgive myself if I profited by his generosity.

. . . .

ELIZABETH — I wonder if you'd be capable of acting like that.

TEDDIE — Acting like what?

ELIZABETH — What would you do if I were married to you and came and told you I loved somebody else and wanted to leave you?

TEDDIE — You have very pretty blue eyes, Elizabeth. I'd black first one and then the other. And after that we'd see.

ELIZABETH — You damned brute!

TEDDIE — I've often thought I wasn't quite a gentleman. Had it ever struck you? (*They look at one another for a while.*)

ELIZABETH — You know, you are taking an unfair advantage of me. I feel as if I came to you quite unsuspectingly and when I wasn't looking you kicked me on the shins.

TEDDIE — Don't you think we'd get on rather well, together?

PORTEOUS — Elizabeth's a fool if she doesn't stick to her husband. It's bad enough for the man, but for the woman — it's damnable. I hold no brief for Arnold. He plays bridge like a fool. Saving your presence, Kitty, I think he's a prig.

LADY KITTY — Poor dear, his father was at his age. I dare say he'll grow out of it.

PORTEOUS — But you stick to him, Elizabeth, you stick to him. Man is a gregarious animal. We're members of a herd. If we break the herd's laws we suffer for it. And we suffer damnably.

LADY KITTY — Oh, Elizabeth, my dear child, don't go. It's not worth it. It's not worth it. I tell you that, and I've sacrificed everything to love.

ELIZABETH — I'm afraid.

TEDDIE — (*in a whisper*). Elizabeth.

ELIZABETH — I can't face it. It's asking too much of me. Let's say good-bye to one another, Teddie. It's the only thing to do. And have pity on me. I'm giving up all my hope of happiness. (*Teddie goes up to her and looks into her eyes.*)

TEDDIE — But I wasn't offering you happiness. I don't think my sort of love tends to happiness. I'm jealous. I'm not a very easy man to get on with. I'm often out of temper and irritable. I should be fed to the teeth with you sometimes, and so would you be with me. I dare say we'd fight like cat and dog, and sometimes we'd hate each other. Often you'd be wretched and bored stiff and lonely, and often you'd be frightfully homesick, and then you'd regret all you'd lost. Stupid women would be rude to you because we'd run away together. And some of them would cut you. I don't offer you peace and quietness. I offer you unrest and anxiety. I don't offer you happiness. I offer you love.

ELIZABETH — (*stretching out her arms*). You hateful creature, I absolutely adore you!

They are in each other's arms now. "Of course, the moment he said he'd give her a black eye, I knew it was finished," Lady Kitty observes wisely as she turns away.

Lord Porteous is convinced that they are a couple of damned fools, but he offers them his car to get away with, if they decide to make a bolt for it right then. That, it appears, had been Teddie's plan from the first. He had taken the precaution to get the car out of the garage and leave it standing by the garden hedge.

PORTEOUS — Do you mean to say that you were going to steal my car?

TEDDIE — Not exactly. I was only going to bolshevize it, so to speak.

PORTEOUS — I'm speechless. I'm absolutely speechless.

TEDDIE — Hang it all, I couldn't carry Elizabeth all the way to London. She's so damned plump.

ELIZABETH — You dirty dog!

PORTEOUS — (*spluttering*). Well, well, well! (*Helplessly*) I like him, Kitty, it's no good pretending I don't. I like him.

TEDDIE — The moon's shining, Elizabeth. We'll drive all through the night.

PORTEOUS — They'd better go to San Michele. I'll wire to have it got ready for them.

LADY KITTY — That's where we went when Hughie and I — (*Falteringly*) Oh, you dear things, how I envy you!

PORTEOUS — (*mopping his eyes*). Now don't cry, Kitty. Confound you, don't cry.

TEDDIE — Come, darling.

ELIZABETH — But I can't go like this!

TEDDIE — Nonsense. Lady Kitty will lend you her cloak. Won't you?

LADY KITTY — (*taking it off*). You're capable of tearing it off my back if I don't.

TEDDIE — (*putting the cloak on Elizabeth*). And we'll buy you a tooth-brush in London in the morning.

LADY KITTY — She must write a note for Arnold. I'll put it on her pincushion.

TEDDIE — Pincushion be blowed! Come, darling. We'll drive through the dawn and through the sunrise.

And now they are off on their way to London with Lady Kitty and Lord Porteous waving their adieux excitedly, but a little sadly. And yet, as Lord Porteous says, it may be that in life it doesn't matter so much what you do as what you are. "No one can learn by the experience of another because no circumstances are quite the same. If we made rather a hash of things, perhaps it was because we were rather trivial people. You can do anything in this world if you're prepared to take the consequences, and consequences depend upon character."

Clive Champion-Cheney and Arnold enter the room, ignorant of all that has occurred. So far as they are aware, Elizabeth is in her room, bitterly, sobbingly, repentant. And they are both sure that Arnold's way with Elizabeth has resulted in her complete change of attitude.

C-C.— I told Arnold exactly what to do and he's done it. What makes a prison? Why, bars and bolts. Remove them and a prisoner won't want to escape. Clever, I flatter myself.

PORTEOUS — You're always that, Clive, but at the moment you're obscure.

C-C.— I told Arnold to go to Elizabeth and tell her she could have her freedom. I told him to sacrifice himself all along the line. I know what women are. The moment every obstacle was removed to her marriage with Teddie Luton, half the allurement was gone.

LADY KITTY — Arnold did that?

C-C.— He followed my instructions to the letter. I've just seen him. She's shaken. I'm willing to bet five hundred pounds to a penny that she won't bolt. A downy old bird, eh? Downy's the word! Downy!

"He begins to laugh. They laugh, too. Presently they are all three in fits of laughter."

The curtain falls

"THE NEST"

A Drama in Four Acts

By Paul Geraldy

(English translation by Grace George)

GRACE GEORGE is beginning to turn her play-hunting disappointments to account. If she cannot find suitable parts for herself she can at least find them for others. And also help to produce the plays containing them.

One such she discovered in Paul Geraldy's "Les Noces D'Argent," ("Silver Weddings") which she renamed "The Nest." Impressed by the human and truthful quality of its drama she arranged immediately for the American rights to the play and set about its translation. When it was ready for production she superintended the engaging of the cast and later supervised the rehearsals. Miss George, of course, has always had a hand in the staging of her own plays, but she never before has taken so complete charge of a production as she did of this one.

"The Nest" was presented at the Forty-Eighth Street Theatre, February 1, 1922. Following an enthusiastic press review, it grew steadily in favor, particularly with matinée audiences, and though it never could fairly be listed with the popular dramatic successes of the season, it was invariably included when the worth-while plays of recent years were under discussion.

The opening act of "The Nest" quite abruptly breaks in upon the confusion following the wedding of Suzanne Hamelin to Henri. Henri, being merely a husband and more or less incidental to the drama, is not given a surname. The ceremony has been held at a neighboring chapel, and the wedding party is about to return to the Hamelin apartment for the home reception.

The scene is Suzanne's room. It is in a state of great disorder. "Clothing, lingerie, hats, parcels, open boxes, etc., are spread over the little brass bed, the chairs, the carpet, everywhere. A profusion of flowers, baskets of white roses and lilacs, trunks and bags — "

Anna, the maid, is trying to set the room in order against the return of the wedding party. Porters are bringing in more flowers than there is room for. The musicians are reported arrived, with no place to go. Eveline Dore, called Marraine by the family, is superintending the preparations for the reception of the guests. She is Mme. Hamelin's best friend, and a sort of older chum of the children and an attractive divorcee of thirty-three. . . . Now the bridesmaid, Jeanne, and Max Hamelin, Suzanne's brother and her groom's best man, have arrived to add to the confusion.

Mme. Hamelin, fearful lest everything will not go as it should, finds time between worries to lament the fact that she is losing her daughter and that at last she is a mother-in-law. Terrible thought! Probably soon she will be losing her son, too. But Max reassures her. Now that Suzanne is gone he will be all the more attentive. They will have ever so many jolly times together.

Max, however, is a bit uncertain. Approaching his twentieth year, he is beginning to rebel at being always treated as a child at home and is eager to be accepted as a man. He objects particularly to Marraine's continued acceptance of him as her "godson." And he dislikes her teasing him whenever she catches him flirting with the younger girls. He is rather fond of his pretty godmother, and has just discovered that she is still young — and beautiful. Under the influence of the wedding festivities, in fact, he is especially attentive to Marraine and she does not know exactly what to do with him.

She does not want Max to make love to her, and yet she finds his spirits infectious and his pleading not displeasing.

MARRAINE — Let's open the windows. There — one can see the chestnut trees in blossom along the avenue. How sweet! Spring has come — (*She leans against the window*) They are going on a wonderful trip, that young couple — oh, the Italian spring! Bomodossola and the descent to the lakes! The aconites and the wild carnations and Pallanza and the villas — oh! Things have changed since I was there and yet — just see that line of automobiles in front of your door. How *smart* you look!

MAX — Marraine, I feel so — so bored.

MARRAINE — Poor dear! What is the matter with you, today?

MAX — I want to go away.

MARRAINE — Where?

MAX — I don't know. I feel lonely here.

MARRAINE — I'm flattered. It must be the spring. How warm it is. (*There is a knock on the door*) That must be my lemonade. (*Max opens the door and Leontine enters on a wave of music.*)

LEONTINE — There is no more lemonade, Madame. I brought a bottle of champagne.

MARRAINE — Thanks. Only you should have brought some water at the same time.

LEONTINE — If Madame wishes —

MARRAINE — Don't bother now. This will do. Thanks. (*Leontine leaves and Max serves the champagne*) Look out for my dress. (*She drinks*) Ah! I was so thirsty. That's good.

MAX — Is it cool?

MARRAINE — It's like a shower — (*She holds her glass out for more*) That's enough. So the gentleman isn't happy. What a pity! Come, tell me all about it.

MARRAINE — Why, upon my word, he has real tears in his eyes. You're not going to cry, I hope. (*He bursts into tears*) And he says he's a man. You big baby — stop — come here! Shall I dry your tears? If anyone came in now, what would they think? Kiss me, stupid, and tell me what's the matter. How can I guess?

MAX — Marraine —

MARRAINE — What is it? What have they done to you? Tell me —

MAX — Nothing. I don't know —

MARRAINE — Then why this sudden change of mood? A little while ago you were quite cheerful.

MAX — My life is so empty.

MARRAINE — Really? Get up. You don't know what you are saying. Go and look for your sister. That will calm you.

MAX — I'm going.

MARRAINE — Wait, you can't go downstairs with those red eyes. Come here. Look at me. Don't look at me like that. What? You're going to cry again?

MAX — (*his head on Marraine's knee*). Oh, if you only knew —

MARRAINE — What?

MAX — Oh, everything — nothing — I wish —

MARRAINE — What do you wish?

MAX — My life is so monotonous. Nothing happens — I wish — that something would happen to me. That somebody would — that they wouldn't always leave me alone. Suzanne is all they ever think of. I am all alone at home, all alone in the streets. I need someone to talk to, to love me. Oh, Marraine, if you knew —

MARRAINE — (*she takes him on her knees*). What does this mean? Kiss me — how big he is. I wish I had a big son like you!

MAX — (*his arms around her neck*). Marraine!

MARRAINE — Does he want to be petted like a little

baby? Don't hold me so tight! You'll suffocate me! Do you hear me?

Max hears, but he is not to be restrained until knocking at the door apprises them that some one is coming. Then, considerably flustered, they make ready to receive the bride.

Suzanne is not excited. Like most brides, she is the calmest person at her wedding, which distresses Jeanne, the bridesmaid, who has been given the exalted privilege of helping her change to her traveling frock.

JEANNE — (*disappointed and almost tearful*). You are not what I expected you'd be.

SUZANNE — But, my dear, that's because I'm in a hurry. Don't think that I'm indifferent. It's sweet of you to be with me and to help me. I'm very grateful for that.

JEANNE — It isn't that. You don't understand.

SUZANNE — (*looking at her wrist watch*). Well, explain, darling!

JEANNE — It's because you look as if everything that is happening to you is quite usual, quite ordinary. Yes, you talk, you walk, you dress — you act like every day. I seem to be the only one who is moved. Even your parents look as if nothing important were happening. I watched your father a little while ago. He talked. Oh, if you only knew. (*She takes Suzanne's hand and places it against her breast*) There, feel.

SUZANNE — That's because you have nothing else to do but think of me. I've had so much excitement this week. In a few days, when we are settled somewhere, I will arrange my thoughts in order. For the present, do you want me to enumerate my impressions? I am happy, I have a headache, I'm afraid we shall miss our train, I wish it were all over!

. . . .

SUZANNE — You mustn't cry, silly. Anyone would say that you are the bride. . . . Now, let them come! These ceremonies are stupid, aren't they? It's like our first communion. You expect to return transfigured and then, after you reach home, a little tired, a little sad, you realize that life is always life. . . . I remember mother scolded because I soiled my white shoes by putting one foot on top of the other —

JEANNE — And yet, it's a little different.

SUZANNE — (*not convinced*). Do you know what mother said to me just now? "Suzanne, stand up straight and watch where you put your feet." (*They laugh and kiss each other*) Do you see all those parcels? They are presents we haven't had time to open.

JEANNE — Oh!

SUZANNE — I got some beautiful things and some horrors! Paper knives and paper weights. Would you believe it? I received nine umbrellas.

JEANNE — Just what did your godmother give you?

SUZANNE — Marraine? She said, "My darling, buy whatever you want," and she gave me a check. There, I'm ready now. I hope Henri will come soon. How heavy my satchel is. Just lift it.

JEANNE — (*lifting it*). Oh!

SUZANNE — If you knew what's inside. Six handkerchiefs, a guidebook, my toilet case, a notebook, films for my kodak, my address-book, two pairs of gloves, a box of candy, my purse and a novel by Anatole France, a veil and a bottle of perfume.

The moment of the final partings has arrived, with everybody trying to be a bit braver than anybody else. There are to be no tears, and everything must be cheerful. Pitifully Mme. Hamelin tries to appear as gay as the others, but it is hard for her.

SUZANNE — My little mamma.

MME. HAMELIN — Don't forget to wear your coat. I know Italy. The nights are cool.

SUZANNE — Yes, Mamma.

MME. HAMELIN—Your gray suit is warm, wear that. Your shoes don't hurt you? They're comfortable?

SUZANNE — Very.

MME. HAMELIN — I gave Henri the check for the large trunk. Leontine took it to the station this morning. Remind him of it.

SUZANNE — Yes, Mamma, dear.

MME. HAMELIN — Leontine could begin to take down the bags. I hope she doesn't forget anything. What about the key to your own bags?

SUZANNE — I have it.

LEONTINE — (*entering*). Here is M. Henri, Madame. He says you've just time enough.

MME. HAMELIN — Let's go.

MARRAINE — You must call her " Madame " from now on, Leontine.

SUZANNE — I haven't got my gloves.

MAX—The car is here!

SUZANNE — My *gloves!* Where are my *gloves?*

MARRAINE — Quick! Quick! Where are her gloves?

MME. HAMELIN — Her gloves? They *were* there. Didn't you take them?

SUZANNE — I *had them* a minute ago.

MARRAINE — Then they can't be far away.

MME. HAMELIN — She can't leave without gloves!

MAX — Here, are these the ones?

SUZANNE — Yes! Yes! There they are! Good-bye!

And in the midst of the final embraces Henri, the groom, rushes in and drags the bride away. A second later the slamming of the outer door sends a sort of shiver through the house. With an effort the elder Hamelins pull themselves together.

MME. HAMELIN — Well, it's all over. They're gone. They didn't even see us.

MARRAINE — (*with a vague gesture*). Yes, that's life.

MME. HAMELIN — Isn't Max here?

MARRAINE — He's gone out to get me a cab.

MME. HAMELIN — What? You're dining with us. It was understood.

MARRAINE — You must excuse me. I have a terrible headache. I'd rather not. Good-bye, you. (*Into M. Hamelin's ear*) She's coming back — be sensible!

M. HAMELIN — (*softly*). Good-bye, Eveline.

MARRAINE — Au revoir, Marie. I'll see you tomorrow.

. . . .

MME. HAMELIN — Well? (*She kisses her husband*) Come, let's be brave.

M. HAMELIN — Brave? But I'm all right.

MME. HAMELIN — I didn't see the Didiers, did you?

M. HAMELIN — (*whose thoughts are elsewhere*). The Didiers?

MME. HAMELIN — They never came. Why doesn't Max come up? (*She pauses*) You haven't said a word about my dress.

M. HAMELIN — It's beautiful.

MME. HAMELIN — Well, you might look at me.

M. HAMELIN — I tell you it's a beautiful dress.

MME. HAMELIN — And the belt?

M. HAMELIN — The belt's all right.

MME. HAMELIN — It doesn't make me look fat?

M. HAMELIN — I think it's perfect.

MME. HAMELIN — I wonder — (*Looking around*) I think I'll give Max this room. He'll like it better than his own. He never gets any sun there, poor boy.

M. HAMELIN — Yes, that's a good idea. In ten minutes they'll be on their way.

MME. HAMELIN — How quiet it is now, after all that noise. (*After a pause she approaches him*) Do you love me?

M. Hamelin — No! (*He hugs her.*)

Mme. Hamelin — (*freeing herself*). I wonder — why — that boy — doesn't — come — back!

The curtain falls

ACT II

It is some weeks later, in the dining room of the Hamelin's home. Monsieur and Mme. Hamelin are at luncheon — a meal that neither has much taste for. The big dining room is lonely without the children.

There have been a letter or two from the bride and groom. Short, formal letters. And several telegrams. They are in Italy now; the weather is beautiful; they are going on to Switzerland; the scenery is wonderful; they are well; they do not know when they will be home! There is not much in such news to cheer the father and mother.

Max is not home for lunch. In fact he has not been home for lunch for several days. He seems strangely preoccupied these last weeks. His mother is worried. After she has left the room Max sneaks in. He has no excuses to make to his father, except that he has been busy. And he would like to have an advance on his allowance. In view of the fact that he has just had his allowance the week before and had previously managed to make it do, M. Hamelin is a little surprised and not at all pleased. It is father's opinion that if Max would work more and spend less he would be a much more satisfactory son. However, he gives him the money and Max is gone again, without so much as inquiring about his mother.

Mme. Hamelin — He didn't come and kiss me, or say a word to me. It looks as if he did everything to avoid me. You see what we've come to, my son and I. He doesn't even say good morning to me now. What have I done to him?

M. HAMELIN — I scolded him severely for not coming home to lunch and I suppose he wanted to escape another lecture.

MME. HAMELIN — (*with tears in her eyes*). I don't know what's the matter with him lately.

M. HAMELIN — We'll soon find out.

MME. HAMELIN — He's never here. Doesn't it seem strange to you, his being out all the time?

M. HAMELIN — He has to go to his classes.

MME. HAMELIN — His classes are in the morning. It's impossible to get him up in the morning. He stays in bed till eleven. It's in the afternoon and evening that he goes out. When does he study? He has an examination in two months.

M. HAMELIN — Two months is time enough if he puts his mind to it.

MME. HAMELIN — And isn't it funny he's always in need of money.

M. HAMELIN — Did he ask *you* for money?

MME. HAMELIN — Fifty francs, yesterday.

M. HAMELIN — You didn't give it to him?

MME. HAMELIN — Yes.

M. HAMELIN — You are right; we've got to keep an eye on that young man.

MME. HAMELIN — He never asks you for any money, does he?

M. HAMELIN — No. No, never!

MME. HAMELIN — He doesn't dare.

Marraine stops in. She is looking especially pretty and cheerful these days, and has taken to wearing such gay colors. She is like a girl of twenty again. The Hamelin's compliments are a little trying to Marraine. She would change the subject if she could. She finds them both looking a little seedy, she thinks. Especially

M. Hamelin. Probably they worry too much about being left alone. They must remember that their children are grown and must live their own lives now. Suzanne is a married woman, and Max — well, Max is much older than they suspect. He should have more liberty. If he is moody and preoccupied, if he spends less of his time at home and seems less interested in family affairs than formerly, it is because they expect too much of him. "Perhaps," she says to Mme. Hamelin, "you're a little to blame."

MME. HAMELIN — I? How?

MARRAINE — He's so sensitive. You don't realize it, but you're very arbitrary sometimes.

MME. HAMELIN — I?

MARRAINE — Yes. He is sensitive and proud. You hurt him without meaning to by your watchfulness and questioning.

MME. HAMELIN — Nonsense! He hasn't got a better friend than I. You know very well that since he was born, I have denied myself parties, visits, everything that might take me away from him. I've been such a good mother that I doubt if I have been a good wife. It's true, I have neglected my husband for this child. I myself, supervised all his studies. I learned to read Greek in order to hear his lessons—

MARRAINE — He'd love you more if you were less strict — less exacting about his duties.

MME. HAMELIN — You are joking.

MARRAINE — He has spoken to me about it several times.

MME. HAMELIN — Ah!

MARRAINE — You know that we are — very friendly. He tells me almost everything.

MME. HAMELIN — Yes.

MARRAINE — Funny, you reproach each other with exactly the same things.

MME. HAMELIN — What?

MARRAINE — Lack of frankness — of understanding.

MME. HAMELIN — He has impudence.

MARRAINE — I, myself — I've noticed that you hurt him sometimes. You answer him abruptly — you snub him.

MME. HAMELIN — I don't see how you —

MARRAINE — You don't take him seriously enough. You still think of him as a little boy who used to steal the jam. That time has passed. Max has developed very much lately, physically and mentally. It's remarkable!

MME. HAMELIN — Possibly. But if you knew what a child he still is in many ways.

MARRAINE — Do you think so? At any rate he is exceptionally intelligent.

MME. HAMELIN — Naturally I agree with you there.

MARRAINE — You should give him more liberty. I believe things will never be right between you unless you meet him halfway. It is always difficult for members of the same family to understand each other.

MME. HAMELIN — I can't let him go on as he is — going out whenever he wishes, coming home at all sorts of impossible hours. At the Law School he has friends that I know nothing about. If they should tempt him — if he should become attached to —

MARRAINE — One of those dreadful creatures, eh? (*She laughs*) My poor Marie, you hurt me. Has motherhood made you as old as that? Well, I'm glad I'm not a mother.

MME. HAMELIN — If it should happen though?

MARRAINE — What?

MME. HAMELIN — Why, that he should have an — affair?

MARRAINE — Well, and what of it?

MME. HAMELIN — Think how young he is.

MARRAINE — He is twenty.

MME. HAMELIN — Not yet. Not until July.

MARRAINE — You make me laugh. Max is a man. You might as well make up your mind to that.

MME. HAMELIN — Max is a child.

MARRAINE — He is a man —

The return of M. Hamelin interrupts them. He brings the morning mail, and leaves them. In the mail there is a letter for Max. It is addressed in a woman's handwriting — the same handwriting that his mother has noticed on several of his letters of late. Even Marraine is a little excited at this. So excited, in fact, that she insists the letter be opened. Surely a mother has a right to know with what women her son is corresponding! Before Mme. Hamelin can stop her she has torn open the letter. A photograph falls out. Of the two women Marraine is much more stunned by the revelations of that letter than Max's mother.

MARRAINE — It isn't possible. It can't be —

MME. HAMELIN — Let me see. No — don't show it to me.

MARRAINE — It's a — letter from a woman. You guessed correctly. A woman's letter — and a photograph — with an inscription!

MME. HAMELIN — What's she like — this woman?

MARRAINE — Oh, a coarse face — a common woman, an actress probably. His mistress of course. (*She breaks down, her strength gone.*)

MME. HAMELIN — Eveline!

MARRAINE — You fool, you! Complaining and nagging instead of watching and guarding him. Twenty! As if a boy of twenty could be trusted not to let his bad instincts get the better of him!

MME. HAMELIN — Why, you yourself said a minute ago — perhaps it is not as bad as —

MARRAINE — Ah! Now you'll make excuses for him!

Give me my hat! I want to get away from here, quick!

MME. HAMELIN — You're trembling like a leaf! Eveline! You terrify me! Do you know something? You're afraid.

MARRAINE — I? What difference does it make to me?

MME. HAMELIN — What a way to speak to me! If you know something you don't want to tell me— Why do you look at that photograph that way? I'm sure you know something. He went to see you very often for the past month. He told you everything. You said so yourself —

MARRAINE — (*at the end of her resources*). I asked for my hat!

MME. HAMELIN — Very well. I am going to give it to you. . . . (*Her suspicions taking form*) Why don't you look at me, Eveline? You drive me crazy. Tell me it is not true! (*Marraine slowly turns towards her, guiltily. The eyes of the two women meet. Marraine staggers. Mme. Hamelin is stunned.*)

MARRAINE — (*with an effort*). Marie!

MME. HAMELIN — Get out! (*Marraine staggers towards the door and as she reaches it —*) No! Not yet! Wait! There are things one cannot grasp so suddenly, which must be explained. Stay and tell me everything. There you stand without saying a word! Surely you are not afraid of words! My child — my little child — you were his —

MARRAINE — His mistress, yes!

MME. HAMELIN — You were — you! Oh! Let me look at you! So these hands — and this mouth! My boy! It was you! You, the friend I believed in like myself. Eveline — Marraine! And to think that it was I who sent him to you so that you would be less lonely in the evenings! Max! A child! Now I understand why, when he came home, he was so distant, so cold! It was because he had left your arms. (*Passionately*)

Ah! I should like to hurt you, tear those arms that have taken him from me!

MARRAINE — That's enough! Be still! Taken? What? What have I taken? I have given, yes, given — given my soul, myself and my reputation to a miserable creature who was running after loose women.

MME. HAMELIN — You gave yourself body and soul to a child to whom you should have been a big sister, a comrade —

MARRAINE — A child! You only know that one word! Look at him the next time you see him. See if he still looks like a child! Ah, I knew it was a mistake, this love — a madness which has ended like all such madness must end, stupidly, miserably.

MME. HAMELIN — You don't suppose I can pity you?

MARRAINE — I don't suppose anything. I am going away — far away — for a long time.

MME. HAMELIN — I hope so.

MARRAINE — But understand this: It is not disgust for me that makes you so unforgiving.

MME. HAMELIN — No? What is it then?

MARRAINE — Jealousy. You can't forgive me that he should be less to you now, that I have liberated him from you — and helped him fly away from the nest in which you held him fast!

MME. HAMELIN — I! Jealous of you! You, whom he has already forgotten, whom he has deserted!

MARRAINE — Yes, it is his mother whom he adores, isn't it? It is his mother for whom he reserves all his heart and tenderness.

MME. HAMELIN — For twenty years he was mine; for twenty years his life was my life, day after day — twenty years that he never went to sleep without a kiss from me.

MARRAINE — The few weeks in which I made him live are more to him than the twenty years of which you speak.

MME. HAMELIN — That's not true.

MARRAINE — These few weeks which he has just thrown away with the careless indifference of youth he will remember later on —

MME. HAMELIN — He never loved you! Never! A boy of his age doesn't love a woman of yours.

MARRAINE — (*her eyes on fire*). You're mistaken! He loved me ardently, passionately!

MME. HAMELIN — You were just a flattering adventure to him, the woman of the world.

MARRAINE — Be still!

MME. HAMELIN — And if he does remember you it will be simply to boast of later on.

MARRAINE — And you say that you are not jealous. . . . You're doing your best to hurt me. He will make *you* suffer too. He will grow farther away from you every day.

MME. HAMELIN — I am not afraid!

MARRAINE — You will soon beg him for the crumbs of his kindness. You will see him give his *best* to women you would be ashamed to touch.

MME. HAMELIN — That is not true!

MARRAINE — The first pretty thing he meets will be more to him than you.

MME. HAMELIN — It's not true! He will always come back to me! Always! I'm sure of that! (*She sobs*) I'm sure!

MARRAINE — If you had spoken to me differently, I'd have been at your feet. Yes, it was a wicked thing. But you don't know what he meant to me, that boy! Love and passion are so closely united. One is easily lost. One can't tell whether it is the body or the soul one desires. You should forgive the sin, Maric, because of the love that prompted it.

MME. HAMELIN — I won't listen to you any more. You disgust me — so much that I couldn't even touch you! Get out!

"Thief! Thief!" the unhappy mother calls after her as she goes.

To M. Hamelin the news of Marraine's relations with Max is a shock, but one of surprise rather than disgust. He feels he understands Max better than she does. He knows men. It is disgusting of him, Mme. Hamelin insists, to take such a stand. His own son —

"I notice you always say 'your son' when you are complaining of him and 'my son' when you are pleased with him," the father rejoins.

He begs her to say nothing to Max. But she is firmly resolved that she shall have a talk with him. Unless she did she would strangle —

But when Max comes, in obedience to her summons, she finds it difficult to say the things she had planned. For years their comradeship has been dear to her; to change it now by accusing him of the things she had in mind to speak about — she can't do that. She chides him with having taken particular pains with his toilet for the dinner engagement he is attending. Guardedly she tells him of Marraine's determination to leave Paris for a long vacation — and is a little startled at his calm acceptance of the news. Evidently Marraine also belongs to Max's rapidly passing past. He is more interested now in getting a latchkey. Not that he expects to be late — but he *might* be. And certainly he is old enough now to have his own key. A little regretfully, but with good spirit, Mme. Hamelin agrees that he is and that he shall have it. Where her boy had stood there now stands a man.

MAX — Papa told you that I couldn't come home for lunch?

MME. HAMELIN — That's all right.

MAX — Then it wasn't for that you sent for me?

MME. HAMELIN — Not at all.

MAX — What did you want to say to me then?

MME. HAMELIN — I don't remember. Nothing.

MAX — But Leontine told me that you asked for me.

MME. HAMELIN — Yes, but — I've thought it over — it wasn't worth while. Go now quickly. Go to your friends! Go — go!

MAX — Au revoir.

MME. HAMELIN — Au revoir.

MAX — Better take an aspirin tablet. (*He leaves. Mme. Hamelin stares at the door through which Max has just passed. A moment later Max reënters with his coat, hat and cane, a card in his hand*) There. A card from Switzerland for father.

MME. HAMELIN — Ah, thanks. Give it to me. (*He hands her the card*) Aren't you going to kiss me?

MAX — Yes. (*He kisses her. She detains him a moment arranging his tie*) Till tomorrow.

MME. HAMELIN — Till tomorrow.

M. HAMELIN — (*entering*). Well?

MME. HAMELIN — (*with a vague motion*) — Oh! (*She hands him the card*) There, a card for you from Suzanne.

M. HAMELIN — (*livening up*). Ah, at last. (*Reading from the card*) "Much love. Are in Zurich. Write Hotel du Lac."

MME. HAMELIN — Is that all?

M. HAMELIN — Yes. You haven't told me. Did you speak to Max?

MME. HAMELIN — Yes — yes —

M. HAMELIN — Well, what happened?

MME. HAMELIN — Oh — nothing.

M. Hamelin is still fingering the card from his absent daughter, as though there might possibly be more to be learned from it if he were able to read it differently. Mme. Hamelin again takes up the photo that had arrived in her son's letter. She looks at it steadily a long minute. "She *is* pretty!" she admits as the curtain falls.

ACT III

Again, in the dining room of their home, the Hamelins are at lunch. And again the absent Max has left the third cover untouched. But he is more or less regularly absent now and his parents have become accustomed to not expecting him. M. Hamelin is inclined to resent the fact that his son no longer takes the trouble to let his parents know whether he expects to be home or not, but Mme. Hamelin is quick to defend him. She understands young men better than she did, and she had much rather have Max as he is than to be the mother of one of those "mama's boys," like Mme. Lorsay's son. "When a young man is refined, sensible and well-bred his escapades are perfectly respectable," she submits as her newer philosophy, which greatly amuses M. Hamelin.

Still, Mme. Hamelin is unable to understand why it is, when they have given Max all the freedom that he prayed for, he still remains so distant from them; why he no longer confides in them, and particularly in his mother. It is a phase of his new-found manhood she does not approve. Still, he will come back to her in time. Of that she is sure.

And as for Suanne, she will be more a daughter than ever when she comes home "To the young girl a mother is like a policeman," Mme. Hamelin concludes; "but to the married woman she is an indispensable friend, *always!*" Suzanne may be home any day now. Six weeks the bride and groom have been away and word of their expected arrival in Paris may come at any time. Their new apartment is being built only a few blocks away. Of course the father and mother have been warned to keep away from it, and not to interfere with the orders given the decorators — but still they are greatly interested. They might walk around now to the new apartment, Mme. Hamelin suggests, just to see how nearly ready it is for the children.

There is a commotion in the hall, and the next minute Suzanne bursts in. "The children" have been home since the day before. They had left Berne in the morning and had dinner in Paris.

MME. HAMELIN — And you never sent us word?

SUZANNE — We meant to wire before we left. But you know how traveling is.

MME. HAMELIN — But after you arrived?

SUZANNE — We were tired — you know what arriving home means.

MME. HAMELIN — But this morning? You were only a few steps away — while we were impatiently longing for you.

SUZANNE — (*a little embarrassed*). That's true — I I should have —

M. HAMELIN — (*to his wife*). Don't bother her. She was busy — her luggage — the first day — (*To Suzanne*) And are we going to see your husband?

SUZANNE — Surely. I told him to call for me. Besides he insisted on seeing you. Only he had to go to his office for a moment. He'll be here.

MME. HAMELIN — Take off your hat You look as if you were on a visit.

SUZANNE — But I am on a visit.

M. HAMELIN — Oh!

SUZANNE — (*quickly*). No, I'll take it off. You see I'm a good girl — I must fix my hair all over again. Isn't Max here?

MME. HAMELIN — No. I don't think he'll be long though.

SUZANNE — Why — uh — I can't stay very long. I have a million things to do.

MME. HAMELIN — Can't I help you? Shall I go with you?

M. HAMELIN — I, perhaps? I have nothing to do.

SUZANNE — It isn't worth while. Henri is going with me. And how is Marraine?

MME. HAMELIN — Marraine has just left Paris.

SUZANNE — No. Where did she go?

MME. HAMELIN — I forget — She'll send you her address. But tell us all about yourself.

But Suzanne is too much interested in her house and her husband to talk about herself. Their trip was wonderful. They had a wonderful time. They are both well. And they are both very happy. Would a light or a dark carpet be better for the apartment? Mother prefers a dark carpet. Papa thinks perhaps a light would be better. So Suzanne thinks Henri had better decide. He will very likely select a medium.

Now she is ready to go, but before she does she makes a casual survey of the room as though appraising the value of its furnishings for the first time. The setting of her own house has given her a new appreciation of such things. She turns to her father.

SUZANNE — I want to ask a favor.

M. HAMELIN — What, my dear?

SUZANNE — There's a large empty panel in our dining room, to the right, as you enter from the drawing room.

M. HAMELIN — Ah, yes. You need something there.

SUZANNE — Yes. That made me think — that commode. (*She points to it*) After all, it isn't of much use to you here and it would look so well there.

MME. HAMELIN — It looks well here, too!

M. HAMELIN — If we gave it to you there would be a large empty panel here.

SUZANNE — (*laughing*). That's true.

MME. HAMELIN — She never thought of that.

SUZANNE — I take it back. But how long Henri is! I must go!

M. HAMELIN — Listen. If your mother would let you have that commode, I —

SUZANNE — No, no! You need it. It's out of the question.

MME. HAMELIN — If you want it very badly —

SUZANNE — I don't want you to be inconvenienced on our account. You've given us enough already.

M. HAMELIN — Would you like it?

SUZANNE — Of course I would, if —

M. HAMELIN — I'll send it over.

SUZANNE — (*hugging him*). How sweet of you. But you are *sure* I'm not depriving you?

MME. HAMELIN — No, oh no!

SUZANNE — Thank you very, very much! Wait. Don't you bother to send it. The men working in my apartment can easily call for it. Henri will be so delighted.

For the first time she notices that her father is thinner than he was. And that her mother looks tired. They should go away for a vacation. A few weeks at the seashore would do them a world of good. And then she notices the clock! What a beautiful clock it is! Funny she had never noticed it before! And, oh, yes — could she borrow Leontine, the maid, for a few days — just while she is getting settled? Certainly. Her mother can easily manage without Leontine.

Henri dashes in for a moment. He, too, is full of house plans and eager to report, more or less privately to Suzanne, his activities of the day. There isn't much time to visit with the Hamelins. Yes, they had a lovely trip. Yes, he found his business in good condition. Yes, he is feeling quite well. No, he does not think Suzanne is looking a little pale. Her health is excellent. Of course, if she wasn't well Henri would consult a physician, even though he does not himself believe in medicines. No, they cannot stay to dinner, seeing they are dining with Henri's parents. The next day? Well, perhaps.

So, after Suzanne has gathered together her music, and asked for her napkin ring — seeing she will no longer have to fold her napkin when she comes *there* to dinner — the newlyweds depart for their own home, pausing in the doorway just long enough for Suzanne to admire a bit of tapestry. "*That's* a pretty screen," says she, significantly.

MME. HAMELIN — Do you know I believe that *sons* remain attached to their parents longer than daughters.

M. HAMELIN — Well —

MME. HAMELIN — What can you expect? A woman's place is with her husband. It *should* be that way. And the boys, in spite of all — I am sure that Max, if we handled him in the right way — Only it seems that *I* cannot ask him his secrets — or even listen to them.

M. HAMELIN — Evidently.

MME. HAMELIN — (*dreamily, leaning on her husband's shoulder*). Henri called me *mother.*

M. HAMELIN — Yes, I noticed.

MME. HAMELIN — How *could* he? "*Mother.*" Imagine. Do you believe that Max could ever call his mother-in-law "mother"?

M. HAMELIN — Max? No! Never!

MME. HAMELIN — (*suddenly*). Oh, we're getting old.

M. HAMELIN — We? Old? My dear, if we were old, all this would seem quite natural to us. We would take it for granted without thinking about it. You are still a very young woman.

Max does not exactly bear out his mother's new confidence in him as a son who really at heart appreciates his home. He comes now, full of excuses for his irregular hours. He is studying for his exams; he is —

But his mother is tired of excuses. She takes him rather more severely to task than is her custom and makes him sit down and talk to her.

MME. HAMELIN — (*forcing him gently but obstinately to turn to her*). What is the matter with you? (*He drops his head*) Tell me! Don't you love me any more? Maybe I *am* in the wrong. I'd like to know! I wanted you to be on time for your meals. I insisted on your keeping regular hours — And then, the other day I opened by mistake a letter addressed to you — the kind of letter I should not have opened. Oh, don't be afraid. I didn't read it. I sealed it at once. Now, is that why you act like this? (*She pauses*) Is it?

MAX — I am always watched; spied on. I have no liberty at all.

MME. HAMELIN — Is that why you act the way you do? Oh, I know well enough that this house is not very gay. I am often tired and in a bad humor. Your father isn't in the best of health.

MAX — Papa?

MME. HAMELIN — He's getting old and you can see how tired he looks.

MAX — Why? Suzanne?

MME. HAMELIN — Yes.

MAX — But she's home now.

MME. HAMELIN — Some home-comings are like departures. All this has made the house seem so empty. I am afraid it has affected your father very much — and I, who have no one but him, feel discouraged, yes, very much discouraged. (*Tears come to her eyes. Max timidly kisses her forehead*) Why don't you talk to your father? It would please him so much. He's so proud of his son. Oh, how hard life is! Max, dear, we've only you. Surely you can confide in your father and mother — you never speak to me any more. Why not? You never were like this. You used to tell me everything. Oh, dearest, where has that time gone?

MAX — I am just about the same, I assure you. Only just now I am worried about — my — exams.

MME. HAMELIN — Don't say that! Don't lie! I will tell you the real reason of your detachment, your stubborness. It's not because you lack conversation. There are things boys don't tell their mothers. You needn't turn your head. Unfortunately, these things are the most important to you. Nothing else — matters — (*She pauses*) Isn't it ridiculous, eh? After what we have been to each other, it should all be over so suddenly? A barrier — strangers — Max, my little Max, don't be foolish.

MAX — Mother —

MME. HAMELIN — You must confide in me, my boy, you must. I'll understand — I want to be my boy's pal. Oh, I know there are mothers who are narrow-minded. But I, Max, I'm not like that, am I? We understand each other — you are in love. You thought I didn't know. Well, what of it? It's natural at your age. My little boy, in love! That doesn't shock me in the least. (*Max lifts his head and looks at her*) That doesn't shock me. Besides, we ought to understand each other, you and I. Your father said to me the other day: "It's surprising how often he has your gestures, expressions." Aunt Martha also noticed it. And a misunderstanding, should we be so far apart? Come now — you will?

MAX — It's harder than you think. Several times I've felt like throwing myself in your arms but something always seemed to stop me. I felt you wouldn't understand. You'd laugh at me.

MME. HAMELIN — How could you think that of me, when I was only waiting for you?

MAX — Yes, perhaps I have been unreasonable, but several times you have said "good morning" to me in a tone that froze me.

MME. HAMELIN — No, no, you misunderstood me.

MAX — And then, there's something paralyzing in the quiet of this house, in the daily routine. After all, Mother, you'll admit it is difficult to be affectionate with one's own people.

MME. HAMELIN — What *are* you saying?

MAX — I tell you it's the truth. You feel that you

know each other too well. You feel ashamed. Remember when Suzanne was engaged, she was bashful before you and father. You told her to kiss Henri. She did, but timidly. But oh, when you weren't there —

MME. HAMELIN — Oh, it could not have been our presence that made her feel that way. She has a way of talking to her husband —

MAX — I don't think that love and family life go together —

MME. HAMELIN — What a philosophy! (*She pauses*) Yet there is some truth in what you say.

MAX — But now I know. I realize that I have been wrong, that I haven't been nice to you. I should have known — I should —

MME. HAMELIN — My boy! Oh, my own boy once more! You see, we must always speak — tell each other things — if you knew how unhappy I've been all this time. (*With joy*) A tear? You're crying, ah, that's good. Come to me like a good child. He was grieved. I knew it — I felt it. Come, be strong and tell me about your sorrow — your love sorrow — tell me — tell me — all about it —

Gradually Max resumes something of his old attitude towards his mother. Little by little he tells her of his great love affair; of how he met the girl of the photograph; of how she is much prettier than any picture could make her and of how remarkably intelligent she is. She is an actress, but a lady and of good family. She has left home only because she must be alone to work, and though she is not playing very big parts now, she is certain to have a big future because of her artistic temperament.

MME. HAMELIN — . . . That's very charming. But tell me; this girl — are you really sure? You understand I don't know her — are you sure? You are very impulsive! Love is a great word, Max!

MAX — (*settles back in his chair*). Oh, don't worry.

MME. HAMELIN—I'm not telling you this to get you away from her. I'm convinced that this girl has fine qualities. Only, she belongs to a different world. A world which amuses you now, because it is new to you, but which might deceive you some day.

MAX — (*confidently*). No danger.

MME. HAMELIN — People older than you and much more experienced have made mistakes, you know!

MAX — But, Mother, there are certain things that I can't possibly tell you. But I assure you I am not a child. I know life.

MME. HAMELIN — Well, in that case —

MAX — I knew a woman of the world — our world. Beautiful and married — well —

MME. HAMELIN — (*quickly*). I believe you, my boy, I believe you. The reason I talk to you like this is because you seemed so nervous to me the past few days — and I wonder if this girl really makes you as happy as you say. (*She pauses*) You just admitted yourself that — you are worried.

MAX — That's because, before she knew me, she had a friend, an actor in the same theatre. Naturally, since she's known me, she's given him up. Now he only sees her at the theatre.

MME. HAMELIN — (*in spite of herself*). What a beautiful world!

MAX — What did you say?

MME. HAMELIN — Nothing. And what did you say about this actor?

MAX — It is perfectly loathsome to see this man always around her.

MME. HAMELIN — I can understand that.

MAX — Not because I'm jealous of what he's been!

MME. HAMELIN — So you're not jealous? What is it then?

MAX — Well, I'm afraid — I'm afraid he'll take her away from me.

MME. HAMELIN — Oh, Max, a person who loves you so?

MAX — (*with superiority*). You can never tell with women!

MME. HAMELIN — Women —

MAX — Besides, I never have any money!

MME. HAMELIN — Money?

MAX — Yes. He has money. Naturally, you understand —

MME. HAMELIN — (*rising*). Yes, I understand. Now, I understand very well.

It is not easy for Max's mother to conceal her loathing for this hopelessly sordid affair of her only son's. She bows her head in her hands and seeks gently to stop his recital of further facts. But her attitude serves only to anger him. "You don't understand," he shouts at her, hiding his shame in anger. "You're trying to humiliate me. Well, I warn you you're wasting your time. She is the only one who understands me. With her, at least, I'm a man — I live! And since you want to know it, I'm happy *only* when I'm with her!"

"You forget that you are speaking to your mother."

"Well, I swear I'll never forget it again!"

"Where are you going?"

"Wherever I please!"

He storms out of the room, slamming the door after him. Weakly his mother tries to call him. Before she can reach the door the men call for the commode. Suzanne has sent them. Before they can take it the commode must be cleared of the Hamelin silver. Leontine will see to that — or would, if Leontine were not herself at Suzanne's.

Resignedly Mme. Hamelin sinks to her knees and begins taking her silver from the commode. . . . Now it is empty and the men are carrying it through the door. Where it stood against the wall the paper has faded to a brownish green. The curtain slowly descends.

ACT IV

In Suzanne's drawing room, Jeanne, who was her bridesmaid, is being shown all the new treasures. Conspicuously placed are the screen, the clock and the commode that have been foraged from mother's house. It is the evening of the first dinner party Suzanne and Henri have given in their new home, delayed a matter of months by the death of M. Hamelin, who seemed never to be quite the same after his daughter's marriage.

JEANNE — Your father was a splendid man.

SUZANNE — Oh, you don't know how good he was. I was everything to him. He was always anxious to give me pleasure. And I — I realize it now. I never was what I should have been to him. Oh, if one only knew. You know, Jeanne, when it is too late, one thinks — and regrets. I was his one thought. And it seemed quite natural. We didn't always agree, especially since my marriage — I often spoke impatiently to him. One shouldn't.

LOUISE — (*entering*). Madame, how many glasses shall I place on the table?

SUZANNE — Wait, I am coming. (*Louise leaves*) Oh, yes, now I feel remorse, but I have made up my mind — I will try to be as good as possible to mother. To go to see her often, not to let her get lonesome, to show her my love. It makes her so happy when I pass a few moments with her. Oh, that reminds me — I promised to go and see her today. She must have waited for me. (*Resolutely*) I'll go tomorrow!

JEANNE — Yes, do go tomorrow.

Marraine calls. She is back in Paris after a considerable stay abroad, looking a little older, but still cheerful with a sort of forced gaiety. There has been a reconciliation between Marraine and Mme. Hamelin. M. Hamelin's death brought the old friends together again.

"Your mother said to me: 'Eveline, I ought to hate you, but I no longer have the strength to hate anyone. Besides, you are all I have left now,'" she says. "What about me?" demands Suzanne. "You don't count as a friend," Marraine explains: "You are her daughter."

Max comes, too. He is in the army now, enjoying a furlough. He meets Marraine frankly, and memories of the past are evidently blotted out between them. He has but the one evening in town, Max explains, and he can't stay to dinner. Neither will he have any time for his mother, and he asks them not to tell Mme. Hamelin that he has been in Paris.

SUZANNE — Really, you might have gone to her for five minutes at least!

MAX — No! I'd rather not go at all than stay only five minutes. You won't say anything? How long since you saw mother?

SUZANNE — I saw her yesterday.

MAX — You should go to see her every day.

SUZANNE — Don't worry about me. Why don't you *write* to her oftener?

MAX — There's an excuse for me, but you live only fifteen minutes away. You shouldn't leave her alone a whole day. You haven't so much to do! I don't think it's considerate of you, you know.

SUZANNE — Well, do you think it's considerate of you to come to Paris today without seeing her?

Max doesn't seem quite sure that it is considerate, but he is convinced it is much more convenient, seeing he has an engagement —

The maid announces Mme. Hamelin! She is waiting in the small reception room. If Max should try to go out that way she would surely see him. So he sneaks a little guiltily out of the servants' entrance at back, while Marraine agrees to entertain Mme. Hamelin and give Suzanne a chance to dress.

Mme. Hamelin quite understands when Marraine explains that Suzanne is dressing and will join them presently. She (Mme. Hamelin) was passing and had dropped in just to say good evening to her daughter. . . .

The talk turns to children and the emptiness of a home without them. "Which of us two, do you believe, is to be envied more? You, who have never had children, or I, who have lost mine?" Mme. Hamelin asks of Marraine.

MARRAINE — Lost?

MME. HAMELIN — Yes. Life took mine from me long ago! Human beings can't divide their affections. They must give it all to one. Well, Suzanne has a husband. Ever since I acquired a son-in-law I feel as if I were the mother-in-law of my own daughter. As for Max — (*She makes a gesture.*)

MARRAINE — Oh. Even if your children are not as near you now as they used to be — they remain as living, palpable souvenirs of your happy days. If a woman is destined to find herself alone some day, is it not better that she have at least something to *remember?*

MME. HAMELIN — Do you believe that those souvenirs are always happy? Oh, Eveline, that day when we come to realize that we are useless — and even a little in the way —

MARRAINE — In the way? What are you talking about? Your children adore you!

MME. HAMELIN — Oh, they do their best to convince me of that! They are very attentive. They are well-bred children and very dutiful. Every day ever since — that unhappy day, either Suzanne or her husband has come to see me — a short visit — they have so much to do, you know. She comes in: "Hello, mamma, I can stay only a minute, I have a thousand things to do," and I never dare start a long story for fear she might be delayed. Sometimes Henri comes in her place. Suzanne has told him: "It's your turn today, I went yesterday." He comes to see me to please her. Once in a while I am invited here, too. Naturally, too, I always wait till — till I'm coaxed — and they insist a little — not too much.

MARRAINE — Ah, you are still the same. You always exaggerate everything that may tend to hurt you.

MME. HAMELIN — You are mistaken. I long for this visit impatiently as the only beautiful moment of the day. Today I expected them all; Suzanne, Henri and Max. They had promised me — and nobody came! Max didn't get his furlough and Suzanne was probably too busy with her dinner. (*She pauses*) Are you dining here?

MARRAINE — No, I was just about to go when you came.

MME. HAMELIN — Ah! (*She lowers her voice*) I came to be invited. I don't know what came over me a while ago. I felt so lonely — so lonely! Just now as I saw you standing at that door I realized — I understood, compared with you I have so much to be grateful for and — today is my wedding anniversary. November seventeenth — our silver wedding! I couldn't stand it any longer. I said to myself, why can't they do something for me? I am going to ask them to have me with them this evening. Lunch alone isn't quite so bad — but dinner — and then the evening — the long evening. (*She makes a despondent gesture*) And in order not to look too mournful in the midst of the scene of youth (*She opens her coat*) I dressed up, you see — it's my crepe de chine dress. It doesn't look too sombre.

MARRAINE—(*deeply moved*). You poor darling!

. . . .

MME. HAMELIN — (*calling to Marraine at the door*). Come back a moment! I've been selfish. I've talked only of myself. I beg your pardon.

MARRAINE — You are very good. Yes, I am very

lonely. But that's my own fault. I spoiled it all myself. In the beginning I expected too much from married life. I was disappointed. Then I tried living alone, but I wasn't strong enough — then I dreamed of wonderful possibilities. They turned out a failure, humiliation, ugliness, our friendship destroyed, my whole life wasted. Ah, you see how dangerous it is not to have children. Without them a woman's life lacks balance. Besides, not to receive anything, that's bearable, but not to be able to give, oh, that's dreadful for a woman. You shouldn't complain. You can give. You, too, have some difficult moments — but still — think of all that.

MME. HAMELIN — You are right. I shouldn't feel unhappy. I have many things to be grateful for. After all, they are good children — they love me. Suzanne is kind and gentle and Max is, too, in spite of his independent airs.

Now Marraine is gone and Henri has arrived home in a rush of excitement. He, too, must hurry and dress. And now Suzanne is dressed and is trying her best to welcome her mother cordially. Won't she stay to dinner? There are only the four couples of "young" people coming! It would be no trouble at all putting on an extra place, if —

But Mme. Hamelin declines. It will be better, she thinks, if she goes home. Leontine is waiting for her — and, besides, she is not dressed — Some other time!

SUZANNE — You would have given us great pleasure. Well, I won't insist because I know you don't feel shy with me.

MME. HAMELIN — Quite right!

SUZANNE — Will you be home tomorrow?

MME. HAMELIN — Yes, all day.

SUZANNE — I'll surely come to see you.

MME. HAMELIN — That's very sweet of you, but if you have something else to do, don't feel yourself obliged to — you have your home, your husband —

SUZANNE — Not at all! Not at all! I am coming to see you tomorrow. You are so much alone at present. The days must seem so long to you.

MME. HAMELIN — Why no, it's not as bad as that. We are never as unhappy as we appear to be. Besides, you know, along with the sadness and solitude life brings us with the years certain powers of resignation which you young folks cannot understand.

SUZANNE — My dear little mother.

MME. HAMELIN — If I had been told that I would be able to survive your father, I wouldn't have believed it. And yet I am here. I've arranged my life in my little corner. The days pass. Don't worry about me. Au revoir, my child. A pleasant evening and enjoy yourself.

SUZANNE — I hate to see you go like this. Shall I send for a cab?

MME. HAMELIN — Why should you? The street car stops right at my door. Don't worry. You are late. You said you had orders to give. Go quickly. Good-bye.

Then Henri rushes in to announce that the Batholles have been waiting in the reception room for ten minutes and Suzanne is whisked away with a hurried renewal of her promise to see her mother surely the next day. For a moment Mme. Hamelin stands deserted in the middle of the floor; then she quietly inspects the arrangement of the flowers, and changes the positions of a chair here and a vase there, to give the finishing touch of an experienced hostess to the room. Louise, the maid, finds her thus engaged when she comes to announce the serving of dinner.

MME. HAMELIN — Louise, madame asked me to tell you, the cheese after the sweets.

LOUISE — Yes, Madame.

MME. HAMELIN — The white wine with the fish and the claret with the roast. You'll remember that?

LOUISE — Yes, Madame.

MME. HAMELIN — Be very careful! There's nothing missing on the table?

LOUISE — No, Madame.

MME. HAMELIN — (*inspecting the table from a distance with the eye of a critic*). Hmm — hmm — well, serve the soup immediately before announcing and don't give it a chance to get cold. Don't lose any time and tell Julie to take care of her roast.

LOUISE — Yes, Madame.

MME. HAMELIN — It must be well seasoned. Not too well done.

JEANNE — (*entering like a flash with flowers in her hands*). What, Madame, you here?

MME. HAMELIN — Shhh — I was just going — I was going —

Slowly she opens the door leading to the servants' quarters and the back stairs. The trail of her skirt is just disappearing through the door as the guests enter, laughingly, from the small drawing room.

The curtain falls

THE PLAYS AND THEIR AUTHORS

"Anna Christie." By Eugene G. O'Neill. Copyright, 1921, by Eugene G. O'Neill. Published by Boni & Liveright, New York. For the second time within three years Mr. O'Neill was awarded the Pulitzer prize of one thousand dollars for the best American play produced during the year. He continues his active coöperation with the Provincetown Players, the group responsible for his introduction to the so-called commercial theatre. Two other plays from his pen, "The Hairy Ape" and "The Straw," met with some success during the 1921-1922 season, and he suffered one failure, "The First Man." He was born in Provincetown, Mass., and is the son of the late James O'Neill, actor. He is the author of numerous short plays. (See "Best Plays of 1919-1920," "Best Plays of 1920-1921.")

"A Bill of Divorcement." By Clemence Dane. Copyright, 1921, by Clemence Dane. Published by the Macmillan Company, New York. Miss Dane is an English actress, though before she went on the stage she studied art and taught school. She has written several novels, one of the war, through which she served as a social worker, called "The Regiment of Women;" another, "Legend," and a third, "First the Blade." She was writing "Will Shakespeare," a drama to be produced in America next season, when the agitation incident to the passage of a new divorce law in England attracted her attention and she left Shakespeare to write "A Bill of Divorcement." Its timeliness of theme, as well as its exceptional power as drama, immediately brought her into prominence.

"Dulcy." By George S. Kaufman and Marc Connelly. Copyright, 1921, by George S. Kaufman and Marc Connelly. Published by G. P. Putnam's Sons, New York. The Messrs. Kaufman and Connelly, inaugurating this season a collaborating partnership that promises much for the theatre, are both young and both newspaper men. Mr. Kaufman is assistant dramatic editor of the *New York Times.* He was born in Pittsburg thirty-two years ago. He tried to study law, he says, and failed. Tried several other things and gave them up. Finally went into newspaper work. Conducted columns on the *Washington Times* and the *Evening Mail,* New York. Did general work for the *New York Tribune,* contributed to *Life* and other magazines; was the co-author of "Someone in the House," adapted "Jacques Duval" for George Arliss and has since written, with Mr. Connelly, "Dulcy," "To the Ladies," and is at work on "Merton of the Movies."

Mr. Connelly is thirty-one, was born in McKeesport, Pa., educated in the public schools and at Trinity Hall, Washington, Pa. He worked as a reporter, assistant dramatic critic and column conductor on Pittsburg newspapers until 1915. He came to New York in 1915 to see the production of a musical comedy for which he had written the lyrics. It failed, and lacking the money to get back to Pittsburg he stayed on in New York. He has done newspaper work, contributed to the magazines, written a vaudeville sketch or two and done some play doctoring.

"Six-Cylinder Love." By William Anthony McGuire. Copyright, 1921, by William Anthony McGuire. Mr. McGuire, born in Chicago, wrote his first play, "The Walls of Wall Street," while he was a student at Notre Dame University in Indiana. It was produced at South Bend and the two leading roles were played by the author and Allan Dwan, now of the movies, but then a professor at the university. Shortly thereafter Mr. McGuire determined upon a career as a playwright, and took a job on the *South Bend News*, which included the writing of dramatic criticisms. He has since written many plays, including "The Heights," for Frank Keenan; "The Divorce Question," an answer to Joseph Medill Patterson's novel, "Rebellion"; "Everyman's Castle," "The Good Bad Woman," and finally "Six-Cylinder Love." He has a new one in rehearsal tentatively called "It's a Boy."

"The Dover Road." By A. A. Milne. Copyright, 1921, by A. A. Milne. The "A. A." in Mr. Milne's name stands for Alan Alexander, and he is well known in England as a journalist, essayist, editor, novelist and, since 1917, playwright. He was graduated from Trinity College, Cambridge, in 1903, and went at once into newspaper work. Three years later he was assistant editor of *Punch*, and remained on the staff of England's favorite humorous weekly until the outbreak of the war, through which he served with the Royal Warwickshire regiment, and about which he wrote many entertaining stories. His first novel, "The Day's Play," was published in 1910; his first play, "Wurzel-Flummery," was written in 1917, and "Belinda," played in America by Ethel Barrymore, followed in 1918. The same year he tossed off two others, "The Boy Comes Home" and "Make Believe." The next year he turned out "Mr. Pim Passes By," in 1920 he did "The Great Broxopp," and last year "The Dover Road" and "The Truth About Blayds." Between times he wrote "The Red House Mystery," described as a new kind of detective story.

"He Who Gets Slapped." By Leonid Nikolayevic Andreyev. Copyright, 1921, by the Theatre Guild Inc., and by the Dial Publishing Company. Published by

Bretano's. Andreyev was the son of humble parents, and was born in central Russia in 1871. He tutored his way through the University of St. Petersburg, following the death of his father. He endured many hardships because of his poverty, and once tried to commit suicide. He was at the law school in Moscow in 1898, making a living by reporting law cases, when some of his short stories were published and attracted attention. He appears to have been considerably influenced by Gorki and Chekhov, and a majority of his plays deal with destiny, the great unknown and the powerful influences of the life force. He is the author of "King Hunger," "Savva," "Anathema," "The Black Maskers," "Life of Man," "The Sabine Women," and "He Who Gets Slapped." In 1919 he wrote "Save Our Souls," an appeal to the allies, and "S O S," another story based on the war and the Russian débacle. Andreyev died in 1919.

"The Circle." By William Somerset Maugham. Copyright, 1921, by William Somerset Maugham. Published by George H. Doran Company, New York. Mr. Maugham was born in Paris in 1874 of English parents. He was educated at King's College, Canterbury, and Heidelberg University and as a young man studied medicine at St. Thomas Hospital in London. His first novel, written in 1897, was "Liza of Lambeth," a story of the London slums growing out of his experiences as a medical student. "Mrs. Craddock," written in 1903, was the most successful of his earlier novels. His first play was "A Man of Honor," which the London Stage Society produced. He followed this with the series of light comedies Charles Frohman brought to America, including "Lady Frederick," "Jack Straw," "Mrs. Dot," "Penelope," and "Smith." "Too Many Husbands" was a wartime comedy, and there also have been "Cæsar's Wife," "Caroline," and "Our Betters" before "The Circle."

"The Hero." By Gilbert Emery. Copyright, 1921, by Gilbert Emery. Mr. Emery is a new writer of plays, though he was well known a few years back as a popular writer of short stories under the name of Emery Pottle. He was born in Naples, New York, and educated in the public schools, the Oneonta Normal School and at Amherst College. He lived abroad for ten years, and as a writer has had experience in newspaper and magazine work. He has a novel, "Handicapped," a book of poems, three short volumes, "The Little House," "My Friend Is Dead" and "The Little Village" to his credit. "The Hero" is his first play, but he has another, "Tarnish," ready for production.

"The Nest." By Paul Geraldy. Copyright, 1921, by Paul Geraldy and Grace George. Geraldy is a French poet. About fifteen years ago he took to playwriting. He has published two volumes of verse, "Small Souls" and "You and I." The latter has achieved such popularity in France that it already has run through 132 editions, though how many copies are included in an edition we do not know. His "The Farce of Families" was produced at the Odeon in 1910. "Silver Weddings," from which Grace George adapted "The Nest," was accepted by the Comedie Français before the war and, after many delays, finally played in 1917. Geraldy is also part author of "Princesse," a romantic tragedy produced at the Odeon, and about three years ago wrote "Aimer," which Miss George has also translated.

"Ambush." By Arthur Richman. Copyright, 1921, by Arthur Richman. Mr. Richman is a native New

Yorker, and attributes his interest in the theatre to the fact that his parents, when he was at the impressionable age of nine, gave him a toy theatre for which he wrote three comedies a day. He was educated mostly by private tutors, and counts himself lucky that he was not sent to college. He never would have graduated, he fears, and would have wasted a lot of perfectly good time. Mr. Richman wrote several plays before he had one produced, and that, "Not So Long Ago," played in 1920. "Ambush" was the second and next season he hopes to have at least two. "The Awful Truth" and a musicalized version of "Not So Long Ago."

PLAYS PRODUCED IN NEW YORK

June 15, 1921 - June 15, 1922

"GOAT ALLEY"

A "drama of primitive love and life" by Ernest Howard Culbertson, produced by Alice Wade Mulhern, at the Bijou Theater, New York, June 20, 1921, with an all-negro cast.

Cast of characters —

Lucy Belle Dorsey.....Lillian McKee
Aunt Rebecca.....Beulah Daniels
Slim Dorsey.....Louis Lang
Lizzie Gibbs.....Daisy Garett
Chick Avery.....Owen Lane
Jeff Bisbee.....Leonard Kennedy
Sam Reed.....Barrington Carter
Jeremiah Pocher.....William H. Smith
Policeman.....Plant Lang
Fanny Dorsey.....Gladys Munroe

Act. I.—Living Room in Lucy Belle Dorsey's House, Goat Alley, Washington, D. C. Evening. Act II.—The Same. One Year Later. Early Afternoon. Act III.—The Same. One Year and a Half Later. Evening. Staged by Cecil Owen.

A study of the human misery ignorance and poverty have bred in a negro section of Washington, D. C. Lucy Belle Dorsey, a hard-working colored girl trying to live decently and remain true to Sam Reed, is finaly forced by circumstances she cannot control to "take up" with other men while Reed is in jail. Forcing a confession from her on his release Reed leaves the girl to support her illegitimate child as best she can.

"ZIEGFELD FOLLIES OF 1921"

A revue in two acts and nineteen scenes; lines and lyrics by Channing Pollock, Gene Buck, Willard Mack, Ralph Spence, and Bud De Silva; music by Victor Herbert, Rudolf Friml and Dave Stamper. Produced at the Globe Theater, New York, June 21, 1921.

Principals engaged —

Raymond Hitchcock	W. C. Fields
Fannie Brice	Mary Eaton
Van and Schenk	M. Tillio
Ray Dooley	Mlle. Mitti
Florence O'Denishawn	Mary Milburn
John Clarke	Vera Michelena
Charles O'Donnell	Jessie Reed

Staged by Edward Royce. Supervised by Florenz Ziegfeld.

"GEORGE WHITE'S SCANDALS"

A revue in two acts and twenty scenes, book by "Bugs" Baer and George White, music by George Gershwin, lyrics by Arthur Jackson. Produced at the Liberty Theater, New York, July 11, 1921.

Principals engaged —

George White	Charles King
Ann Pennington	Lou Holtz
George Lemaire	Olive Vaughan
Lester Allen	Harry Rose
George Bickel	Bert Gordon
"Aunt Jemima"	Gene Ford

Staged by George White.

"THE SKYLARK"

A domestic comedy in three acts by Thomas P. Robinson. Produced by Henry Stillman at the Belmont Theater, New York, July 25, 1921.

Cast of characters —

Katherine	Helen Odell
Arville	Marion Blackton
Daisy	Charlotte Walker
Tokio Toss	G. P. Patrimmo

John....................................Fred Eric
Ellery....................................Eric Maxon
Elsie....................................Marguerita Sylva
Arthur....................................Eugene Lockhart
Peter....................................E. S. Colling

Act. I.—Daisy's Drawing-room in New York. Late Afternoon in September. Act. II.—The Same. Noon. Early the Following June. Act III.—Ellery's Camp on Long Island. Late the Same Night. Play Produced by Henry Stillman and Fred Eric.

Daisy and John, married five years and a little tired of the experience, decide to try a temporary divorce, during the operation of which they will remain married in name only, free to go their respective ways and without protest or interference. Daisy elects to return to dancing "The Skylark," a diversion of her flapper days, and John looks for amusement in several directions. Elsie, a widow and wise, acts as a sort of chaperon until Daisy grows jealous and calls off the separation.

"THE TEASER"

A comedy in four acts by Martha M. Stanley and Adelaide Matthews. Produced by William A. Brady at the Playhouse, New York, July 27, 1921.

Cast of characters —

Teddy Wyndham....................................Jane Grey
Annie Barton ....Faire Binney
Lois Caswell....................................Rose Winter
Janet Wheelden....................................Paula Shay
Edmunds....................................Mariette Hyde
Geoffrey Loring....................................Leonard Willey
James MacDonald....................................Bruce Elmore
Roddy Caswell....................................John Cromwell
Perry Grayle....................................Homer Barton
Subi....................................Allen Atwell

Act I.—Teddy Wyndham's Living Room. Late Afternoon. Act II.—Same. About 8 o'clock in the Evening. Five Months Later. Act III.—Library in Roddy Caswell's House. A Little Later the Same Evening. Act IV.—Same as Act Act I. The Following Morning. Time—Present. Place—New York. Staged by John Cromwell.

Annie Barton, sixteen, pretty and flirtatious, visits her aunt Theodora Wyndham, in New York, and "teases" all aunty's men friends until they invite her upon all sorts of parties. One finally induces her to have supper with him in his rooms, which, as all heroines should know, is a risky thing to do. Annie is rescued by aunty in time, however, and everybody is much relieved, when next day this incorrigible flapper marries a traveling salesman she met on the train.

"GETTING GERTIE'S GARTER"

A farce comedy in three acts by Wilson Collison and Avery Hopwood. Produced by A. H. Woods at the Republic Theater, New York, August 1, 1921.

Cast of characters —

Pattie Walrick............................Dorothy Mackaye
Billy Felton....................................Lorin Raker
Nanette.......................................Adele Rolland
Gertie Darling...................................Hazel Dawn
Allen ....Walter Jones
Ken Walrick...........................Donald MacDonald
Teddy Darling.................................Louis Kimball
Barbara Felton..............................Eleanor Dawn
Algy Riggs...Ivan Miller

Act I.—The Lounging Room of the Darling Bungalow. Act II.—The Barn. Act III.—Same as Act I. Time—A June Evening. Place—The Darling Estate in Westchester. Staged by Bertram Harrison.

Gertie Darling, who has just married Teddy Darling, is trying to return to Ken Walrick the diamond studded garter, with his picture in the buckle, which he had given to her the year before. The idea being that if either Mr. Darling or Mrs. Walrick hear about it there will be trouble. The pursuit of the garter covers a good deal of ground and occupies two hours' time.

"TANGERINE"

A musical comedy in two acts by Philip Bartholomae and Guy Bolton; lyrics by Howard Johnston; music by Carlo Sanders. Produced by Carle Carlton at the Casino Theater, August 9, 1921.

Cast of characters —

A Warden....................................P. A. Leonard
Jack Floyd....................................Harry Puck
Lee Loring....................................Billy Rhodes
Fred Allen..............................Joseph Herbert, Jr.
Dick Owens................................Frank Crumit
Shirley Dalton..............................Julia Sanderson
Kate Allen....................................Edna Pierre
Elsie Loring..................................Becky Cauble
Mildred Floyd................................Gladys Wilson
Noa ....Jeannetta Methven
Clarence ....Wayne Nunn
King Home-Brew.........................John E. Hazzard
Akamai ....Mary Collins
Hulu......................................Victoria Miles
Kulikuli....................................Helen Frances
Pilikia....................................Nerene Swinton
Ukola....................................Carolyn Hancock
Polihu....................................Ruth Rollins
Aloha....................................Hazel Wright
Aoha Oe..................................Grace De Carlton
Tangerine Police Force.....................California Four

Act I.—Scene 1—Alimony Jail, New York. Scene 2—Lanai of the King. Act II.—Main Street, Tangerine. Staged by George Marion and Bert French.

Jack Floyd, Lee Loring and Fred Allen are all in Ludlow Street Jail from choice. They had rather be there than pay their respective ex-wives alimony. Along comes Dick Owens with an offer to transport them to a South Sea island where the women do all the work and man's place is in the home. Owens also schemes to get the divorced wives there and bring about a general reconciliation. The men soon tire of their freedom and the wives are ready to remarry at the finale.

"HONORS ARE EVEN"

A comedy in three acts by Roi Cooper Megrue. Produced by the Selwyns, at the Times Theater, New York, August 10, 1921.

Cast of characters —

Belinde....................Lola Fisher
Vaughan Outerbridge....................Horace Sinclair
The Chair Man....................Laurence Redmond
Ralph Kingsland....................Paul Kelly
A Man....................Ambrose Martin
Neigel Gordon....................Henry Mowray
John Leighton....................William Courtenay
Parker....................Horace Pollock
Lucile Berkeley....................Eleanor Woodruff
Georgy Haile....................Boots Wooster
David Carter....................Clifford Dempsey
Luigi....................Ralph Simone
Hannah....................Mable Stanton

Act I.—Incident 1—Man Proposes. The Boardwalk. Summer. Incident 2—Woman Disposes. The State Road. Autumn. Incident 3—Man Proposes. The Beach. Winter. Incident 4—Woman Chooses. The Country Place. Spring.
Act II.—Several Incidents in His Rooms, a Week Later.
Act III.—And a Finale in the Country Place. The Next Day.
Staged by the Author.

Belinde, heart whole and fancifully imaginative, rejects many proposals of marriage while she is waiting for the great thrill. Finally she meets John Leighton, who writes plays. She knows him to be the man. But John, knowing heroines, professes to be indifferent, and Belinde feels she must pay him in kind. So, after he proposes she pretends she is about to run away with the villain. With "honors even" they decide to marry.

"MARCH HARES"

A satirical comedy in three acts by Harry Wagstaff Gribble. Produced by Lee and J. J. Shubert at the Bijou Theater, August 11, 1921.

Cast of characters —

Ethel....................Gertrude Purcell
Mrs. Janet Rodney....................Lucile Watson

Edgar Fuller....................................Brandon Peters
Geoffrey Wareham...........................Alexander Onslow
Oliver....................................Charles Warburton
Janet Rodney...........................Adrienne Morrison
Claudia Kitts...............................Norma Mitchell
The Cook.....................................Nellie Griffen
Mr. Brown ....Frank Dekum
Act I.—Just About Dinner Time. Act II.—Just About Bed Time. Act III.—Just About Luncheon Time. Staged by W. H. Gilmore.

Geoffrey Wareham and Janet Rodney are teachers of elocution. Also engaged to be married. Likewise extremely temperamental and always getting on each other's nerves. Resenting Geoffrey's attitude of seeming indifference Janet invites Claudia Kitts, an "affinity," to visit her. To get even Geof invites Edgar Fuller to visit him. In the clash that follows Geof and Janet grow jealous of each other, Geof declares himself and they are again happily engaged.

"DULCY"

A comedy in three acts by George S. Kaufman and Marc Connelly. Produced by George C. Tyler and H. H. Frazee, at the Frazee Theater, New York, Aug. 13, 1921.

Cast of characters —

William Parker.................................Gregory Kelly
Henry...Harry Lillford
Gordon Smith..................................John Westley
Tom Sterrett..................................Elliott Nugent
Dulcinea.....................................Lynn Fontanne
Schuyler Van Dyck...........................Gilbert Douglas
C. Rogers Forbes...............................Wallis Clark
Mrs. Forbes.............................Constance Pelissier
Angela Forbes..................................Norma Lee
Vincent Leach.............................Howard Lindsay
Blair Patterson..............................George Alison
Act I.—Just Before Dinner on a Friday Night. Act II.—Immediately After Dinner. Act III.—The Following Morning. Staged by Howard Lindsay.

Dulcinea Smith has a heart of gold but a rubber stamp

mind; a loquacious bromide with a passion for making everybody happy. In trying to help her husband put through a business deal she muddles everything by talking too freely and too often. But "all's well that ends well," agrees Dulcinea, "and every cloud has a silver lining." (See page 96.)

"THE NIGHTCAP"

A mystery comedy in two acts by Guy Bolton and Max Marcin. Produced by Max Marcin at the 39th Street Theater, New York, Aug. 15, 1921.

Cast of characters —

Charles	Ronald Colman
Policeman	John Wray
Jerry Hammond	John Daly Murphy
Col. James Constance	Jack Raffael
Lester Knowles	H. Dudley Hawley
Mrs. Lester Knowles	Elizabeth Risdon
Anne Maynard	Flora Sheffield
Fred Hammond	Grant Mills
Robert Andrews	Jerome Patrick
George Rainsford	Walter Horton
Rev. Dr. Forbes	Wilson Day
Coroner Watrous	Halbert Brown
Seldon	W. W. Shuttleworth

The action takes place at the home of Robert Andrews, in a suburb of Chicago. Staged by the Authors.

Robert Andrews, president of a bank, is a half million dollars short in his accounts. To protect his fellow directors, his depositors and his ward, Anne Maynard, he plans to have himself murdered that his recently accumulated life insurance may save the bank. There are several possible, but inexperienced, would-be murderers in the cast. One of them attempts the job, but gets the wrong man. Suspicion points to several innocent people until the mystery is cleared up and the bank president finds a way to repay the bank without dying. Then he marries Miss Maynard.

"SONYA"

A romantic play in three acts, adapted from the Polish of Gabryela Zapolska by Eugene Thomas Wyckoff. Produced by Marc Klaw, Inc., at the 48th Street Theater, New York, Aug. 15, 1921.

Cast of characters —

Peter .... Charlson Smith
Jakov .... Jay Fassett
Prince Paul .... Edward Emery
Count Victor Dukas .... France Bendtsen
Prince Michael .... William H. Thompson
Prince Alexander .... Otto Kruger
Sonya .... Violet Heming
King Stefan .... Joseph Macauley
The Court Chamberlain .... Rexford Kendrick
The Ambassador of Romatia .... Wallis Roberts

Act I.—The apartment of Prince Alexander, the heir apparent. An evening in May. Act II.—The same. Afternoon, one month later. Act III.—The same. Evening of the same day.

The action of the play takes place in the last quarter of the Nineteenth Century, in the Palace Royal of a Kingdom in Eastern Europe. Staged by Harrison Grey Fiske.

Sonya is the solo dancer and a star trapeze performer at the circus. Prince Alexander is the handsome heir apparent to the throne of a kingdom in eastern Europe. Prince Paul, seeking to embarrass his royal cousin, smuggles Sonya into Prince Alexander's apartments disguised as a boy. To outwit the opposition the young people agree to pretend that the girl becomes the mistress of the Prince. A month later they have fallen in love with each other, and when a royal marriage is arranged for the Prince, on the eve of his accession to the throne, he rebels and swears he will marry Sonya or no one. And gets his way.

"SONNY"

A melody play in three acts by George V. Hobart; music by Raymond Hubbell. Produced by the Selwyns, at the Cort Theater, New York, August 16, 1921.

Cast of characters —

Buddy....................Carl Randall
James....................Russell Medcraft
Florence....................Berta Donne
Nora....................Georgie Laurence
Harper Craig....................Richie Ling
Mrs. Crosby....................Emma Dunn
Charlie Crosby....................Ernest Glendinnig
Madge....................Esther Howard
Jasper....................Bert Melville
Henry....................Horace James
Joe Marden....................Ernest Glendinning
Alicia....................Mabel Withee
Thomas....................James Kilpatrick
Zeke....................Jack Fox
Zach....................Joseph Evans
Dick....................Robert Pollock
Harry....................Wm. Meredith
Martin....................Fred Grod
Donald....................Nate Goodwin
Rose....................Violet Gray
Rosemary....................Dorothy Clark

Act I.—Scene 1—The Exterior of the Home of the Crosbys in Pelham Manor. Time—1917. Scene 2—The Exterior of Joe Marden's Garage in Granby, Michigan. Time—1917. Scene 3—A Room in a Base Hospital in France. Time—1918. Scene 4—Part of the Deck of a Transport Homeward Bound. Time—Spring, 1919. Act II.—The Living Room in the Home of the Crosbys in Pelham Manor. Time—Early Summer, 1919. Act III.—The Same as Act II. Time—Eight days later. Staged by the Author.

Charlie Crosby leaves his blind mother in Pelham Manor and goes to war. In France he meets Joe Marden, who is enough like him to be his twin brother. Charlie is mortally wounded, but before he dies he makes Joe promise that he will return to Pelham Manor and pretend to be Charlie Crosby, that the blind mother may never know her son was killed. In Pelham Joe has a time of it convincing the neighbors that he is Charlie, but just as he is about to get into serious trouble the mother tells him she knew him all the time. He and

Charlie, it appears, were indeed twin brothers who had been separated in infancy when the Crosby yacht went down in Lake Michigan.

"THE MIMIC WORLD"

A revue in two acts, lines and lyrics by Harold Atteridge, James Hussey and Owen Murphy; music by Jean Swartz, Lew Pollack and Owen Murphy. Produced by the Shuberts at the Century Promenade, New York, Aug. 15, 1921.

Principals engaged —

Clarence Harvey
Lou Edwards
Frank Masters
Albert Wiser
Wm. Moran
Cliff Edwards
Mae West
Gladys James
El Brendel
Flo Burt
Peggy Brown
Beth Stanley

Staged by Allen K. Foster.

"NOBODY'S MONEY"

A farce comedy in three acts by Willian Le Baron. Produced by L. Lawrence Weber at the Longacre Theater, New York, Aug. 17, 1921.

Cast of characters —

Mrs. Judson....................Helen Lowell
An Expressman....................John Ryan
Francis R. Carey....................Frederick Raymond, Jr.
Carl Russell....................Robert Strange
Helen Carey....................Jean Robertson
Grace Kendall....................Regina Wallace
John W. Hamilton....................Wallace Eddinger
Eddie Maloney....................Will Deming
Annette Riley....................Shirley De Me
Henry Kendall....................Howard Gould
Bertram Miller....................Philip Lord
George Kelly....................William J. Brady

Act I.—Living Room of the House Occupied by Carey and Russell. Act II.—Henry Kendall's Library. Act III.—Same as Act I. About Two Weeks Later. The Action of the Play Occurs in a Large Middle Western City in the Present Year.

Frances Carey and Carl Russell, writers, to outwit the publishers who control their exclusive output, create a mythical author who becomes more popular than either of them. When they overlook an item or two in this young man's income tax return the internal revenue officers descend upon them and they are obliged to produce him in person. They hit upon the scheme of hiring John W. Hamilton, an alleged book agent, to impersonate the author. After John W. gets them into and out of many scrapes, it transpires that he is a tired business man seeking adventure as the pal of a burglar, whom they know as his secretary.

"THE SCARLET MAN"

A farce comedy in three acts by William Le Baron. Produced by Charles Dillingham at the Henry Miller Theater, New York, Aug. 22, 1921.

Cast of characters —

Daniel G. Talbot	William Morris
Margaret	Beatrice Tremaine
Mrs. Talbot	Olive May
Helen Clarke	Patricia Morris
Wilbur Lawrence	John Cumberland
Mrs. Delafield	Alice Putnam
Mary Talbot	Frances Carson
Richard Talbot	Don Borroughs
Jackson	John Gray

Act I.—The Talbots' Living Room in Putnam, Westchester County, New York. (During Act I. the curtain will be lowered for thirty seconds to mark the passing of two hours.) Act II.—Living Room of Wilbur Lawrence's Apartment in New York. Later, the Same Evening. Act III.—Scene 1—Same as Act I. The Next Morning. Scene 2—Same. One Week Later. Staged by Ira Hards.

Richard Talbot is engaged to marry Helen Clarke, when he learns that a year before she had been the subject of a village scandal. Missing the last boat at a picnic she had remained all night on an island alone with a young man. Richard, at the request of his shocked parents, promptly breaks his engagement, which so angers his sister Mary that she determines to "lose her own reputation" and see what her family will do about that. Making her way to the bachelor apartment of Wilbur Lawrence, a timid lad to whom she is engaged, she insists on staying the night there that she may be properly compromised. Wilbur is terribly upset, especially next day, when his friends begin to cut him, his club requests his resignation and he loses his job as a result of the "scandal" forced upon him. It is the man who pays and pays and pays, decides Wilbur. A general family compromise clears up the complications.

"THE MASK OF HAMLET"

A melodrama in three acts by Ario Flamma. Produced by the Excelsior Drama Corporation at the Princess Theater, New York, Aug. 22, 1921.

Cast of characters —

Paschensko	Cecil Owen
Trofin	Ashmead Scott
Katia	Laura Walker
Powell	John Todd
Father O'Fallen	John R. Amory
Marx Marvin	Harmon MacGregor
Mrs. Marvin	Leah Winslow
Margaret	Francesca Rotoli
Mr. Marvin	George Berry

Act I.—The Apartment of Marx and Katia. Greenwich Village. Act II.—Living Room in the Home of the Marvins. On Long Island. Act III.—The Same as Act II.—A Few Minutes Later. Time—September 22, 1920. Staged by Cecil Owen.

A crude melodrama seeking to place the blame for the Wall street bomb outrage of a year ago at the door of a visionary bolshevik, who, on learning that his own father was among the victims, committed suicide.

"THE DETOUR"

A domestic drama in three acts by Owen Davis. Produced by the Messrs. Shubert, at the Astor Theater, New York, Aug. 23, 1921.

Cast of characters —

Stephen Hardy....Augustin Duncan
Helen....Effie Shannon
Kate....Angela McCahill
Tom Lane....Willard Robertson
Dana Lamont....Harry Andrews
Dora Lamont....Eva Condon
Ben Clenny....Claude Cooper
Weinstein....James Waters
Jake....Leon Watsky

Act I.—Mrs. Hardy's Kitchen, Act II.—The Veranda. That Afternoon. Act III.—The Kitchen. A Little Later. Time—The Present. Place—Near Northport, L. I. Staged by Augustin Duncan.

For ten years Helen Hardy, the patiently plodding wife of a Long Island truck farmer, has secretly been saving her butter and egg money that her daughter Kate may go to New York and study the art for which she has given evidence of possessing some talent. But the day the great venture seems to have been made possible Farmer Hardy puts his foot down. He doesn't believe in paintin' nohow, and he needs whatever savin's the family may have to buy more land and put his truck farm on a paying basis. The wife rebels, and is even ready to leave both home and husband, when a visiting artist convinces her that her daughter's talent isn't really worth cultivating. Pathetically she settles back into the old rut, the money goes into the farm and the daughter decides to marry the village garage owner.

"THE TRIUMPH OF X"

A domestic drama in four acts by Carlos Wupperman, produced by Lee Shubert and Jessie Bonstelle at the Comedy Theater, New York, August 24, 1921.

Cast of characters —

Phillis.....Helen Menken
Ralph Armstrong.....Robert Keith
Jenny.....Mrs. Jacques Martin
Robert Knowles.....Frank Morgan
William Taylor.....Fred Burt
Paul.....Frank J. Kirke
Mrs. Armstrong.....Mrs. Herbert Gresham
Colonel Prout.....Ben Hendricks
Marjorie Prout.....Alma Moeller
Christine.....Margaret Knight
A Man.....Benedict McQuarrie

Act I.— Robert Knowles' Study. April. Act II.— Dining Room in the Home of the Armstrongs. A Few Days Later. Act III.— Scene 1 — Robert Knowles' Study. Next Day. Scene 2 — At the End of the Crooked Street. November. Act IV.— Robert Knowles' Study. Staged by W. H. Gilmore and Jessie Bonstelle.

Phillis, "born in sin," is adopted in infancy by her father's chum, Robert Knowles, a professional youth twenty years her senior, and reared in guarded respectability. Grown to young womanhood Phillis becomes engaged to Ralph Armstrong, son of a prominent scientist who holds firmly to the theory that hereditary tendencies cannot be overcome by the influences of environment, and regrets the betrothal. When Phillis, at her engagement dinner party, becomes tipsy on champagne, her fiancé, angered and disgusted, turns on her and reveals to her the facts of her past, whereupon Phillis decides to "laugh her way to hell" to join her parents. Her guardian, who loves her, determines to keep her company, but in the end Phillis finds herself and is able to reclaim her foster parent. The "X" of the title represents the unknown quantity in the soul that, the author claims, inevitably shapes the destiny of a human being, dominating both hereditary tendencies and environment.

"SIX-CYLINDER LOVE"

A comedy in three acts by William Anthony McGuire, produced by Sam H. Harris, at the Sam H. Harris Theater, New York, August 25, 1921.

Cast of characters —

Geraldine Burton	Eleanor Gordon
Richard Burton	Donald Meek
Phyllis Burton	Betty Linley
Mary	Fay Walker
Margaret Rogers	Hedda Hopper
Bertram Rogers	Calvin Thomas
Harold Winston	Kenneth Hill
William Donroy	Ralph Sipperly
Marilyn Sterling	June Walker
Gilbert Sterling	Ernest Truex
George Stapleton	Berton Churchill
Smith	Harry Hammill
Tom Johnson	Howard Hull Gibson

Act I.— Suburban Homes of Richard Burton and Gilbert Sterling, Long Island. Sunday Morning. Act II.— Living Room of the Sterling Residence. Several Months Later. Evening. Act III.— Interior of Sterling's Home. Two Months Later. Staged by Sam Forrest.

(See page 163.)

"PERSONALITY"

A comedy drama in three acts by Philip Bartholomæ and Jasper Ewing Brady, produced by William A. Brady, at the Playhouse, New York, August 27, 1921.

Cast of characters —

(In the Order of Their Appearance)

Dennis Hogan	Freddie Lawshe
Simpson	John Cromwell
A Window Cleaner	Frank Peck
John C. Kent	Dodson Mitchell
Judge Lawton	Albert Sackett
Ruth Kent	Dorothy Bernard
Mary Murdock	Eveta Nudsen
Robert Wainwright	Louis Bennison
Leary	Henry E. Dixey
Franklin	William J. Florence
Jenkins	Robert Vivian

Prologue — Ruth Kent's Bedroom. Midnight. Act I.— John C. Kent's Office. The Next Morning. Act II.— Robert

Wainwright's Apartment. Two Years Later. (During Act II the curtain will be lowered for one minute to denote the passing of an hour.) Act III.— Same as Act II. Three Months Later. The Action Occurs in New York City. Staged by Frank Peck.

Ruth Kent, awakened in the night by a burglar, hurls her bedroom slipper at him and buries her face in the bedclothes. Next day she meets and is greatly attracted to a young man down on his luck, who has applied to her father for a job in answer to an advertisement for a $50,000-a-year man. Afterward she falls in love with this youth, Robert Wainwright, but decides that his amazing ego, superinduced by his quick success, must be broken. She conspires with her father to bring about his failure. But Wainwright outwits them and is himself the conqueror, whereupon he admits he also was the burglar and has always kept the slipper, which satisfies Ruth that he's the boy for her.

"THE WHEEL"

A drama in four acts by Winchell Smith, produced by John Golden, at the Gaiety Theater, New York, August 29, 1921.

Cast of characters —

Theodore Morton....Frank Burbeck
Theodore Morton, Jr....Charles Laite
Edward Baker....Thomas W. Ross
Harry Parke....Stuart Fox
Sam Marks....Harold Waldrige
Stella Wittstein....Margot Williams
Kate O'Hara....Ida St. Leon
Norah Rooney....Leila Bennett
Bridget Rooney....Josephine Williams
Jack LeRoy....J. Francis O'Reilly
Mr. D....Richard Malchein
Mr. S....Herbert Saunders
Mr. G....John Clements
Dave....Frank Keogh
Charlie....Rodney Thompson
Fred....David Sabel
Jake....George Spelvin
Monty....Albert Roccardi
George....Julius Johnson
Tony....Frank Miller

Act I.— Kate's Millinery Shop, West of Broadway, New York, Early September, 6 P.M. Act II.— Apartment of the Mortons. The Following May. Noon. Act III.— Baker's Gambling Apartment in Park Avenue. A Week Later. 9 P.M. Act IV.— Same as Act II. Mid-July. 8 P.M. Play Staged by Winchell Smith.

Kate O'Hara, an attractive and self-reliant Fifth Avenue milliner, marries Theodore Morton, Jr., a young society man, and discovers him to be addicted to gambling. He can't leave the roulette wheel alone. Contriving a way to teach him the costliness of his passion and the absurdity of his theory that some day he will make a big winning and then quit, Kate conspires with Edward Baker, a professional gambler who loves her, to fit up a gambling room and invite Theodore there to play. The boy plays, loses everything, and when he sends for the "boss" to ask for credit discovers his wife occupying that rôle. The shock cures him and he agrees never to play again. The self-sacrificing Baker, having made Kate happy, gracefully retires.

"THE POPPY GOD"

A melodrama in a prologue and three acts by Leon Gordon, Leroy Clements and Thomas Grant Springer, produced by the Selwyns at the Hudson Theater, New York, August 29, 1921.

Cast of characters —

THE PROLOGUE

Mrs. Bennett	Marion Grey
Stanley Bennett	Ralph Morgan
Major Hawley	J. Malcolm Dunn
Higgins	Wallace Ford
Exley	King Calder
Leighton	Glenn Hopkins
"Tubby"	George Pembroke
Steward	Robert Peel

Scene—Bennett's Stateroom on the S.S. *Ventura*, en route from Hong Kong to San Francisco. Time — Evening, November, 1914.

THE PLAY

Hop Lee....................................Harold Seton
Gin Long...................................Harry Mestayer
Wo Ling Wo.................................Geo. MacQuarrie
Stanley Bennett............................Ralph Morgan
Suie Ming..................................Edna Hibbard
Joe ....Nick Stark
Sadie ....Doris Marquette
"Hick" Lewis...............................Frank Allworth
"Doc" ....H. Conway Wingfield
Billy Grant................................Robert Brister
Margery Dean...............................Ruby Gordon
First Tough................................Donald Strebig
Second Tough...............................James Millward
Detective ....Judson Langill
Workman ....Victor Goddard

Act I.— The House of Wo Ling Wo in Marin County — Across the Bay From San Francisco. Summer, 1915. Act II.— "Joe's" Saloon on the Barbary Coast, San Francisco, April, 1917. Act III.— Suie Ming's Room — Waverly Place, San Francisco's Chinatown. Staged by Leon Gordon.

Stanley Bennett, born a coward and trying to fight down the handicap, has lived for many years in China. When the Great War breaks he starts for his native England with the hope that he will have courage enough to join the army. He gets as far as San Francisco where he quits and hides in Chinatown. Here he meets, loves and seduces the wife of his Chinese host, who elects to avenge his honor by condemning Bennett, not to a quick death, but to a slow, torturous one as an opium fiend. Bennett passes out pitifully in the last act.

"BACK PAY"

A drama in three acts and an epilogue by Fannie Hurst, produced by A. H. Woods, at the Eltinge Theater, New York, August 30, 1921.

Cast of characters —

Angie Simms................................Mary Shaw
Rufus Giles................................Edward L. Walton
Hester Bevins..............................Helen MacKellar
Gerald Fishback............................Frank M. Thomas
Philip Gordon..............................Leo Donnelly
J. G. Wheeler..............................E. F. Bostwick
Lottie ....Lucille LaVerne
Kitty ....Hermione Shone

Babe....................................Carmen Nesville
Queenie ....Judith Vosselli
Vida ....Maureen Olsen
Chris Morrison....................................John T. Dwyer
T. Blackton....................................John Charles
M. M. G....................................Donald Hall
H. Messmore....................................William Rhodes
Interne ....Edward Power
Major Hamilton....................................Harry C. Bradley

Act I.— Living Room in the Home of Angie Simms, Demopolis, Ohio. 1914. Act II.— Room in an Apartment on Riverside Drive, 1919. Act III.— Scene 1 — Waiting Room in a Brooklyn Base Hospital. Next Morning. Scene 2 — Same as Act II. One Hour Later. Epilogue — Same as Act II. Two Weeks Later. Staged by Elwood F. Bostwick.

Hester Bevins, reared in a house of ill repute conducted by her aunt in a small Ohio town, grows up to hate cotton and love silk. She has a crepe de chine soul, she says, and must live. She cannot wait for the boy she loves to make enough money to marry her and runs away with a traveling salesman who sells pink silk camisoles. In New York she becomes one of the most successful of the Riverside Drive mistresses. Then she hears that her early love, wounded in France, has been brought to a New York hospital. Deserting a rowdy party of which she is hostess she searches him out, finds him blinded and dying, orders him taken to her apartment, throws out her wealthy paramour and his friends, marries the boy and nurses him until he dies. Then, haunted by the blind eyes that continue to stare at her, she goes back to an honest job as a clerk in a store.

"TWO BLOCKS AWAY"

A character comedy in three acts by Aaron Hoffman, produced by Charles Dillingham, at the George M. Cohan Theater, New York, August 30, 1921.

Jane ....Marie Carroll
Captain Maggie....................................Alice Endres
Robert Ives....................................John Rutherford
Bill Lewis....................................John Cope
Nathaniel Pommerantz....................................Barney Bernard

Nora Finnegan..............................Kate Morgan
Tom Roland..................................Robert Craig
Guiseppe ....William Morlin
Martin ....Wallace Erskine
Mrs. Watson..................................Jessie Nagle
Molly Finnegan...........................Hope Sutherland
Officer Donovan.........................Charles Henderson
Jimmy Finnegan..............................Clyde Dilson

Act I.—Shop and Living Room of Nate Pommerantz, Second Avenue, New York. Time—About 5.30 on a Hot Saturday Afternoon in July. (During the act the curtain will be lowered for a few seconds to denote the lapse of about two hours.) Act II.—Two Blocks Away. (Residence of Mr. Nathaniel Arange.) Another Saturday a Year or so Later. Act III.— Time—The Action of Act III takes place a few minutes before the end of Act II. The Same Night.

Nathaniel Pommerantz, a gentle and a generous Jew, is a cobbler on New York's East Side, living with an adopted daughter and loving everybody. Quite unexpectedly he inherits a fortune and moves two blocks away to Fifth Avenue. Here his nature quickly undergoes a change. He forgets all his old friends and grows greedily ambitious. Threatened bankruptcy and a slight attack of brain fever bring him back to normal, and everybody is rich and happy.

"GREENWICH VILLAGE FOLLIES"

A revue in two acts. Lyrics by Arthur Swanstron and J. M. Anderson, music by Carey Morgan, produced by The Bohemians, Inc., at the Shubert Theater, New York, August 31, 1921.

Principals engaged—

Irene Franklin
Robert Pitkin
Rosalind Fuller
Peggy Hope
Ted Lewis
Robert Bold
Donald Kerr
James Watts
Al Herman
Dore
Addie Rolfe
Gretchen Eastman

Production devised and staged by John Murray Anderson.

"DADDY'S GONE A-HUNTING"

A drama in three acts by Zoe Akens, produced by Arthur Hopkins, at the Plymouth Theatre, New York, August 31, 1921.

Cast of characters —

Julien Fields	Frank Conroy
Edith	Marjori Rambeau
Janet	Frances Victory
Walter Greenough	Lee Baker
Theodore Stewart	Hugh Dilman
Mrs. Dahlgren	Helen Robbins
Mrs. Price	Winifred Wellington
Oscar	Manart Kippen
Olga	Olga Olonova
Laura	Jean Wardley
Knight	John Robb

Staged by Arthur Hopkins.

Edith Fields, and Janet, her six-year-old daughter, eagerly await the home-coming of Julian, the husband and father, who has, thanks to the interest and generosity of a wealthy patroness, been studying art in Paris. But when Julian comes he is a changed man. Paris and its artistic life have whetted his desire to be "free," and he would be rid of all family obligations. Edith, momentarily crushed by this startling revelation, accepts it as gracefully as possible. Later she tries to jolt Julian into a fuller realization of what he is doing by first pretending to accept and later accepting the patronage of a wealthy man who loves her and is eager to marry her. But not even the death of the daughter, and a sudden panic of loneliness can reclaim her husband for long, and Edith is left at the play's conclusion sadly facing an empty future.

"SWORDS"

A drama in three acts by Sidney Howard, produced by Brock Pemberton, at the National Theater, New York, September 1, 1921.

Cast of characters —

Amina	Sophie Wilds
Giovanna	Lillian Dix
Madelina	Helen Forrest
Cannetto	José Ruben
Jacopone	John Saunders
Captain of the Garrison	Edward Mackay
Ugolino	Charles Waldron
Papal Nuncio	Montague Rutherford
Maria	Jane Darwell
Fiamma	Clare Eames
Fiorenzo	Catherine Roberts
Damiano	Raymond Bloomer

Staged by Brock Pemberton.

Fiamma, a beautiful lady of Italy, in the days following the Crusades, is imprisoned in the castle of Ugolino, a German noble, at war with the papish party in Italy. It is Ugolino's intention to bend Fiamma to his will, but so heavy handed and awkward is he that a crafty friend, one Cannetto, deftly takes his place in carrying on the conspiracy. Cannetto forces Fiamma, through threats of torturing her husband and her son, to promise obedience to his desires. But with her loved ones set free Fiamma deftly murders Cannetto the moment he crosses the door of her chamber. Then, with the blessings of the people, who hail her as "Madonna," she walks out of her prison.

"TARZAN OF THE APES"

A melodrama in four acts by Major Herbert Woodgate and Arthur Gibbons, based on the novel of the same title by Edgar Rice Burroughs. American version by George Broadhurst, produced by George Broadhurst, at the Broadhurst Theater, New York, September 7, 1921.

Cast of characters —

Lord Greystoke.............................Lionel Glenister
Lady Greystoke.............................Alice Mosley
Webb ....Howard Kyle
Big Michael..............................John F. Morrisey
Kala, the mother ape......................Edward Sillward
Kerchak ....Alfred Arno
Tarzan, the child...........................John Grattan
Tarzan, the boy..........................Lawrence Marks
Lady May Greystoke....................Minna Gale Haynes
Lady Alicia Clayton..................Greta Kemble Cooper
Bobby, Lord Greystoke.......................Boyd Clarke
Edward Ainslee............................Lionel Glenister
Charles Porter..........................Forrest Robinson
Jane Porter.................................Ethel Dwyer
Parkinson ....Ford Chester
Tarzan, the man..........................Ronald Adair.

Act I.— On the West Coast of Africa. Act II.— A Room in Greystoke Castle, England. Act III.— On the West Coast of Africa. Act IV.— In Greystoke Castle. Staged by Mrs. Trimble Bradley.

Lord and Lady Greystoke, put ashore in Africa by a mutinous crew, are killed by apes. Their infant son, however, is adopted by a mother ape who has dropped her own infant out of a tree and killed it. Grown to manhood and called Tarzan in Apese, the young Greystoke is found by a searching party sent out to discover trace of his parents and, being taught to talk and wear pants, marries Dr. Porter's daughter and succeeds to the Greystoke estates.

"GET TOGETHER"

A vaudeville revue produced at the Hippodrome, New York, by Charles Dillingham, September 3, 1921.

Principals engaged —

Fokine
Fokina
Bert Levy
Ferry Corwey
Five Kaeths
Three Bobs
Charlotte
Katie Schmidt
Paul Kreckow
Howard Nicholson
Jack Hanley
Moron
Marceline

Staged by R. H. Burnside.

"THE SILVER FOX"

A domestic drama in three acts by Cosmo Hamilton, adapted from the original by Ferencz Herczeg, produced by Lee Shubert, at the Maxine Elliott Theater, New York, September 5, 1921.

Cast of characters —

Frankie Turner..........................Vivienne Osbourne
Edmund Quilter........................Lawrence Grossmith
Major Christopher Stanley...............William Faversham
Helen ....Violet Kemble Cooper
Captain Douglas Belgrave........................Ian Keith

The Scene of the Three Acts is Laid in the Living Room of Quilter's House in the Country. Staged by William Faversham.

Major Christopher Stanley, life-long friend of Edmund Quilter, novelist, has lived for three years in the home of the Quilters, during which time he has fallen deeply in love with Mrs. Quilter. She, as much in love with him, seeks to bring the matter to an issue by seeming deliberately to compromise herself in the eyes of both her husband and his friend. As a result, she is about to lose them both, when Quilter, quite willing to free his wife, whom he does not love, in order that he may marry the younger and more vivacious Frankie

Turner, divorces Mrs. Quilter, who soon thereafter convinces Major Stanley that she is still a good woman and just the mate for him.

"THE HERO"

A domestic drama in three acts by Gilbert Emery, revived by Sam H. Harris, in the Belmont Theater, New York, September 5, 1921.

Cast of characters —

Andrew Lane.............................Richard Bennett
Hester Lane.............................Alma Belwin
Sarah Lane.............................Blanche Friderici
Andrew Lane, Jr.............................Joseph Depew
Oswald Lane.............................Robert Ames
Marthe Roche.............................Fania Marinoff

Act I.— The Dining Room. Act II.— The Sitting Room. Sunday Night, Three Months Later. Act III. The Following Morning. Time—1919. The Scenes Are Laid in the Home of the Lanes in a Small Suburban Town Near New York City.. Staged by Sam Forrest.

(See page 199.)

"THE MERRY WIDOW"

A revival of the operetta in three acts, music by Franz Lehar, lyrics by Adrian Ross, produced by Henry W. Savage, at the Knickerbocker Theater, New York, September 5, 1921.

Cast of characters —

Raoul de St. Brioche.............................Ralph Soule
Natalie.............................Dorothy Francis
Camille de Jolidon.............................Frank Webster
Khadja.............................Charles Angelo
Nova Kovich.............................William H. White
Olga.............................Marie Wells
Nish.............................Jefferson de Angelis
Popoff.............................Raymond Crane
Prince Danilo.............................Reginald Pasch
Sonia.............................Lydia Lipkowska
Marquis Cascada.............................Georges Dufranne
Melitza.............................Margaret Schilling

Praskovia ....Blanche Seymour
Little Willie.................................Weslyn Hull
Head Waiter.................................John Yorke
Orchestra Leader at Maxim's.................Bert V. Elias
Zo-Zo ....Yvette DuBois
Fi-Fi ....Peggy Arthur
Lo-Lo ....Gwyn Stratford
Do-Do ....Evelyn Dorn
Jou-Jou ....Dorothy Gilbert
Frou-Frou ....Margery Wall
Clo-Clo ....Frances Romana
Margot ....Esther Morris

Act I.—The Marsovian Embassy in Paris. Act II.—Gardens of Sonia's Residence in Paris. Act III.—Café Maxim, Paris. Staged by George Marion.

"THE EASIEST WAY"

An American drama in four acts by Eugene Walter, revived by David Belasco, at the Lyceum Theater, New York, September 6, 1921.

Cast of characters —

John Madison.................................Robert Kelly
Willard Brockton.................................Joseph Kilgour
Jim Weston.................................John P. Brawn
Laura Murdock.................................Frances Starr
Elfie St. Clair.................................Laura Nelson Hall
Annie ....Marion Kirby
Mrs. Williams.................................Pauline Moore

Act I.—Mrs. Williams' Ranch House or Country Home, Perched on the Side of the Ute Pass, Near Colorado Springs, Colorado. Time—Late in an August Afternoon. Act II.—Laura Murdock's Furnished Room, Second Story, Back, New York. Time—Six Months Later. Act III.—Laura Murdock's Apartments, New York. Time—Two Months Later. In the Morning. Act IV.—The Same as Act III. Time—The Same Afternoon. Staged by David Belasco.

Laura Murdock, having lived as the mistress of Willard Brockton, a rich New Yorker, for a number of years, goes west and meets an honest newspaper reporter named John Madison. Finding themselves in love, Laura and John confess their respective pasts, agree to overlook each other's slips and marry as soon as they can save the money. Apprised of Laura's determination to go straight, Brockton agrees to release her. Back in New York Laura finds living honest a severe strain, and after facing starvation for weeks goes back to Brockton. Madison, striking it rich in Nevada, comes finally to get her, discovers that she has lied to him and leaves her. Brockton also quits, and Laura, contemplating suicide, changes her mind and decides to get all there is to get out of the rest of her life.

"DON JUAN"

An ironic comedy adapted from Henri Bataille's "L'Homme a la Rose" by Lawrence Langner, produced by Frank Reicher, at the Garrick Theater, New York, September 5, 1921.

Cast of characters —

Consuelito ....Mary Moore
Don Juan....................................Lou Tellegen
Manuel ....Richard Ranier
Duke de Nunez....................................Paul McAllister
Chaplain ....Leonard Rowe
Officer ....J. Herbert Frank
1st Soldier....................................Harry English
2nd Soldier....................................Howard Claney
Alonso ....Henry Mortimer
Fashionable Woman....................................Joan Clement
Countess de Angasturo....................Katherine Atkinson
Barbadillo ....Leonard Rowe
Isabel ....Myra Murray
Unknown Woman....................................Helen Sheridan
1st Tavern Girl....................................Estelle Paul
2nd Tavern Girl....................................Henrietta York
3rd Tavern Girl....................................Elaine Bonton
4th Tavern Girl....................................Elaine Revallos
Beatrice ....Miriam Stoddard
Countess Vera de Lopez....................................Gladys Carr
Juanito ....Robert Schilling
De Molino ....Walter Howe
Oltaro ....Millie Butterfield
Young Girl....................................Alison Bradshaw
Pepilla ....Stella Larrimore
The Traveler....................................Walter Howe
Recapo ....J. Herbert Frank
The Draper....................................Howard Claney
The Innkeeper....................................Leonard Rowe
Barbara ....Henrietta York
Ines ....Theresa Maxwell Conover
The Shepherd....................................Addie Williams

Act I.—The Castle of Nunez Near Seville, About the Year 1620. Act II.—Seville Cathedral. A Few Days Later. Act III.—A Tavern in Andalusia. Five Years Later.

Don Juan, Spain's great lover, arranges an assignation with Consuelito for his friend Manuel. Consuelito's husband returns unexpectedly and kills Manuel, thinking him Don Juan. The latter, furnishing the body with certain marks for identification, permits the rumor to spread that he has been assassinated. Attending his own funeral he overhears the spoken eulogies of his mourning sweethearts, but when shorn of his fame he seeks to renew his easy conquests of the fair sex, he discovers he is no longer popular. It is not he but his legend they worship. Also time is exacting its toll, and he is getting old. In the end he who had been a king of love is forced to buy the favors of a serving wench.

"THE ELTON CASE"

A melodrama in four acts by William Devereux, produced by George Broadhurst, at the Playhouse, New York, September 10, 1921.

Cast of characters —

Donald Hayston.............................Charles Waldron
Robert Elton.................................Byron Beasley
Charles Ramsey..................................Stuart Sage
Frederick Newsome..........................Richard Farrell
George Arthur...............................Edward Poynter
John MacChesney.............................Albert Barrett
Inspector Harris........................John F. Morrissey
District Attorney Russell...................Bernard McOwen
Thompson ....John Jennings
Marjorie Ramsey.............................Chrystal Herne
Josephine Hayston...........................Kathleen Lowry
Lady Anstruther...............................Florence Fair
Mme. Cecile Florent............................Jetta Coudal
Mrs. Griggs.................................Anne Sutherland
Jenny ....Joan Taber
Mrs. ———.................................Genevieve Hayes

Act. I.—The Living Room in the Home of Marjorie Ramsey. Evening. Act II.—The Scene is the Same as Act I. The Next Afternoon. Act III.—The Living Room in the Home of Robert Elton. The Same Night. Act IV.—The Scene is the Same as Act III. Next Morning About 10 O'clock. Staged by Mrs. Trimble Bradley.

Marjorie Ramsey, a friend of Robert Elton, famous as a bridge whist expert, learns that her younger brother,

Charles, having misappropriated the funds of his firm, is likely to be sent to jail if he does not recover $10,000 within a few hours. To help him Marjorie agrees to play Elton for $5 a point. In place of winning she loses. Elton agrees to give her another chance to win. He makes the condition, however, that if she loses a second time she will accept the necessary money from him and become his mistress. Marjorie agrees, but when she visits the Elton apartments she suddenly determines that anything were preferable to dishonor, and shoots Elton dead as he is about to attack her. Confessing the murder to the district attorney, that worthy agrees not to prosecute, first, because of the prominent people who would be involved and second, because he knows he could not secure a conviction.

"THE CIRCLE"

A comedy in three acts by Somerset Maugham. Produced by the Selwyns, at the Selwyn Theatre New York, September 12, 1921.

Cast of characters —

Arnold Champion-Cheney, M.P. .... Robert Rendel
Footman .... Charles L. Sealy
Mrs. Shenstone .... Maxine MacDonald
Elizabeth .... Estelle Winwood
Edward Luton .... John Halliday
Clive Champion-Cheney .... Ernest Lawford
Butler .... Walter Soderling
Lord Porteous .... John Drew
Lady Catherine Champion-Cheney .... Mrs. Leslie Carter

Act I.—Morning. Act II.—Afternoon. Two Days Later. Act III.—Evening of the Same Day. The Scene is Laid in the Drawing Room at Aston-Adley, Arnold Champion-Cheney's House in Dorset, England. Staged by Clifford Brooke.

Lady Catherine Champion-Cheney and Lord Porteous, who had eloped thirty years before, return to England after a lengthy exile in Italy. Taking pity upon them, Elizabeth, the wife of Lady Catherine's son — the son she had deserted when he was five — invites them to visit the old Champion-Cheney estate. There they inadvertently meet the husband from whom her ladyship bolted, and also learn that Elizabeth is seriously contemplating repeating the family history by running away with a young man, whom she greatly prefers to her priggish young huband. Lady Catherine seeks to dissuade the young people, frankly offering her own experience and the misery of her social ostracism as a horrible example. But they will not be convinced. And the circle is completed when the young elopers borrow the old elopers' machine to carry them to London. (See page 311.)

"ONLY 38"

A comedy in three acts by A. E. Thomas. Produced by Sam H. Harris, at the Cort Theater, New York, September 13, 1921.

Cast of characters —

Mrs. Stanley....................................Mary Ryan
Mrs. Newcomb................................Kate Mayhew
Mrs. Peters..............................Helen Van Hoose
Mrs. Sanborn.................................Percy Pollock
Robert Stanley...............................Neil Martin
Lucy Stanley.................................Ruth Mero
Mary Hadley.........................Margaret Shackelford
Syd Johnson...........................Leon Cunningham
Professor Giddings.......................Harry C. Browne

Act I.—Library of the Parsonage; the Stanley Home in Lebanon, a Small New England Town. Act II.—The Stanley Home in Sinclair, a Small College Town. (During this act the tableau curtain will be lowered to indicate the passing of a few days.) Act III.—Same as Act I. Some Weeks Later. (During this act the tableau curtain will be lowered to indicate the passing of a few hours.) Staged by Sam Forrest.

Mrs. Stanley is a minister's widow, recently left with $3,000 life insurance and eighteen-year-old twins. She was the reverend gentleman's second wife and twenty odd years his junior. With the help of her father she puts the children in a small New England college and gradually emerges from the gloom that has always enveloped her. Past the period of respectful mourning she even indulges in a few pretty frocks, and stirs up a romance by attracting the attention of one of the bachelor professors. But the children will have none of such frivolousness and force her back into black. In due time, however, the professor, who loves her, finds a way of overcoming the tyrant children's opposition, and happiness impends.

"THE BLUE LAGOON"

A spectacular melodrama in four acts by Norman MacOwen and Charlton Mann. Produced by the Messrs. Shubert, in association with Basil Dean, at the Astor Theater, New York, September 14, 1921.

Cast of characters —

Mr. Lestrange.............................David Classford
Dick (his son, a child)...............Andrew J. Lawlor, Jr.
Emmeline (his niece, a child)................Lorna Volare
Paddy Button...................................Cecil Yapp
Capt. La Farge.............................Henry Morrell
Dick (a youth).............................Harold French
Emmeline (a girl)..........................Frances Carson
Guy Neborg (a castaway)...................Harry Plimmer
Mrs. Fountain.................................Selma Hall
Mr. Wannamaker.............................Henry Morrell
Capt. Fountain............................Edmund Gurney

Act I.—The Deck of the Sailing Ship *Northumberland*.
Act II., III. and IV.—The Island of the Blue Lagoon.
Staged by Basil Dean.

In this dramatization of H. De Vere Stackpoole's novel of the same name Dick and Emmeline are shipwrecked in the South Seas when he is approximately five and she three. They grow to manhood and womanhood, being protected in their early youth by an Irish seaman. Left alone by the sailor's death they manage to do for themselves, finally discover their love of each other and are so contented in their modern Eden that the uncle who eventually locates them is of a mind to leave them there rather than bring them back to civilization.

"THE WHITE-HEADED BOY"

An Irish comedy in three acts by Lennox Robinson. Produced by Charles Dillingham at the Henry Miller Theater, New York, September 15, 1921.

Cast of characters —

Mrs. Geoghegan....Maureen Delany
George....Sydney Morgan
Peter....Harry Hutchison
Kate....Norah Desmond
Jane....Suzanne McKernan
Baby....Maire Slade
Denis....Arthur Shields
Donough Brosman....John O'Rourke
John Duffy....Arthur Sinclair
Delia....Gertrude Murphy
Hannah....Christine Hayden
Aunt Ellen....Marie O'Neill

Act I.—Evening. Act II.—Night. Act III.—Next Morning. Scene—Mrs. Geoghegan's House in Ballycolman. Staged by J. B. Fagan.

Denis Geoghegan, the youngest of six and his mother's particular pet, is the " white-headed boy " of the Geoghegan family. For his comfort and advancement all the family is sacrificed. They plan to make a doctor of Denis, and marry him to Delia Duffy, the village belle. But when he fails periodically in his examinations at Trinity College the other children rebel. As a result Denis is brought home and plans are made to ship him to Canada, where he is to shift for himself. Before they can get him away, however, the Duffys are heard from. Either Denis will go through with his promise to marry Delia, or there will be an action for breach of promise. To meet which situation Denis promptly marries Delia and takes a job at home as a street laborer, which is so much of a blow to the Geoghegan and Duffy pride that they are of mind to give the boy anything he wants if he will only promise not to disgrace them. So they find Denis a fine position and the play leaves him as much master of the situation as he ever had been.

"LAUNCELOT AND ELAINE"

A poetic drama in four acts by Edwin Milton Royle. Produced by the Playwright and Players' company, at the Greenwich Village Theater, New York, September 12, 1921.

Cast of characters —

King Arthur.................................Gerald Rogers
Queen Guinevere..............................Selena Royle
Sir Launcelot............................Pedro de Cordoba
Sir Modred.................................J. Arthur Young
Sir Gawain....................................W. Lawrence
The Voice of Lyonesse................Margaret Fareleigh
Lord of Astolot..........................Charles Harbury
Sir Torre.....................................John Hendricks
Sir Lavaine...................................Lee Leonard
Elaine.......................................Josephine Royle
The Servitor.............................Bertram Marburgh
The Hermit.......................................Karl Stall
Lady Vivian.....................................Elsie Esmond
Lady Margaret.............................Martha Messinger
Lady Ysolde...............................Margaret Fareleigh
Lady Melissa..............................Francesca Di Stinti
Lady Rosamund...........................LaGarda Harling
Knights.......................Bosley Hiss and H. B. Dee

Prologue—A Glen in the Trackless Wastes of Lyonesse. Act I.—The Queen's Garden in King Arthur's Court. Act II.—Courtyard of the Castle of the Lord of Astolot. Act III.—Same as Act II. Act IV.—Sunken Garden of Arthur's Palace on the Banks of the Thames. Staged by Edward Elsner.

A dramatization of episodes from Tennyson's "Idylls of the King," involving Launcelot's worldly love for Guinevere and his spiritual love for the lily maid of Astolot, beginning with the Knights of the Round Table swearing fealty to King Arthur and ending with the death of Elaine and the appearance of the funeral barge at the castle landing.

"BLUEBEARD'S EIGHTH WIFE"

A comedy in four acts adapted by Charlton Andrews from the French of Alfred Savoir. Produced by William Harris, Jr., at the Ritz Theater, New York, September, 19, 1921.

Cast of characters —

The Marquis de Briac....................Ernest Stallard
Lucienne....................Anne Meredith
John Brandon....................Edmund Breeze
Monna....................Ina Claire
Albert De Marceau....................Barry Baxter
Mlle. George....................Leonore Harris
M. Kay....................Jules Epailly
A secretary....................Philip Tonge

Act I.—At Biarritz, a Hotel. October. Act II.—The Brandon's Drawing Room in Paris. Six Months Later. Act III.—Monna's Boudoir. That Night. Act IV.—The Same. Six Months Later. Staged by Lester Lonergan and Robert Milton.

Monna de Briac, daughter of an impoverished French nobleman, knowing that John Brandon, the richest American in the world, is dickering with her father for her "purchase," agrees to sell herself to Brandon on his usual terms — that he will marry her, and, in the event of his tiring of her, will divorce her and give her a handsome allowance — an allowance just double that he has given his seven previous wives. After the ceremony, however, Monna refuses to live with Brandon, whom she secretly loves. Finally, to teach him a lesson and force him to divorce her, she plans to have him find an innocent but drink-befuddled young man in her bed when he returns unexpectedly to his home. Brandon, who really loves Monna, is crushed by the revelation of Monna's apparent faithlessness. With her freedom and her self-respect restored Monna voluntarily remarries Brandon.

"BLOOD AND SAND"

A drama in four acts adapted by Tom Cushing from the novel by Blasco Ibanez bearing the same title. Produced by Charles Frohman, Inc., at the Empire Theater, New York, September 20, 1921.

Cast of characters —

Garabato	John Rogers
A Room Attendant	Edward Norris
Dr. Ruiz	Louis Calvert
Alvarez	F. D. Dalton
Juan Gallardo	Otis Skinner
Don Jose	William Lorenz
Antonio	Guy Nichols
Encarnacion	Octavia Kenmore
Senora Josefina	Edna Vaughn
Rosario	Madeline Delmar
Juanillo	Fred. Verdi
Pepe	Martin Broder
Dona Sol	Catherine Calvert
El Nacional	Romaine Callender
Marques De Miura	Chas. N. Greene
Condesa De Torrealta	Shirley Gale
Dona Sarasate	Cornelia Skinner
Monsenor	Claude Gouraud
Don Ernesto	James Church
Dona Luisa	Eleanor Seybolt
Dona Emilia	Genevieve Delaro
A Servant	Robert Brinton
Pedro	Victor Hammond
Senora Angustias	Clara T. Bracy
Mariana	Devah Morel
A Picador	William Gaylord
A Priest	Carlos N. Gray
El Fuentes	Nathan Edward
An Attendant	Kenneth Kipling

Act I.—El Gallardo's Sitting Room in the Hotel of the Rising Sun, Madrid. Act II.—The Salon of Dona Sol. Act III.—The Patio of La Rinconada in Andalusia. Act IV.—Scene 1—The Salon of Dona Sol. Scene 2—The Chapel of the Virgin of the Dove at the Plaza de Toros in Madrid.

Juan Gallardo, the favorite toreador of Spain, at the height of his popularity in Madrid, meets and is fascinated by Dona Sol, a great lady with the instincts of a vampire, who first accepts and later repulses him. After making vain attempts to restore himself to the lady's graces Juan is killed in the bullring and dies in the chapel adjoining the arena. He dies with his faithful wife's kisses, but Dona Sol's name, on his lips.

"THE MAN IN THE MAKING"

A drama in four acts by James W. Elliott. Produced by John Meehan, Inc., at the Hudson Theater, New York, September 20, 1921.

Cast of characters —

Jimmy Carswell....................Donald Gallagher
Grace Whiting....................Kathleen Comegys
Aunt Lou....................Suzanne Willis
Mrs. Carswell....................Leah Winslow
Cliff Whiting....................Francis Byrne
J. Z. Carswell....................Paul Everton
Lester Toomey....................Robert Fisk
Stanley Sheridan....................Raymond Hackett
Traveling Salesman....................Joseph Guthrie
Al Wayman....................William B. Mack
Slim Peters....................Duncan Harris
Dolan....................Edwin Walter
Teddy Barco....................Justin Lees
The Clam....................Billie Bergh
Theodore Barco....................Fraser Coulter

Prologue—Home of J. Z. Carswell. Act I.—Same. Act II.—Mezzanine floor of a San Francisco hotel. Act III.—The home on the hill. Act IV.—A small town in the Middle West. Staged by John Meehan.

J. Z. Carswell, a pushing, forceful, self-made man, is determined that this son Jimmy shall enjoy the educational advantages he missed. Against thc advice of his best friend, who insists four years of college life will ruin any boy who is "sent" there before he has found himself in real work and appreciates what a college education means, J. Z. ships Jimmy to a big institution of learning —and receives him back four years later with a fine taste for liquor and parties, but none for labor. Whereupon J. Z. cuts Jimmy off at the pockets and sends him out to "make good or make room." Jimmy goes from bad to worse, falls in with crooks and such like, but is finally reclaimed and builds a last act city in which boys are privileged to earn their educations and everybody lives by success mottoes.

"THE RETURN OF PETER GRIMM"

A psychic drama in four acts by David Belasco. Revived by Mr. Belasco, at the Belasco Theater, New York, September 21, 1921.

Cast of characters —

Peter Grimm	David Warfield
Frederik	John Sainpolis
James Hartman	George Wellington
Andrew MacPherson	Joseph Brennan
Rev. Henry Batholommey	William Boag
Colonel Tom Lawton	John F. Webber
Willem	Richard Dupont
Kathrien	Miriam Doyle
Mrs. Batholommey	Marie Bates
Marta	Marie Reichardt
The Clown	David Malcom

The First Act takes place at eleven o'clock in the morning on a fine Spring day. The Second Act ten days later. The Third Act on the Same Night. The scene of the play is laid in the living room of Peter Grimm's home in Grimm Manor, a small town in New York State, founded by early settlers from Holland.

Peter Grimm, a Dutch horticulturist and early settler in New York state, jokingly makes a compact with his friend, Andrew MacPherson, who is greatly interested in psychical phenomena, that whichever dies first shall come back and report progress to the other. Peter passes out shortly after, and though he does return, and works earnestly to get his messages across, both to Andrew and his adopted daughter, he has a difficult time making them understand. Finally, working through a "sensitive," a small boy who is himself near death, Peter is able to expose the dishonorable record of a nephew of whom he was inordinately proud while he was alive, and bring happiness to those he loved most.

"THE SPRING"

A drama in a prologue and three acts by George Cram Cook. Produced by the Provincetown Players at the Princess Theater, New York, September 21, 1921.

Cast of characters —

Nam-e-qua....................................Jeanie Begg
Singing Bird....................................Jeanne Powers
Na-som-see....................................Andrew Fraser
Elijah Robbins I....................................Donn Miller
John Street....................................Iden Thompson
Black Hawk....................................Harlod McGee
Wai-tai-sai....................................Em Lo
Ti-a-ma.................................... C. J. Matthews
Village crier of Sauk-e-nauk....................................Alan MacAteer
Ira Robbins....................................Harold McGee
Mrs. Caroline Robbins....................................Kirah Markham
William Chantland....................................Howard F. Smith
Esther Chantland....................................Ruth Rickaby
Elijah Robbins III....................................William S. Rainey
Dr. Hadley....................................Andrew Fraser
Johnson....................................Donn Miller
Nurse....................................Greta Hoving
Louis Williams....................................Eugene Lincoln
Dr. Sheldon....................................Henry O'Neill
Judge Parsons....................................Alan MacAteer

In a Sauk village, 1813. Acts I., II. and III.—Same location 100 years later. Staged by George Cram Cook.

A psychological drama in which the spirit of a Sauk Indian, taking temporary possession of the body of a descendant a century after its owner's passing, gets several persons, including a youthful and progressive professor of psychology, into serious trouble with those conservative investigators who look upon the demonstration as proof of the heroine's insanity. The young professor is able, by the practice of hypnotism, finally to straighten out the tangle.

"MUSIC BOX REVUE"

A topical revue in two acts, words and music by Irving Berlin. Produced by Sam H. Harris at the Music Box, New York, Sept. 22, 1921.

Principals engaged —

Irving Berlin
William Collier
Sam Bernard
Joseph Santley
Ivy Sawyer
Rose Rolando
Rene Riano
Hugh Cameron
Margaret Irving
Florence Moore
Wilda Bennett
Paul Frawley
Emma Haig
Mlle. Marguerite
Frank Gill
Richard W. Keene
Aleta

Staged by Hassard Short.

"WAIT 'TIL WE'RE MARRIED"

A comedy in three acts by Hutcheson Boyd and Rudolph Bunner. Produced at the Playhouse, New York, by Oliver Morosco, Sept. 26, 1921.

Cast of characters —

Kate Livermore.........................Maud Turner Gordon
Marshall.................................Gerald Oliver Smith
James Twells...............................Robert Strange
Marion Livermore...........................Marion Coakley
Connie Temple..................................Jean Shelby
William Plumb..................................Henry Duffy
Aunt Carrie...................................Adah Sherman
Aunt Betsy....................................Lucy Beaumont
Aunt Meridian...............................Edna May Oliver
Tom Hatch..................................James Spottswood
Uncle Kester..................................Rapley Holmes
Felix...Robert Hawkins

Act I.—Reception Hall of Mrs. Kate Livermore's Country House Near Tuxedo. Act II.—Lapse of One Month. Garden of William Plumb's Home on Staten Island. Act III.—One Year Later. The Same. Staged by Oliver Morosco and John McKee.

Marion Livermore, a society girl and rich, fishes William Plumb, a war hero, but shy, out of a river when he is about to drown. Taking a personal interest in William after that Marion decides she would like to marry him, but would prefer that he be made over first that he may cut a better figure in her social set. William, pure and high-principled, does not take gracefully to the suggested reforms, and Marion finally gives him up as a bad job, only to repent a year later when she discovers that, taking her at her word, he has acquired all the monkey tricks of her society friends. Bill was only shamming, however, so they kiss and make up.

"BLOSSOM TIME"

A musical comedy in three acts, adapted from the German by Dorothy Donnelly. Produced by the Messrs. Shubert, at the Ambassador Theater, New York, September 29, 1921.

Cast of characters —

Mitzi.......................................Olga Cook
Bella Bruna..................................Zoe Barnett
Fritzi...................................Dorothy Whitmore
Kitzi.....................................Frances Halliday
Mrs. Kranz.................................Ethel Branden
Greta.......................................Emmy Niclas
Baron Franz Schober........................Howard Marsh
Franz Schubert...........................Bertram Peacock
Kranz.....................................Wm. Danforth
Vogl..Roy Cropper
Kuepelweiser...................................Paul Kerr
Von Schwind..............................Eugene Martinet
Binder.......................................Lucius Metz
Erkmann.....................................Perry Askam
Count Sharntoff..............................Yvan Servais
Hansy.......................................Irving Mels
Novotny...............................Robt. Payton Gibbs
Rose.......................................Mildred Kay
Mrs. Coberg..................................Erba Robeson

Founded on the life of Franz Schubert, with numerous liberties taken as to dates, etc., this operetta introduces the composer as a young man just achieving a little prominence in Vienna. In the first act he dashes off the famous "Serenade" on the back of a menu card and meets Mitzi Kranz, daughter of one who is later to become his patron. He loves Mitzi, but when he dedicates his "Song of Love" to her he asks his friend, Baron Schober, to sing it. The Baron obliges and Mitzi promptley transfers her affection to him. Whereupon Franz is hard hit, and out of his misery writes the "Unfinished Symphony."

"POT LUCK"

A comedy in three acts by Edward Childs Carpenter.
Produced by Kilbourn Gordon Inc., at
the Comedy Theater, New York,
September 29, 1921.

Cast of characters —

Lester Scanlon	Junius Matthews
Sarah Penfield	Beth Franklyn
Martha Holcomb	Helen Reimer
Amy Jewell	Clara Moores
William Farley	Frank Allworth
Hilda Wren	Frances Kennen
Mrs. Wren	Jennie Dickerson
Phoebe Lyman	Helen Stewart
Jim Patterson	Rockliffe Fellowes
Stephen McCauley	James Rennie
Judge Penfield	Howard Nugent
Roscoe Brown	Percy Moore
Wilbur Holcomb	Frank E. Jamieson
David Crum	Douglas Bright

Acts I., II. and III.—Home and phonograph parlor of Amy Jewell, in Hebron, Conn.

Amy Jewell, slipping into her middle twenties, still unmarried, and recently jilted, determines to advertise for a husband. As a result of the ad she exchanges photographs with a likely looking prospect and invites him to call upon her at her phonograph parlor in Hebron, Conn. The applicant, who turns out to be a professional crook, brings with him a young newspaper man who is temporarily "in bad" as the result of a little rum-running adventure across the Canadian border. Amy refuses to marry the crook, but takes kindly to his more literate friend. Inasmuch as all the crooks want is the girl's money, it doesn't matter which of them marries her, so the newspaper lad takes over the assignment. Married he falls in love with Amy and is eager to protect her, but he is hounded by his pal, until a way is found to be rid of him.

"BEWARE OF DOGS"

A comedy in three acts by William Hodge. Produced by Lee Shubert, at the Broadhurst Theater, New York, October 3, 1921.

Cast of characters —

Nick....................Gustave Rolland
Mrs. Williams....................Mrs. Chas. G. Craig
George Oliver....................William Hodge
Florence Arnold....................Ann Davis
Mr. Appleton....................George W. Barbier
Henry Shaw....................Leighton Stark
Mrs. Appleton....................Edith Shayne
Mr. Jennings....................John Webster
Camille DuBarry....................Julia Burns
John Winford....................Philip Dunning
Mimi....................A. Pekingese
Dynamite....................An English Bull

Acts I., II. and III.—George Oliver's Home, Just Off the Boston Post Road, Greenwich, Conn. Time—The Present.

George Oliver, renting a place in the country in which to care for an invalid sister, assumes with it the proprietorship of a boarding kennel for dogs. Being a trusting soul he does not suspect that his hired man is robbing him of his hen's eggs, or that his cook is running a blind tiger. And he is quite upset when he learns that the dog owners who have been in the habit of using the first floor front are not Mr. and Mrs. Appleton at all, but Mr. Appleton and his lady friend, Camille Du Barry. Learning these things Mr. Oliver rises up and smites the sinners, thus quieting the neighborhood scandal that has been started, and convinces Florence Arnold that he is worth marrying.

"THANK YOU"

A comedy in three acts by Winchell Smith and Tom Cushing. Produced by John Golden at Longacre Theater, New York, October 3, 1921.

Cast of characters —

Hannah	Helen Judson
Miss Blodgett	Dickie Woolman
Joe Willetts	Albert Hyde
David Lee	Harry Davenport
Andy Beardsley	Frank McCormack
Mrs. Jones	Alice Johnson
Gladys Jones	Frances Simpson
Monte Jones	Theodore Westman, Jr.
Diane	Edith King
Kenneth Jamieson	Donald Foster
Cornelius Jamieson	Frank Monroe
Leonard Higginbotham	Charles Goodrich
Abner Norton	George Schiller
Dr. Andrew Cobb	William Post
Judge Hasbrouck	Herbert Saunders
Hiram Swett	Frederick Malcolm
Morton Jones	Alfred Kappeler
Alfred Watrous	George Spelvin
Griggs	Leslie Palmer

Act I.—The Study at St. Mark's Rectory, Dedham, Conn. Mid-Winter. Act II.—Same. Spring. Act III.—Same. Autumn. Staged by Winchell Smith.

The Rev. David Lee, pastor of St. Mark's church in Dedham, Conn., is living on a salary of $800 a year "and donations." His niece, Diane, who has been brought up in Paris, comes to live with him and is properly shocked to find uncle dependent upon the "tips" of his congregation. She keeps at him until she strengthens his courage to demand a living wage and refuse all gratuities, and starts something of a scandal when she takes charge of the housekeeping and shows to what straits the pastor is reduced when he tries to live on his salary. The vestry, stung by the unsavory notoriety, seeks to force the Rev. Lee's resignation, at which juncture a rich business man, whose son the pastor has saved, steps in and provides the pastor with a bank account. A year later, his self-respect re-established and his church a great success, the Rev. David gives his niece in marriage to the rich man's son.

"LIKE A KING"

A comedy in three acts by John Hunter Booth. Produced by Adolph Klauber at the Thirty-Ninth Street Theater, New York, October 3, 1921.

Cast of characters —

Thomas H. Coffin	Charles Esdale
Norah Smuts	Margaret Wiltshire
Nathaniel Artemus Alden	James Gleason
Dan Riordan	Hale Norcross
Policeman	John Hardtap
Mrs. Alden	Mina Gleason
Phyllis Weston	Ann Harding
Abigail	Lucille Parker
Robert Alden	James Seeley
Arabella Alden	Frances Howard
General Wade Weston	Robert E. Homans
Samuel Pemberton	E. L. Duane
Calvin Lowe	Edward Poland
J. W. Savage	Max Waizman
William Chubb	Arthur Allen
George W. Grubble	Dodson Mitchell

Act I.—Scene 1—A corner in Central Park, New York City. Midnight. Scene 2—The Alden home. Lower Falls, Mass. Act II. and III. The living room.

Nathaniel Alden, back from France and broke, is ashamed to go home to Lower Falls, Mass., because he has let his folks think he has achieved a great success as a big business man. Ruminating in Central Park he walks in front of a passing motor car and is knocked down. In the chauffeur he recognizes an old buddy of the army, who, hearing Nat's story, proposes borrowing his employer's Rolls-Royce for a week and rolling Nat into Lower Falls "like a king." They try the experiment, the village accepts Nat as the rich and powerful man he looks to be, and he is invited to take over the rebuilding of the town. Several times he is threatened with being completely exposed, but by a lucky twist of fate, gets through successfully, is betrothed to the girl next door and holds in his hand a check for $50,000 advanced by a man who wants to get in on the town's boom as the curtain falls.

"THE O'BRIEN GIRL"

A musical comedy in two acts, music by Lou Hirsch, book and lyrics by Otto Harback and Frank Mandel. Produced by George M. Cohan at the Liberty Theater, New York, October 3, 1921.

Cast of characters —

Mrs. Hope	Finita DeSoria
Alice O'Brien	Elizabeth Hines
Joe Fox	Alexander Yakovleff
Lawrence Patten	Edwin Forsberg
Humphrey Drexel	Robinson Newbold
Mrs. Drexel	Georgia Caine
Eloise Drexel	Ada Mae Weeks
Larry Patten	Truman Stanley
Wilbur Weathersby	Andrew Tombes
Gerald Morgan	Carl Hemmer
Minerva	Kitty Devere
Lucille	Vera O'Brien
Aline	Kathleen Mahoney
Estelle	Gretchen Grant
Wolf	Harry Rose
Bear	George Page
Eagle	Lou Lesser
Owl	George Hurd
Mickey	M. Cunningham
Dickey	Hazel Clements

Act I.—The Exterior of a Fashionable Hotel on a Lake in the Adirondacks. Act II.—Scene 1—A room adjoining the Ballroom; same hotel. Scene 2—Exterior of Ballroom. Staged by Julian Mitchell.

Alice O'Brien, stenographer and secretary to Humphrey Drexel, acquiring $800 quite suddenly and unexpectedly, determines to spend it all on one good time at a fashionable Adirondack lake resort. All goes well until she meets her employer, who is married to a jealous and suspicious wife. To protect himself, Mr. Drexel is forced to keep the O'Brien girl's secret. At the lake Alice meets Larry Patten, a son of riches, and though his people are not keen about his marrying a common stenographer, he succeeds in convincing them that Alice is altogether uncommon, and likewise an excellent soprano.

"LILIES OF THE FIELD"

A drama in three acts by William Hurlburt. Produced by Garrick Productions, at the Klaw Theater, New York, October 4, 1921.

Cast of characters —

Suki....................Y. Mimura
Nettie....................Gertrude Clemens
Maisie Lee....................Josephine Drake
Florette Ellwood....................Alison Skipworth
Doris Carter....................Pauline Garon
Walter Harker....................Roy Walling
Gertrude Ainlee....................Cora Witherspoon
Amy Van Epps....................Evelyn Duncan
Mildred Harker....................Marie Doro
A Manicurist....................Alice Cavanaugh
Pink Cortney....................Mary Phillips
Lewis Willing....................Norman Trevor
James Overstreet....................J. Cleneay Mathews
Louise....................Dorothy Day
Rose....................Elfin Finn
A Private Detective....................Dan Day

Act I.—In Maisie's New York Apartment. Act II.—One Year Later. The Same. Act III.—One Year Later in Mildred's Apartment in New York. Staged by Harry McRae Webster.

Mildred Harker, unjustly divorced by her husband, who wished to be rid of her that he might take up with another woman, is denied the custody of her two-year old daughter. In her extremity she turns to an old school friend, Maisie Lee, who happens to be one of a group of "lilies of the field," who toil not and spend their days spinning fairy stories to extract money from their lovers. Mildred, staunch in her determination to live worthily for her child's sake, gives up when she is told of the baby's death, and accepts the patronage of one Lewis Willing, the richest and likewise the kindest man in New York. For a year she lives gorgeously with Willing, and learns to love him deeply. Then she hears that her child is alive, that she has been tricked by her ex-husband. She determines to steal the child and run away, but decides to stay when Willing agrees to marry her; and her husband, admitting his wrongs, allows the child to stay with her.

"THE FAN"

A satirical comedy in three acts adapted by Pitts Duffield, from the French of Robert de Flers and Robert de Caillavet. Produced at the Punch and Judy Theater, New York, October 3, 1921.

Cast of characters —

Therese....................................Rosalie Mathieu
Pierre.......................................Jackson Dunn
Marc d'Arnot...............................Edward H. Wever
Germaine de Landeve.....................Eva Leonard-Boyne
Jacques de Landeve.........................Harold Heaton
Blanch Bertier...............................Beatrice Miller
Garin-Miclaux...............................Frank Sylvester
Madame Oviedo.............................Margaret Dumont
Monsieur Oviedo..............................Horace James
François Trevoux..............................Ian Maclaren
Giselle Vaudrey...............................Hilda Spong
Michel...J. A. Osborne

Act I.—Late Afternoon. (The curtain will be lowered for two minutes to denote a lapse of three hours.) Act II.—Evening, Week Later. Act III.—Next Morning. Locale: Cheneviette Manor, the Country Seat of Count de Landeve, in Normandy. Staged by Edgar MacGregor.

Giselle Vaudrey, an attractive widow and a born flirt, visiting her school day friend, Germaine de Landeve, discovers there the only man she ever loved, really,—one François Trevoux. Also she finds Germaine more or less upset because her own husband is inclined to look upon the rouge when it is red on other cheeks than hers; and a trusting ingenue who is beset with worry because her young man will not propose. Giselle agreeably settles all these little affairs and then attaches herself to François.

"THE LOVE LETTER"

A musical comedy in three acts, adapted from a play by Franz Molnar ("The Phantom Rival"), book and lyrics by William Le Baron, music by Victor Jacobi. Produced by Charles Dillingham, at the Globe Theater, New York, October 4, 1921.

Cast of characters —

Michael	Townsend Ahern
Julien	Henry White
Head Waiter	Charles Lawrence
Eugene Bernard	Will West
Countess Irma	Marjorie Gateson
Miriam Charlot	Carolyn Thomson
Madame Charlot	Katharine Stewart
Richard Kolnar	Fred Astaire
Aline Moray	Adele Astaire
Philip Delma	John Charles Thomas
Waiter	Elliott Roth
Bus-Boy	Roger Davis
Marie	Alice Brady
Gina	Irma Irving
Zena	Dorothy Irving
Betty Parker	Jane Carroll
Ambassador	Tom Fitzpatrick

Act I.—The Restaurant. Act II.—Scene 1—The Boudoir. Scene 2—The Dream Ball. Act III.—Countess Irma's Party.
Staged by Edward Royce.

Miriam Charlot, being forced by her socially ambitious mother to marry a fat man, rebels and dreams of the lover who had left her some years before, promising in his last letter to return to her — perhaps as a victorious soldier, a great statesman, a fine artist, or, it might be, as a lowly lackey, or one who begged in the streets. In the dream she sees the lover in each of these characters — and then meets him at the party that night as none of them, but as a successful business man whom mother is perfectly willing she should sing duets with the rest of her life.

"MAIN STREET"

A drama in four acts, adapted by Harvey O'Higgins and Harriet Ford from the novel of Sinclair Lewis, produced by the Messrs. Shubert, at the National Theater, New York, October 5, 1921.

Cast of characters —

Dave Dyer	Bert Melville
Sam Clark	Wm. T. Clark
Adolph Valborg	Chas. P. Bates
Vida Sherwin	Marie Pettas
Juanita Haydock	Marion Hutchins
Cy Bogart	Cliff Heckinger
Myrtle Cass	Marvee Snow
Rita Simons	Ruth G. Clark
Maud Dyer	Eva Lang
Erik Valborg	Norval Keedwell
Guy Pollock	Everett Butterfield
Dr. Will P. Kennicott	McKay Morris
Carol	Alma Tell
Mrs. Clark	Maud Nolan
Ezra Stowbody	Elmer Grandin
Harry Haydock	Boyd Agin
Ella Stowbody	Helen Cromwell
Bea Sorenson	Hilda Helstrom

Act I.—Corner Main Street and Railroad Avenue, Gopher Prairie, Minn. Act II.—Living Room at the Kennicott's. Scene 2—The Bedroom. Act III.—Living Room. Act IV.—Same.

Carol Kennicott, having married a small town doctor, arrives in Gopher Prairie, Minn, and is amazed, not to say shocked, to find it so utterly unpromising a place in which to live. The immediate reformation of its benighted citizens, and the rebuilding of the ugly town along artistic lines becomes her favorite obsession. Gopher Prairie needs culture, and the forces of the uplife must be aroused. All of which the townsfolk resent, causing Carol, in her defiance, to consider leaving

Dr. Will, her husband, and running away with Erik Valborg, a young electrician with a soaring soul. She does go away for a year, but not with Erik, and then returns temporarily chastened and eager to have another try at Gopher Prairie and its people.

"BOMBO"

A musical revue in two acts, book and lyrics by Harold Atteridge, music by Sigmund Romberg. Produced by the Messrs. Shubert, at Jolson's Fifty-ninth Street Theater, New York, October 6, 1921.

Principals engaged —

Al Jolson	Gladys Caldwell
Franklyn A. Batie	Janet Adair
Forrest Huff	Fritzi Von Busing
Bertie Beaumont	Bernice Hart
Frank Bernard	Irene Hart
Russell Mack	Vivien Oakland
William Moore	Mildred Keats
Cortez and Peggy	Janette Dietrich

Staged by J. C. Huffman, under the personal supervision of J. J. Shubert.

"THE WREN"

A comedy in three acts by Booth Tarkington, produced by George C. Tyler and A. L. Erlanger, at the Gaiety Theater, New York, October 10, 1921.

Cast of characters —

Cap'n Olds.................................George Fawcett
Mrs. Freehart..............................Marion Abbott
Frazee...John Flood
Francis...Sam Reed
Mrs. Frazee...............................Pauline Armitage
Roddy.......................................Leslie Howard
Seeby...Helen Hayes

The Scene of the Three Acts is "Cap'n Olds' Place" on the New England Coast; the Time, an Afternoon and Evening and the Following Morning. Staged by Howard Lindsay.

Eusebia ("Seeby") Olds is the "general manager" of Cap'n Olds' Place, a summer boarding house on the New England coast. Mr. Roddy is a young Canadian artist who spends his summers there. Until Mrs. Frazee arrived Roddy seemed to be interested in Seeby. But Mrs. Frazee seemed to fascinate the boy and he was by way of being "lost" until Mr. Frazee appeared and caused a bit of a row. Then, naturally, he turned back to Seeby, who really had been sorta managin' the whole affair — knowin' men were mostly like children, any how, and needed a lota managin'.

"A BILL OF DIVORCEMENT"

A drama in three acts by Clemence Dane, produced by Charles Dillingham, at the George M. Cohan Theater, New York, October 10, 1921.

Cast of characters —

Margaret Fairfield	Janet Beecher
Hester Fairfield	Ada King
Sydney Fairfield	Katharine Cornell
Bassett	Lillian Brennard
Gray Meredith	Charles Waldron
Kit Pumphrey	John Astley
Hilary Fairfield	Allan Pollock
Dr. Alliot	Arnold Lucy
The Rev. Christopher Pumphrey	Fred Graham

Act I.—Christmas Morning. Act II.—Early in the Afternoon. Act III.—Sundown. Scene—A Room in a Small Country House. Staged by Basil Dean.

Scene, England. Time, 1932. Certain amendments to the existing divorce laws are presumed to have been made. Hilary Fairfield, who had married Margaret the year of the Great War, suffered severely from shell shock and was sent to a sanitarium. Several years later he was pronounced incurably insane and Margaret, in love with Gray Meredith, divorced Hilary and was preparing to marry Gray during the New Year holidays. On Christmas day Hilary walked out of the sanitarium, apparently a well man, and sought out his wife and the seventeen-year-old daughter, Sydney, he had never seen. It develops that the shell shock was merely a contributing cause to his mental derangement and that there was insanity in his family. Margaret is torn between her pity for Hilary and her love for Gray. It is Sydney who solves the problem for her. Realizing that it would be wrong for her to marry, with insanity in her family, she sends her own lover away and plans to devote her life to her father, leaving Margaret free to marry Gray. (See page 63.)

"AMBUSH"

A drama in three acts by Arthur Richman, produced by the Theater Guild, Inc., at the Garrick Theater, New York, October 10, 1921.

Cast of characters —

Walter Nichols..............................Frank Reicher
Harriet Nichols..............................Jane Wheatley
Harry Gleason..............................Charles Ellis
Margaret Nichols..........................Florence Eldridge
Seymour Jennison..............................John Craig
Mrs. Jennison..............................Katherine Proctor
A Chauffeur..............................Edwin R. Wolfe
Alan Kraigne..............................Noel Leslie
Howard Kraigne..............................Edward Donnelly
George Lithridge..............................George Stillwell

Acts I., II. and III.—The Home of Walter Nichols, in Jersey City.

Walter Nichols, a clerk earning a moderate salary and trying to live within it, is something of an old-fashioned stickler for the old-fashioned virtues of family honor and the self-respect that is bred by a strict adherence to definite ideals. Neither his wife, Harriet, nor his daughter, Margaret, are able to appreciate his stand in these matters. Margaret is bound she will have pretty clothes and a good time and her mother upholds her in her ambition, with the result that Margaret accepts the patronage of rich men, deliberately selling herself for the things her father can't afford. Trying to make good with his family Nichols speculates and loses. Finally he is beaten, spiritually and physically, his job, his savings, his self-respect gone. The final curtain leaves him accepting money to pay the rent from his daughter's current lover. (See page 271.)

"THE CHILDREN'S TRAGEDY"

A tragedy in three acts by Carl Schoenherr, English text by Benjamin F. Glazer, produced by Arnold Daly at the Greenwich Village Theater, New York, October 10, 1921.

Cast of characters —

The Elder Brother.............................Phillips Tead
The Younger Brother.........................Sidney Carlyle
The Sister..................................Nedda Harrigan

Act I.—The Living Room in the Home of a Forester in a Tyrolean Village. Act II.—The Attic. Act III.—A Clearing in the Forest.

The three children of a Tyrolean forester, becoming suspicious of their mother, whom they have seen flirting with a stranger recently come to the neighborhood, have their suspicions confirmed after they are sent to the attic to get them out of the way. From the window above they observe the approach of their mother's lover in response to the signal set to apprise him of the father's absence. Later in the forest the young brother manages the killing of the lover and drops dead of shock. The sister is attacked by those who threaten to spread the scandal if she tell, and the elder brother is screaming for help through the forest as the curtain falls.

"LOVE DREAMS"

A "melody drama" in three acts by Ann Nichols, lyrics by Oliver Morosco, music by Werner Janssen, produced by Oliver Morosco, at the Times Square Theater, New York, October 10, 1921.

Cast of characters —

Larry Pell....................................Tom Powers
Billy Parks....................................Maurie Holland
Dr. Duncan Pell....................................Orrin Johnson
Cadillac Packard....................................Harry K. Morton
Renee d'Albret....................................Vera Michelena
Stage Manager....................................Charles Yorkshire
Hildegard....................................Maude Eburne
Cherry O'Moore....................................Marie Carroll
Premier Dancer....................................Amelia Allen
Pauline....................................Pauline Maxwell
Grace....................................Grace Culvert
Irene....................................Irene Novotney
Jean....................................Jean Warner
Ann....................................Ann Pauley
Grace....................................Grace Elliott
Maude....................................Maude Lydiate
Charmine....................................Charmine Essley

Act I.—Dr. Pell's New York Apartment. Act II.—Scene 1—Green Room of Theatre Where Renee d'Albret is appearing. Next Day. Act III.—Renee's Home in the Country. A Few Days Later. Staged by Oliver Morosco and John McKee.

Renee D'Albret, presumed to be the wickedest, as she is the barest, musical comedy queen in New York, is in reality a good girl who supports an invalid sister and permits her press agent to tell lies about her for the good of the advertising that will help her make more money. To avenge an insult she becomes engaged to young Larry Pell while Larry is drunk. Later she discovers that he loves her sister, who is made well by Dr. Pell, Larry's brother, and gives him up. She is listening to the doctor's suggestion that they get married, some time, as the curtain falls.

"THE CLAW"

A tragedy in four acts by Henri Bernstein, English version by Edward Delaney Dunn and Louis Wolheim, produced by Arthur Hopkins, at the Broadhurst Theater, New York, October 17, 1921.

Cast of characters —

Jules Doulers	Charles Kennedy
Paul Ignace	E. J. Ballantine
Antoinette	Irene Fenwick
Marie	Marie Bruce
Achille Cortelon	Lionel Barrymore
Vincent Leclerc	Giorgio Majeroni
Anne Cortelon	Doris Rankin
Nathaniel	Joseph Granby
A Doorman	Ian Wolfe
Guy Germain-Leroy	Harold Winston
A Police Officer	S. B. Tobias

Act I.—Home of Doulers. Act II.—(Two Years Later.) Home of Cortelon. Act III.—(Ten Years Later.) Studio of Anne Cortelon. Act IV.—(Four Years Later.) Drawing Room in the Ministry. Staged by Arthur Hopkins.

Achille Cortelon, famous as a journalist and leader of the radical wing of the Socialist party in France, takes as his second wife, Antoinette Doulers, twenty-eight years his junior, the daughter of one of his sub-editors who, with the girl, and unknown to Cortelon, has been scheming for years to bring the match about. Once married to her great catch, Antoinette proceeds to influence him in the interests of herself and her father, plunges him into such extravagances that he is forced to compromise with his enemies, and finally to accept bribes from them in order to maintain his home. Gradually she works his complete moral and physical undoing. Then she trips gayly away to Italy with the newest of her lovers, leaving Cortelon to face the gathering political storm he has brought down upon his head. Outside the ministry a jeering mob has gathered and as he leaves for the chamber of deputies to defend himself he falls dead in the center of his office.

"A BACHELOR'S NIGHT"

A farce comedy in three acts by Wilson Collison, produced by John Cort, at the Park Theater, New York, October 17, 1921.

Cast of characters —

Cleetie....................Amy Ongley
Frederica Dill....................Leila Frost
Vivian Barnes....................Vera Finlay
Lilly Carnes....................Dorothy Smoller
Trixie Moulton....................Lilyan Tashman
Dicky Jarvis....................William Roselle
Gildy Barnes....................Herbert Yost
Amelia Annesley....................Luella Gear
Mrs. Jarvis....................Isabel Irving

The Action of the Play Occurs in the Lounging Room of Dicky Jarvis' Town House, New York City. An Evening in the Early Spring. Staged by Harry Andrews.

Dicky Jarvis, out of town for a vacation, returns to find that Cleetie, his comic maid, has rented a room in his apartment to Frederica Dill, young and pretty. The efforts of Frederica to escape, and Cleetie's attempt to keep her hidden while Dicky is trying to give a party to certain of his low-cut lady friends provide the action.

"THE DEMI-VIRGIN"

A farce comedy in three acts by Avery Hopwood, based on a French original, produced by A. H. Woods, at the Times Square Theater, New York, October 18, 1921.

Cast of characters —

Estelle St. Marr....................Marjorie Clements
Gladys Lorraine....................Mary Salisbury
Dot Madison....................Mary Robinson
Fay Winthrop....................Helen Flint
Cora Montague....................Constance Farber
Bee La Rose....................Sascha Beaumont
Amy Allenby....................Peggy Coudray
Wanda Boresca....................Mildred Wayne
Aunt Zeffie....................Alice Hegeman
Betty Wilson....................Helen Cunningham

Chicky Belden....................................Charles Ruggles
Gloria Graham....................................Hazel Dawn
Sir Gerald Sydney................................Kenneth Douglas
Wally Dean.......................................Glenn Anders
A Director.......................................Charles Mather
Owen Blair.......................................John Maroni
Jack Milford.....................................Ralph Glover

Act I.—A Motion Picture Studio in Hollywood. Act II.—At Gloria's Home, El Paradiso. A Week Later. Act III.—The Same Night. Staged by Bertram Harrison and Charles Mather.

The night Gloria Graham and Wally Dean, motion picture celebrities, were married, a former sweetheart of Wally's called him from Gloria's side at 1 a.m., which made Gloria so mad she promptly left Wally and applied for a divorce. The scandalmongers of Hollywood called her the "demi-virgin" after that. Gloria and Wally are forced to agree to finish the picture they were making when the separation occurred and during this episode Wally, insisting that he has been misjudged, determines to force Gloria to take him back, which he does.

"AS YE MOULD"

A domestic drama in three acts by Charles Mackay, produced by Geoffrey Stein, Inc., at the People's Theater, New York, October 19, 1921.

Cast of characters —

Capt. Thos. Lanford, U.S.N.......................Charles Hammond
Paul Driscoll....................................Geoffrey C. Stein
Mrs. Lanford.....................................Alice Fleming
Mrs. J. Lomax Graham.............................Helen Lackaye
Ella Bates.......................................Leonora Bradley

The action takes place in the living room of the Lanford's home near Newport News.

Mrs. Lanford is the mother of Paul Driscoll's ten-year-old son, a fact she has deemed it wise, seeing she had never married Paul, to keep from her husband, Capt. Lanford, to whom she has been married but a few years. Driscoll, who has been keeping an eye on the boy, has a chance of marrying the rich Mrs. Graham and would be rid of his nameless son. Therefore he proposes to the boy's mother that she ask her husband's permission to adopt him. Mrs. Lanford hesitates, fearing Lanford's discovery of her past, but later agrees. The arrangement is barely consummated, however, before both Capt. Lanford and Mrs. Graham learn the truth. Instead of kicking up the conventional row both are willing to take the boy, who goes to the Lanfords, and only the slimy Driscoll is kicked out.

SOTHERN-MARLOWE SEASON

Revival of Shakespearean plays, presented at the Century Theater, by the Messrs. Lee and J. J. Shubert, during October, November and December, 1921.

"TWELFTH NIGHT"

Cast of characters —

Orsino	Frederick Lewis
Sebastian	Sydney Mather
Antonio	Frank Peters
A Sea Captain	V. L. Granville
Curio	James Hagen
Valentine	Frank Howson
Sir Toby Belch	Rowland Buckstone
Sir Andrew Aguecheek	Albert Howson
Malvolio	Mr. Sothern
Fabian	France Bendtsen
Feste	Vernon Kelso
A Priest	Jerome Collamore
First Officer	Frank Howson
Second Officer	Harold Webster
Olivia	Alma Kruger
Viola	Miss Marlowe
Maria	Lenore Chippendale
Page to the Duke	Elaine Sims
Attendants on Olivia	Lillian Gray, Carolyn Ferriday, Dina Schleicher
Musicians	Helen Besley, Eleanor Wells, John Abrams

"THE TAMING OF THE SHREW"

Cast of characters —

Baptista ....Frank Peters
Vincentio....................................Frank Howson
Lucentio....................................Frederick Lewis
Petruchio....................................Mr. Sothern
Hortensio, Suitor to Bianca..................V. L. Granville
Gremio, Suitor to Bianca..................France Bendtsen
Tranio, Servant to Lucentio....................Vernon Kelso
Biondello, Servant to Lucentio...............Albert Howson
A Pedant....................................Sydney Mather
Tailor....................................Jerome Collamore
Haberdasher....................................J. W. Latham
Grumio....................................Rowland Buckstone
Katharina....................................Miss Marlowe
Bianca....................................Lenore Chippendale
Widow....................................Alma Kruger
Curtis, A Servant to Petruchio.................James Hagen
A Priest....................................Constantine Zazzali
Lady Attendants at Wedding.....Lillian Gray, Maud Walker,
Carolyn Ferriday, Dina Schleicher
Page to Baptista....................................Elaine Sims
Musicians........Eleanor Wells, Helen Besley, John Abrams
Servants to Petruchio......William Adams, Harold Webster,
Elaine Sims, Frank Howson

"THE MERCHANT OF VENICE"

Cast of characters —

Duke of Venice....................................Frank Peters
Prince of Morocco..............................Albert Howson
Prince of Arragon.............................France Bendtsen
Antonio....................................Sydney Mather
Bassanio....................................Frederick Lewis
Salanio....................................Frank Howson
Salarino.................................. Jerome Collamore
Gratiano....................................V. L. Granville
Lorenzo ....Vernon Kelso
Shylock....................................Mr. Sothern
Tubal....................................James Hagen
Launcelot Gobbo...........................Rowland Buckstone
Old Gobbo....................................William Adams
Leonardo....................................Harold Webster
Balthazar....................................Carolyn Ferriday
Portia....................................Miss Marlowe
Nerissa ....Alma Kruger
Jessica....................................Lenore Chippendale
Ladies of Portia's House......Lillian Gray, Dina Schleicher
Pages....................................Elaine Sims, Helen Besly
Serenade Singers.............Messrs. Lathan, Rabon, Kelso,
Webster, Adams
Attendant to Morocco..............................John Abrams

"THE RIGHT TO STRIKE"

A drama in four acts by Ernest Hutchinson, produced by Richard Walton Tully, at the Comedy Theater, New York, October 24, 1921.

Cast of characters —

Elizabeth	Katherine Rober
Dr. Miller	David Torrence
Dr. Eric Miller, his son	Schuyler White
Mary Miller	Gipsy O'Brien
Rose Ormerod	Cynthia Latham
Dr. Wrigley	Edmond Lowe
Gordon Montague	Harry Mestayer
" Tubby "	V. R. Beecroft
" Sidey "	Leslie R. Benson
Dr. Donald	Nevin Clark
Ben Ormerod	Ronald Adair
Walter Dewhurst, M.P.	Geo. E. Riddell
Sir Roger Pilkington	Byron Russell
Mr. James	John H. Brewer
Alfred Watson, K.C., M.P.	E. W. Laceby

Act I.—The Home of Dr. Miller, Valleyhead, Lancashire, England. Act II.—The Infirmary. Act III.—Home of Ben Ormerod.

The railroad workers of a small hill-surrounded community in Lancashire, England, entirely dependent upon its one line of railway, walk out on strike. The young doctors of the community hospital serve as strike breakers, and when one of them is killed the other doctors determine to call a strike of their own. So long as the strike lasts not a doctor will respond to the call of a striker or any of his kin. The strike leader's wife is near to death in childbirth before a compromise is effected, and even then the leading young surgeon is loath to call quits and go to her aid. He is moved finally by the plea of the dead doctor's widow, made in the name of humanity and the greater love.

"THE SIX-FIFTY"

A comedy drama in three acts by Kate McLaurin, produced by Lee Kugel, at the Hudson Theater, New York, October 24, 1921.

Cast of characters —

Gramp.....Reginald Barlow
Dan Taylor.....Leonard Willey
Hester.....Lillian Albertson
Steward.....Harold Healy
Walter.....Wilbur Cox
Gaston Hedges.....Wm. T. Hays
Marie Louise Hall.....Lillian Ross
Ann Seymour.....Hazel Turney
Christine Palmer.....Lolita Robertson
Mark Rutherford.....John Merkyl
Jim Armstrong.....E. Maxwell Selser
Bob Marshall.....Harry Knapp

Act I.—The Farm of the Taylors, New Hampshire. Scene 2—Interior of Dining Car. Acts II. and III.—Taylor Farm.

For seven years Hester Taylor has been reduced to the slavery of the average farmer's wife, with nothing to stir her imagination but the nightly passing of "The Six-Fifty." One day the train is wrecked and a carload of interesting passengers are dumped in upon Hester. One of them is a fascinating young man who finds her pretty and desirable and proposes that when the train is righted they go away together, which Hester agrees to do. But after she is all dressed up and ready to start she remembers her poor but patient husband and decides to stick it out on the farm. At which juncture it is discovered that the railroad will have to have a new right of way across the farm, and that the money will give Hester her chance of moving into town for a spell.

"THE WANDERING JEW"

A spectacle drama in seven scenes by E. Temple Thurston, produced by David Belasco and A. L. Erlanger, at the Knickerbocker Theater, New York, October 26, 1921.

Cast of characters —

Judith.....Helen Ware
Rachel.....Thais Lawton
Mathathias.....Tyrone Power
Du Guesclin.....Ralph Theodore
Boemond.....Robert Noble
Godfrey.....Bishop Dickinson
Raymond of Toulouse.....Lionel Adams
Issacher.....Howard Lang
A Page.....Augustus Anderson
Joanne de Beaudricourt.....Miriam Lewes
The Unknown Knight.....Tyrone Power
Phirous.....Melville J. Anderson
Mario.....Chas. W. Burrows
Andrea Michelotti.....Albert Bruning
Matteo Battadio.....Tyrone Power
Gianello Battadio.....Adele Klaer
Pietro Morelli.....Lionel Adams
Al Kazar.....Robert Noble
Tazzaro Zapportas.....Sidney Herbert
Maria Zapportas.....Virginia Russell
Arnaldo Zapportas.....Augustus Anderson
Matteos Battadios.....Tyrone Power
Ollalla Quintana.....Belle Bennett
Gonzales Ferara.....Edward Kent
Alonzo Gastro.....Howard Boulden
Juan de Texeda.....Howard Lang
Councillor.....Emmet Whitney
Councillor.....Chas. W. Burrows
Officer of the Inquisition.....Bishop Dickinson
Officer of the Inquisition.....Melville J. Anderson

The Scenes—In Jerusalem the Day of the Crucifixion; in Syria at the Time of the First Crusade; in Sicily in the Thirteenth Century; in Spain in the Middle Ages.

Mathathias, representing the scoffer who taunted and spat upon Jesus and was set wandering the world until the second coming of Christ, is shown in Jerusalem the day of the crucifixion. Later he appears in Syria in the time of the First Crusade, where he is a victorious Unknown Knight at a tourney, but, his identity being discovered by the lady he loves, he is promptly repulsed by her. In Sicily in the thirteenth century, though he is a humble and helpful citizen, he is deserted by his wife, who embraces the Christian church to be rid of him. In Spain, at the time of the inquisition, he is condemned as heretic and Jew and is burned at the stake, thus achieving temporary relief from the curse.

"THE MADRAS HOUSE"

A drama in four acts by Harley Granville Barker, produced at the Neighborhood Playhouse, New York, October 29, 1921.

Cast of characters —

Henry Huxtable....Whitford Kane
Katherine Huxtable....Evelyn Carter Carrington
Laura Huxtable....Aline Macmahon
Minnie Huxtable....Agnes B. Morgan
Clara Huxtable....Beatrice Sackett
Julia Huxtable....Marie Pinckard
Emma Huxtable....Esther Mitchell
Jane Huxtable....Katherine Sayre
Major Hippisley Thomas....Dennis Cleugh
Philip Madras....Warburton Gamble
Jessica Madras....Margaret Linden
Constantine Madras....Montague Rutherford
Amelia Madras....Eugenia Woodward
Eustace Perrin State....Eugene Powers
Marion Gates....Ernita Lascelles
Mr. Brigstock....John Roche
Mrs. Brigstock....Marie de Becker
Miss Chancellor....Katherine Brook
Mr. Windlesham....Albert Carroll

Act I.—At the Huxtables, London. Act II.—Waiting Room at Roberts and Huxtables. Act III.—Rotunda of Madras House. Act IV.—At the Home of Philip Madras.

A plotless play discussing the woman problem in England, with exhibits to emphasize the author's contention that it (the problem) is serious. These include the six anaemic daughters of a London draper without hope of finding husbands; a shopgirl who "goes wrong" deliberately, being denied marriage; a group of mannikins from Paris, imported to prove the lure of the draped female; the nagging wife of a man milliner who turns to Mohammedanism in sheer desperation, and the flirtatious wife of a good but neglectful male. The author's conclusion being that until the sex problem is settled some way there will be little useful work done in the world.

"THE GRAND DUKE"

A comedy in three acts by Sacha Guitry, produced by David Belasco, at the Lyceum Theater, New York, November 1, 1921.

Cast of characters —

Grand Duke Feodor Michaelovitch............Lionel Atwill
Michel Alexis..............................Morgan Farley
Vermillon..................................John L. Shine
A Servant..............................H. Percy Woodley
A Hotel Page...............................Edwin Dupont
Mlle. Martinet............................Lina Abarbanell
Marie Vermillon............................Vivian Tobin

Act I.—A Salon in M. Vermillon's Apartment. Act II.—The Studio of Michel Alexis. Act III.—The Grand Duke's Suite at the Hotel du Rhin. Staged by David Belasco.

The Grand Duke Feodor Michaelovitch, cousin to the czar, having been chased from Russia by the intemperate Bolsheviki, finds himself in Paris seeking a position as a teacher of languages. While tutoring Marie Vermillon, daughter of a profiteering French plumber grown rich during the war, the duke meets Mlle. Martinet, the young woman's singing teacher, and recognizes in her an opera singer with whom, as a young man, he had spent many pleasant months. He also meets young Michel Alexis, mademoiselle's son, born, as it transpires, but a few months after the duke's departure for Russia in the old days. Without officially recognizing his son, the duke manages to show him some little preference, helps him to marry the rich plumber's daughter and finally sees the little opera singer comfortably paired with the plumber himself.

"GOOD MORNING DEARIE"

A musical comedy in two acts, music by Jerome Kern, book and lyrics by Anne Caldwell, produced by Charles Dillingham, at the Globe Theater, New York, November 1, 1921.

Cast of characters —

Florrie....................Ruth Williamson
Cherry....................Lilyan White
Pat....................Patricia Clark
Margie....................Pauline Hall
George Mason....................John Price Jones
Ruby Manners....................Peggy Kurton
Madame Bompard....................Ada Lewis
Billy Van Cortlandt....................Oscar Shaw
Gimpy....................John J. Scannell
Rose-Marie....................Louise Groody
Chesty Costello....................Harland Dixon
Steve Simmons....................William Kent
Cutie....................Marie Callahan
Kirby....................Raymond Moore
Sing Lee....................Otis Harper
Hoi Fat....................Irving Jackson
Lim Ho....................Edouard Le Febvre
Pierre....................Joseph Viau
Gigi....................Daniel Sparks
Mrs. Greyson Parks....................Roberta Beatty
Miss Hetherington....................Ingrid Zanders
Pauline....................Hebe Halpin
Dorothy....................Miriam Miller
Muriel....................Muriel Harrison
Winters....................Spaulding Hall
Sylvia — Harriet....................Darling Twins

Maurice and Hughes in Their New Dance Creations

Act I.—Scene 1—Workroom of Madame Bompard's Shop. Scene 2—Exterior of the Dance Hall. Scene 3—Interior of Hell's Bells Dance Hall. Act II.—Scene 1—Showroom of the Toddle Shop. Scene 2—Fragonard. Scene 3—Terrace at Mrs. Greyson Parks' Home. Staged by Edward Royce.

Rose-Marie, a pretty milliner, attracts the attention of Billy Van Cortlandt, who promptly nominates himself her champion, after which he fights for her at the Hell's Bells dance hall and finally becomes engaged to her at Mrs. Greyson Parks' lawn fete.

"GOLDEN DAYS"

A comedy in four acts by Sidney Toler and Marion Short, produced by George C. Tyler and A. L. Erlanger, at the Gaiety Theater, New York, November 1, 1921.

Cast of characters —

Betsy	Jo Wallace
Miss Slissy	Florence Earle
Mrs. Simmonds	Blanche Chapman
Mary Anne	Helen Hayes
Mrs. Kirkland	Minna Gale Haynes
Felice	Camille Pastorfield
Richard Stanhope	Donald Gallaher
Trella Webb	Ruth Harding
Elaine Jewett	Selena Royle
Lloyd Helderson	S. Iden Thompson
William Barclay	Robt. Fiske
Pattie Ellison	Jean May
Teddy Farnum	Russell Medcraft
Charlie Mason	Alexander Clark, Jr.
Edgar Allen	Justin Lees
Annabelle Greely	Minna Henderson
Florence Austin	Marion Buckler
Walter Moore	Wellman Parsons
Jessica Devine	Ann Wallace
Frank Marvin	Arthur Christian

Act I.—Sitting Room in the Simmonds' Home, Farmdale, Conn. Act II.—Parlor of the New Hotel, Farmdale. Act III.—A Room in Mrs. Kirkland's Home, New York City. Act IV.—Same as Act I. Staged by Sidney Toler.

Mary Anne, having apparently been jilted by William Barclay because his father has made a lot of war money, enlists the sympathy of her rich aunt, Mrs. Kirkland, who dresses her up in fine feathers and sends her to the ball with handsome young Dick Stanhope. Dick pretends to be in love with Mary Anne, to help the game, but finds when he goes away to war that his love is something more than pretense. When he comes back he finds Mary Anne waiting, although young Barclay has repented and tried to recover his lost sweetheart.

"ANNA CHRISTIE"

A drama in four acts by Eugene G. O'Neill, produced by Arthur Hopkins, at the Vanderbilt Theater, New York, November 2, 1921.

Cast of characters —

Johnny-the-Priest............................James C. Mack
First Longshoreman............................G. O. Taylor
Second Longshoreman..........................John Hanley
A Postman...............................William Augustin
Chris. Christopherson......................George Marion
Marthy Owen................................Eugenie Blair
Anna Christopherson.........................Pauline Lord
Mat Burke..................................Frank Shannon
Johnson......................................Ole Anderson
Three Sailors...........Messrs. Reilly, Hansen and Kennedy

Act I.—Johnny-the-Priest's Saloon Near the Waterfront, New York City. Act II.—The Barge, *Simeon Winthrop*, at Anchor in the Harbor of Provincetown, Mass., Ten Days Later. Acts III. and IV.—Cabin of the Barge, at Dock in Boston, a Week Later.

(See page 22.)

"THE INTIMATE STRANGERS"

A comedy in three acts by Booth Tarkington, produced by Florenz Ziegfield, A. L. Erlanger and Charles Dillingham, at the Henry Miller Theater, New York, November 7, 1921.

Cast of characters —

The Station Master..........................Charles Abbe
Ames..Alfred Lunt
Isabel...Billie Burke
Florence...................................Frances Howard
Johnnie White...............................Glenn Hunter
Henry.......................................Frank J. Kirk
Aunt Ellen..............................Elizabeth Patterson
Mattie.......................................Clare Weldon

Act I.—A Railway Station. Night. (During Act I the curtain will be lowered to denote the lapse of a few hours.) Act II.—The Living Room at Isabel's. The Next Morning. Act III.—The Same. That Afternoon. Staged by Ira Hards.

Isabel, a maiden lady going on thirty or thereabouts, is marooned in an up York state railway station for twenty-four hours because of wrecks, washouts and other "acts of God." Marooned with her is an attractive but cautious bachelor person, one Ames. Becoming a little better than well acquainted the two are sentimentally interested in each other by the time they are rescued. Then Isabel, eager to test the seriousness of her Ames' proposal, bedevils him for a day about her possible age, and throws him, as a further test, into intimate touch with her flashy young niece. The bachelor lover is amusingly puzzled, but comes through the ordeal still in love with Isabel.

"THE SKIRT"

A farce comedy in three acts by Howard Hickman, produced by Richard Herndon, at the Bijou Theater, New York, November 7, 1921.

Cast of characters —

Jimmy Newman..........Vincent J. Dennis
Grace Warren..........Ruth Hammond
Ching Lee..........Irving Brooks
Ma Preston..........Merle Stanton
Bill Preston..........F. J. Woods
Betty Price (Bob)..........Bessie Barriscale
Jack Warren..........Paul Harvey
Slumber..........William Friend
Gabby..........Howard Hickman
Mushy..........Leo Curley
Shorty..........Phil Bishop
Silent..........Harry Buchanan
Red Kirby..........Louis Hendricks
Denver Red..........Frank Fanning

Acts I., II. and III.—On the Warren Ranch in Arizona, and in a Revamped Saloon in Town.

Betty (Bob) Price, having quarreled with her sweetheart, Jack Warren, in Chicago, determines to visit him on his Arizona ranch in the hope of effecting a reconciliation. To save her pride she disguises herself as a boy. The ranchmen, easily penetrating the disguise, "frame a rough party for Bob," in which there is considerable shooting and a little fun. Betty resumes her organdie and camisole in the last act and accepts Jack's apology for the quarrel.

"THE GREAT WAY"

A drama in four acts by Horace Fish and Helen Freeman, produced at the Park Theater, New York, November 7, 1921.

Cast of characters —

Prologue....................................Reginald Pole
Lola....................................Beatrice Wood
Jaime....................................H. Ellis Reed
Isabel....................................Martha Messinger
Auntie....................................Charlotte Granville
Jose Luis....................................Moroni Olsen
Dulce....................................Helen Freeman
"Y"....................................Eva Benton
La Velera....................................Ysobel Del Rey
Manager....................................Kraft Walton
Impressario....................................Max Rossi
Maestro....................................Juan de la Cruz
A Gitana....................................Marian Marcus Clarke
Jane....................................Duval Dalzell
Don Quixote....................................J. C. Hyde
Sancho Panza....................................Gus Alexander
Cleanboots....................................Elfin Finn
A Bullfighter....................................Paul Gregory
The Proprietor....................................Wiliam Anker
First Waiter....................................George Morgan
Second Waiter....................................Pietro Pelletz
Chief of Police....................................Domani Homann
A Coal Heaver....................................Thomas J. Coyne
A Stout Woman....................................Rena Armstrong
Her Escort....................................Ray Savich
Her Friend....................................Helen Fields
A Spanish Lady....................................Aurora Cortez
A Postcard Vendor....................................David Belbridge
A Man Servant....................................George W. Dear

Act I.—Scene 1—Barcelona "Ramblas." "Spanish Clay." Act II.—Dulce's Room in "Calle del Carmen." "On the Wheel." Act III.—Scene 1—A Small Street in Cadiz. Scene 2—Isabel's Apartment at "Hotel del Francia." "Firing the Glaze." Act IV.—Scene 1—Dressing Room in Opera House, Barcelona. Scene 2—Same. Scene 3—Montserrat. "The Perfect Cup." Time—Modern. Place—Modern Spain. Staged by Helen Freeman and Reginald Pole.

Dulce, a lady love who takes to the pavements in Barcelona, meets an engaging Spaniard, Jose Luis, who is wounded in a fight with her lover. She takes him to her rooms, holds him for a week until his wound is healed, falls desperately in love with him and is heartbroken when he leaves to return to the English girl to whom he is engaged. Dulce, determined to keep herself worthy until Jose returns, takes up music and becomes a great prima donna. The night of her triumph in Barcelona she meets for the first time the husband of the woman who has long been one of her best friends. He is Jose Luis. Still undefeated, Dulce climbs to the top of Montserrat and promises God she will go on being worthy.

"THE PERFECT FOOL"

A revue in two acts, book, music and lyrics by Ed Wynn, produced by A. L. Erlanger, at the George M. Cohan Theater, New York, November 7, 1921.

Principals engaged —

Ed Wynn
Flo Newton
True Rice
John Dale
Guy Robertson
Janet Velie
Aline McGill
Estelle Penning
Fred Ardath
The Meyakos

Staged by Mr. Wynn.

"THE MAD DOG"

A drama in three acts by George Scarborough, produced by Lee and J. J. Shubert, at the Comedy Theater, New York, November 8, 1921.

Cast of characters —

Jimmie Taylor.......................... Raymond Van Sickle
Blue Quail.................................... Margaret Knight
Padre Francolon........................... Forrest Robinson
Maria.. Helen Menken
Sanger... Charles Krause
Rab Mobley................................. Conway Tearle
Sheriff Gilson.............................. William Harcourt

A Room in the Mission of San Pablo, Seven Miles This Side the Mexican Border.

Rab Mobley, sentenced to serve a life term for the murder of a faithless sweetheart in Colorado, escapes from the state penitentiary and makes his way toward the Mexican border. Entering the San Pablo Mission he finds Maria, a ward of the good Padre Francolon, alone and unprotected. The sight of her, after seven years in prison, maddens him. . . . The following day Mobley escapes to Mexico, eluding the sheriff. But his conscience hurts him, Maria's voice haunts him, and he comes back to San Pablo to atone. He begs the girl to shoot him, which, fearing a second attack, she does. All day they both pray that Mobley may die, but the priest returns and he gets well. He has been regenerated by the experience, and when he leaves for Mexico a second time, he takes Maria with him.

"WE GIRLS"

A comedy in three acts by Frederic and Fannie Hatton, produced by Marc Klaw, at the Forty-Eighth Street Theater, New York, November 9, 1921.

Cast of characters —

Louisa	Minna Phillips
Mrs. Carter Durand	Mary Young
Frances Waite	Frances Neilson
Harriet Durand	Juliette Day
Richard I. A. Ryan	John McFarlane
Pilgrim	William Lennox
Doctor Tom Brown	Warren Krech
James Stedman	A. J. Herbert
Mrs. Embree	Cordelia MacDonald
Lucy Darragh	Marguerite Forrest
Winthrop Hale	Edward Fielding
Lawrence Ferris	Ray Wilson
Samuel Welsh	Thos. A. Rolfe

The Entire Action Takes Place in Mrs. Durand's Sitting Room in Her House in New York City. Staged by Priestly Morrison.

Mrs. Carter Durand, forty-six, having had her face peeled, steamed, lifted and realigned, doesn't look over thirty and is determined to remain thirty. Harriet, her nineteen-year-old daughter, who has been parked in a convent, finally rebels and comes home, demanding that she be at once acknowledged and treated as a grown-up should be. Failing to move her mother, Harriet introduces herself as a country cousin, flirts with all her mother's admirers and finally has to threaten to marry and make Mrs. Durand a grandmother before she can make her ageless parent behave.

"THE STRAW"

A drama in four acts by Eugene G. O'Neill, produced by George C. Tyler, at the Greenwich Village Theater, New York, November 10, 1921.

Cast of characters —

Bill Carmody	Harry Harwood
Nora	Viola Ormonde
Tom	Richard Ross
Billy	Norris Millington
Dr. Gaynor	George Woodward
Fred Nicholls	Robert Strange
Eileen Carmody	Margola Gilmore
Stephen Murray	Otto Kruger
Miss Gilpin	Katherine Grey
Miss Howard	Dothea Fisher
Mrs. Abner	Nora O'Brien
Miss Bailey	Alice Haynes
Mrs. Turner	Grace Henderson
Dr. Stanton	George Farren
Mrs. Brennan	Jennie Lamont

Act I.—The Carmody Home. Acts II., III. and IV.—A Sanitorium in Connecticut for the Treatment of Tuberculosis.

Eileen Carmody, eldest daughter of an Irish widower, is ordered into a sanitorium by the family physician who hopes thus to check the progress of the lung trouble with which she is afflicted. At the sanitorium she meets Stephen Murray, a young newspaperman, with whom, during the succeeding months, she falls deeply in love. Murray, responding to treatment, is ready to leave a few months later. On the eve of his departure Eileen confesses her love for him. He is grateful, but unresponsive. A few weeks later he visits the sanitorium and finds Eileen dying. She has lost all desire to live. Her only chance of lingering more than a few months happily is to have some new interest. Murray realizes that the sacrifice is up to him. He asks Eileen to marry him, professing a love he did not know he felt until he is in the midst of his confession. Then the thought of what her dying will mean to him so unnerves him that the girl reads her own doom in the expression of his eyes. He recovers control of his nerves and the play leaves them facing the future more hopefully than circumstances warrant.

"THE TITLE"

A satirical comedy in three acts by Arnold Bennett, produced by Richard G. Herndon, at the Belmont Theater, New York, November 14, 1921.

Cast of characters —

John Culver....Robert Harrigan
Hildegarde Culver....Shiela Courtenay
Tranto....Noel Tearle
Mrs. Culver....Selene Johnson
Mr. Culver....Lumsden Hare
Parlor Maid....Agnes Atherton
Miss Starkey....Emily Lorraine
Sampson Straight....Ernest Cossart
Acts I., II. and III.—Mr. Culver's House in London.
Staged by Lumsden Hare.

John Culver, an English gentleman and minor politician of note, is convinced that many shady reputations are being whitewashed by the government. Rich tradesmen and others who have been generous in their donations to the government or the political party in power have been placed on the title list as a reward. Finding himself offered a baronetcy he promptly refuses it, being backed up in his decision by his progressive son and daughter. But Mrs. Culver's social aspirations, coupled with a certain feminine diplomacy, force Culver finally to accept the title.

"NATURE'S NOBLEMAN"

A farcical comedy in three acts by Samuel Shipman and Clara Lipman, produced by William A. Brady, at the Apollo Theater, New York, November 14, 1921.

Cast of characters —

Carl Schnitzler....................................Louis Mann
Dora Schnitzler....................................Louise Beaudet
Dan Schnitzler....................................John Roche
Effie Schnitzler....................................Sue McManamy
Wilhelm Brand....................................Hans Hansen
Belle Brand....................................Helen Lowell
Rose Brand....................................Mary Brandon
Charles Johnson....................................Morgan Wallace
Josephine Johnson....................................Allyn Gillyn
Fred Tanner....................................Leonard Doyle
Morgan Rockefeller Wells....................................Clarke Silvernail
Shag....................................Kenneth Lee
Freda....................................Frances Harland

Acts I. and II.—Schnitzler's Hotel. Acts III. and IV.—Foyer of the Hotel. Staged by Louis Mann.

Carl Schnitzler (and dialect), running a tourist hotel in the Catskills, seeks to prevent his son from falling in love with a married woman. He doesn't succeed.

"THE VERGE"

A drama in three acts by Susan Glaspell, produced by the Provincetown Players, at the Provincetown Theater, New York, November 14, 1921.

Cast of characters —

Anthony....................................Louis Hallet
Harry Archer....................................Edward B. Reese
Hattie....................................Jeanie Begg
Claire (Mrs. Archer)....................................Margaret Wycherly
Dick Demming....................................Harold West
Tom Edgeworthy....................................Henry O'Neill

Elizabeth.................................Marion Berry
Adelaide.................................Blanche Hays
Dr. Emmons.................................Andrew Fraser

Act I.—In the Greenhouse. Act II.—In the Tower. Act III.—In the Greenhouse.

"THE GREAT BROXOPP"

A comedy in a prologue and three acts by A. A. Milne, produced by Iden Payne and Lavarack, Inc., at the Punch and Judy Theater, New York, November 15, 1921.

Cast of characters —

Nancy Broxopp.................................Pamela Gaythorne
Mary.................................Marie Davenport
James Broxopp.................................Iden Payne
Benham.................................John M. Troughton
Alice.................................Eula Guy
Honoria Johns.................................Margaret Nybloc
Jack Broxopp.................................Alfred Shirley
Iris Tenterden.................................Betty Linley
Sir Roger Tenterden.................................George Graham
Nora Field.................................Mary Ricards
Ronny Derwent.................................Kenneth Thomson

Prologue—Broxopp's Lodgings in Bloomsbury, London. Act I.—Den in Broxopp's House, Queen's Gate, London. Act II.—Hall in Broxopp's Country Home. Act III.—Broxopp's Home in London. Staged by Iden Payne.

James Broxopp is a flaring egotist with a passion for advertising. Buying an interest in an infants' food he places it upon the market as "Broxopp's Beans for Babies" and eventually accumulates a fortune. Twenty years later his grown son, eager to marry the daughter of a nobleman, objects to being known as the original "Broxopp baby" and induces his father to retire and change his name to Chilingham. The old man wilts in the country house atmosphere to which he is consigned until his wife, realizing his unhappiness, purposely permits certain sharpers to take away his fortune. Then Broxopp (now Chilingham) goes back to the modest apartment from which he started, puts "Chilingham's Cheese for Chickens" on the market and is in a fair way of making another fortune when the play ends.

"THE MAN'S NAME"

A drama in three acts by Marjorie Chase and Eugene Walter, produced by A. H. Woods, at the Republic Theater, New York, November 14, 1921.

Cast of characters —

Wong.......................................T. Tamamoto
Mrs. Marvin..........................Dorothy Shoemaker
Marshall Dunn.............................Felix Krembs
Hal Marvin...............................Lowell Sherman
Acts I., II. and III.—In the Marvin Cabin, Colorado.
Staged by Bertram Harrison.

Hal Marvin, a young writer of promise, is stricken with tuberculosis in his eastern home. His wife, young and attractive, knowing that he must be taken west if his life is to be saved, meets the crisis by borrowing three thousand dollars from her former employer, Marshall Dunn, a publisher, and, in a manner of speaking, gives herself as security. Dunn follows the Marvins to Colorado, finds Marvin recovered and Mrs. Marvin still attractive. He seeks to resume his friendly relations with the wife, is repulsed, arouses the suspicions of the husband and is finally brought to an acknowledgment of the truth. Marvin, being of a mind to kill Dunn, decides to do no more than "brand him as the rat he is," which he does by shooting the publisher in the hand. Then he forgives Mrs. Marvin and returns to his writing.

"EVERYDAY"

A comedy in three acts by Rachel Crothers, produced by Mary Kirkpatrick, at the Bijou Theater, New York, November 16, 1921.

Cast of characters —

Judge Nolan..............................Frank Sheridan
Fannie Nolan...............................Minnie Dupree
Phyllis Nolan..........................Tallulah Bankhead

Mrs. Raymond..............................Lucille Watson
May Raymond..............................Mary Donnelly
T. D. Raymond..............................Don Burroughs
John McFarlane..............................Henry Hull

Acts I., II. and III.—The Living Room in Judge Nolan's Home. A Small Town in the Middle West. Staged by Miss Crothers.

Phyllis Nolan, nineteen, is sent in charge of a chaperon for a tour of Europe that extends over a period of two years. The chaperon happens to be a superior sort of intellectual who gives Phyllis an entirely new outlook upon life. Returning to the everyday affairs of her home in Missouri, Phyllis is shocked to find it the ugly, gold and plush affair it is. The discovery also that her father is a domineering and bigoted type of successful politician, her mother a pathetic little brow-beaten woman, and that she (Phyllis), is expected to marry the state's political boss is also more or less disturbing. For a time Phyllis tries to readjust herself to the old conditions, but finally revolts, delivers herself of a new declaration of independence and marries the son of the town butcher, a wounded warrior back from France and the only honest idealist among them.

"ZIEGFELD MIDNIGHT FROLIC"

A revue in two acts, music and lyrics by Gene Buck and Dave Stamper, produced by Florenz Ziegfeld, on the roof of the New Amsterdam Theater, New York, November 17, 1921.

Principals engaged—

Will Rogers
Leon Errol
Carl Randall
Alexander Grey
Carlos and Inez
Carletta Ryan
Gloria Foy
Muriel Stryker
Athea
Shaw Sisters

Staged by Leon Errol.

"MARIE ANTOINETTE"

A drama in three acts by "Edymar," produced at the Playhouse, New York, November 22, 1921.

Cast of characters —

Louis XVI., King of France.......................Fred Eric
Joseph II., Emperor of Austria..............Walter Ringham
Duc d'Orleans...................................Douglas Wood
Count Axel Fersen........................Pedro de Cordoba
Caspierre...Basil West
Sacques......................................Herbert Ashton
Maillard......................................John Cromwell
Pinnet.....................................Rexford Kendrick
Leonard......................................H. Paul Doucet
Toulan...Craig Ellis
Augeard.......................................Austin Huhan
Marie Antoinette, Queen of France.............Grace George
Madame de Genlis.............................Harda Daube
Countess de Noailles.......................Florence Edney
Princess de Lamballe..........................Bettie Wales
De Beauvert....................................Agnes Dunphy
Louis, Duke of Normandy, the Dauphin........Jack Grattan
Marie Therese, the Princess Royal.............Lorna Valare
Madame Mouchy...............................Frances Young
Swiss Guards..............Roy Adams and Henri de State.
Ushers....................H. W. Rathke and Victor La Salle
Tirewomen..............Jean Eastman, Floria de Martimprey
and Jane Page

Act I.—Marie Antoinette's Bedchamber in the Petit Trianon, 1777. "The Queen Dances." Act II.—Gardens of the Trianon. "The Queen Gambles." Act III.—The Queen's Antechamber in the Palace of Versailles. Some Years Later. "The Queen Pays." Staged by Grace George and John Cromwell.

A slightly altered historical account of Marie Antoinette's friendship for and with Count Axel Fersen, divided into three acts in which (I) "The Queen Dances," and flirts with the count, who is much too noble to add fuel to the flames of scandal already started; (II) "The Queen Gambles," playing faro recklessly and losing millions of francs when Fersen continues to advise her to remain true to the vacillating and shallow-pated Louis XVI, and (III) "The Queen Pays," bartering with the revolutionists to sacrifice her own life if they will save Louis and her children. Thus she goes direct from Versailles to the guillotine.

"THE DREAM MAKER"

A melodrama in four acts by William Gillette, from a story by Howard E. Morton, produced by Charles Frohman, Inc., at the Empire Theater, New York, November 21, 1921.

Cast of characters —

Charles Frederick Farrar	William Morris
Rena Farrar	Myrtle Tannehill
Geoffrey Cliffe	Frank Morgan
Finch. Larsen	Harry E. Humphrey
Mrs. Kenneth Bruce	Miriam Sears
Dave Bruce	Charles Laite
Nora	Marie Haynes
Dr. Paul Clement	William Gillette
Buck Watson	Arthur J. Wood
Joseph C. Bates	Arthur Ebenhack

Acts I., II. and III. and the Second Scene of Act IV.—Living Room of the Bruce Cottage. First Scene of Act IV.—Parlor of the Farrar Cottage. The Action is Laid at a Seaside Resort Not Far From New York. Staged by David Burton.

Cherishing a tender memory of Marian Bruce's mother, with whom he was once in love, Dr. Paul Clement seeks out the daughter at a seaside resort near New York. He finds her, with her husband away, surrounded by a gang of blackmailing crooks who are planning to trap her into a compromising situation and then force her to buy their silence. Dr. Paul, who is a little like an aging Sherlock Holmes, determines to protect Marian, and after the blackmailers have sprung their traps he succeeds in twisting them into such knots they are glad to confess and escape.

"SUZETTE"

A musical comedy in two acts, book by Roy Dixon, music by Arthur Gutman, produced by the Suzette Producing Company, at the Princess Theater, New York, November 24, 1921.

Cast of characters —

Armand..John Cherry
Tony..Frank Lalor
Suzette..Marie Astrova
Dora Dolores................................Marjorie Booth
Max Kalman................................Victor Morley
Paul Huntley..........................James R. Marshall
Mme. Bimboula..............................Carola Parson

Act I.—A Montmartre Cafe, Paris. (Evening.) Act II.—A Garden Party, Deauville. (Next Evening.)

Suzette, a flower girl, fascinates Paul Huntley, an American millionaire, when they meet in a Montmartre café. From there they go to a garden party at Deauville where Tony, the comic waiter, arrives disguised as a Turk, and Suzette substitutes for a missing prima donna.

"THE WILDCAT"

A Spanish music drama in three acts by Manuel Penella, produced by John Cort, at the Park Theater, New York, November 26, 1921.

Cast of characters —

Solea..Dorothy South
Sena Frasquita....................................Vera Ross
Loliya..Grace Hamilton
Father Anton...............................W. H. Thompson
Rafael..Sam Ash
Hormigon....................................Carlos Villarias
Caireles....................................Max Gonzales
Gipsy..Louise Barnolt
Juanillo, the "Wild Cat"......................Marion Green
Gipsy Dancers...........Conchita Piquer and Pilar Torralba
A Shepherd....................................Russell Ash
A Flower Seller............................Conchita Piquer
El Pezuno............................Oliver T. McCormick
Alguacil..Fred Rogers

Act I.—The Macareno's Farmhouse near Seville. (An Afternoon in Summer.) Act II.—Scene 1—Patio of the Macareno's House in Seville. (The Following Sunday.) Scene 2—Interior of the "Plaza de Toros" in Seville. (The Same Afternoon.) Act III.—Scene 1—The Macareno's Farmhouse at Night. (Two Weeks Later.) Scene 2—A Cave in the Mountains. The Hiding Place of the "Wild Cat." (The Same Evening.) Time—Present. Place—Andalusia, Spain. Staged by Manuel Penella.

Juanillo, called "The Wildcat," by the neighbors who had seen him sneaking down from his bandit cave in the mountains to sing love songs to Solea, was a good young man until he was unjustly jailed for having killed a man in a duel. In love with Solea, a gipsy, he refuses to give her up to Rafael, a toreador, even though he cannot marry her himself. Rafael, being reckless, is killed in the bullring and Solea dies of grief, whereupon Juanillo comes for the girl's body and bears it away to his cave. Pursued by Solea's friends, the bandit bids one of his own men shoot him through the heart and dies embraced by the cold arms of his true love's corpse.

"THE WIFE WITH THE SMILE" AND "BOUBOUROCHE"

A tragi-comedy in two acts by Denys Amiel and Andre Obey, and a farce in two acts by Georges Courtcline, adapted from the French by Ruth Livingstone, produced by the Theater Guild, at the Garrick Theater, New York, November 28, 1921.

"THE WIFE WITH THE SMILE"

Cast of characters —

Mme. Beudet....................Blanche Yurka
Marguerite Prévot....................Catherine Proctor
Mme. Lebas....................Katherine Clinton
Eugénie....................Jeanne Wainwright
Gabrielle....................Maud Brooks
M. Beudet....................Arnold Daly
M. Lebas....................Willard Bowman
Jacques Dauzat....................Edwin R. Wolfe
A Clerk....................Philip Loeb

Staged by Frank Reicher.

"BOURBOUROCHE"

Cast of characters —

Boubouroche	Arnold Daly
Old Gentleman	J. Monte Crane
André	Robert Donaldson
Roth	Carl Anderson
Potasse	Edwin R. Wolfe
Fouettard	Willard Bowman
Henri	Philip Loeb
Cashier	Katherine Clinton

Staged by Philip Moeller.

"The Wife With the Smile" is Mme. Beudet, who has been bedevilled into a state of nerves by her husband, a small-town bully given to boasting of his commercial success and smacking his lips over vulgar stories. He also has a joking way of flourishing an unloaded revolver and snapping it at the cavity in which his brains should be lodged to illustrate what he would do should his wife ever deceive him. After a particularly irritating scene Mme. Beudet loads the revolver and awaits the "accident" that will blow off her hated husband's silly head. She later repents, but before she can recover the gun, M. Beudet, up to his old jokes, suddenly changes his mind, levels it at her and pulls the trigger. The bullet misses the lady and smashes a mirror. A family reconciliation follows. "Boubouroche" is the story of a kindly old simpleton whose sponging friends and trusted mistress deceive him with impunity.

"HER SALARY MAN"

A comedy farce in three acts by Forrest Rutherford, produced by John Cort, at the Cort Theater, New York, November 28, 1921.

Cast of characters —

A Bellboy	Mae Washburne
Burton	H. B. Thomas
"Sponge" Ferris	Dudley Clement
Montaine Grey	Hedley Hall
Dick Barry	Thomas F. Jackson
Mrs. Sophie Perkins	Edna May Oliver

Emily Sladen.....Ruth Shepley
John Brown—"Bunny".....A. H. Van Buren
George Hunter.....Will Deming
Drusilla Willis.....Grace Carlyle
Jessie Van Alstyne.....Hope Sutherland
Mrs. Warton Van Alstyne.....————
Franklyn Willis.....Donald Hall
Patterson Pomeroy.....Donald Call
A Maid.....Nina Gleason

Act I.—Semi-Lounging Room Between Two Suites on Second Floor of a Southern California Hotel. Act II.—Library in the Franklyn Home. (Five Months Later.) Act III.—Emily's Boudoir in the Willis Home. (The Same Evening.) Staged by Harry Andrews.

Emily Sladen, willed to the care of a comic aunt until she (Emily) is safely married, announces her willingness to "hire" a husband, and pay him so much a year if he will marry her and then keep away from her. A reporter overhears Emily, prints the story and immediately the place is overrun with applicants. Walking into the lobby of her hotel, and mistaking "Bunny" Brown, a rich bachelor who is a fellow guest, for one of her would-be husbands, Emily practically proposes to him, is accepted and the marriage performed according to agreement. Five months later, however, "Bunny" is back. He has returned his "salary" and, being in love, is of a mind to demand his marital rights, which, after a series of comedy complications, he successfully accomplishes.

"KIKI"

A comedy farce in three acts, adapted from the French of Andre Picard by David Belasco, produced by David Belasco, at the Belasco Theater, New York, November 29, 1921.

Cast of characters —

Victor Renal.....Sam B. Hardy
Baron Rapp.....Max Figman
Brule.....Thomas Findlay
Joly.....Sidney Toler
Sinette.....Saxon Kling

Adolphe.....................................Thomas Mitchell
The Doctor.................................Harry Burkhardt
Paulette.....................................Arline Fredricks
Lolotte..Pauline Moore
Susanne..Florence Lee
Claire..Gertrude Bond
Marcel..Mignon Ranseer
Florine..Jean Scott
The Cook.......................................Frances Kyle
Kiki..Lenore Ulric

Act I.—Renal's Office in the "Follies Monplaisir" Music Hall. The Door Being Open, Kiki Drifts In. Act II.—A Week Later. The Drawing Room in Renal's Apartment—From Which Kiki is Requested to Drift Out. Act III.—A Few Hours Later. A Room in the Same Apartment is Made the Scene of Kiki's Last Stand When Renal Returns at Midnight From Supper. Kiki Explains Herself. The Scenes of the Episodes in the Vagrant Life of Kiki Are Laid in Paris. Staged by David Belasco.

Kiki (pronounced "Keeky") is a Parisian gamine who becomes infatuated with the manager of the music hall in which she is sometimes employed. She worships him from afar so long as she can stand it, and then forces her way into his office. When his assistants try to eject her she bites and scratches. Finally, amused by her persistence, the manager takes her to dinner and later to his apartment. She is deeply grateful, but when he tries to kiss her she resumes her kicking. For ten days Kiki refuses to be dislodged, even when the manager's divorced wife is ready to return to him, and when force is resorted to she contrives to simulate catalepsy so perfectly even the physicians are fooled. Her later confession of love, pathetically linked with the story of her life on the streets, through all of which she has managed to keep herself "good," induces the manager to accept her love.

"THE VARYING SHORE"

A drama in a prologue, three acts and an epilogue by Zoe Akins, produced by Sam H. Harris, at the Hudson Theater, New York, December 5, 1921.

Cast of characters —

Laura....Sylvia Gough
Marie....Margot Rieman
Roger....Harris Gilmore
Tom....Donald Bethune
Larry Sturgis....Charles Francis
The Ghost of Madame Leland....Elsie Ferguson
Garreth Treadway....Paul Everton
An Englishman....Herbert Evans
Hester....Geraldine O'Brien
Richard....Rollo Peters
Madame Leland (Julie Venable)....Elsie Ferguson
Vernon Baird....Clyde North
Kitty....Blythe Daly
Joe Leland....James Crane
Tom....Charles Baldwin
Julie....Elsie Ferguson
Governor Venable....Wright Kramer
John Garrison....Rollo Peters
Mrs. Venable....Maidel Turner
William Blevins....Norman Houston
Julie Venable....Elsie Ferguson

The Prologue—At Monte Carlo. Time—Today. Act I.—Madame Leland's Suite, Paris. Time—1870. Act II.—Joe Leland's Country Place Near New York. Time—1859. Act III.—Governor Venable's Home, Richmond. Virginia. Time—1847. The Epilogue—Same as the Prologue. Time—Today. Staged by Sam Forrest.

The ghost of Mme. Leland, who has died the night before, reappears to her last lover, Larry Sturgis, as he sits sipping coffee in a hotel garden at Monte Carlo and seeks pleasantly to explain, if not to justify, the life she has led. It has been a life in which she has died many times, she says, so that her real death came as a sort of benediction. As she recalls the important crises in her life they are re-enacted. First she is forty, and sacrifices the life she was leading in Paris that her son's name may not be smirched. Then she is thirty and living outside New York with her first lover, Joe Leland. Again she sacrifices herself that Joe may marry respectably and well. Finally she is a girl of sixteen, in love with John Garrison, who is the father of her child. But rather than see him give up his career to make her an "honest woman," she runs away — and starts upon the career the prologue saw ended in Monte Carlo.

"THE HAND OF THE POTTER"

A tragedy in four acts by Theodore Dreiser, produced by the Provincetown Players, at the Provincetown Theater, New York, December 5, 1921.

Cast of characters —

Aaron Berchansky..........................Nathaniel Freyer
Rebecca..................................Dosha Rubinstein
Masha....................................Dorothy Sawyer
Rae......................................Esther Stockton
Joe......................................Lutha J. Adler
Isadore..................................J. Paul Jones
Esther (Mrs. Greenbaum)..................Jane March
Tillie Greenbaum.........................Mary Stephens
Kittie Neafie............................Millie Beland
Mrs. John Neafie.........................Amelie Barleon
George Greenbaum.........................Milton J. Bernd
Mrs. Lersch..............................Sarah Fishman
Mrs. McHugh..............................Conway Sawyer
Eddie McHugh.............................Beatrix Loughran
Rutger B. Miller (District Attorney)..........Harold McGee
Emil Daubenspeck.........................Alexander Boije
Foreman of the Grand Jury..................H. B. Kroeger
Clerk of the Grand Jury...................Francis H. Valtair
Thomas Bush (An Expressman)..............Harry Gottlieb
Samuel Elkas (A Landlord).................Lutha J. Adler
Hagar Elkas...............................Billie Rudell
Ed. Armsby (Reporter).....................James Meighan
Stephen Leach (Reporter)..................Ernest Freeman
Dennis Quinn (Reporter)...................F. S. Merlin
Officer Thomas McKagg.....................John Ferris
McGranahan (Detective)....................Patrick Barnum
Wallstein (Detective).....................Luigio Balestro

Acts I. and II.—Berchansky's Home on the Upper East Side of New York. Act III.—Grand Jury Room. Act IV.—Furnished Room in Lower East Side Rooming House.

"THE FAIR CIRCASSIAN"

A romantic comedy in four acts by Gladys Unger, produced by Miss Newell, at the Republic Theater, New York, December 6, 1921.

Cast of characters —

His Excellency, Prince Mirza Fatoullah Khlan...Claude King
Moussa Beg..............................John H. Brewer
Ismael Beg............................Berkley Huntington
Ionides..................................Robert Fischer
Lala.......................................John Smith
H. R. H., The Prince Regent..............Louis Wolheim
Lord Ripley..............................Stanley Hewlett
Lord Ottery...............................Henry Carvill
The Hon. Claude Faulconhurst................Dennis King
Mr. Fitzjames..............................Echlin Gayer
The Hon. Charles Hill.......................Harry Green
Capt. Richard Wingham...................Messenger Bellis
Portleight..................................Roy Cochran
James....................................William Nelson
John.....................................Gilbert Rooney
The Duchess of Darlington...............Kathleen Molony
Lady Ottery..................................Ethel Dane
The Hon. Georgina Faulconhurst................Fay West
Lady Blandish..........................Nellie Graham-Dent
Miss Priscilla Hart.......................Helene Sinnott
Zora....................................Margaret Mower

Act I.—A Reception Room in the East Wing of Lord Ottery's House in London. A Foggy Day in April. Act II.—A Reception Room in the West Wing of Lord Ottery's House in London. A Bright Morning in June. Act III.—The Same, the Same Evening. Act IV.—A Room in the Persian Ambassador's House in London. The Next Afternoon. Period—1819. Staged by Clifford Brooke.

The first Persian ambassador to the English court in 1819, Prince Mirza Fatoullah Khlan, brings as a gift from the shah to the king a beautiful slave girl, Zora. Finding that the king is a bit balmy, he decides to transfer the gift to the prince regent. Balked in this, because the English law frowns upon harems, he thinks some of keeping Zora for himself. But the girl learns that she is technically free so long as she remains on English soil and eludes him — only to return to him when she realizes how much nicer he is than any of the Englishmen she meets.

"BOUGHT AND PAID FOR"

A drama in four acts by George Broadhurst, revived by William A. Brady, at the Playhouse, New York, December 7, 1921.

Cast of characters —

Robert Stafford....................Charles Richman
James Gilley....................Capt. Wm. Harrigan
Oku....................Allen Atwell
Virginia Blaine....................Helen MacKellar
Fanny Blaine....................Marie Nordstrom
Josephine....................Katya Prevon

Act I.—Robert Stafford's Apartments. Act II.—Mrs. Stafford's Boudoir. Act III.—Same as Act II. Act IV.—James Gilley's Flat. Place—New York City. Time—The Present. Staged by John Cromwell.

Robert Stafford, falling in love with Virginia Blaine, a telephone operator, marries her and takes her to his expensive apartments to live, Robert being excessively wealthy. He is a fine man with but one besetting sin. He will drink, and when he drinks he is a brute. The night he announces that his wife is his, because he bought and paid for her, and breaks down the door to her bedroom after she has tried to keep him out, she leaves him and goes back to work as a shopgirl. In time, Robert, repentant and reformed, finds her out and they are reunited.

"ALIAS JIMMY VALENTINE"

A melodrama in four acts by Paul Armstrong, based on an O. Henry short story, "A Retrieved Reformation," revived by George C. Tyler, at the Gaiety Theater, New York, December 8, 1921.

Cast of characters —

Handler....................Harold Hartsell
Smith....................Archie Curtiss
Blickendolfenbach....................Emil Hoch
Doyle....................Emmett Corrigan
Bill Avery....................Edmund Elton

Mrs. Webster.....Mary Boland
Mrs. Moore.....Grace Henderson
Robert Fay, Lieut.-Gov. of New York.....William Ingersoll
Rose Lane.....Margalo Gillmore
"Blinky Davis".....Edward Wonn
"Dick the Rat".....J. J. Hyland
Lee Randall.....Otto Kruger
Red Joclyn.....Earle Brown
William Lane.....George Farren
Bobby Lane.....Andrew Lawlor
Kitty Lane.....Lorna Volare
A Bank Clerk.....John Kennedy

Act I.—Warden's Office, Sing Sing Prison, New York. Act II.—Parlor in Hotel at Albany, New York. Act III.—Assistant Cashier's Office, First National Bank, Springfield, Ill. Act IV.—Interior of Bank. Time—Present. Staged by Hugh Ford.

Lee Randall, a gentleman safe breaker, is released from Sing Sing through the influence of the lieutenant-governor's daughter, Rose Lane, whom he had befriended. Determined to go straight Randall (alias Jimmy Valentine) fights off his tempting crook friends and eludes the police, who are unable to break down his perfect alibi — until the little daughter of his employer gets herself locked in the bank vault. Then Jimmy risks re-arrest by opening the vault. The detective sees him, but turns his back. And Jimmie marries Rose.

"THE CHOCOLATE SOLDIER"

An opera bouffe in three acts, music by Oscar Straus, libretto, based on Bernard Shaw's "Arms and the Man," by R. Bernauer and L. Jacobson, English version by Stanislaus Stange, revived by the Messrs. Shubert, at the Century Theater, New York, December 12, 1921.

Cast of characters —

Nadina Popoff, Daughter of Col. Popoff.....Tessa Kosta
Aurelia Popoff, Her Mother.....Mildred Rogers
Mascha, Aurelia's Cousin.....Virginia O'Brien
Lieutenant Bumerli, "The Chocolate Soldier"...Donald Brian
Captain Massakroff, of the Bugarian Army....Detmar Poppen

Louka, Popoff's Servant....................Beauton O'Quinn
Stephen, Popoff's Servant............Jay Carlton McCormack
Col. Kasimer Popoff, of the Bulgarian Army..John Dunsmure
Major Alexius Spiridoff, of the Bulgarian Army,
betrothed to Nadina...............John Humbird Duffey

Act I.—Scene—Nadina's Sleeping Apartment in Popoff's House. Act II.—Scene—Gardens of Popoff's House. Act III.—Scene—Same as Act II. Sunset. Time—1885. Place—Near the Dragoman Pass, Bulgaria.

Lieut. Bumerli, a professional soldier escaping capture by the Bulgarians while he is fighting with the Serbs, climbs the trellis and hides himself in the sleeping room of Nadina Popoff, daughter of Col. Popoff of the Bulgarians. Completely exhausted, he also goes to sleep there. Likewise he falls in love with Nadina, and she with him. There are complications attending his concealment, and later, when the war is over and he is recognized, he has some little difficulty lying himself into the good graces of his prospective father-in-law.

"THE MOUNTAIN MAN"

A comedy in three acts by Clare Kummer, produced by Charles L. Wagner, at the Maxine Elliott Theater, New York, December 12, 1921.

Cast of characters —

Wellington, a Servant of the Delaneys'....Lawrence Eddinger
Mary Vaughan, Aaron's Cousin by Marriage.....Lucia Moore
Lulie, Her Daughter........................Marjorie Kummer
Virginia Delaney, Her Sister....................Grace Reals
Aaron Winterfield, From High Mountain, Heir to the
Winterfield Estate.......................Sidney Blackmer
Major Miles McCloud, Del's Uncle................Fred Karr
Carey, a Distant Connection of Aaron's.......Chester Morris
Delaney McCloud, "Del"...............Catherine Dale Owen
Jess, a Mountaineer..........................George Fawcett
Laura Bayne, a Neighbor.....................Marion Abbott
Stephen Bayne...............................Leonard Rowe
General Verterin, a French Army Officer.....E. J. DeVarney

Scenes 1 and 2—Parlor of the Delaney Home, Laurel, Va. Scene 3—The Hall of Aaron Winterfield's Home at Winterfield, Va. Scene 4—Same as Scene 1. Scene 5—Aaron's Cabin on High Mountain. Staged by Clare Kummer and Edward Elsner.

Aaron Winterfield, a Virginia mountaineer, inherits the fortune his pappy spurned and is brought down from the hills into a Virginia town to take his place at the head of the family. There he finds a mess of relatives planning to marry him to a dimly distant kin, Delaney McCloud, just returned from Paris. Aaron doesn't mind marrying, seeing he immediately takes a fancy to the girl, but when he hears that there is another gentleman waiting for her to return to France his temper rises. He feels like killin', he says, and he allows he will go to France where killin' is legal, the war having just started. Returned from the front three years later Aaron is a hero and glad to find out he was mistaken about the girl and her French admirer.

"THE IDLE INN"

A folk tale in three acts by Peretz Hirshbein, adapted by Isaac Goldberg and Louis Wolheim, produced by Arthur Hopkins, at the Plymouth Theater, New York, December 20, 1921.

Cast of characters —

Schakne	Whitford Kane
Esther	Joanna Roos
Bendet	Louis Wolheim
Mendel	Edward G. Robinson
Maite	Eva MacDonald
Hyenne	Mary Shaw
Eisik	Ben-Ami
Leibush	Sam C. Jaffe
1st Maiden	Margaret Fareleigh
2nd Maiden	Juliet Brennon
3rd Maiden	Bella Nodell
4th Maiden	Ottie Wetter
5th Maiden	Alice Kiesler
6th Maiden	Daisy Rieger
7th Maiden	Shirley Albert
1st Woman	Elizabeth Hunt
2nd Woman	Ellen Larned
3rd Woman	Maud Sinclair
4th Woman	Gertrude Mann
5th Woman	Lucy English
Eisik's Companions	Andrey Lensky and Leon Seidenberg
Peasant Musicians	William Schukin and Leo Witko

Guests......Jacob Kingsberry, George Casselberry, A. M. Bush, David Leonard, Bennie Wagschall, Philip Scherman, Julius Bliech and Henry Simons
1st Merchant............................Lionel Hogarth
2nd Merchant............................Stanley Howlett
3rd Merchant............................Henry Sharp
4th Merchant............................Anton Grubman
5th Merchant............................Gregory Robbin
6th Merchant............................Boris Weiner
7th Merchant............................Frohman Foster
Act I.—Outside Bendet's House. Act II.—The Wedding. Act III.—Near the Idle Inn.

Eisik is a bad boy but handsome and romantic. Maite knows she is fascinated by him, but seeks to remain loyal to her family and the traditions of her people and marry the yokel they select for her. At the wedding feast, however, Eisik and his pals appear and, during the dance, deftly steal the bride away. On the highroad, near the "Idle Inn," a haunted caravansary the thrifty parents intend as a dwelling place for the young people, Maite seeks to turn back, but Eisik's tempestuous love-making is too much for her and she reluctantly surrenders.

"DANGER"

A domestic drama in three acts by Cosmo Hamilton, produced by Carle Carleton, at the Thirty-ninth Street Theater, New York, December 22, 1921.

Cast of characters —

Mrs. Sturgess............................Gilda Leary
Percy Sturgess............................Leslie Howard
Mrs. Scorrier............................Marie Goff
Elizabeth............................Ruth Hammond
Mary Hubbard............................Kathlene MacDonell
John Fitzroy Scorrier............................H. B. Warner
Albert............................Stapleton Kent
Hon. Algernon Meakin, M.P............................Knox Orde
Act I.—The Sturgess Bungalow. Act II.—Scorrier's Study. Act III.—A Cottage. Staged by Carle Carleton.

Following the wedding supper Mrs. Scorrier tells her impetuous young husband that her ideas of marriage and his are quite different. To her marriage is merely a partnership, entered into for the social, political and business advancement of the contracting parties. She has no intention of devoting herself to her home, and she refuses to be one of those catlike women whose earthly function it is to crawl into warm straw and litter the place with kittens. Mr. Scorrier, considerably upset, takes the blow standing, and the wife retires behind a locked door. A year later, his love dead, his spirit broken, Scorrier is thinking of suicide when his typist, Mary Hubbard, a pretty girl and brave, stays his hand. Learning that Mary loves him Scorrier leaves his wife and lives openly with Mary in the high hills. Later he willingly sacrifices his career, when Mrs. Scorrier refuses him a divorce, rather than desert his true love.

"THE DOVER ROAD"

A comedy in three acts by A. A. Milne, produced by Guthrie McClintic, at the Bijou Theater, New York, December 23, 1921.

Cast of characters —

Dominic.......................................George Riddell
The Staff.................Phyllis Carrington, Ann Winslow, Edwin H. Morse and George Nolan
Latimer.......................................Charles Cherry
Leonard.......................................Reginald Mason
Anne.......................................Winifred Lenihan
Eustasia.......................................Molly Pearson
Nicholas.......................................Lyonel Watts

Acts I., II. and III.—At Mr. Latimer's Home on the Dover Road.

On the road to Dover — the road eloping couples take when they leave London for Paris or the south of France — there lives a certain Mr. Latimer. Rich, and a bit eccentric, he conceives the plan of stopping the runaways, detaining them by gentle force in his home and keeping them apart, yet together, for a week. Thus he gives them an opportunity of seeing each other as they really are — especially at breakfast — and a chance to change their minds if they want to. Usually, he finds, they are quite content to return home. The quartet of would-be elopers with whom the play is directly concerned — Anne and Leonard, Nicholas and Eustasia — are thus enlightened. With Leonard out of the way, Anne stays on to comfort the lonely Latimer — and we fear she broke up his admirably helpful institution by marrying him. (See page 237.)

"TRILBY"

A comedy in three acts by George Du Maurier, produced by the Coöperative Players, Inc., at the National Theater, New York, December 23, 1921.

Cast of characters —

Mme. Vinard	Jeffreys Lewis
Talbot Wynne	George Nash
Alexander McAllister (The Laird)	Joseph Allen
William Bagot (Little Billee)	Edmond Lowe
Trilby	Charlotte Walker
Svengali	Wilton Lackaye
Gecko	Harry Mestayer
Angele	Ruth Harding
Honorine	Violet Anderson
Mrs. Bagot	Carrie Radcliffe
Rev. Thos. Bagot	Frank Doane
Duc de la Rochemartel	Ignacio Martinetti
Theodore de la Farce	Wilton Lackaye, Jr.
Anthony	Desmond Gallagher
Lorimer	Cyril Ring
Musette	Diana Gray
Mimi	Geneva Harrison
Bebe	Laura Walters
Fifi	Rose Le Vere
Col. Kaw	I. B. Johnson
Phillippe	Harry Kittredge

Acts I. and II.—The Studio. Act III.—Foyer of the Cirque de Bashibazouks. Act IV.—Trilby's Apartments.

A revival of the Du Maurier story of the Latin Quarter model, Trilby O'Farrell, who became a great prima donna under the hypnotic influence of Svengali, but was finally rescued by her three artist friends, Taffy, the Laird and Little Billee.

"THE MARRIED WOMAN"

A comedy in three acts by C. B. Fernald, produced by Norman Trevor, at the Princess Theater, New York, December 24, 1921.

Cast of characters —

Mrs. Temple............................Mrs. Edmund Gurney
Alice Matthewson............................Margaret Dale
William Temple............................Grant Stewart
George Herbert............................Percy Waram
Henry Matthewson............................Marsh Allen
Sylvia Temple............................Beatrice Maude
Maidservant at William Temple's..............Anna Gaston
Hugh Dellamy............................Norman Trevor
Footman at George Herbert's................Edmond Norris
Manservant at Hugh Dellamy's..............Charles Herbert
Maidservant at Hugh Dellamy's................Ida Molthen

Act I.—At William Temple's. Act II.—At George Herbert's. Two Years Later. Act III.—At Hugh Dellamy's. Two Weeks Later. Staged by C. A. De Lima.

Sylvia Temple, about to marry George Herbert, pauses, as you might say, at the threshold of the church to inquire of her friends just why it is "the story always ends there?" Why should the romantic love of courtship and honeymoon days die practically at the altar? Why can't it be carried all through the married life of two who love each other? None of her friends can tell her. All about her she sees the unhappy results of unhappy marriages and she is troubled. Only one, Hugh Dellamy, a philosophic bachelor, offers an answer. "Romantic love," says he, "is mostly bunk; a pinkish fog that blinds the young and the sentimental." Sylvia marries and a year later knows her marriage is as great a failure as any of them, so she leaves Herbert to establish her economic independence — and turns in time to Dellamy.

"THE WHITE PEACOCK"

A melodrama in three acts by Mme. Olga Petrova, produced at the Comedy Theater, New York, December 26, 1921.

Cast of characters —

Anna.....Ludmilla Toretzka
Marietta.....Doris Carpenter
Don Miguel di Ribera y Santallos.....Leon Gordon
Rafael Roderiguez.....E. L. Fernandez
Revette di Ribera y Santallos.....Madame Petrova
The Countess Wyanock.....Letha Walters
Captain Hubert Lang.....George C. Thorpe
Don Cæsar di Mendoza Gonzales.....Malcolm Fassett
Joselito.....Charles Brokaw
Pedro.....Judson Langill

Act I.—Sleeping Room in the Home of Revette. Act II.—Studio in the Home of Revette. Act III.—Room in the House of Don Miguel. Place—Seville, Spain. Staged by Leon Gordon.

Revette di Santallos, married to the brutal and otherwise quite impossible Don Miguel, premier of Spain, leaves him and proceeds to earn her way by painting. One night her sleeping room is invaded by Don Cæsar Gonzales, a handsome youth seeking vindication for wrongs done him by Don Miguel. It is his purpose to harm Revette and thereby be even with the premier, instead of which he falls immediately in love with her and sleeps the night through by the fire. Later Revette is also attracted to Don Cæsar, and Don Miguel seeks to use the situation to his advantage. His wife is far too clever for him, however, and he is forced finally to give her up. Two or three sudden deaths clear the way for the lovers.

"THE SQUAW MAN"

A drama in four acts by Edwin Milton Royle, revived by Lee Shubert, at the Astor Theater, New York, December 26, 1921.

Cast of characters —

Henry Wynnegate, Earl of Kerhill..........J. Malcolm Dunn
Diana, His Wife, Countess of Kerhill..................
Julia Hoyt (Mrs. Lydig Hoyt)
Lady Elizabeth Wynnegate, His Mother......Winifred Harris
Lady Mabel Wynnegate, His Sister.........Elizabeth Bellairs
Capt. James Wynnegate, His Cousin, Afterwards Known as Jim Carston.........................William Faversham
Malcolm Petrie, His Solicitor..............H. Cooper Cliffe
Bates, His Butler..........................George Schaeffer
Sir John Applegate, Diana's Cousin............Frank Hollins
Rev. Belachazar Chiswick.....................Gerald Rogers
Lieut. Markwell....................Raymond Van Rensselaer
Lieut. Crosby..............................Ralph Sumpter
Big Bill, Foreman of Carston's Ranch........Burr McIntosh
Shorty, Cowboy on Carston's Ranch.....Emmett Shackleford
Andy, Cowboy on Carston's Ranch.....Bertram A. Marburgh
Grouchy, Cowboy on Carston's Ranch........Herbert Ashton
Baco White...............................Herbert Farjeon
Tab-Y-Wana, Peace Chief of the Utes...........Riley Hatch
Nat-U-Ritch, His Daughter..................Josephine Royle
Little Hal, Her Son........................Bernard Durkin
Cash Hawkins...........................Willard Robertson
Nick, Barkeeper of "The Long Horn Saloon"...........
Edmund Soraghan
Bud Hardy, County Sheriff................William Frederic
Pete, A Cowboy.............................Harry Hanlon
Parson......................................Frank Lyon
McSorley, Engineer of the Overland Limited..........
Chauncey Causland
Parker, Conductor of the Overland Limited....Murray Darcy
Mrs. Hiram Doolittle........ ....Emily Lorraine
Mr. Hiram Doolittle.......................Wiiliam T. Hays
Punk, A Chinaman...........................Curley Judge

Act I.—The Terrace of Maudsley Towers, England. Act II.—The Long Horn Saloon, Maverick. Act III.—Red Butte Ranch. Act IV.—The Same, at Daybreak the Following Morning. Staged by Mr. Faversham.

A revival of the sixteen-year-old story of Capt. James Wynnegate, the younger son of a noble English family, who shoulders the blame of his cousin's crime for the sake of the woman he loved and comes to America to become a western cattleman. Years later, as Jim Carston, he marries an Indian chief's daughter and becomes a "squaw man," which embarrasses him not a little when the situation at home is cleared up and he becomes heir to the title. Nobly again he sacrifices himself and sends his half-breed son to take his place at Maudsley Towers. But before the boy can get away the little Indian mother, Nat-U-Ritch, conscious of standing in the way of her son's and her husband's happiness, shoots herself.

"FACE VALUE"

A comedy in three acts, adapted from the Italian of Sabatino Lopez by Solita Solano, produced by Lee Shubert, at the Forty-ninth Street Theater, New York, December 26, 1921.

Cast of characters —

Henry..M. A. Kelly
Edward Barton..................................Lee Millar
Jose Henriquez.............................Leo Ditrichstein
Alexis Borozouff............................Alexis Polianov
Harry Stewart..............................Hugh O'Connell
Mrs. Rose Jennings.....................Josephine Hamner
Alma Curtis...........................Frances Underwood
Dr. Frederick Curtis, Her Husband.............Orlando Daly
Arabella Mapes...............................Clara Mackin
Miss Farrell.................................Mary Duncan

Act I.—Reception Room of Mrs. Jennings' Family Hotel. Act II.—Sitting Room of Dr. Curtis' Apartment on the Ground Floor of the Hotel. Act III.—Henriquez's Office in the Wall Street District. Time—The Present. Early Fall. Place—New York.

Jose Henriquez is a homely Cuban stock broker in New York — so homely none of the ladies ever notice him and none of the men suspect him of being a rival. It is his boast, however, that having nothing in the way of good looks to depend upon he has been obliged to sharpen his wits and that given half a chance — a mirrorless room, say, and a romantic lady who will listen but not look at him — he can hold his own with the handsomest of lovers. He makes good his boast when he wins the flirtatious Alma Curtis away from the handsome Edward Barton. And though Mrs. Curtis' husband unexpectedly interrupts him, he slides gracefully from the predicament when the lights are turned up. He is too homely even to be suspected of being a successful rival. Out of this scrape Henriquez is happy to discover that his ward loves him despite his ugliness.

"BULLDOG DRUMMOND"

A melodrama in four acts by "Sapper," produced by Charles B. Dillingham, at the Knickerbocker Theater, New York, December 26, 1921.

Cast of characters —

Capt. Hugh Drummond....................A. E. Matthews
Algy Longworth..........................Geoffrey Millar
Peter Darrell.......................H. Franklyn Bellamy
Carl Peterson..............................Sam Livesey
Dr. Lakington..........................C. H. Croker-King
Jas. Handley...........................St. Clair Bayfield
W. Hocking..............................Wm. W. McNeill
Wm. G. Travers...........................George Barraud
Denny.....................................Edward M. Favor
Derbyshire................................Thomas Gillen
Marcovitch................................Wallace Hickman
Brownlow..................................Jas. A. Boshell
A Chinese Mute............................G. Tracy Barlow
Hospital Attendants......J. W. Albaugh, Jr. and J. H. Hunt
Irma Peterson..............................Mary Robson
Maid.......................................Augusta Davis
Phyllis Benton.............................Dorothy Tetley

Act I.—Scene 1—A Room in Captain Drummond's Flat in Half Moon Street. Scene 2—Room at "The Larches," Godalming. Act II.—Scene 1—A Sitting Room at "The Elms," Godalming. Scene 2—Captain Drummond's Cottage at Goring. Act III.—The Central Room at "The Elms." Act IV.—The Same. Staged by Fred G. Latham.

Capt. Hugh Drummond, a year out of the army and dying of boredom, advertises for any kind of a job that promises excitement. Phyllis Benton, sister of an old buddie of Drummond's, answers the ad. She is living next door to what it is claimed is a sanitarium. Frequently she hears screams. Oftener than that the leading "physician" of the sanitarium comes to her house and seems to have some hold upon her aged uncle. Drummond promises to investigate and next act is on the trail of a desperate gang of crooks who are holding a multi-millionaire American captive. With the help of his pals Drummond fights the gang and eventually emerges victoriously with one good arm with which to hold Phyllis.

"CAPTAIN APPLEJACK"

A farcical comedy in three acts by Walter Hackett, produced by Sam H. Harris, at the Cort Theater, New York, December 30, 1921.

Cast of characters —

(In the Order of Their Appearance)

Lush	John Gray
Poppy Faire	Phoebe Foster
Mrs. Agatha Whatcombe	Marie Wainwright
Ambrose Applejohn	Wallace Eddinger
Anna Valeska	Mary Nash
Mrs. Pengard	Helen Lackaye
Horace Pengard	Ferdinand Gottschalk
Ivan Borolsky	Hamilton Revelle
Palmer	Maud Andrew
Dennett	Walter F. Scott
Johnny Jason	Harold Vermilye

Act I.—The Adventure. Act II.—The Dream. Act III.—The Romance. In the Library of Ambrose Applejohn's House at Polperren, Cornwall. Staged by the Author.

Ambrose Applejohn, a youthful English squire, is vegetating on his place in Cornwall. Determined that he should go in search of life and adventure he advertises the place for sale. At ten o'clock a few nights later strange persons call. Ambrose believes they are prospective purchasers. They are really crooks in search of a pirate's treasure supposed to be hidden in the house. Learning this, Ambrose determines to sit up all night to guard the house. He falls asleep and dreams himself his piratical ancestor. Waking, he has further adventure with the would-be crooks and finally beats them off, about which time he discovers that he is also in love with the young Poppy Faire, who has been living there all the time. So Ambrose finds both romance and adventure without need of travel.

"THE S. S. TENACITY"

A character comedy in three acts from the French of Charles Vidrac, produced by Augustin Duncan, at the Belmont Theater, New York, January 2, 1922.

Cast of characters —

Therese	Marguerite Forrest
Widow Cordier	Jennie Dickerson
Bastien	George Gaul
Segard	Tom Powers
Hidoux	Augustin Duncan
An English Sailor	Claude Cooper
A Young Workman	Howard Claney
Another Workman	Robert H. Forsythe
An Old Workman	R. Henry Handon

The Story is Enacted in a Little Restaurant in a Seaboard Town in France. Staged by Augustin Duncan.

Bastien and Segard are typesetters. Discharged from the army, they find the after-the-war conditions in Paris unpleasant and start for a seacoast town to take ship for Canada. It is Bastien's scheme, he being the strong-willed, decisive one. Segard is more inclined to dream. Arrived at the seacoast they find the sailing of the *Tenacity* delayed. They stop a fortnight at the village inn. They both fall in love with Therese, the pretty waitress who serves them. Segard talks to her of spring and roses and little farms that they may know some day. Bastien talks to her of love and wine and the fleeting hours. Bastien wins. With Therese he starts for Paris, leaving Segard to sail on the *Tenacity* alone.

"LAWFUL LARCENY"

A melodramatic comedy in a prologue and three acts by Samuel Shipman, produced by A. H. Woods, at the Republic Theater, New York, January 2, 1922.

Cast of characters —

Marion Dorsey.......................... Margaret Lawrence
Andrew Dorsey.......................... Allan Dinehart
Judge Perry.......................... Felix Krembs
Mrs. Davis.......................... Martha Mayo
Mrs. French.......................... Ida Waterman
Vivian Hepburn.......................... Gail Kane
Celeste.......................... Bijoute La Violette
Guy Tarlow.......................... Lowell Sherman
Marion Sylvester.......................... Margaret Lawrence
Mr. French.......................... John Stokes
Mr. Davis.......................... Frazier Coulter
Nora.......................... Sara Haden
Detective Farrel.......................... John Sharkey

Prologue.—Andrew Dorsey's Home. Act I.—Vivian Hepburn's Apartment. Act II.—Same as Act I. Act III.—Andrew Dorsey's Home. Staged by Bertram Harrison.

Marion Dorsey, back from a trip to California, learns from the confession of her husband that during her absence he had been seduced and robbed by Vivian Hepburn, a fascinating woman who runs an exclusive gambling salon. Refusing to forgive him, Marion determines to be revenged upon the woman who has robbed her. She engages herself to Miss Hepburn as secretary and not only manages to steal back all her husband's money and securities, and everything else in the safe, but to win the love of the gambling siren's latest and most popular lover as well. Cornered in her own home, Marion dares Miss Hepburn to press the charge of theft against her, but is horrified to learn that while she (Marion) can be sent to prison for stealing money, her enemy can only be brought to trial in a civil action for stealing a husband, and cannot be jailed. "You spend millions of dollars on a police force to protect the furniture, but any clever wanton can steal the heart and soul of the home and go scot free." She offers to go to trial to expose the rottenness of such a system, but is not permitted to do so. There is a promise that, having her revenge, she will later forgive her husband.

"DRIFTING"

A melodrama in six scenes by John Colton and D. H. Andrews, produced by W. A. Brady, at the Playhouse, New York, January 2, 1922.

Cast of characters —

Mrs. Cook	Jane Corcoran
Deacon Cook	H. Mortimer White
Dr. Hepburn	Burr Curruth
Willie Bates	Barry Fitz Patrick
Ernie Crockett	H. D. Bogart
Cassie Cook	Alice Brady
Mrs. Polly Voo Frances	Florence Short
Foo Chow Lizzie	Blanche Wallace
Rangoon Rose	Winnifred Lawshé
Number One Mafu	William Blaisdell
Number Two Mafu	Cornelius Bull
Number Three Mafu	Olaf Laven
Molyneaux	Leward Meeker
Flock	Maxwell Driscoll
Monsieur Repin	Franklyn Fox
Badlands McKinney	Robert Warwick
Dr. Li Shen Kueng	Lumsden Hare
Lady Beamish	Selene Johnson
Cyril Trenwyth	Leonard Cary
A China Boy	Edwin Thompson
The Woman of Tung Kow	Mme. Marguerite de Marhanno
A Priest of Buddha	Edwin Thompson
A Sorceress	Geraldine McCreery
A Monger of Lost Dolls	Jane Corcoran
A Holy Beggar	Edwin Thompson
A Road Woman From Nowhere	Eve Ware
First Husband	Leward Meeker
Second Husband	Edwin Thompson
Third Husband	Humphrey Bogart
Coolie	Barry Fitz Patrick
Chu Che La Lu	Millie Beland
Tommy Hepburn	Master Jack Grattan
Wang	Allen Atwell
Komisky	Frank Backus
The Jhanzi Kahn	H. Mortimer White
Capt. Jack John Micheljohn	Harry Davies
Ramirez	William Blaisdell
A China Boy	Barry Fitz Patrick
First Body Servant	Barry Fitz Patrick
Second Body Servant	Olaf Laven

Scene I.—Somewhere in America. Scene II.—Shanghai, China, Cabaret. Scene III.—In the Hills of Tung Kow. Scene IV.—Ruins of Christian Mission. Scene V.—In Tsin Sein. Scene VI.—Aboard the *Hester Blount*. Staged by John Cromwell.

Cassie Cook, unjustly treated by her father, a Methodist deacon in Waltham, Mass., determines to live the rest of her life dangerously and in defiance of all the conventions. For a start she goes to China with some friendly missionaries traveling that way, leaves them, becomes a cabaret singer and dancer in Shanghai, later is plunged into a Tartar insurrection in Tung Kow, meets and is saved by Badlands McKinney, a derelict American soldier unjustly cashiered from the army, falls in love with him and finally confesses to him all that she is and has been. He, being in much the same boat, accepts her love and the two, regenerated by their meeting and subsequent experiences, determine to go the rest of the way together.

"ABOVE THE CLOUDS"

A musical comedy in three acts, libretto and lyrics by Will B. Johnstone, music by Tom Johnstone, produced by Joseph M. Gaites at the Lyric Theater, New York, January 9, 1922.

Cast of characters —

Archie Dawson............................Hal Van Rensallear
Curtis Dawson..............................Walter Walker
Betty Dawson...............................Florence Hedges
Ferdie Simpson.................................Mark Smith
Jeffreys.......................................Page Spencer
Ruby Airedale............................Gertrude O'Connor
Millicent Towne............................Gladys Coburn
Bud Usher..................................Skeet Gallagher
Louise...June Roberts
J. Herbert Blake............................Wm. N. Bailey
Jean Jones....................................Grace Moore
Gypsy Venue...............................Dorothy Smoller
Gerald..Angelo Romeo
Wm. Tuttle....................................Van J. Melino

Will Tuttle....................................John J. Weis
Willie Tuttle....................................Roy Alexander
Premier Danseuse....................................June Roberts
Character Dancer....................................Arthur Corey
Classical Dancers..........Melissa Ten Eyck and Max Weily

Jean Jones, a popular movie star on the Pacific coast, hearing that J. Herbert Blake, who is running a movie school in the east, is cheating a gullible public of young movie aspirants and using her name to help his schemes along, travels to New York from Hollywood to investigate. Her investigations lead her to the home of the Dawsons, where she becomes acquainted with young Archie, a demobilized soldier with an ambition to do something fine for America in the line of a propaganda picture to be called "The Birth of America." Remaining incognito she helps Archie and puts a twist in the schemes of Director Blake, who was mismanaging the school and trying to steal the Dawson idea.

"HE WHO GETS SLAPPED"

A tragedy in four acts, adapted from the Russian of Leonid Andreyev by Gregory Zilboorg, produced by the Theater Guild, at the Garrick Theater, New York, January 9, 1922.

Cast of characters —

Tilly....................................Philip Leigh
Polly....................................Edgar Stehli
Briquet....................................Ernest Cossart
Mancini....................................Frank Reicher
Zinida....................................Helen Westley
Angelica....................................Martha Bryan Allen
Estelle....................................Helen Sheridan
Francois....................................Edwin R. Wolfe
He....................................Richard Bennett
Jackson....................................Henry Travers
Consuelo....................................Margalo Gillmore
Alfred Bezano....................................John Rutherford
Baron Regnard....................................Louis Calvert
A Gentleman....................................John Blair
Wardrobe Lady....................................Kathryn Wilson
Usher....................................Charles Cheltenham
Conductor....................................Edwin R. Wolfe

Pierre....................................Philip Loeb
A Sword Dancer..............................Renee Wilde
Ballet Master...............................Oliver Grymes
Ballet Girls....Vera Tompkins, Anne Tonerri, Marguerite Wernimont and Frances Ryan
Actresses in Circus Pantomime......Adele St. Maur and Sara Enright
Thomas......................................Dante Voltaire
A Snake Charmer.............................Joan Clement
A Contortionist.............................Richard Coolidge
A Riding Master.............................Kenneth Lawton
A Juggler...................................Francis G. Sadtler
Acrobats....................Sears Taylor and Luigi Belastro

Act I.—Rehearsal. Act II.—Performance. Act III.—Next Day. Act IV.—Consuelo's Benefit Performance. The Action of the Play Takes Place in a Room Off the Ring of Briquet's Circus in One of the Large Cities of France. Staged by Robert Milton.

Into a general meeting room off the ring of a continental circus a French nobleman wanders, and applies for a job, suggesting that he play a clown — the clown who gets slapped. Given the place he also asks that his anonymity be preserved; that he be known simply as "He." During his subsequent adventures with the circus it is revealed that "He" has evidently been robbed of the love of his wife and the work of his brain by a false friend; that, the world having slapped him, he extracts a martyr-like joy by continuing the game while the world laughs. In the circus he meets Consuelo, the little bareback rider, and appoints himself her spiritual guardian. When he learns that she is about to be sold by a vicious foster father to a licentious old baron, "He" poisons the girl's wine at her farewell supper, and, drinking of the potion himself, dies with her. (See page 126.)

"ROSA MACHREE"

A comedy drama in four acts by Edward E. Rose, produced by the Hudson Productions Company, at the Lexington Opera House, New York, January 9, 1922.

Cast of characters —

Brian Delaney	Clarence Derwint
Rachel Goldran	Sonia Marcelle
Gordon Brae	Ryder Keane
Lucius Marley	Charles Esdale
Cyril Lardon	Harry Green
Rosa Goldran	Julia Adler
Ellen Carew	Mabel Allen
Lady Ethel Carew	Lucy Beaumont
Lord Ragdon	Fuller Mellish
Binks	By Himself
Wharton	Austin Huhan

Another attempt to prove that nothing on earth can beat a combination of the Irish and the Jews. An English lordling elopes with a Hebrew servant girl. When their baby is a grown daughter her English grandfather agrees to adopt her if she will leave her mother. She agrees tentatively, but when mother learns the separation may be made permanent she crosses to England and takes a place in his lordship's kitchen. Mother and daughter thus find each other and grandfather is made to see the sentimental error of his melodramatic ways.

"THE BLUE KITTEN"

A musical comedy in three acts, adapted from "Le Chasseur de Chez Maxim's" by Otto Harbach and William Cary Duncan, produced by Arthur Hammerstein, at the Selwyn Theater, New York, January 13, 1922.

Cast of characters —

Louis	Bill Hawkins
Giglain	Victor Morley
Theodore Vanderpop	Joseph Cawthorn

Durand....................................George Le Soir
Octave....................................Robert Woolsey
Fifi......................................Betty Barlow
Cri Cri...................................Marion Sunshine
Marcelle..................................Carola Parson
Totoche...................................Lillian Lorraine
Armand Duvelin............................Douglas Stevenson
Mme. Lucile Vanderpop.....................Jean Newcombe
Madelaine Vanderpop.......................Lorraine Manville
Popinet...................................Dallas Welford

Act I.—The Foyer of "The Blue Kitten." Act II.—At Vanderpop's Chateau at Fontainebleu. Act III.—"The Blue Kitten" Cafe. Staged by Edgar Selwyn, Leon Errol and Julian Mitchell.

Theodore Vanderpop, porter and head waiter at "The Blue Kitten," has acquired a fortune which his wife and daughter believe he has earned as a night editor. When he is about to retire, because of the approaching marriage of his daughter, Madelaine, to Armand Duvelin, he discovers that Armand is one of "The Blue Kitten's" best patrons. His effort to pretend that he is not the same Vanderpop Armand knows as a porter, and also to prevent Armand marrying Madelaine, serve to interrupt the songs and dances and rest the chorus.

ELSIE JANIS AND HER GANG

A revue in two acts by Elsie Janis, produced by Elsie Janis, at the Gaiety Theater, New York, January 16, 1922.

Principals engaged —

Jurien Thayer
Charlie Lawrence
Monk Watson
Duane Nelson
Lane McLeod
Gus Shy
Bradley Knoche
Herbert Goff
Frank Miller
James F. Nash
W. Dornfeld
Red Murdock
Lewis Reid
Dan Walker
Chester Grady
Elizabeth Morgan
Maude Drury
Inez Bauer
Elva Magnus
Margaret Sousa

FRITZ LEIBER SEASON

Revival of Shakespearean Plays, presented by George Ford, at the Forty-eighth Street Theater, New York, beginning January 16, 1922.

"MACBETH"

Cast of characters —

Duncan, King of Scotland....................William Daniels
Malcolm, His Son....................Frank Howard
Macbeth....................Fritz Leiber
Banquo....................John Burke
MacDuff, a Nobleman....................Louis Leon Hall
Ross....................Philip D. Quin
Lennox....................W. Leonard Gordon
Fleance, Banquo's Son....................Constance Kingsley
Seyton....................James Hendrickson
A Wounded Messenger....................Richard Allen
A Doctor....................Harold Rand
A Drunken Porter....................Robert Strauss
A Messenger....................Waldron Smith
Another Messenger....................Frederic Drake
A Murderer....................Richard Allen
Another....................Arthur Rowley
First Witch....................Virginia Bronson
Second Witch....................H. Rand
Third Witch....................Harry Williams
Gentlewoman....................Caroline Kohl
Lady Macbeth....................Olive Oliver

"JULIUS CAESAR"

Cast of characters —

Julius Cæsar....................Philip D. Quin
Marc Anthony....................Fritz Leiber
Casca....................Richard Allen
Trebonius....................Frank Howard
Marcus Brutus....................Louis Leon Hall
Cassius....................John Burke
Decius Brutus....................James Hendrickson
Metellus Cimber....................Herman Thomas
Popilius Lena....................Waldron Smith
Cinna, a Senator....................Fredric Drake
A Soothsayer....................W. Leonard Gordon
Pindarus....................James Hendrickson
Metellus....................Arthur Rowley
Octavius Cæsar....................Harold Rand
First Citizen....................Robert Strauss
Lucius....................Constance Kingsley
Portia....................Olive Oliver
Calpurnia....................Virginia Bronson

"ROMEO AND JULIET"

Cast of characters —

Romeo....................................Fritz Leiber
Benvolio, His Friend.......................Frank Howard
Mercutio, Friend of Romeo...............Louis Leon Hall
Capulet.....................................Richard Allen
Paris.................................W. Leonard Gordon
Tybalt..John Burke
Friar Lawrence...........................Philip D. Quin
Balthasar...................................Harold Rand
An Apothecary.............................Fredric Drake
Peter, Capulet's Servant.................Robert Strauss
Chorus.............................James Hendrickson
Nurse to Juliet............................Mary Williams
Lady Capulet.................................Olive Oliver
Juliet, Daughter to Capulet...............Virginia Bronson

"THE NATIONAL ANTHEM"

A drama in four acts by J. Hartley Manners, produced by A. L. Erlanger and George C. Tyler, at the Henry Miller Theater, New York, January 23, 1922.

Cast of characters —

Marian Hale...............................Laurette Taylor
Madeline Trent.....................Lillian Kemble Cooper
Maud Ethel......................................Jo Wallace
Etta.................................Greta Kemble Cooper
Arthur Carlton..............................Ralph Morgan
John K. Carlton...........................Dodson Mitchell
Tom Carroll...............................Frank M. Thomas
Reuben Hale...................................Richie Ling
Jim Picket...................................Robert Hudson
Ned Scoofy......................................Ray Wilson
Dr. Virande...................................Paul Porcasi
Waiter...................................William Armstrong

Act I.—Northchester. Summer. Act II.—New York. Winter. Act III.—Paris. Spring. Act IV.—The Same. The Afternoon of the Tenth Day. Staged by the Author.

Marian Hale, in love with Arthur Carlton, marries him despite the warning of the boy's father that he (Arthur) is no good. Both Marian and Arthur are members of the lively younger set, much given to jazzing around the country clubs near New York, and Arthur is a good two-fisted drinker. Marian's belief that she can reform him bears fruit the first six months of their marriage, but after that Arthur slips back into his old ways and carries Marian with him. They go to Paris and continue the mad pace there until, befuddled by liquor, Marian takes bichloride of mercury, thinking it a headache medicine and Arthur, rushing for a doctor, is killed in a motor-car smashup. There is a promise of happiness for Marian in the love of Tom Carroll, who has been patiently waiting for her.

"MARJOLAINE"

Louis N. Parker's "Pomander Walk" set to music by Hugo Felix, book by Catherine Chisholm Cushing, lyrics by Brian Hooker, produced by Russell Janney, at the Broadhurst Theater, New York, January 24, 1922.

Cast of characters —

Admiral Sir Peter Antrobus............... Albert G. Andrews
Jim... Royal Cutter
Mrs. Pamela Poskett......................... Daisy Belmore
The Rev. Jacob Sternroyd, D.D............. Colin Campbell
The Eyesore.................................. E. L. De Brocq
Punch and Judy Man.......................... Paul Warren
Miss Barbara Sternroyd........................ Mary Hay
Mr. Basil Pringle.......................... Maurice Holland
Jerome Brooke-Hoskyn, Esq.................. Lennox Pawle
Jane.. Merle Stevens
Madame Lucie Lachesnais...................... Nellie Strong
Nanette.. Olga Treskoff
Lieut. The Hon. Jack Sayle.................. Irving Beebe
Tom... Irving S. Finn
Joe... Addeson Youngs
John Sayle, Tenth Baron Otford........... Worthe Faulkner
Mlle. Marjolaine Lachesnais.................. Peggy Wood

Act I.—Saturday Afternoon, May 25. Act II.—Saturday Morning, June 1. Act III.—The Same. Two Hours Later. The entire action takes place in Pomander Walk, "out Chiswick Way," in London, in the year 1805. Staged by Russell Janney and W. H. Post. Dances by Bert French.

Marjolaine Lachesnais, living in Pomander Walk with her mother, meets Lieut. Jack Sayle when that gay young naval officer comes in search of an old friend. Their love for each other is strong and immediate, but both Jack's father, the Baron Otford, and Marjolaine's mother object. The baron had once been engaged to Lucie Lachesnais and jilted her. It isn't possible to keep the young folk apart longer than an act or two, however, at which time their parents also decide to renew their old romance.

"THE DELUGE"

A drama in three acts, adapted by Frank Allen from the Swedish of Henning Berger, revived by Arthur Hopkins, at the Plymouth Theater, New York, January 27, 1922.

Cast of characters —

Stratton, a Saloonkeeper..............Robert E. O'Connor
Charlie, a Waiter........................James Spottswood
First Customer............................Arthur Hurley
Frazer, a Promoter........................Robert McWade
Another Customer..........................John Ravold
Adams, a Broker...........................Charles Ellis
O'Neill, a Lawyer.........................Lester Lonergan
Nordling, an Immigrant................Edward G. Robinson
Higgins, an Actor.........................William Dick
Sadie...................................Kathlene MacDonell

Acts I., II. and III.—The Barroom of a Saloon in a Middle Western City.

Seven men and a girl are caught in the barroom of a basement saloon during a cloudburst in a city located on the banks of the Mississippi River. The storm continues, the river overflows, and finally, with the steel shutters up and all doors barred, the trapped customers find themselves shut off from all communication with the outside world and facing probable death by suffocation. In their extremity the natures of all eight undergo definite reactions. Alcoholically stimulated, a cheating broker becomes fanatically inspired by the thought of forming a great human chain of brotherhood; a philosophical "shyster" lawyer preaches eloquently the claims of the soul; a self-seeking and inordinately ambitious broker admits to the girl of the streets imprisoned with them, whom he had known in his clerkship days, that she is the only woman he ever loved, and that he left her to marry a rich girl to give him power in the business world. With their respective souls shriven the storm ceases and release follows. Within a half hour they have reverted to type and are as tricky as they were before — selfish, human, honest or tricky, according to their kind.

"THE NEST"

A drama in four acts, adapted by Grace George from Paul Geraldy's "Les Noces d'Argent," produced by William A. Brady, at the 48th Street Theater, New York, January 28, 1922.

Cast of characters —

Marie Hamelin..............................Lucile Watson
Eveline Dore (Called Marraine)..........Christine Norman
Jacques Hamelin............................Frank Burbeck
Max Hamelin..............................Kenneth MacKenna
Suzanne....................................Juliette Crosby
Henri.......................................Bruce Elmore
Jeanne......................................Ruth Gillmore
Leontine..................................Marjorie Oakley
Anna.......................................Florence Mack
Louise.....................................Helen Cromwell

Act I.—At the Hamelins'. Suzanne's Room. Act II.—At the Hamelins'. Act III.—At the Hamelins'. The Dining Room. Act IV.—At Suzanne's Home. Time—Today. Place—Paris. Staged by Edward Elsner.

(See page 346.)

"THE VOICE FROM THE MINARET"

A drama in a prologue and three acts by Robert Hichens, produced by Marie Löhr, at the Hudson Theater, New York, January 30, 1922.

Cast of characters —

Andrew Fabian.............................Herbert Marshall
Selim.....................................E. Rayson-Cousens

Father Elsworthy............................C. M. Hallard
Lady Caryll..................................Marie Löhr
A Muezzin...............................Jacques Chapin
Mrs. Fabian.............................Vane Featherston
Miss Rodd............................Content Paleolobue
A Waiter....................................Basil West
Sir Leslie Caryll..........................Edmund Gwenn
Astley..................................E. Rayson-Cousens

Prologue—Sitting Room in a Hotel in Damascus. Act I.—Sitting Room at the Vicarage, Drobridge-on-Sea. Act II.—Sitting Room at the Lord Gordon Hotel, Drobridge-on-Sea. Act III.—Sir Leslie Caryll's Flat in Savoy Court. Staged by Marie Löhr.

Lady Caryll, on her way from India back to London following a quarrel with her "beast of a husband," meets Andrew Fabian, a young theological student, on his way to the Holy Land, preliminary to taking orders. They love each other and linger in Damascus for weeks, desperately happy. But gradually her ladyship discovers that the call of the church — as symbolized by the voice of the Muezzin calling the people to prayer from the minaret—still has a stronger claim upon her young lover than her love and leaves him. Lady Caryll returns to her beastly husband. Andrew goes into the church. Six years later they meet in London. She hears him preach and is tempted to visit him in the vicarage late at night. Sir Leslie Caryll, learning of the meeting, grows suspicious and finally uncovers the love adventure in Damascus, which both her ladyship and the young rector bravely acknowledge. Sir Leslie's death puts him out of the way, but the priest and the lady decide to go their separate ways.

"MR. FAUST"

A drama in four acts by Arthur Davison Ficke, produced by Ellen Van Volkenburg, at the Provincetown Theater, New York, January 30, 1922.

Cast of characters —

Brander......................................Byron Foulger
Oldham...Robert Bell

Mr. Faust..................................Maurice Browne
The Butler..................................Jack Gude
Nicholas Satan..................................Moroni Olsen
The Holy One..................................Henry O'Neill
Midge..................................Janet Young
The Doctor..................................Harold McGee

Act I.—Mr. Faust's Library, New York. Act II.—A Deserted Temple in India. Act III.—A Gothic Cathedral. Act IV.—Mr. Faust's Library, New York. Time—Today.

"THE CZARINA"

An historical comedy in three acts, adapted by Edward Sheldon from the Hungarian of Melchior Lengyel and Lajos Biro, produced by Charles Frohman, Inc., at the Empire Theatre, New York, January, 31, 1922.

Cast of characters —

The Czarina..................................Doris Keane
Annie Jaschikova..................................Lois Meredith
Marie..................................Phyllis Alden
The Chancellor..................................Frederick Kerr
The French Ambassador..................................Ian Keith
Count Alexei Czerny..................................Basil Rathbone
Nicholas Jaschikoff..................................Kenneth Thompson
Ronsky..................................William Devereux
Dymow..................................Richard Malchien
Kaschumowsky..................................Edwin Noel
Malakoff..................................William H. Thompson
Yvonne..................................Blanche Gervais
Maids.........Jane Page, Miriam Stoddard, Virginia Trabue and Elizabeth Collins
Lackeys.............William Marr, Bertram Hanauer, Stuart Kemp, Guy Standing, Jr. and Charles Frank

Act I.—An Afternoon in Springtime. Act II.—Four Weeks Later. In the Summer. Act III.—Eight Days Later. The action of the play takes place in the Inner Audience Chamber of the Imperial Palace at St. Petersburg in 1765. Staged by Gilbert Miller.

A comedy of court intrigue and romance built around certain episodes in the life of the amorous Catherine II of Russia. This particular adventure concerns her meeting with the dashing ruffian, Count Alexei Czerny, who rides from the western front to warn her of a nobles' plot to dethrone her. The handsome Alexei wins his sovereign's gratitude and likewise her heart, and by her command stays on at court for several weeks.

Then he, in turn, humiliated by Catherine's treatment of him as a sort of male mistress, rebels and is condemned to death while the empress turns her come-hither gaze upon the new French ambassador. She later forgives Alexei, however, pardons him and gives him an estate.

"PINS AND NEEDLES"

An English musical revue in two acts, book by Albert de Courville, Wal Pink and Edgar Wallace, lyrics by Ballard MacDonald, Rupert Hazel and I. Ceasar, music by James Hanley and Frederick Chappelle, produced by Albert de Courville, at the Shubert Theater, New York, February 1, 1922.

Principals engaged —

Edith Kelly Gould
Harry Pilcer
Maisie Gay
Jimmy Nervo
Howard Knox
Jack Morrison
Tommy Mostol
Amy Verity
Jane Taylor
Geneva Marlowe
Ewart Scott
Alice Pollard
Teddy Knox

"THE PIGEON"

A fantasy in three acts by John Galsworthy, revived by Edward Goodman, at the Greenwich Village Theater, New York, February 2, 1922.

Cast of characters —

Ann Wellwyn..............................Louise Treadwell
Cristopher Wellwyn..........................Whitford Kane
Guinevere Megan..............................Edna James
Ferrand..................................Georges Renavent
Timson.....................................Hubert Druce
Alfred Calway...........................Edward Jephson
Sir Thomas Hoxton.......................Marshal Vincent
Rory Megan.................................Gordon Blyth
First Humble Man.........................Frederic Monti
Second Humble Man.......................Wellman Parsons

Third Humble Man............................Alan McAteer
A Police Constable.......................Charles L. Douglas

Act I.—Christmas Eve. Act II.—New Year's Day. Act III.—The First of April. The action passes in Wellwyn's Studio and the Street Outside, by the Embankment in London. Staged by Edward Goodman.

Christopher Wellwyn, a sentimental artist, living in studios facing the Embankment, London, is sorely distressed at his inability to alleviate the suffering of the human derelicts constantly appealing to him for help. Like the gentle pigeon that he is he is pretty thoroughly plucked by the wild birds he seeks to aid. The law and the church are found equally incompetent to deal with the problems of the poor when their aid is sought, and, finding no practical remedy, the pigeon goes on being a pigeon to the end.

"CHAUVE-SOURIS"

A Russian vaudeville organized by M. Nikita Balieff, presented by F. Ray Comstock and Morris Gest, at the 49th Street Theater, New York, February 4, 1922.

Principals engaged—

Mmes.	Birse	MM.	Balieff
	Ershova		Wavitch
	Dianina		Gorodetsky
	Karabanova		Birse
	Deykarhanova		Borco
	Fechner		Davidoff
			Kochetovsky
			Malakoff
			Marievsky
			Pons
			Stoianovsky
			Salama
			Dalmatoff

"The Bat Theater of Moscow," organized first by the players from Stanislavsky's Art Theater for their own diversion, was afterward expanded into a sort of impromptu vaudeville for the entertainment of the public.

A mixed Russian Lambs' club gambol, consisting of Russian folk songs and dances and burlesque dramatic skits. The New York engagement followed successful appearances in London and Paris.

"THE LAW BREAKER"

A melodrama in four acts by Jules Eckert Goodman, produced by William A. Brady, at the Booth Theater, New York, February 1, 1922.

Cast of characters —

Father Spalding	Frank Sheridan
Ewing Fowler	Clifford Dempsey
Walter Homer	John Cromwell
Tom Fowler	Frederick Bickel
Jim Thorne	William Courtenay
Bill Dobbs	Morgan Wallace
Gibson	Frank Sylvester
Donovan	John Milton
Griggs	Herbert Rathke
Joan Fowler	Blanche Yurka
Kit Grey	Marguerite Maxwell

Ewing Fowler's bank has been robbed of sixty thousand dollars. The theft has been traced to Jim Thorne. Fowler is eager to send Thorne to prison until he learns that his own son, Tom, has been craftily woven into the plot of the robbery by Thorne. Even then he is willing to push the prosecution until his daughter, Joan, a settlement worker with theories respecting society's responsibility for crime and criminals, suggests another solution. There is only one way to reform criminals, says Joan, and that way to develop their sense of moral responsibility. She therefore offers to pledge her seventy-five thousand dollar pearl necklace that Jim Thorne, if properly trusted, will, of his own accord, return the sixty thousand dollars he has stolen. Thorne considers the adventure a good joke at first, but later the thought of Joan's faith in him becomes oppressive and he loses his nerve as a crook. Finally he returns the money to buy back his "freedom." After which he plans to steal the necklace. But the reform idea gets him. He doesn't marry Joan, however, but his little pal, Kit, a darned good "come-on" for a badger game, and eager to go straight.

"THE BLUSHING BRIDE"

A musical comedy in two acts, book and lyrics by Cyrus Wood, based on a play by Edward Clark, music by Sigmund Romberg, produced by Lee and J. J. Shubert at the Astor Theater, New York, February 6, 1922.

Cast of characters —

Paul Kominski	Robert O'Connor
Flower Girl	Violette Strathmore
Cigarette Girl	Kitty Flynn
Francois	Harold Gwynne
Schwartz	David Belbridge
Cazazza	George Craig
Christopher Pottinger	Tom Lewis
Alfred	Clarence Nordstrom
Rose	Edythe Baker
Justine	Beatrice Swanson
Lorraine	Marcella Swanson
Coley Collins	Cecil Lean
Lulu Love	Cleo Mayfield
Judge Redwood	Harry Corson Clarke
Doris Mayne	Jane Carroll
Mrs. Pottinger	Gertrude Mudge

Specialty Entertainers—
Ma-Belle, Miss Stoneburne and Mr. Wm. Holbrooke

Act I.—The Cabaret of Paul Kominski. Act II.—The Home of Mr. and Mrs. Pottinger. Staged by Frank Smithson.

To revive his dying cabaret business, Paul Kominski engages Lulu Love to serve the coat and hat checks. Lulu is a snappy little chorus girl turned Quaker because her "yea, verilys," and "nay, bo's" seem to please the men. Among her suitors is Coley Collins, a good tout but broke. To be near her Coley agrees to act as a professional "third party" in the Kominski place. When somebody's husband wants to dine with somebody else's wife the third party sits at table with them. He sees nothing, hears nothing, but eats a lot, and is on call if discovery makes it advisable for a chaperon to be present. Coley is a comic third party in the first act and after shooing several fiirtatious baldheads away from Lulu in the second act finishes as an eager bridegroom to the blushing bride.

"FRANK FAY'S FABLES"

A revue in two acts, book, lyrics and ideas by Frank Fay, produced by Harry L. Cort, at the Park Theater, New York, February 6, 1922.

Principals engaged —

Frank Fay
Bernard Granville
Eddie Carr
Helen Groody
Robert Cummings
Fania Marinoff
Olga Steck
Geogiana Hewitt
The Fifer Trio
Herbert Corthell
Louis Cassavant
"Olivette"
Donald Lee Roberts

"THE CAT AND THE CANARY"

A melodrama in four acts by John Willard, produced by Kilbourn Gordon, Inc., at the National Theater, New York, February 7, 1922.

Cast of characters —

Roger Crosby....................................Percy Moore
"Mammy" Pleasant..........................Blanche Friderici
Harry Blythe..................................John Willard
Susan Sillsby..................................Beth Franklin
Cicely Young..............................Jane Warrington
Charles Wilder...............................Ryder Keane
Paul Jones.......................................Henry Hull
Annabelle West...........................Florence Eldredge
Hendricks.................................Edmund Elton
Patterson..............................Harry D. Southard

The heirs of the late Ambrose West are summoned to Clifton Castle on the Hudson to hear his will read at twelve o'clock midnight on the twentieth anniversary of his passing. Mr. West was a trifle eccentric and feared a strain of insanity in his family. The will reveals Annabelle West as the sole heir, but provides that should she give any sign of mental unsoundness a second envelope should be opened and a second heir named. The rest of the evening is spent in trying to frighten the wits out of Annabelle with mysterious disappearances, murders, tales of escaped lunatics, etc. Everyone of the heirs is suspected, but the mystery is not cleared until the final scene.

"FEDORA"

A tragedy in four acts by Victorien Sardou, revived by Marie Löhr, at the Hudson Theatre, New York, February 10, 1922.

Cast of characters —

Count Loris Ipanoff........................Herbert Marshall
Jean de Seriex................................C. M. Hallard
Pierre Boroff..................................Edward Lester
Dr. Loreck.....................................Charles Esdale
Gretch..Edmund Gwenn
Desire..E. Vivian Reynolds
Boleslav Lasinski.............................Sydney Ellis
Tchileff...E. Rayson-Cousens
Kirill...George Sydenham
Boris...Max Brent
Dmitri...Junius Matthews
Ivan..William Grayson
Basil...Howard Edwardes
Countess Olga Soukareva.....................Hilda Spong
Marka...Vane Featherston
Princess Fedora Romazova....................Marie Löhr

Act I.—Count Vladimir's Study, Russia. Act II.—Reception Room in the House of the Countess Soukareva, Paris. Act III.—Princess Fedora's House, Paris. Act IV.—The Same. Staged by Miss Löhr.

Princess Fedora Romazova, believing Count Loris Ipanoff a nihilist and responsible for the murder of her fiancé, trails him to Paris and there, after extracting a confession from him as a result of his passionate love for her, notifies the secret police of her success. A moment later she learns that Loris was justified in killing her lover, seeing he had betrayed Mme. Ipanoff. Realizing also that she loves the man she has condemned, Fedora poisons herself rather than suffer death at his hands for having betrayed him to the authorities.

"MONTMARTRE"

A drama in four acts, translated from the French of Pierre Frondaie by Benjamin Glazer, produced by the Players' Assembly, at the Belmont Theater, New York, February 13, 1922.

Cast of characters —

Henri	James Meighan
Edmond	Karl Carmen
Georges	Frank Huyler
An Announcer	Oliver Putnam
A Girl in Gray	Virginia Sale
A Girl	Margaret Hawkins
An Englishman	Leslie J. Spiller
The Man with the Monocle	Gerald Randall
Simonne	Mabel Frenyear
Eve-Adam	Dorrit Kelton
Suzanne	Rose Winter
Big Alfred	Wells Spaulding
A Girl	Helen Stransky
A Girl	Dora Matthews
A Flower Girl	Marjorie Urquehart
A Cigarette Girl	Alta Mearkle
A Waiter	Billy Francis
Another Waiter	Emile Collins
A Gendarme	Vashti Bockmiller
Gaston Logerce	Frank Doane
Gabriel Montinat	Lucille Wall
Elaine de Morennes	Mae Hopkins
Pierre Marechal	Arthur Hohl
Jean Tavernier	Brandon Hurst
Madame Berthe	Bertha Skner
Marie-Claire	Galina Kopernak
Camille	Helen Lowell
Parmain	John Anthony
Charlotte	Helen Ware
Saint-Serge	Frank Connor
Levy-Brach	Frank Martins
A Maid	Mona Bundoon
A Gypsy Violinist	Clarke Silvernail
Claude	Roy Bucklee
Edgar	William Leonard
A Girl with the Red Coat	Mildred Gibson
Duchess de Grival	Helen Lowell
Mme. Claron	Nina Herbert

M. Claron.................................Edward M. Grace
A Woman...................................Virginia Duncan
Juliette..................................Gail Webster
Aiser.....................................Winifred Harris
Robert....................................Clarke Silvernail
Patrons..............Anne Morris, Teddy Solpult, Bertha Diamond, Frankie Holden
Dancers..................Marguerite Sinclair, Maxine Henry

Act I.—The Garden of the Moulin-Rouge. Act II.—Pierre Marechal's Flat in the Rue de Lille. Act III.—Gaston Logerce's Villa at Ostend. Act IV.—The Garden of the Moulin-Rouge. Staged by Clarke Silvernail.

Marie-Claire, born of an obscure mother and a cab-driving father, in the Montmartre district of Paris, meets and loves Pierre Marechal at the "Red Mill." Pierre is a struggling artist, but pure, and it is his idea that when he has money enough he will marry Marie-Claire. Temporarily they try apartment life, of which Marie-Claire soon tires, finding herself out of harmony with Pierre's musical friends. Soon she runs back to Montmartre and takes up with a rich man. Then back to Pierre when he finds her again. But back to Montmartre and the gay life finally when decency again becomes a bore, and there Pierre is forced to leave her, a lost and wasted soul. It may be something of the Christ-spirit in men that urges them to try to make a madonna of a harlot, suggests the author. But it seldom is a successful venture.

"DESERT SANDS"

A drama in three acts by Wilson Collison, produced by Shelton Wheeler, at the Princess Theater, New York, February 13, 1922.

Cast of characters —

Hugh Berndon................................Norman Trevor
Pickering (Otherwise Arthur Landran)........Edmond Lowe
Kadra.......................................Anzonetta Lloyd
Lady Alicia Marchbanks..............Virginia Hammond
Camel Boys...............Herbert Bellmore, Miano, Raffa, Rubenstein, Corne

The Action Takes Place at Hugh Berndon's Camp in the Great Sahara Desert Between Moonrise and Dawn. Staged by Harry Andrews.

Hugh Berndon, arriving at the home of Lord Marchbanks a few moments after his lordship had been killed in a struggle with another of Lady Marchbanks' admirers, is accused of the crime and, rather than start a scandal, goes to jail for seven months. At the end of that time the suicide theory is accepted and Berndon is released. To escape the notoriety aroused by the case, and also to get away from Lady Marchbanks, with whom he is in love, Berndon goes to Africa. There, a year later, he meets Arthur Landran, the real murderer of Marchbanks, and extracts a confession from him. Also he meets an Arab dancing girl and takes her into the desert as his mistress. Also Lady Marchbanks, coming in search of him, meets all three of them, is disgusted with Berndon and his dancing girl, is attacked by Landran, who is in turn killed by the dancing girl, and finally is ready to overlook Berndon's sin if he will return to England and marry her, which he agrees to do.

"MADAME PIERRE"

A comedy in three acts, adapted from the French of Eugene Brieux by Arthur Hornblow, Jr., produced by William Harris, Jr., at the Ritz Theater, New York, February 15, 1922.

Cast of characters —

Pierre Cottrel.................................Roland Young
Ferdinand Brochot.............................Marsh Allen
Henri Limouzin.................................Cecil Yapp
Bodier..Fuller Mellish
A Boatman.....................................Stanley Jessup
Charlotte.....................................Estelle Winwood
Isabelle......................................Marjorie Wood
Phrasie..Alice John
Mme. Bodier......................Evelyn Carter Carrington

Acts I., II. and III.—In the Living Room of the Cottrel Apartment, in Paris. Staged by Robert Milton.

Pierre Cottrel, botanist and nature student, has been for three years the intimate friend of Mlle. Charlotte.

For the last year they have been keeping house together. Now they are beginning to get upon each other's nerves. M. Pierre would welcome his freedom, which he finds it as difficult to secure as though he were married to Mlle. Charlotte. She, though she is not above flirting with M. Pierre's friends with a view to establishing other arrangements if the need arise, is still in love with M. Pierre and determined not to lose him as a provider so long as she can hold on. Thinking to strengthen her hold Charlotte leaves Pierre temporarily, sending back pathetic stories of her plans to drown herself in the Seine to which he pays not the slightest attention. Finally she does jump into the river, but within easy reaching distance of a handy boatman's hook. She is rescued and returned to M. Pierre, who weakly takes her back on the old terms. "Madame Pierre" is taken from M. Brieux's twelve-year-old comedy, "Les Hannetons," the "hanneton" being a sort of clinging beetle.

"TO THE LADIES"

A comedy in three acts by George S. Kaufman and Marc Connelly, produced by George C. Tyler and A. L. Erlanger, at the Liberty Theater, New York, February 20, 1922.

Cast of characters —

Leonard Beebe	Otto Kruger
Elsie Beebe	Helen Hayes
Chester Mullin	Percy Helton
Mrs. Kincaid	Isabel Irving
John Kincaid	George Howell
A Truckman	J. J. Hyland
Another Truckman	Albert Cowles
The Toastmaster	William Seymour
The Politician	Wm. F. Canfield
A Photographer	Albert Cowles
Tom Baker	Robert Fiske
The Stenographer	Norma Mitchell
The Barber	John Kennedy
The Bootblack	John Maroni
The Manicure	Grace Morgan

Act I.—The House of the Beebes in Nutley, New Jersey. Act II.—Annual Dinner of John Kincaid's Sons, Hotel Commodore, New York. Act III.—The Office. Staged by Howard Lindsay.

The Leonard Beebes are living in Nutley, N. J., after having been married for six months and are trying to get along on Leonard's salary as a salesman for the Kincaid Piano Company. Being a self-confident youth of high ambitions and small talent he is given to spending the family savings on visionary schemes promising quick riches, such as grape fruit farms in Florida. Elsie Beebe, a sane child-wife from Mobile, sees that if they are ever to get anywhere she will have to take up the management of Leonard without his knowing it. The head of the Kincaid Piano Company, calling to thank Leonard for having stamped out a fire in the factory, meets Mrs. Beebe. Also Mrs. Kincaid meets Mrs. Beebe. Between them the women silently and secretly conspire to promote the young man. Mrs. Kincaid manages to have young Beebe invited to a company banquet, and when he falls down with his speech, Mrs. Beebe makes it for him and saves the day. His promotion follows and finally a promise of success. Hence the author's salaam, "To The Ladies."

"THE FRENCH DOLL"

A comedy in three acts, adapted from the French of MM. Armont and Gerbidon by A. E. Thomas, produced by Ray Goetz at the Lyceum Theater, New York, February 20, 1922.

Cast of characters —

Baroness Mazulier....................Adrienne D'Ambricourt
A Furniture Mover............................James Hunter
Rene Mazulier...............................Eugene Borden
Baron Mazulier.............................Edouard Durand
Georgine Mazulier............................Irene Bordoni
Melanie.......................................Laura Lussier

Jackson.......................................Will Deming
T. Wellington Wick.............................Thurston Hall
Emily Morrow...................................Edna Hibbard
Philip Stoughton...............................Don Burroughs
James Allen....................................William Williams

Act I.—Living Room in the Studio Apartment of the Mazuliers, New York. Act II.—Drawing Room in the Hotel Suite of the Mazuliers, Palm Beach, Fla. Act III.—Same as Act II.—Staged by W. H. Gilmore.

The family of the Baron Mazulier is stranded in New York, making a precarious living selling faked antiques from "the old chateau." Georgine Mazulier, the handsome daughter, is the family's last hope. If she can marry a rich American all may yet be well. If not the worst is threatened. For which reason Georgine worms herself into favor with T. Wellington Wick, a self-made American millionaire, and lands him after a Palm Beach campaign financed on borrowed money. Midway in the game, however, Georgine believes herself in love with Philip Stoughton, a youth of her own age, and thus considerable suspense is developed before the story is happily concluded.

"FOR GOODNESS SAKE"

A musical comedy in two acts, book by Fred Jackson, lyrics by Arthur Jackson, music by William Daly and Paul Lannin, produced by Alex A. Aarons, at the Lyric Theater, New York, February 20, 1922.

Cast of characters —

Teddy Lawrence, in Love with Suzanne.........Fred Astaire
Suzanne Hayden...............................Adele Astaire
Vivian Reynolds, Perry's Wife.............Marjorie Gateson
Joseph, a Servant at the Reynolds' Place.....Harry R. Allen
Count Spinagio..............................Charles Judels
Perry Reynolds..............................John E. Hazzard
Marjorie Leeds..............................Helen Ford
Jefferson Dangerfield, a Lawyer............Vinton Freedley

Act I.—Veranda of the Reynolds' Place on Lake Content, N. Y. Act II.—Drawing Room of the Reynolds' Place. Staged by Priestly Morrison and Allan K. Foster.

Perry Reynolds, caught by his wife, Vivian, separating an attractive widow from a cinder in her eye, is suspected of being a flirt and becomes mighty unpopular at home. Also Vivian takes to flirting on her own account to be even with Perry. To re-establish himself Perry plans to disappear temporarily, leaving the inference to be drawn that he has committed suicide. Vivian overhears the plot, refuses to get excited and Perry, sneaking back home for food and shelter, has a sad time hiding under the piano and the dinner table.

"THE RUBICON"

A comedy in three acts, adapted from the French of Edouard Bourdet by Henry Baron, produced by Henry Baron, at the Hudson Theater, New York, February 21, 1922.

Cast of characters —

Germaine Glandelle............................Violet Heming
Georges Glandelle........................Warburton Gamble
Francois Maurel.................................Kenneth Hill
Madame Sevin............................Minna Gale Haynes
Monsieur Sevin..............................Walter McEwen
Yvonne Sainclair............................Dorothy Tierney
Jacques Sainclair..........................Edwin Strawbridge
The Stage Manager...........................George Vivian
Jeanne Caumont..............................Elisabeth North
Madeleine Derval...............................Ruth Tausig
Louise Baudier..................................Ann Byrnes
A Guest.......................................Walter McEwen
Elise..Mary Cecil
Baptiste.......................................Arthur Bowyer

Act I.—A Morning in September. Act II.—A Month Later. Act III.—The Next Morning. At the Apartment of the Glandelles in Paris. Staged by Clifford Brooke.

Germaine Glandelle, having married Georges Glandelle to be revenged upon the man she really loves, Francois Maurel, returns from her honeymoon with the proud report that she is a wife in name only. Her parents and her husband are distressed. Likewise Maurel. He had secretly hoped to be accepted as a lover, but under the circumstances he feels that it would be extremely imprudent of him to assume so completely the obligations of a husband. He therefore joins the family in advising Germaine to accept Georges as her lawful mate — at least temporarily, which Germaine does. And immediately thereafter bids Francois good-by forever.

"MRS. WARREN'S PROFESSION"

A tragi-comedy in four acts by George Bernard Shaw, revived by Mary Shaw, at the Punch and Judy Theater, New York, February 22, 1922.

Cast of characters —

Vivie Warren....Agnes Atherton
Mr. Praed....Edwin Martyn
Mrs. Warren....Mary Shaw
Sir George Crofts....Lynn Pratt
Frank Gardner....Everett Butterfield
Rev. Samuel Gardner....Edward Poland

Act I.—A Garden at Hindhead View, England. Summer. Act II.—A Room at Mrs. Alison's Cottage at Hindhead View. Act III.—A view of the Garden Adjoining the Rectory. Act IV.—Frazer and Warren's Chambers, London. Staged by Miss Shaw.

During this engagement Miss Shaw also revived Ibsen's "Ghosts."

"BAVU"

A melodrama in three acts by Earl Carroll, produced by Earl Carroll, at the Earl Carroll Theater, New York, February 25, 1922.

Cast of characters —

Kuroff....Charles Wray Wallace
Piplete....Maude Eburne
Bavu....Henry Herbert
Olga....Carlotta Monterey
Michka....William H. Powell
Annia....Helen Freeman

Scene—In the Russian Town of Balta. In the Attic of Bavu. Staged by Earl Carroll.

Bavu is a renegade half-caste Turk who becomes mixed up with the Committee of Ten in the Russian Revolution. Acquiring a fortune in loot he plans to wall it up in an old fireplace in his attic in Balta, Russia, escape to Roumania and return and salvage it when the commune is no more. His plans, however, are frustrated by a young aristocrat turned revolutionist who is seeking to get his sweetheart, a Russian princess, over the border. In his effort to be rid of the aristocrat, claim the princess and make his escape Bavu is variously successful until his final defeat, in which he discovers that in place of walling up his enemy in the fireplace, he has imprisoned his own Russian sweetheart.

"BACK TO METHUSELAH"

A philosophic fantasy in five parts by Bernard Shaw, produced by the Theater Guild, at the Garrick Theater, New York, in three divisions, February 27, March 6 and 13, 1922.

Cast of characters —

PART I.—IN THE BEGINNING

Adam....................George Gaul
Eve....................Ernita Lascelles
The Voice of the Serpent....................Margaret Wycherly
Cain....................Dennis King

Act I.—The Garden of Eden. Act II.—An Oasis in Mesopotamia, a Few Centuries Later.

PART II.—THE GOSPEL OF THE BROTHERS BARNABAS

Franklyn Barnabas....................Albert Bruning
Conrad Barnabas....................Moffat Johnston
The Parlor Maid....................Margaret Wycherly
Haslam....................Stanley Howlett
Savvy....................Eleanor Woodruff
Joyce-Burge....................A. P. Kaye
Lubin....................Claude King

Franklyn Barnabas' Study, Hampstead Heath, London, Shortly After the War. Staged by Alice Lewisohn and Agnes Morgan.

PART III.—THE THING HAPPENS

Burge-Lubin, President of the British Isles.......A. P. Kaye
Barnabas, the Accountant General...........Moffat Johnston
Confucius, the Chief Secretary................Claude King
The Minister of Health.......................Mary Lawton
The Archbishop of York...................Stanley Howlett
Mrs. Lutestring, the Domestic Minister....Margaret Wycherly

The Official Parlor of the President of the British Isles in the Year 2170 A.D.

PART IV.—THE TRAGEDY OF AN ELDERLY GENTLEMAN

The Elderly Gentleman......................Albert Bruning
The Woman.................................Ernita Lascelles
Zozim...Claude King
Zoo.......................................Eleanor Woodruff
Napoleon....................................George Gaul
The Oracle..............................Margaret Wycherly
The Envoy.....................................A. P. Kaye
The Envoy's Wife............................Shirley King
The Envoy's Daughter...................Martha-Bryan Allen

Act I.—Burrin Pier on the South Shore of Galway Bay in Ireland in the Year 3000 A.D. Act II.—Courtyard Before the Temple. Act III.—Inside the Temple. Staged by Frank Reicher.

PART V.—AS FAR AS THOUGHT CAN REACH

Strephon....................................Dennis King
A Maiden..................................Eleanor Woodruff
The He-Ancient............................Moffat Johnston
Acis..Walter Abel
The She-Ancient..........................Margaret Wycherly
Ecrasia.................................Clelia Benjamin
Arjillax................................Stanley Howlett
Martellus...................................Claude King
The Newly-Born........................Martha-Bryan Allen
Pygmalion.....................................A. P. Kaye
The Male Figure.............................George Gaul
The Female Figure.......................Ernita Lascelles
The Ghost of Adam...........................George Gaul
The Ghost of Eve........................Ernita Lascelles
The Ghost of Cain...........................Dennis King
The Voice of the Serpent...............Margaret Wycherly
Lilith......................................Mary Lawton

Before the Temple, 31920 A.D. Staged by Philip Moeller.

"YOUR WOMAN AND MINE"

A drama in four acts by Cleves Kinkead, produced by Lee Kugel, at the Klaw Theater, New York, February 27, 1922.

Cast of characters —

Thomson, the Governor's Servant...............Fred Eckhard
Mrs. Ward, the Governor's Sister.................Helen Gill
Governor Gilbert Moreland..................Byron Beasley

Clem Prewitt.............................Reginald Barlow
Sally Jackson.............................Regina Wallace
Hon. Amos T. Glossup.....................Bertram Marburgh
Dawson, a Detective..................George Stuart Christie
Abby Prewitt, the Wife of Clem..............Minnie Dupree
Joe Harney.................................Henry Mortimer
The Speaker of the House.......................Dan Pennell
Clerk of the House.........................Royal C. Stout
Hon. Timothy McClosky...................James L. Kearney
Tom Graves....................................Louis Fierce
Chester Graves............................Malcolm Duncan

Act I.—The Governor's Mansion. Act II.—Scene 1—Prewitt's Home. Scene 2—The Same. Act III.—Chamber of the State House of Representatives. Act IV.—The Schoolhouse. Staged by Daniel Pennell.

Governor Moreland refuses to pardon Joe Harney, county clerk, when it is discovered that Joe has "borrowed" money to help Clem Prewitt, a legislator. Prewitt explains that no theft was intended, that the money was used by Mrs. Prewitt to get him to a hospital when he was seriously ill and the county will lose nothing. Still the governor upholds the law. Whereupon Prewitt learns that there is something still unexplained about the "suicide" of a former suitor of Sally Jackson, whom the governor is going to marry. On the floor of the state legislature he accuses the governor of having murdered his rival. Subsequent revelations clear all parties and prove that any man, governor or farmer, will fight for his woman.

"THE FIRST MAN"

A tragi-comedy in four acts by Eugene O'Neill, produced by Augustin Duncan, at the Neighborhood Playhouse, New York, March 4, 1922.

Cast of characters —

Curtis Jayson..............................Augustin Duncan
Martha.....................................Margaret Mower
John Jayson.................................Harry Andrews
John, Jr.....................................Gordon Burby
Richard.......................................Alan Bunce
Esther (Mrs. Mark Sheffield)............Margherita Sargent
Lily......................................Marjorie Vonnegut
Mrs. Davidson...............................Marie L. Day

Mark Sheffield..............................Eugene Powers
Emily..............................Eva Carder
Richard Bigelow..............................Frederic Burt
A Maid..............................I. Hill
A Trained Nurse..............................Isabel Stuart

Act I.—Living Room in Home of Curtis Jayson, Bridgetown, Conn. Act II.—Curtis' Study. Act III.—The Same. Act IV.—The Same as Act I. Staged by Augustin Duncan.

Because of the death of his two baby daughters while they were still young, Curtis Jayson and Martha Jayson, his wife, agree that there shall be no more children born to them. Some years later, returned to Bridgetown, Conn., from the west, Jayson, who is a scientist, is about to set forth with an expedition to Asia which expects to uncover the bones of the first man, when Mrs. Jayson, who has always acted as his secretary, informs him that she will be compelled to stop at home. The hope of presenting him with a son has been born within her, and she has broken her part of their compact. Angered at the interference of fate with his plans Jayson curses his luck and frankly hopes the child will be born dead. The mother dies giving birth to a lusty boy, but Jayson refuses to look upon the face of "the little murderer." His attitude is accepted by his New England friends as proof that he suspects the parentage of the child. Then, out of loyalty to his memory of his wife, he accepts the boy and turns defiantly against the scandal spreaders.

"MADELEINE AND THE MOVIES"

A melodramatic farce by George M. Cohan, produced by George M. Cohan, at the Gaiety Theater, New York, March 6, 1922.

Cast of characters —

Garrison Paige..............................James Rennie
Harvey..............................Frank Hollins
Madeleine..............................Georgette Cohan
Aggie..............................Ruth Donnelly
Madigan..............................Edward Nannery
Tony Burgess..............................Harry Mestayer

...ts ...and
...ppear ...s a joke
...him ...y to fight. See-
...ds ... into Madeleine seeks
...here ...nly in getting him in
...he ... happens to be a way
...es... (for he has taken a great
...cape. Then there occurs a
...ing how Madeleine and her
friends became mixed up in the plot.

"BROKEN BRANCHES"

A comedy drama in three acts by Emil Nyitray and Herbert Hall Winslow, produced by Arthur G. Delamater, at the Thirty-ninth Street Theater, New York, March 6, 1922.

Cast of characters —

Arthur Weldon	Wallace Ford
Mary	Amy Ongley
Larry Martens	Raymond Hackett
Emilie Martens	Beatrice Allen
Elsie McCann	Aileen Poe
John McCann	H. R. Irving
Karl Martens	Hyman Adler
Mr. McCann	J. M. Kerrigan
Mr. Fox	Russell Johnstone

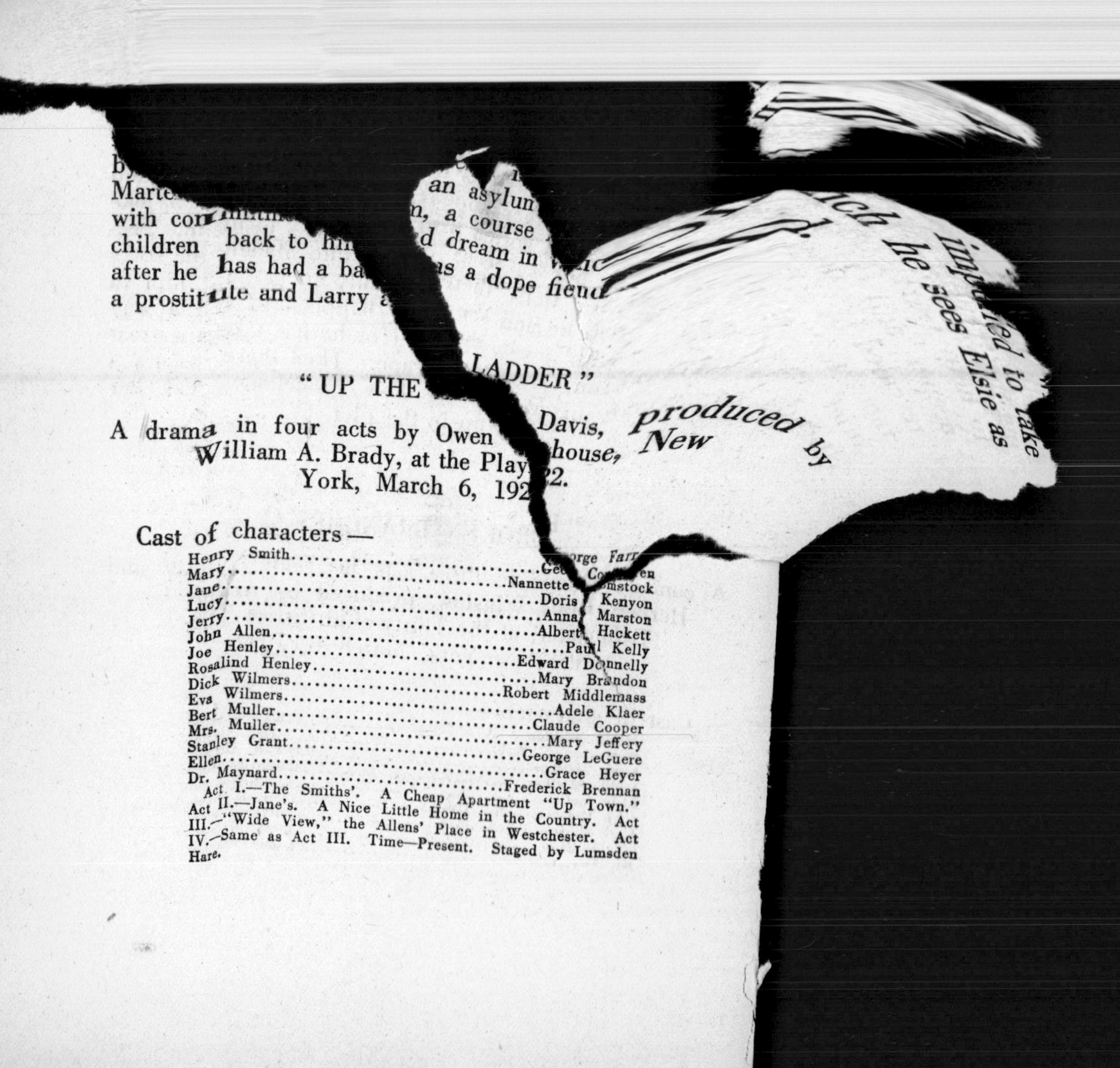

by ... an asylum ...
Marte...
with co... n, a course ...
children back to hi... d dream in ...
after he has had a ba... as a dope fiend
a prostitute and Larry a...

... impelled to take ... ich he sees Elsie as ...

"UP THE ... LADDER"

A drama in four acts by Owen ... Davis, produced by William A. Brady, at the Play...house, New York, March 6, 192...2.

Cast of characters—

Henry Smith..George Farr...
Mary..Ge... Co...en
Jane..Nannette ...mstock
Lucy..Doris Kenyon
Jerry..Anna Marston
John Allen..Albert Hackett
Joe Henley..Paul Kelly
Rosalind Henley..Edward Donnelly
Dick Wilmers..Mary Brandon
Eva Wilmers..Robert Middlemass
Bert Muller..Adele Klaer
Mrs. Muller..Claude Cooper
Stanley Grant..Mary Jeffery
Ellen..George LeGuere
Dr. Maynard..Grace Heyer
....Frederick Brennan

Act I.—The Smiths'. A Cheap Apartment "Up Town." Act II.—Jane's. A Nice Little Home in the Country. Act III.—"Wide View," the Allens' Place in Westchester. Act IV.—Same as Act III. Time—Present. Staged by Lumsden Hare.

Jane Smith, self-supporting, shies at marrying the young bond salesman, John Allen, whom she loves, because she fears he will not accept her as an equal partner. She submits finally and together they start "up the ladder of success." Soon, however, Jane notices that John, ambitious for power, is getting ahead of her, and going on alone. Soon they are making money but losing their self-respect. Now they are in the punch and party set and soon they are doing roadhouse twosomes and riding for a financial and moral fall. Then John checks his pace, outwits his enemies and, theoretically, at least, promises to reform. America is all right as a melting pot, the author declares, but we have all been too busy to skim the scum from the boiling mess, and as a result American character and American ideals are rapidly disintegrating. Hence such situations as those the Allens are called upon to solve.

"THE ROSE OF STAMBOUL"

An operetta in three acts, music by Leo Fall and Sigmund Romberg, book and lyrics by Harold Atteridge, produced by the Messrs. Shubert, at the Century Theater, New York, March 7, 1922.

Cast of characters —

Kemel Pasha.................................Henry Warwick
Kondja Gul, His Daughter.....................Tessa Kosta
Achmed Bey...................................Marion Green
Howard Rodney Smith..........................Jack McGowan
Bob, His Valet...............................James Barton
Midili, Kondja's Dearest Friend..............Mabel Withee
Desiree, Kondja's Companion..............Elizabeth Reynolds
Abdul, Guard of the Harlem...................Lon Hascall
Rodney Smith, Howard's Father................Rapley Holmes
Bul-Bul......................................Elmira Lane
Saada..Ottilia Barton
Maada..Sibylla Bowhan
Baada..Emma Wilcox
Guzela.......................................Maude Satterfield
Fatima.......................................Belle Mazelle
Durlane......................................Lillian Wagner
Emire..Marjorie Wayne
Haidee.......................................Zita Lockford

Hassan....................................Naro Lockford
Neidjal....................................John V. Lowe
Desha....................................Mlle. Desha
Felicia....................................Felicia Sorel
Helen....................................Helen Nelidova
Jack....................................Jack Scott

Act I.—The Harem of Kemel Pasha at Stamboul, Turkey. Act II.—In the Palace of Achmed Bey, a Few Days Later. Act III.—On the Riviera. Staged by J. C. Huffman.

Kondja, the daughter of Kemel Pasha, is promised in marriage to the Achmed Bey, though she really loves a young poet. She has never met the poet, but he has written her many ardent love letters. She marries the Bey, but escapes the night of the wedding thinking to elope with the poet, only to find in Act III that they are one and the same.

"THE HAIRY APE"

A tragi-comedy in eight scenes by Eugene O'Neill, produced by the Provincetown Players, at the Provincetown Theater, New York, March 9, 1922.

Cast of characters —

Robert Smith "Yank"....................................Louis Wolheim
Paddy....................................Henry O'Neill
Long....................................Harold West
Mildred Douglas....................................Mary Blair
Her Aunt....................................Eleanor Hutchinson
Second Engineer....................................Jack Gude
A Guard....................................Harry Gottlieb
A Secretary....................................Harold McGee

On the Deck and in the Stokehold of an Atlantic Liner. On Fifth Avenue, New York. In a New York Jail. At the Headquarters of the I. W. W. and in a Public Zoölogical Garden.

"Yank" is a stoker on an Atlantic liner, a huge man and rough, whose pride it is that he is strong like steel; a part of the active, primitive forces that move the world. Into the stokehold ventures the silk-draped daughter of a director of the steamship line, curious to see how the men live. She catches Yank angrily cussing an underofficer and as he turns on her, flushed with anger and dripping with perspiration, she withers him with the cry, "You beast!" at which Yank throws his shovel and a few choice epithets after her retreating form. Ashore, Yank, smarting under the insult, seeks to be even by battling society, but finds himself powerless to reach the "dirty bums." Jailed as a nuisance, refused as a would-be dynamiter by the peaceable I. W. W., he wanders into the zoo, meets another "hairy ape," the gorilla, thinks together they might even matters with society, releases the animal and is crushed to death.

"THE FIRST FIFTY YEARS"

A drama in seven scenes by Henry Myers, produced by Lorenz Hart and Irving Strouse, at the Princess Theater, New York, March 13, 1922.

Cast of characters —

Martin Wells.................................Tom Powers
Ann Wells....................................Clare Eames

In the Harlem Apartment of the Wells, at the Celebrations of Their Paper, Wooden, Tin, Crystal, Silver and Golden Weddings.

Martin and Anne Wells are married and go to live in Harlem, swearing eternal devotion and agreeing, at the behest of a friend, to "search their hearts" at each of their anniversaries. At their paper wedding, the first year, they quarrel. At their wooden wedding they sweartogawd never to speak to each other again. They spend their tin wedding in stubborn silence. At the crystal wedding he is ill and they patch up a truce. At the silver wedding they are resigned, but strangers still, and by the time they reach their golden wedding they are mumbling childishly over their game of euchre. The Wellses are the only two persons in the cast.

"THE HOTEL MOUSE"

A musical comedy in three acts, the book adapted from a French source by Guy Bolton, lyrics by Clifford Grey, music by Armand Vecsey and Ivan Caryll, produced by the Messrs. Shubert, at the Shubert Theater, New York, March 13, 1922.

Cast of characters —

Dolly	Cynthea Perot
Burroughs	Barnett Parker
Tiny	Lois Wood
Bob Biddle	Al Sexton
Lola	Fay Marbe
Don Esteban	Stewart Baird
Wally Gordon	Taylor Holmes
Cæsar	Richard Temple
Mauricette	Frances White
Detective	Frank Green
Victor	James Smith
Marquis de Santa Bella	Frank Green
Albert, Dancer	Elliott Taylor
Adele, Dancer	Cynthea Perot
Suzanne	Violet Duval
Marie	Edna Duval
Jeanne	Marion Phillips
Iote	Amy Frank

Act I.—Wally's Suite at the Hotel des Anglais. Act II.—Garden of the Hotel des Anglais. Act III.—Terrace of Don Estaban's Villa. Staged by John Harwood.

Mauricette, a good girl at heart, but taught to be a thief from her childhood, is known to the police as "The Hotel Mouse" because of her uncanny skill in sneaking into and out of Riviera hotels to collect the jeweled knick-knacks of the rich patrons. Once only is she defeated, and that the night she is penned in with an optimistic baritone who is charmed with her demureness and protects her from the detectives waiting in the hall by permitting her to sleep in his pajamas, and likewise his bed, while he snuggles up on the floor outside. During the last duet, or thereabouts, Mauricette reforms.

"THE TRUTH ABOUT BLAYDS"

A tragi-comedy in three acts by A. A. Milne, produced by Winthrop Ames, at the Booth Theater, New York, March 14, 1922.

Cast of characters —

Oliver Blayds.................................O. P. Heggie
Isobel.....................................Alexandra Carlisle
Marion Blayds-Conway.....................Vane Featherston
William Blayds-Conway................Ferdinand Gottschalk
Oliver Blayds-Conway.........................Leslie Howard
Septima Blayds-Conway......................Frieda Inescort
A. L. Royce...................................Gilbert Emery
Parsons..Mary Gayley

Act I.—Afternoon. Act II.—Morning, Four Days Later. Act III.—Afternoon, Three Days Later. Scene—A Room in Oliver Blayds' House. Staged by Winthrop Ames.

For seventy years Oliver Blayds has been worshipped by literary England as the last of the great Victorian poets. On his ninetieth birthday, after he has been reverently honored both by his family and by a famous critic who brings an address from the younger writers, Blayds confesses to his younger daughter that he is in fact an impostor. All the poetry he has ever published, except a single volume which was severely criticized, was written by a young genius who had died practically in his arms when they were lads together. A few days later Blayds dies, and the family's efforts to arrive at a decision as to whether or not the truth about his life should be told furnish material for the concluding two acts. A satisfactory compromise is finally settled upon. A bit of romance circles about the youngest daughter, Isobel, who has given up her life and refused to marry the man she loved out of a sense of loyalty to the lovable old faker.

"THE HINDU"

A drama in a prologue and three acts by Gordon Kean and Carl Mason, produced at the Comedy Theater, New York, March 21, 1922.

Cast of characters —

Maharajah....................................Don Richfield
Hari....................................Maurice Barrett
Shirza....................................Mignon McClintock
Clarice Cartright....................................Sydney Shields
Denton Morgan....................................Ian Maclaren
Prince Tamar....................................Mr. Whiteside
A Priest....................................Stanley G. Wood
Princess Yashda....................................Maude Allan
Ghinzi....................................Grant Sherman
Gautamar....................................William Cooray
Gupta....................................S. Pazumba

In the palace of Prince Tamar, Somnouth, India. Staged by John Harwood.

In an effort to stamp out the cause of rebellion being fostered in India by a certain mysterious "master mind," Clarice Cartwright, a Scotland Yard operative, is sent to the scene of the disturbances. In the palace of Prince Tamar, a crafty oriental, she meets with numerous adventures, including an unwelcome attack by the prince, a threatened forced marriage with a renegade Englishman, and a final death in a bed of quicklime. With comparatively little effort, however, she squeezes through and is a party to the final outwitting and capture of the "master mind," who is not at all the person you suspect.

"VOLTAIRE"

A romantic comedy in three acts by Leila Taylor and Gertrude Purcell, produced by Arthur Hopkins, at the Plymouth Theater, New York, March 21, 1922.

Cast of characters —

Francois Marie Arouet de Voltaire....................Arnold Daly
Jean Le Rond d'Alembert....................Lionel Hogarth

Aristide Freron....................Frederick Truesdell
Le Duc de Navailles....................Horace Braham
Marquis de Villette....................Leslie Austen
Father Adam....................John S. O'Brien
Moisnel....................George Le Guerre
Wagniere....................Howard Claney
Janvier....................Marcel Rousseau
Mlle. Clairon....................Carlotta Monterey
Mme. Denis....................Jane Wheatley
Marie Corneille....................Marguerite Forrest
At the Home of Voltaire in Ferney, France, 1865.

Voltaire, at seventy-one, is living quietly at his place in Ferney, surrounded by refugees and relatives. He is still actively liberal, and Mlle. Clairon of the Comédie Française begs him to assist in the escape of Moisnel, a young atheist thrown into the Bastille because he had failed to uncover during the passing of a Corpus Christi procession. Voltaire secretes the boy from Freron, the police agent, and eventually succeeds in smuggling him across the border into Switzerland, employing him, incidentally, to carry certain libelous verses, written by Frederick of Prussia and corrected by Voltaire, back to the scribbling monarch, thus averting another war between Germany and France.

"JUST BECAUSE"

A musical comedy in two acts, book and lyrics by Anne Wynne O'Ryan and Helen S. Woodruff, music by Madelyn Sheppard, produced by Just Because, Inc., at the Earl Carroll Theater, New York, March 22, 1922.

Cast of characters —

Cherry Bartlett....................Priscilla Paul
Bluebell....................Ruth Williamson
Syringa....................Queenie Smith
Wisteria....................Jean Merode
Mr. Cummings....................Frank Moulan
Mrs. Bennett....................Nellie Graham-Dent
Claude Wellington....................Charles Trowbridge
Mignonette....................Jane Richardson
Susan....................Mary Hotchkiss

Sarah...Ann Dale
Foster Phillips.................................Olin Howland
Leonard Wall.....................................Edgar Nelson
Rev. Dr. Bombig...............................Charles Froom
Daisy...Violet Mack
Fuschia...[illegible]
Clematis...Ethel Duffield
Magnolia.....................................Florence Kingsley
Marigold.....................................Gwendolyn Gordon
Ruth...Lillian Hazel
Elizabeth...Blanche Terrell
Sophia...Claire Martin
Martha...Maud Lydiat
Kate...Jeanette Dixe
Nora...Isabelle Bennett
Ann..Naomi Johnson
Matilda..Dawn Wolfe
Francis Savage..................................H. M. Arden
John Brown..Jean Barney
Peter Dale..Gayle Mays
Philip Duke.....................................William Wilson
William Benton................................Charles Froom
Joseph Crown..John Daly
Albert Stone....................................Harold Wheeler

Act I.—Adjoining Gardens of the Wellingtons' and Cummings'. Act II.—Scene 1—Knoll Overlooking the River. Scene 2—Garden Wall on Cummings' Estate. Scene 3—Parlor of the Cummings' Homestead. Staged by Oscar Eagle.

Suburban neighbors near New York are Mr. Cummings and his nine marriageable daughters and Claude Wellington who, having been disappointed in love, has adopted an orphan asylum. The youngest of the Cummings girls, deciding to marry the bachelor Wellington, disguises herself as an orphan and joins his group. Her plan, meeting with some lyrical opposition, is finally successful.

"CANDIDA"

A comedy in three acts by Bernard Shaw, revived by Maurice Browne, at the Greenwich Village Theater, New York, March 22, 1922.

Cast of characters —

The Rev. James Mavor Morell.................Moroni Olsen
Miss Proserpine Garnett...........................Janet Young
The Rev. Alexander Mill....................Charles Webster
Mr. Burgess.......................................Harry Neville
Candida...............................Ellen Von Volkenburg
Eugene Marchbanks...........................Byron Foulger

Acts I, II and III.—The Drawing Room of St. Dominic's Parsonage, London, a Fine Morning in October.

One of the best-liked of the Shaw comedies — that in which Candida, the parson's wife, brings about a minor domestic crisis in her home by taking in and mothering Marchbanks, an adolescent poet. It is a crisis which Candida is quite capable of handling, however, and is finally and completely solved by the withdrawal of the poet.

"TABOO"

A drama in three acts by Mary Hoyt Wiborg, produced by Augustin Duncan, at the Sam H. Harris Theater, New York, April 4, 1922.

Cast of characters—

Aunt Angy....................................Marie Stuart
Mammy Dorcas....................Fannie Belle de Knight
The Child..........................Master Junior Tiernan
Mrs. Gaylord...........................Margaret Wycherly
Charles..Henry O'Neill
Sadie...Ruth Taylor
Tom...Alex Rogers
Jim...Paul L. Robeson
Steve..............................Harold E. Simmelkjaer
Lemuel Johnson..............................Milton S. Dees
Joseph..F. H. Wilson
Cartwright...................................Harold McGee
Wheeler.....................................Walter Downing
Dr. Elder...................................David A. Leonard
The Beze..................................C. Kamba Simango

The Gaylord child, eight years old, is still subnormal, and has been dumb from birth. The grandmother, having tried all other suggested cures, listens to her negroes' opinion that the child is bewitched and can be cured if a "luck ball" is prepared under the proper voodooistic auspices. She visits a meeting of the "True Believers," and is given the "luck ball." The scene changes to one along the Guinea coast of Africa, the play tracing, through the dream of a sleeping negro, the origin of the voodooistic superstitions of the colored people. In the dream, the dreamer sees himself as the king and Grandmother Gaylord as the queen of a tribe that sacrifices an Albino child to the flames because of the abnormalities developed after its birth. And when she faces the negro of the dream, bringing the child home from the swamp, she dies of the shock. The plantation help threaten the innocent negro, but the dumb child recovers his speech and saves him.

"THE GREEN RING"

A comedy in four acts from the Russian of Zinaida Hippius, produced at the Neighborhood Playhouse, New York, April 4, 1922.

Cast of characters —

Ivan Yasvein	Ian Maclaren
Helena Vozzhin	Pamela Gaythorne
Sophia Vozzhin	Joanna Roos
Sergei Tarasof	Albert Carroll
Anna Tarasova	Frances Neilson
Vassili Vozzhin	Stanley Forde
Roussya Shapovola	Esther Mitchell
Marfusha	Millie Butterfield
Matilda	Aline MacMahon
Nickolai	Junius Mathews
Marrousya	Lily Lubell
Lyda	Paula Trueman
Vera	Frances Diamond
Boris	Robert Forsyth
Sacha	Philip Mann
Volodya	Edwin Kasper
Andrei	John McGovern

Act I.—The Flat of Vassili Vozzhin. Act II.—Uncle Mike's Study. Act III.—Apartment of Helena Vozzhin. Act IV.—Same as Act I.

Sophia Vozzhin, seventeen, has her heart set on reuniting her father and mother who have been separated for several years. But the Vozzhins are perfectly content to stay separated, the father being consoled by an agreeable widow and the mother having flown to the arms of an eager lover. In her search for a solution for her particular problem Sophia discovers "The Green Ring," an organization of would-be intellectuals, ranging in years from eighteen to twenty-three, who have taken upon themselves the correction of the mistakes of the older generation. The "Ring," which is fathered by Ivan Yasvein, a middle-aged philosopher, seeks to find some way to help Sophia, but finally can think of none unless she marries "Uncle Ivan." He can at least serve as a temporary husband, granting her the protection of his name and his home and leaving her free to look around for something better. "Uncle Ivan" is a bit staggered, but agrees to the plan.

"LETTY PEPPER"

A musical comedy in two acts, book by Oliver Morosco and George V. Hobart, music by Werner Janssen, based on a comedy by the late Charles Klein called "Maggie Pepper," produced by Oliver Morosco, at the Vanderbilt Theater, New York, April 10, 1922.

Cast of characters —

(In the Order of Their Appearance)

Hattie....................Jane King
Abe Greenbaum....................Paul Burns
Imogene....................Mary King
Mrs. Hatch....................Josie Intropidi
James Van Ness....................Thomas Walsh
Hutchinson....................Hallam Bosworth
Joseph Colby....................Ray Raymond
Letty Pepper....................Charlotte Greenwood
Billy....................Master Gabriel
Carolie Van Ness....................Vera Hellaire
Margery....................Frances Victory
Tony Barrillobatso....................Stewart Wilson
Mack....................William Balfour

Act I.—Stock Room in Colby & Company's Store. Act II.—Display Room in Colby & Company's Store. Staged by George V. Hobart.

Letty Pepper, risen from her beginnings as a cash girl in Colby & Co.'s department store, hopes to be appointed to a vacancy in the ranks of the buyers. The store superintendent, jealous of her progress, fires her instead. Meeting the youthful proprietor of the store just returned from Europe, and mistaking him for a drummer, Letty tells him her troubles and makes so great a hit that he re-engages her and gives her the coveted position. From this point of vantage she makes a real store of Colby's, and defeats all the superintendent's schemes to dislodge her.

"MAKE IT SNAPPY"

A revue in two acts, book and lyrics by Harold Atteridge, music by Jean Swartz, produced by the Winter Garden Company, at the Winter Garden, New York, April 13, 1922.

Principals engaged—

Eddie Cantor	Nan Halperin
Lew Hearn	Lillian Fitzgerald
J. Harold Murray	Margaret Wilson
Joe Opp	Muriel De Forest
Teddy Webb	Marie Burke
Georgie Hale	Tot Qualters
John Byam	Dolly Hackett
Cleveland Bronner	Ingrid Solfeng
Carlos and Inez	The Eight Blue Devils

Staged by J. C. Huffman and Allan K. Foster; supervised by J. J. Shubert.

, "SOME PARTY"

A revue in two acts arranged by R. H. Burnside, music by Silvio Hein, Percy Wenrich and Gustave Kerker, produced at Jolson's Fifty-ninth Street Theater, New York, April 15, 1922.

Principals engaged—

DeWolf Hopper	Lew Dockstader
Harry C. Browne	Jefferson De Angelis

John E. Henshaw	Sam Ash
Jed Prouty	Scott Welch
Herbert Waterous	John Hendricks
William Courtleigh	William B. Mack
Nannette Flack	Louise McIntosh
Primrose Caryll	Virginia Futrelle
John Abbott	George Averill
Bert Bowlen	William Grant
Ruth Adair	Percy Haswell

Staged by R. H. Burnside.

"THE GOLDFISH"

A comedy in three acts, adapted by Gladys Unger from the French of Armont and Gerbidon, produced by the Messrs. Shubert, at the Maxine Elliot Theatre, New York, April, 17, 1922.

Cast of characters —

Magnolia	Lucille La Verne
Amelia Pugsley	Norma Mitchell
Jenny	Marjorie Rambeau
Jim Wetherby	Wilfred Lytell
Count Stanislaus Nevski	Wilton Lackaye
Herman Krauss	Ben Hendricks
Ellen	Rhy Derby
Casimir	John De Silva
Hamilton J. Power	Robert T. Haines
Wilton	John Robb
The Duke of Middlesex	Dennis Cleughs

Act I.—A Flat in 24th St. Act II.—An Apartment on Riverside Drive. Act III.—The Lounge in an Apartment in Park Avenue. Staged by Stuart Walker.

Jenny, having married Jim Wetherby, a song writer, after a Coney Island courtship, meets Count Nevski, a down-at-the-heel Pole, who inspires her with confidence that she can be somebody socially and financially if she will permit him to give her lessons in deportment and thereafter trade on her beauty. She fights with Jim and "gives him the goldfish," which is to be the signal used by the first to tire of their married life, indicating that he or she is through. A year later she is married to Herman Krauss, living on Fifth Avenue, continuing her deportment lessons and looking higher. A year or so after that she has married Hamilton Power, who is Krauss' employer and a millionaire, and is living in great style on Park Avenue. Having achieved riches and society, however, Jenny—become Guinevere—longs for poverty and Jim. So, having buried Power, she is free to return to her first love when he comes calling. In Paris the comedy was called "A School for Cocottes."

"LADY BUG"

A farce in three acts by Frances Nordstrom, produced by Philip Klein, at the Appollo Theater, New York, April 17, 1922.

Cast of characters—

Robert Manning..............................Fleming Ward
Pauline Manning.............................Lilyan Tashman
J. Claude Ruthford..........................Leon Gordon
Dorothy Meredith............................Leila Frost
Tutwiller Thornton..........................John Cumberland
Julia.......................................Hilda Vaughan
Viddlars....................................Denman Maley
Marion Thornton.............................Marie Nordstrom
Daniel Dill.................................Edward Poland
Cook..Ida Fitzhugh

Acts I, II and III—At the Thorntons'. Staged by Priestly Morrison.

Marion Thornton, faddist, is interested in the "Second Chance" society, organized to give criminals a new start. She populates her home with ex-convicts and her pet of the moment is a murderer recently released from Sing Sing. To cure her, Tutwiller, her husband, bribes the butler to hide in the garret and let it be thought the murderer has murdered him. But the butler gets drunk and exposure follows.

"THE CHARLATAN"

A mystery melodrama in three acts by Leonard Praskins and Ernest Pascal, produced by Adolph Klauber, at the Times Square Theater, New York, April 24, 1922.

Cast of characters —

Mason Talbot	William Ingersoll
Eric Stark	Craufurd Kent
Bryce	Lewis Broughton
Jagi-Nama	William Podmore
Annie	Florence Johns
Dhima	Fania Marinoff
Cagliostro	Frederick Tiden
Avril Penniston	Olive Wyndham
Florence Gilly-Smythe	Margaret Dale
Herbert Deering	Purnell Pratt
Dr. Paynter	Edward Powers
Jane Farrell	Jane Thompson
Walter Knapp	Howard Ragsdale

The Drawing Room of Mason Talbot's Country House in Florida One Evening in Spring. Staged by Ira Hards.

Cagliostro, a magician who has lived long in India, is induced to give an exhibition at the country home of Mason Talbot in Florida. Among his other illusions is that of the disappearing lady. He places Mme. Cagliostro in the cabinet and she disappears. When she fails to reappear search is made for her and she is discovered in the secret compartment of the cabinet, dead. She has been stabbed in the back with a needle soaked in a powerful Hindu poison. The magician is immediately suspected of the murder, though various false scents are thrown out, and there is much verbal and physical dodging during the district attorney's investigation. Finally it is revealed that Cagliostro is an American, that he went to India to hunt down the villains who had betrayed his father; that he traced them back to the Talbot house; that he had here located the necessary proofs of his father's innocence, and that the real murderer of Mme. Cagliostro was — But that would be telling. The least suspected member of the cast, you may be sure of that.

"THE SHADOW"

A drama in three acts by Eden Phillpotts, produced by Marc Klaw, Inc., at the Klaw Theater, New York, April 24, 1922.

Cast of characters —

Nanny Coaker.....Kate Morgan
Sarah Dunnybrig.....Louise Randolph
Willes Gay.....Dallas Welford
Thomas Turtle.....J. M. Kerrigan
Elias Waycott.....Noel Leslie
Johnny Slocombe.....Barry Macollum
Hester Dunnybrig.....Helen MacKellar
Phillip Blanchard.....Percy Waram

Act I.—In a Country Store. Acts II and III.—In the Living Room of the Blanchards' Cottage, Devonshire, England.

Hester Dunnybrig is wooed by two men, Elias Waycott, educated and gentle, and Phillip Blanchard, a butcher's helper, rough but impassioned. After she has married Phillip, influenced by her greater love for him, Elias is accused of murdering his uncle, a cruel man who had disappeared some months before. With Elias in jail, Phillip admits to Hester that he (Phillip) committed the crime and stands ready to confess should Elias be convicted on circumstantial evidence. Elias is convicted, Phillip prepares his confession and is about to shoot himself when word comes that Elias, for love of Hester, has himself made the sacrifice, and the wife pleads successfully with Phillip to live on for her sake.

"THE BRONX EXPRESS"

A fantastic comedy in three acts by Ossip Dymow, translated from the Russian by Samuel Golding, adapted by Owen Davis, produced by the Coburns, at the Astor Theater, New York, April 26, 1922.

Cast of characters —

David Hungerstoltz.....Charles Coburn
Sarah, His Wife.....Bertha Creighton

Leah, His Daughter........................Hope Sutherland
Sammy, His Son........................Sidney Salkowitz
Reb Kalmon Lippe........................James H. Lewis
Joseph Hayman........................Joseph Sterling
Jacob Katzenstein........................James R. Waters
Casey........................Thomas Williams
Miss Mason........................Mrs. Coburn
Jack Flame........................John G. Bertin

David Hungerstoltz, twenty-six years a button-maker below Canal Street, objects to his daughter marrying a scribbling youth with few prospects. The girl, leaving her home in the Bronx, threatens to elope with her lover. David, going in search of her, boards the Bronx express, meets an old friend who has been successful in business, listens to the latter's tale that all success in America is built on bluff and advertising, as represented by the huge fortunes built up by the advertisers pictured around the car and falls asleep. He dreams that the characters on the cards come to life, and attends a reception at Mr. Pluto Water's home, where the Wrigley boys, the Pompeian massage lady, the Gold Dust Twins, the Smith Brothers, etc., are guests. Here he learns more of bluff and advertising. Awake he finds his daughter has come home a married woman and most of his other troubles are pleasantly dissipated.

"THE NIGHT CALL"

A melodrama in four acts by Adeline Hendricks, produced by the Players' Assembly, Inc., at the Frazee Theater, New York, April 26, 1922.

Cast of characters —

Alice Dodge........................Elsie Rizer
The Man From Out of the Storm........Charles Trowbridge
Martha Stuart-Scott........................Helen Lowell
Jerry Thompson........................Jay Hanna
Mollie Braden........................Nellie Burt
George Dodge........................Dodson Mitchell
Bob Braden........................Earle Mitchell
Edward Howe........................Brandon Hurst
The Other Man........................Wells Spalding

Acts I, II and III.—Living Room in an Old Mansion on the New Jersey Coast. Act IV.—Scene 1—A Tunnel. Scene 2—Living Room.

Alice Dodge finds herself with her maid marooned in a huge house on the New Jersey coast. A storm comes up, the telephone wires are cut, a strange young man makes his appearance followed by other strange men, murder is done and everybody in the cast is suspected. As it turns out the house is the headquarters of a band of wealthy and influential rum runners; the man murdered was one of them and had threatened to tell. The girl's father is implicated, none too honorably, and the strange young man had his reasons for appearing as an investigator. The conclusion is mystery-clearing and satisfying.

"CHAINS OF DEW"

A comedy in three acts by Susan Glaspell, produced by the Provincetown Players, at the Provincetown Theater, New York, April 27, 1922.

Cast of characters —

Nora Powell....................................Marion Berry
Leon Whittaker....................................Rollo Lloyd
James O'Brien....................................Harmon MacGregor
Seymour Standish....................................Edward Reese
Dotty, Seymour's Wife....................................Louise Treadwell
Mrs. Standish....................................Agnes McCarthy
Mrs. MacIntyre....................................Josephine Wehn
Edith....................................Eda Heinemann
Dean Davis....................................Henry O'Neill
Maid....................................Lillian Ward Grant

Act I.—Nora Powell's Office in New York. Acts II and III.—The Standish Home in River Bluff. Staged by Ralph Stuart.

Seymour Standish, a mid-western poet, feels that his genius is shackled to the environment in which he is forced to live. There is little chance for soulful expression in River Bluff, particularly when one is married to a shallow wife and burdened, as it were, with a misunderstanding mother. In New York Standish finds the intellectual companions he feels he needs and they, also convinced that he should be freed from his home restraints, take it upon themselves to follow him home to River Bluff, where they purpose to do anything necessary — even to the starting of a scandal — to break the ties of convention that tie Standish to the earth. But in River Bluff they discover that the young Mrs. Standish is ever so eager to go any lengths to let her husband soar, and that the mother, too, is much more understanding than they suspected. Standish, they discover, is held only by "chains of dew." Relieve him of his fancied martyrdom and all incentive to succeed would be stripped from him. Therefore he is left as found.

"WHAT THE PUBLIC WANTS"

A comedy in four acts by Arnold Bennett, produced by the Theater Guild, at the Garrick Theater, New York, May 1, 1922.

Cast of characters —

Sir Charles Worgan........................Charles Dalton
Francis Worgan..............................Claude King
John Worgan...............................Moffat Johnston
Saul Kendrick...............................Malcom Dunn
Holt St. John................................Louis Calvert
Samuel Cleland.............................George Frenger
Simon Macquoid............................Stanley Howlett
James Brindley..............................Harry Ashford
Emily Vernon..........................Margaret Wycherly
Mrs. Cleland................................Jane Wheatley
Annie Worgan.................................Shirley King
Mrs. Worgan...............................Marietta Hyde
Mrs. Downes................................Emily Fitzroy
Directed by Louis Calvert.

Sir Charles Worgan, having gained control of forty different publications in England, and made them all successful by printing in them "what the public wants," is a little tipsy with power when he meets Emily Vernon, a widow and an intellectual who is trying to be an actress in support of a new art theater movement. Becoming interested in Emily, Sir Charles agrees to modify, at her earnest request, his attitude toward certain aspects of yellow journalism. Also he takes an interest in the art theater and succeeds in putting it on its feet. He is still hopelessly bourgeois, however, and when Emily realizes that she is winning him to her way of thinking, not by convincing but rather by caressing him, she decides she cannot go through with her promise to marry him. So Sir Charles is left still groping for an explanation of the intellectuals' dislike and misunderstanding of him.

"PARTNERS AGAIN"

A comedy in three acts by Montague Glass and Jules Eckert Goodman, produced by the Selwyns, in association with A. H. Woods, at the Selwyn Theater, New York, May 1, 1922.

Cast of characters —

Marks Pasinsky....Lee Kohlmer
Mawruss Perlmutter....Alexander Carr
Abe Potash....Barney Bernard
Leon Sammett....Cameron Clemens
Mrs. Sammett....Mabel Carruthers
Dan Davis....Louis Kimball
Mozart Rabiner....James Spottswood
Officer Miller....Jack C. Grey
Rosie Potash....Jennie Moscovitz
Tilly....Helen Reimer
Hattie....Adele Rolland
Gibbs....Robert Gleckler
Bates....Frank Allworth
Schenckmann....Edwin Mordant
Kennedy....James F. Ayres
Smith....John F. Morrissey
Feldman....Max Waizman
U. S. Commissioner....John T. Dwyer

Act I.—Office and Salesroom of Potash & Perlmutter Motors, Ltd. June. Act II.—Office and Salesroom of Potash & Perlmutter Motors, Ltd. September. Act III.—Office of the U. S. Commissioner. Six Weeks Later. Staged by Bertram Harrison.

Abe and Mawruss, in bad with the agency for the Schenckmann Six, turn to the exploitation of the Climax Four. After selling a half million dollars' worth of stock they find themselves the victims of sharpers and face investigation at the hands of the government authorities. A substitute gasoline, patented by Dan Davis, a young plant foreman they have befriended, is suddenly found to be exceedingly valuable and saves the day.

"THE ADVERTISING OF KATE"

A comedy in four acts by Annie Nathan Meyer, produced by Lee Kugel, at the Ritz Theater, New York, May 8, 1922.

Cast of characters —

Miss Wanda	Maud Sinclair
Mr. Dell	Louis Fierce
Brandeth	Frederick J. Waelder
Sam	Gardner James
Wally Ziegler	Bertram U'Ren
Robert Kent	Leslie Austen
Sadie Ryan	Fay Courteney
Thaddeus Knox	Byron Beasley
Kate Blackwell	Mary Boland
Diana Verulman	Helen Gill
Aunt Maisie	Mrs. Thomas Whiffen
Miss Levinsky	Gertrude Mann
Mrs. Muldoon	Peggy Doran
Thomas Luce	Ray Wilson
Edgar Leroy	Bernard Thornton
Daisy Towne	Isabel Lamon
Madge Leslie	Jessie Nagle
Butler	Louis Stewart

In the Offices of Kent & Blackwell, and at the Home of "Aunt Maisie."

Kate Blackwell, succeeding to a partnership in her father's advertising business, soon finds herself achieving her desire to be treated in business as a man's equal. About which time she also discovers that she is in love with her partner and that he is paying not the least attention to her. Whereupon she determines to quit advertising goods and begin advertising Kate. As a result she not only wins the love of her partner, but of several less worthy men as well. Disgusted with her success as a salesman of sex she is ready to go back to business and spinsterhood for the rest of her life, when the young partner takes a hand and effects a satisfactory compromise.

"THE RED GERANIUM"

A tragi-comedy in four acts by Ruth M. Woodward, produced by the Greenwich Village Producing Company, at the Princess Theater, New York, May 8, 1922.

Cast of characters —

Larry	William S. Rainey
Mary	Florence Rittenhouse
Bill	Mary Ricard
Sallie	Eleanor Coates
Mid	Robert J. Adams
Jane	Marion Lord
Elizabeth	Kirah M[illegible]kham
Beatrice	Mary D[illegible]elly
John Dawson	Benjamin [illegible]auser
The Dope	George Burton
The Doctor	Frank Andrews
Mary's Mother	Mina Gleason
Policeman	Edward Fetbroth

Act I.—Apartment on Edge of Greenwich Village. Act II.—Mid's Studio. Act III.—The Broomstick Tea Room. Act IV.—A Private Room in a Hospital. Staged by Reginald Travers.

Mary, a country school teacher, comes to New York to take the summer course at Columbia. She is most eager, however, to see Greenwich Village. Secretly she longs for the freedom and adventure the village suggests. John Dawson, her fiancé, who has come to town with her to see her settled, is induced to leave her at the studio of a mutual friend until eleven in the evening. Before that time Mary has met the leading free lover of the village, bobbed her hair, been held as a material witness when a dope fiend dies suddenly in the studio of one of her new friends, and agreed to keep house for the free love apostle. Months later, discovering that her lover is tired of her and that she is to become a mother, she hurls herself from the window of a hospital to which she has been removed.

"GO EASY, MABEL"

A musical comedy in three acts by Charles George, produced by the Hudson Productions Company, Inc., at the Longacre Theater, New York, May 8, 1922.

Cast of characters —

Ted Sparks	Will J. Deming
Mabel Sparks	Estelle Winwood
Mabel Montmorency	Ethel Levey
Edward Drenton	James C. Marlowe
Mrs. Edward Drenton	Margaret Dumont
Bruce Drenton	Russell Mack
George Macdonald	Arthur Aylesworth
Tessie Claire	Eileen Van Biene

Acts I., II. and III.—A Room in the Sparks' Home. Staged by Bertram Harrison and Julian Alfred.

The Ted Sparkses, having ceased to sparkle, are variously advised by friends as to how to recover their lost romance. Mrs. Sparks' friends advise her to flirt with her husband's best friend. Mr. Sparks' best friend advises him to introduce a professional stenographer into his house to do his typing and then bribe her to add a line of love making to her duties. They try the new cures with variously comic results. Mabel Montmorency, as the hired stenog, not only flirts with Mr. Sparks, but with his father-in-law, his brother-in-law and all his friends.

"BILLETED"

A comedy in three acts by F. Tennyson Jesse and H. M. Harwood, revived by Grace Griswold, at the Greenwich Village Theater, New York, May 9, 1922.

Cast of characters —

Rose	Mary Hughes
Emmaline Lipptrott	Sally Williams

Rev. Ambrose Lipptrott........................Harold Vizard
Penelope Moon..............................Selena Royle
Betty Taradine..............................Lois Bolton
Col. Preedy.................................Lumsden Hare
Mr. MacFarlane...........................Marshall Vincent
Capt. Rymill............................H. Langdon Bruce
Mrs. Brace..................................Kate Mayhew
The Three Acts in the Sitting Room of Mrs. Taradine's Cottage in Rural England.

Betty Taradine, two years separated from a husband who objected to her thoughtless extravagances, is notified that she is to have two army officers billeted with her. The religious folk of the neighborhood question the propriety of the situation, inasmuch as Betty is not a real widow. To satisfy the gossips Betty decides to kill off the absent husband and sends herself a telegram confirming his demise. Whereupon he turns up as one of the billeted officers under the assumed name of Rymill. Amusing complications are followed by reasonable settlements.

"FANNY HAWTHORN"

A drama in three acts by Stanley Houghton, produced by the Vanderbilt Producing Company, at the Vanderbilt Theater, New York, May 11, 1922.

Cast of characters —

Mrs. Hawthorn..........................Nellie Graham Dent
Christopher Hawthorn......................Whitford Kane
Fanny Hawthorn..............................Eileen Huban
Mrs. Jeffcote..........................Alice Bellmore Cliffe
Nathaniel Jeffcote..........................Herbert Lomas
Ada...Nannie Griffin
Alan Jeffcote...............................Gordon Ash
Sir Timothy Farrar..........................Walter Edouin
Beatrice Farrar.............................Gilda Leary
Act I.—Scene 1—Kitchen of the Hawthorns' House, 137 Burnley Road, Hindle. Bank Holiday, Monday, August 6, 9 P.M. Scene 2—Breakfast Room of the Jeffcotes' House, Bank Top, Hindle Vale. Acts II. and III.—The Same, Tuesday Evening.

This is "Hindle Wakes," a drama written by the late Stanley Houghton for Miss Horniman's stock company in Manchester, England, a matter of a dozen years ago. The new title was attached on the occasion of the play's revival in New York on the theory, evidently, that it would create a new interest in the play. The story is of Fanny Hawthorn, a weaver, who returns to her home on a bank holiday after having spent the week end with Alan Jeffcote, the rich young man of Hindle Vale, in a neighboring town. Caught in the lie she tells her family to clear herself, Fanny confesses. To the simple Lancashire folk there is but one way to set the matter straight, and that is to force Alan to make Fanny "an honest woman." The wedding is finally arranged, with every one satisfied except Fanny. She frankly rebels. She is able to take care of herself, and she will. And they can all make what they care to of it. Whereupon she walks out of the family council and leaves them.

"KEMPY"

A comedy in three acts by J. C. and Elliott Nugent, produced by Richard G. Herndon, in the Belmont Theater, New York, May 15, 1922.

Cast of characters —

Ruth Bence	Ruth Nugent
"Dad" Bence	J. C. Nugent
"Ma" Bence	Jessie Crommette
Jane Wade	Helen Carew
Katherine Bence	Lotus Robb
Ben Wade	Robert Lee Allen
"Kempy" James	Elliott Nugent
"Duke" Merrill	Grant Mitchell

Acts I., II. and III.—Living Room in "Dad" Bence's Home in a Small New Jersey Town. Staged by Augustin Duncan.

James Kemp, called "Kempy," is studying architecture, but he is forced temporarily to take a job as a plumber's helper in a New Jersey town. He had learned plumbing in the army. Called to the home of "Dad" Bence to fix a leaky pipe in the kitchen, he arrives just after Katherine Bence has quarreled with "Duke" Merrill, her fiancé. To assert her independence and be even with "Duke," Katherine induces Kempy, who has expressed an admiration for the one book she has written, to marry her and drags him to a justice of the peace before he has time to change his mind. That night Kempy sleeps on the living room sofa with the dog and Katherine retires to her own room to think things out. Next morning, when both Kempy and Katherine have decided they had acted a little hastily, "Duke" Merrill, who is a lawyer, finds a way out of the muddle.

"FROM MORN TILL MIDNIGHT"

A tragi-comedy in seven scenes by Georg Kaiser; translation by Ashley Dukes, produced by the Theater Guild at two subscription performances in the Garrick Theater, New York, May 14, 1922. Added to regular repertoire June 5, 1922.

Cast of characters —

Cashier....................................Frank Reicher
Stout Gentleman..........................Ernest Cossart
Clerk..Sears Taylor
Messenger Boy.............................Francis Sadtler
Lady...Helen Westley
Bank Manager..............................Henry Travers
Muffled Gentleman..........................Allyn Joslyn
Serving Maid...............................Adele St. Maur
Porter...................................Charles Cheltenham
The Lady's Son...............................Edgar Stehli
The Cashier's Mother.....................Kathryn Wilson
His Daughters.................Lela May Aultman, Julia Cobb
His Wife...................................Ernita Lascelles
First Gentleman.........................Walton Butterfield
Second Gentleman............................Philip Leigh
Third Gentleman.............................Charles Ellis
Fourth Gentleman...........................Samuel Baron
Fifth Gentleman...........................William Crowell
Salvation Lass............................Helen Sheridan
Waiter.......................................Edgar Stehli
First Mask...............................Clelia Benjamin
Second Mask.................................Frances Ryan
Third Mask..............................Caroline Hancock
Fourth Mask.................................Joan Clement

First Guest....................................Sears Taylor
Second Guest....................................Allyn Joslyn
Third Guest....................................Sam Rosen
Officer of the Salvation Army...............Ernita Lascelles
First Soldier of Salvation Army................Philip Leigh
First Penitent....................................Charles Ellis
Second Soldier of Salvation Army........Camille Pastorfield
Second Penitent..............................Helen Westley
Third Soldier of Salvation Army.............Henry Travers
Third Penitent..............................Ernest Cossart
Fourth Soldier of Salvation Army..........William Crowell
Policeman.....................................Stanley Howlett

Scene I.—The Interior of a Provincial Bank. II.—The Writing Room of a Hotel. III.—A Field in Deep Snow. IV.—The Parlor in the Cashier's Home. V.—The Steward's Box at a Velodrome During Bicycle Races. VI.—A Private Supper Room in a Cabaret. VII.—A Salvation Army Hall.

The cashier of a provincial bank in Germany, depressed by a life of drudgery, his head momentarily turned by the appearance of a beautiful woman at the bank, steals sixty thousand marks and pursues the lady. Repulsed by her he embarks upon a more or less systematic debauch, seeking to put selfish humanity to various tests of soul and character floating hazily in his mind. He finds the world rotten and its people shallow, avaricious and mean. At midnight he shoots himself in a Salvation Army hall.

"THE ROTTERS"

A satirical comedy in three acts by H. F. Maltby, produced by the Messrs. Morris and Clarke, at the Thirty-ninth Street Theater, New York, May 22, 1922.

Cast of characters —

Councillor John Clugston, J.P.........Harry Corson Clarke
Mrs. Clugston, His Wife.....................Janet Murdoch
Percy Clugston, His Son.................Harry McNaughton
Winnie Clugston, His Spinster Daughter..Margaret Dale Owen
Estelle Clugston, His Flapper Daughter......Kathleen Flynn
Charles Berry, His Chauffeur..................Louis Hector
Phoebe, His Servant...........................Selma Hall
Police Inspector Wick....................George Suydenham
Emma, the Cook...........................Marian Marcus

Acts I., II. and III.—In the Clugston Living Room. Staged by Harry Corson Clarke.

John Clugston, a blustering justice of the peace in a provincial English village, has long made a boast, as well as a political slogan, of his own and his family's "respectability." Suddenly there are revelations. His spinster daughter is caught flirting outrageously with the chauffeur, his youngest daughter is expelled from boarding school, his son is arrested in a raid on a "pub," his wife acknowledges having been married once before and his own past rises to smite him in the person of his own first wife, come to demand her unpaid alimony. Clugston is forced to pay heavily to silence the threats of exposure made by his pretty respectables.

"SALOME"

An elaborated version of the short play by Oscar Wilde, produced by the Players' Forum, at the Klaw Theater, New York, May 22, 1922.

Cast of characters —

Narraboth.......................................Paul Doucet
Damasco.......................................Harold West
Tigellinus.......................................Horace Milleron
Naaman.......................................Lyman Grant
Salome.......................................Thelma Harvey
Tamoura.......................................Lilas Foret
Johanaan.......................................Noel Leslie
Herod Antipas.......................................Fred Eric
Herodias.......................................Alma Kruger
Manassa.......................................T. Morse Koupal

Act I.—Before Midnight. Act II.—After Midnight. Act III.—A Few Moments Later. A Room Adjoining the Banquet Hall in the Palace of Herod. Staged by Fred Eric.

"ABIE'S IRISH ROSE"

A comedy in three acts by Anne Nichols, produced at the Fulton Theater, New York, May 23, 1922.

Cast of characters —

Mrs. Isaac Cohen.......................................Mathilde Cottrelly
Isaac Cohen.......................................Bernard Gorcey
Dr. Jacob Samuels.......................................Howard Lang

Solomon Levy.............................Alfred Wiseman
Abraham Levy.............................Robert B. Williams
Rosemary Murphy.............................Marie Carroll
Patrick Murphy.............................John Cope
Father Whalen.............................Harry Bradley
Flower Girl.............................Dorothy Grau

Act I.—Solomon Levy's Apartment, New York City. Act II.—Same. Act III.—Abie and Rosemary's Apartment, New York. Staged by Laurence Marston.

Abraham Levy, whose father's heart is set on his marrying a nice little Jewish girl, brings home as his bride Rosemary Murphy, whom he met in France when he was with the A. E. F. and she was an entertainer. To appease his father's first wrath Abie introduces Rosemary as Rosie Murphyski. Father Levy is fooled until Rosie's father arrives, and turns out to be Patrick Murphy. Right there a comic war is started. Abie and Rose, having been married by a Methodist minister, are married again by a rabbi to please Levy, and a third time by a Catholic priest to satisfy Murphy. Rosie's wisdom in having twins, a girl to be called Rebecca and a boy to be known as Patrick Joseph, halts the family feud long enough to bring the play to a close.

"MAKERS OF LIGHT"

A drama in four acts by Frederick Lansing Day, produced at the Neighborhood Playhouse, New York, May 23, 1922.

Cast of characters —

Mrs. Nellis.............................Eva Condon
Willis Button.............................Junius Mathews
Agnes Chatley.............................Esther Mitchell
David Nellis.............................Ian Maclaren
Sally Morton.............................Adrienne Morrison
James Grupton, Sr.............................Herbert Ashton
Jimmy Grupton.............................Albert Carroll
John McCleary.............................Frederick Lloyd
Joseph Prine.............................John Francis Roche
Peters.............................Edwin H. Kasper
Florence.............................Polaire Weissmann
Pearl.............................Paula Trueman
Ruth.............................Lily Lubell
Alice.............................Anne Schmidt

Lucy....................Eleanor Carroll
Bertha....................Elsie Brown
Tom....................John McGovern
Charlie....................Augustin Sweeny
Michael....................Ace Angline

Act I.—Living Room at the Nellis'. Act II.—Scene 1—Miss Morton's Room in the Millville High School. Scene 2—The Principal's Office. Act III.—Same as Act I. Scene—Millville, a New England Town, 1920.

Sally Morton, teaching Latin in the high school of a small New England town, and trying to support herself, her mother and a younger sister on the meager salary allowed by the school board, grows moody, depressed, lonely and rebellious. In this state of mind she drifts into a sympathetic friendship with seventeen-year-old Jimmy Grupton, a student in her class and son of the school board's president. Later their affair grows more intimate and Miss Morton discovers she will be forced to leave town to avoid a scandal. Jimmy, a "queer" youth, misunderstood at home, learns his teacher's secret and begs that she let him go with her. When she refuses because she is twelve years older than he, Jimmy kills himself. Running through the play is a plea for a living wage for underpaid teachers, that they may have sufficient to live decently, maintain their self-respect and not suffer from the effects of a weakened morale as did this heroine.

"RED PEPPER"

A musical comedy in two acts, book by Edgar Smith and Emily Young, lyrics by Howard Rogers and Owen Murphy, music by Albert Gumble and Owen Murphy, produced by the Messrs. Shubert, at the Shubert Theater, New York, May 29, 1922.

Cast of characters —

Juniper Berry, Colored Gentleman of Misfortune, James McIntyre
Jimpson Weed, Get-Rich-Quick Wallingford of the Colored Race....................Thomas Heath

Lilly Rose, Colored Highbrow..................Mabel Elaine
Nokomis..................................Vivian Holt
Wah Letka..............................Lillian Rosedale
Col. Shelby Bright, Kentucky Colonel..........Dan Quinlan
Sally, His Daughter.....................Florence Rayfield
Richard Pitney, Owner of Race Horses....Barrett Greenwood
Dolly Pitney, His Sister, and Owner of Red Pepper,
Ferne Rogers
Lord Gathe-Coyne, English Lord and Owner of Sir
Robert................................Charles Brown
Scotty, Race Track Tout...................... Bob Nelson
Babe Stringer, Stranded Chorus Girl.........Gladys Fooshee
Billie Bull, Her Pal.........................Sybil Fooshee
Jimmy Swift, an American Jockey.............Dan Brennan
Tommy Dodd, an English Jockey..................Hal Sands
Lariat Ike, Western Cowboy..................Bee Ho Gray
Nan, a Western Cowgirl...................Ada Summerville
R. R. Attorney.........................George Youngman
Rembrandt, a High-toned Colored Gentleman,
George Youngman
Ramonda, a Mexican...........................Escamilio

Act I.—Scene 1—Cafe of the Casino, Havana, Cuba. Scene 2—Grove of Palms and Poncianas in Havana, Cuba. Scene 3—Interior of Stables at Race Track, Havana, Cuba. Scene 4—Lawn in Front of Clubhouse, Havana, Race Track. Act II.—Scene 1—Pitney's Ranch and Corral in Arizona. Scene 2—The Golf Links of the Dingeville Country Club. Scene 3—Gold Room in Colonel's Mansion. Scene 4—Mansion of Colonel Bright in Georgia. Staged by Frank Smithson.

"THE DRUMS OF JEOPARDY"

A mystery melodrama in five scenes by Howard Herrick and Harold MacGrath, produced by Alfred E. Aarons, at the Gaiety Theater, New York, May 29, 1922.

Cast of characters —

Kuroki.................................Emmet O'Reilly
Boris Karlov..............................Paul Everton
Cutty..............................William Courtleigh
Edward Burlingame.......................Bernard Reinold
Kitty Conover...........................Marion Coakley
Antonio Bernini.........................George Frenger
Stemmler..................................John Colvin
John Hawksley..........................C. Henry Gordon
Patrick Conroy...........................M. Tello Webb
Dr. Richard Harrison....................Victor Harrison
Stepan Gregory.........................Reginald Barlow
Chauffeur...............................George Golden

Scene 1—Cutty's Apartment on the Eighteenth Floor of an Office Building in New York City. Scene 2—Kitty Conover's Flat. Scene 3—Cutty's Apartment. Scene 4—Karlov's Attic in an Old Building. Scene 5—Cutty's Apartment. Staged by Ira Hards.

John Hawksley, a noble Russian, escapes with what is left of the family jewels when the Bolsheviki put his family out of commission. Among the jewels are the "Drums of Jeopardy," two sizable emeralds declared to bring the possessor all manner of bad luck. Bolsheviki agents trail Hawksley to New York, where circumstances place him under the protection of Kitty Conover, a likable newspaper woman, and "Cutty," her godfather, who is also a secret service agent. The chase of the emeralds places the cast in jeopardy for four scenes. They are extricated in the fifth and Kitty engages herself to John. The play is a dramatization of Mr. MacGrath's story bearing the same title.

"A PINCH HITTER"

A comedy in four acts by H. M. Harwood, produced by Allan Pollock, at the Henry Miller Theater, New York, June 1, 1922.

Cast of characters —

Millicent Thannay..........................Pamela Gaythorne
Nigel Bellamy..........................Charles Waldron
Page..........................Gordon Gunniss
Mr. Prothero..........................J. M. Kerrigan
Dennis Lestrange..........................Allan Pollock
Archibald Hannay..........................Edgar Kent
Joyce Traill..........................Helen Stewart

Act I.—Mr. Prothero's Office in Bond Street. Act II.—The Hall at Heron's Court. Act III.—The Same. Act IV.—The Same.

Dennis Lestrange, an English gentleman financially on his "beam ends," accepts an assignment to serve as a professional corespondent so Millicent Hannay may get a divorce from Archibald Hannay, leaving her free to marry Nigel Bellamy, M.P. Lestrange is invited to the Hannay place, where he discovers Bellamy to be a bounder, Hannay a decent sort, and Mrs. Hannay merely restless and feeling neglected. Incidentally the women of the household are all charmed by Lestrange and he ends by proposing to Mrs. Hannay's niece, Joyce Traill, and Mrs. Hannay returns to her husband.

ZIEGFELD FOLLIES, 1922

Music by Victor Herbert, Louis A. Hirsch and Dave Stamper, book and lyrics by Ring Lardner, Gene Buck and Ralph Spence, produced by Florenz Ziegfeld, Jr., at the New Amsterdam Theater, New York, June 5, 1922.

Principals engaged —

Will Rogers
Al Shean
Ed Gallagher
Andrew Tombes
Brandon Tynan
Jimmy Nervo
Teddy Knox
Grant Simpson
Muriel Stryker
Evelyn Law
Serge Pernikoff
Gilda Gray
Mary Eaton
Lulu McConnell
Mary Lewis
Rita Owin
Martha Lorber
Thelma Connor
Velma Connor
Jessie Reed
Tiller Girls

Staged by Ned Wayburn.

"THE RIVALS"

A comedy in three acts by Richard Brinsley Sheridan, revived by the Players' Club of New York, at the Empire Theater, New York, June 5, 1922.

Cast of characters —

Sir Anthony Absolute....Tyrone Power
Captain Absolute....Robert Warwick
Faulkland....Pedro de Cordoba
Acres....Francis Wilson
Sir Lucius O'Trigger....John Craig
Fag....Henry E. Dixey
David....James T. Powers
Mrs. Malaprop....Mary Shaw
Lydia Languish....Violet Heming
Lucy....Patricia Collinge

Act I.—Scene 1—The Drawing Room in Mrs. Malaprop's House. Scene 2—Captain Absolute's Lodgings. Act II.—Scene 1—The North Parade. Scene 2—The Drawing Room in Mrs. Malaprop's House. Scene 3—Acres' Lodgings. Act III.—Scene 1—The Drawing Room in Mrs. Malaprop's House. Scene 2—King's Mead Fields. The action of the play takes place at Bath. Staged by William Seymour.

"RAYMOND HITCHCOCK'S PINWHEEL"

A "Kaleidoscopic Revel" in twenty parts, whirled by Michi Itow, produced by Richard G. Herndon, at the Earl Carroll Theater, New York, June 15, 1922.

Principals engaged—

Raymond Hitchcock
Frank Fay
Michi Itow
Zoltan Hecht
Senia Gluck
Yuji Itow
Louise Riley
Margaret Petit
Isabel Vernon
Maria Montero
Felicia Sorel
Rosalind Fuller
Eva Clark
Anita Enters
Ragina Devi

STATISTICAL SUMMARY

(June 15, 1921–June 15, 1922.)

Plays	*Performances*
*Abie's Irish Rose	28
Advertising of Kate, The	24
Alias Jimmy Valentine	46
Ambush	98
Anna Christie	177
Bachelor's Night, A	8
Back to Methuselah	25
Back Pay	79
Bavu	25
Beware of Dogs	88
Billeted	23
Bill of Divorcement, A	173
Blood and Sand	71
Blossom Time	295
Blue Kitten, The	140
Blue Lagoon, The	21
Bluebeard's Eighth Wife	155
Blushing Bride, The	144
Bombo	219
Bought and Paid For	30
Broken Branches	16
Bulldog Drummond	162
*Bronx Express	58
Candida	43
*Captain Applejack	195
*Cat and the Canary, The	148
Chains of Dew	16
*Charlatan, The	61
Chauve-Souris	153
Children's Tragedy, The	8
Chocolate Soldier, The	83
Circle, The	175
Claw, The	115
Creditors, The	7
Czarina, The	136
Danger	79
Daddy's Gone-a-Hunting	129
Deluge, The	45
Demi-Virgin, The	268
Desert Sands	16
Detour, The	48
Don Juan	14
*Dover Road, The	204
Dream Maker, The	82
Drifting	63
Drums of Jeopardy, The	8
Dulcy	246

Plays	*Performances*
Easiest Way, The	63
Elsie Janis and Gang	56
Elton Case, The	17
Everyday	30
Face Value	41
Fair Circassian, The	7
Fan, The	32
Fanny Hawthorne	36
Fedora	12
First Fifty Years, The	48
First Man, The	27
For Goodness Sake	103
Frank Fay's Fables	32
French Doll, The	120
Friar's Jamboree	12
*From Morn Till Midnight	
George White's Scandals	97
Getting Gertie's Garter	120
Ghosts	21
Get Together	397
Goat Alley	5
Go Easy, Mabel	16
Golden Days	40
*Goldfish, The	70
*Good Morning, Dearie	265
Grand Duke, The	131
Great Broxopp, The	66
Great Way, The	8
Green Ring, The	30
Greenwich Village Follies	167
*Hairy Ape, The	108

Plays	*Performances*
Hand of the Potter, The	21
Hero, The	80
Her Salary Man	32
*He Who Gets Slapped	182
Hindu, The	71
Honors Are Even	70
Hotel Mouse, The	88
Idiot, The	3
Idle Inn, The	25
Intimate Strangers	91
Just Because	46
*Kempy	38
*Kiki	233
Lady Bug	5
Launcelot and Elaine	32
Lawbreaker, The	90
*Lawful Larceny	190
Letty Pepper	32
Like a King	16
Lillies of the Field	169
Liliom	16
Love Dreams	40
Love Letter, The	31
Madame Pierre	37
Mad Dog, The	15
Madeleine and the Movies	80
Madras House, The	80
Main Street	86
*Make It Snappy	77
Makers of Light	21
Man in the Making, The	22
Man's Name, The	24

Plays	*Performances*
March Hares	60
Marie Antoinette	16
Marjolaine	136
Married Woman, The	51
Mask, The	8
Merry Widow, The	56
Mimic World, The	27
Montmartre	112
Mountain Man, The	163
Mr. Faust	15
Mr. Pim Passes By	16
Mrs. Warren's Profession	25
*Music Box Revue, The	313
National Anthem, The	114
Nature's Nobleman	74
Nest, The	161
Nightcall, The	29
Nightcap, The	96
Nobody's Money	29
O'Brien Girl, The	164
Oh, Marion	56
Only 38	88
*Partners Again	53
*Perfect Fool, The	256
Personality	9
Pigeon, The	92
*Pinch Hitter, The	17
Pins and Needles	46
Pinwheel Revue	1
Poppy God, The	16
Pot Luck	28
Put and Take	34
Red Geranium, The	16
*Red Pepper	22

Plays	*Performances*
Return of Peter Grimm, The	78
Right to Strike, The	8
Rivals, The	8
Rosa Machree	8
Rose of Stamboul	111
Rotters, The	16
*Rubicon, The	132
Salome	8
Scarlet Man, The	16
Shadow, The	16
Silver Fox, The	112
*Six-Cylinder Love	344
Six-Fifty, The	24
Skirt, The	8
Skylark, The	32
Snapshots of 1921	24
Some Party	17
Sonny Boy	31
Sonya	101
Spring, The	21
Steamboat *Tenacity*, The	67
Straw, The	20
Squaw Man, The	50
Suzette	4
Swords	36
Taboo	3
Tangerine	337
Tarzan of the Apes	14
Teaser, The	29
Thank You	257
Title, The	16
To The Ladies	128
Trilby	12
Triumph of X, The	30

Plays	*Performances*
True to Form	15
*Truth About Blayds, The	108
Two Blocks Away	47
Up in the Clouds	89
*Up the Ladder	117
Varying Shore, The	66
Verge, The	38
Voice from the Minaret	13
Voltaire	16
Wandering Jew, The	69
We Girls	30
Wife With a Smile, The	41
Wild Cat, The	74
What the Public Wants	24
Wheel, The	49
White Headed Boy, The	60
White Peacock, The	102
Wren, The	24
Your Woman and Mine	48
Ziegfeld Follies, 1921	119
Ziegfeld Midnight Frolic	123
Ziegfeld Follies, 1922	13

*Still running June 15, 1922.

PLAYS THAT HAVE RUN OVER FIVE HUNDRED PERFORMANCES ON BROADWAY

Lightnin'	1291
The Bat	867
The First Year	760
Peg o' My Heart	692
East is West	680
Irene	670
A Trip to Chinatown	657
Adonis	603
Sally	570
The Music Master	540
The Boomerang	522
Shuffle Along	504

WHERE AND WHEN THEY WERE BORN

Abarbanell, Lina	Berlin	1880
Adams, Maude	Salt Lake City, Utah	1872
Adelaide, La Petite	Cohoes, N. Y.	1890
Allen, Viola	Huntsville, Ala.	1869
Ames, Robert	Hartford, Conn.	1893
Anglin, Margaret	Ottawa, Canada	1876
Arbuckle, Maclyn	San Antonio, Texas	1866
Arliss, George	London, England	1868
Arthur, Julia	Hamilton, Ont.	1869
Atwell, Roy	Syracuse, N. Y.	1880
Atwill, Lionel	London, England	1883
Bacon, Frank	Marysville, Cal.	1864
Bainter, Fay	Los Angeles, Cal.	1893
Barbee, Richard	Lafayette, Ind.	1887
Barrymore, Ethel	Philadelphia, Pa.	1883
Barrymore, John	Philadelphia, Pa.	1880
Barrymore, Lionel	London, England	1878
Bates, Blanche	Portland, Ore.	1873
Bayes, Nora	Milwaukee, Wis.	1880
Beban, George	San Francisco, Cal.	1873
Beecher, Janet	Chicago, Ill.	1884
Belasco, David	San Francisco, Cal.	1862
Ben-Ami, Jacob	Minsk, Russia	1890
Bennett, Richard	Cass County, Ind.	1872
Bennett, Wilda	Asbury Park, N. J.	1899
Bernard, Sam	Birmingham, England	1863
Bernhardt, Sarah	Paris	1844
Bingham, Amelia	Hickville, Ohio	1869
Binney, Constance	Philadelphia, Pa.	1900
Blinn, Holbrook	San Francisco, Cal.	1872
Boland, Mary	Detroit	1880

Brady, Alice............New York............1896
Brady, William A........San Francisco, Cal......1865
Breese, Edmund.........Brooklyn, N. Y.........1871
Brian, Donald...........St. John's, Newfoundland...............1880
Brooks, Virginia Fox.....New York............1893
Burke, Billie............Washington, D. C.......1886
Byron, Arthur...........Brooklyn, N. Y.........1872
Cantor, Eddie...........New York............1894
Carle, Richard..........Somerville, Mass.......1871
Carlisle, Alexandra......Yorkshire, England....1886
Carter, Mrs. Leslie.......Lexington, Ky.........1862
Cawthorne, Joseph.......New York............1868
Chatterton, Ruth.........New York............1893
Claire, Ina.............Washington, D. C.......1897
Clarke, Marguerite.......Cincinnati, Ohio.......1887
Coghlan, Rose..........Petersboro, England....1850
Cohan, George M........Providence, R. I.......1878
Collier, Constance.......Windsor, England......1882
Collier, William.........New York............1866
Collinge, Patricia........Dublin, Ireland........1894
Corthell, Herbert........Boston, Mass..........1875
Courtenay, William.....Worcester, Mass........1875
Courtleigh, William.....Guelph, Ont...........1867
Cowl, Jane.............Boston, Mass..........1884
Crane, William H........Leicester, Mass.........1845
Craven, Frank..........Boston, Mass..........1875
Crews, Laura Hope......San Francisco, Cal......1883
Crosman, Henrietta......Wheeling, W. Va.......1865
Crothers, Rachel.........Bloomington, Ill.......1878
Cumberland, John.......St. John, N. B.........1880
Dale, Margaret..........Philadelphia, Pa.......1880
Dalton, Charles.........England 1864
Daly, Arnold...........New York............1875
Dawn, Hazel...........Ogden, Utah..........1891
Day, Edith.............Minneapolis, Minn......1899
De Angelis, Jefferson....San Francisco, Cal......1859

Dean, Julia	St. Paul, Minn.	1880
De Belleville, Frederic	Belgium	1857
De Cordoba, Pedro	New York	1881
Dickson, Dorothy	Chicago, Ill.	1898
Dinehart, Alan	Missoula, Mont.	1889
Ditrichstein, Leo	Temesbar, Hungary	1865
Dixey, Henry E.	Boston, Mass.	1850
D'Orsay, Lawrence,	Northamptonshire, Eng.	1860
Dodson, John E.	London, England	1857
Donnelly, Dorothy Agnes	New York	1880
Dresler, Marie	Cobourg, Canada	1869
Drew, John	Philadelphia, Pa.	1853
Drew, Louise	New York	1884
Dunn, Emma	England	1875
Dupree, Minnie	San Francisco, Cal.	1875
Duse, Eleanora	Vigerano, Italy	1859
Eagels, Jeanne	Kansas City, Mo.	1892
Eames, Clare	Hartford, Conn.	1896
Eddinger, Wallace	New York	1883
Edeson, Robert	Baltimore, Md.	1868
Elliott, Maxine	Rockland, Me.	1871
Ellsler, Effie	Philadelphia, Pa.	1898
Eltinge, Julian	Boston, Mass.	1883
Emerson, John	Sandusky, Ohio	1874
Errol, Leon	Sydney, Australia	1881
Ewell, Lois	Memphis, Tenn.	1885
Fairbanks, Douglas	Denver, Colo.	1883
Farnum, Dustin	Hampton Beach, N. H.	1875
Farrar, Geraldine	Melrose, Mass.	1883
Faversham, William	Warwickshire, England	1868
Fawcett, George	Virginia	1860
Ferguson, Elsie	New York	1885
Fields, Lewis	New York	1867
Findlay, Ruth	New York	1897
Fisher, Lola	Chicago, Ill.	1892
Fiske, Minnie Maddern	New Orleans, La.	1867
Forbes, Robertson, Sir J.	London, England	1853

Frederick, Pauline	Boston, Mass.	1884
Frohman, Daniel	Sandusky, Ohio	1850
Fulton, Maude	St. Louis, Mo.	1883
Garden, Mary	Scotland	1876
George, Grace	New York	1883
Gillette, William	Hartford, Conn.	1856
Gilmore, Margalo	England	1901
Glaser, Lulu	Alleghany, Pa.	1874
Glendinning, Ernest	Ulverston, England	1884
Hackett, James K.	Wolfe Island, Ont.	1869
Haines, Robert T.	Muncie, Ind.	1870
Hajos, Mitzi	Budapest, Hungary	1891
Hale, Louise Closser	Chicago, Ill.	1872
Hamilton, Hale	Fort Madison, Ia.	1883
Hampden, Walter	Brooklyn, N. Y.	1879
Hawtrey, Charles	Eton, England	1858
Hayes, Helen	Washington, D. C.	1902
Hedman, Martha	Ostersund, Sweden	1888
Heggie, O. P.	South Australia	1879
Heming, Violet	Leeds, England	1894
Herbert, Victor	Dublin, Ireland	1859
Herne, Chrystal	Boston, Mass.	1883
Hilliard, Robert S.	New York	1860
Hitchcock, Raymond	Auburn, N. Y.	1870
Hodge, William	Albion, N. Y.	1874
Hopper, DeWolf	New York	1858
Hopper, Edna Wallace	San Francisco, Cal.	1874
Holmes, Taylor	Newark, N. J.	1872
Huban, Eileen	Loughrea, Ireland	1895
Hull, Henry	Louisville, Ky.	1893
Illington, Margaret	Bloomington, Ill.	1881
Janis, Elsie	Delaware, Ohio	1889
Joel, Clara	Jersey City, N. J.	
Jolson, Al	Washington, D. C.	1883
Keane, Doris	Michigan	1885
Keightley, Cyril	New South Wales	1875
Kennedy, Madge	Chicago	1884

[illegible]ta, Tessa	Chicago, Ill.	1895
Kruger, Otto	Toledo, O.	1885
Lackaye, Wilton	Virginia	1862
Larrimore, Francine	Russia	1888
La Rue, Grace	Kansas City	1882
Lawrence, Margaret	Trenton, N. J.	1889
Lawton, Thais	Louisville, Ky.	1881
LeGallienne, Eva	London, England	1900
Lewis, Ada	New York	1871
Lord, Pauline	Hanford, Cal.	1893
MacDonell, Kathleen	Toronto, Canada	1894
Mack, Andrew	Boston, Mass.	1863
Mack, Willard	Ontario, Canada	1873
Mackay, Elsie	London, England	1894
MacKellar, Helen	Spokane	1888
Mann, Louis	New York	1865
Mantell, Robert B.	Ayrshire, Scotland	1854
Marinoff, Fania	Russia	1892
Marlowe, Julia	Caldbeck, England	1870
Matthison, Edith Wynne	England	1875
Maude, Cyril	London, England	1862
McIntyre, Frank	Ann Arbor, Mich.	1879
McRae, Bruce	London, England	1864
Melba, Nellie	Melbourne, Australia	1866
Mercer, Beryl	Seville, Spain	1882
Miller, Henry	London, England	1859
Miller, Marilyn	Dayton, Ohio	1900
Mitchell, Grant	Columbus, Ohio	1874
Moores, Clara	Omaha, Neb.	1897
Morris, Clara	Toronto, Canada	1846
Murphy, Tim	Rupert, Vt.	1860
Nazimova, Mme.	Crimea, Russia	1879
Nielsen, Alice	Nashville, Tenn.	1876
Olcott, Chauncey	Providence, R. I.	1862
O'Neill, Nance	Oakland, Cal.	1875
O'Ramey, Georgia	Mansfield, Ohio	1886
Painter, Eleanor	Iowa	1890

Pennington, Ann	Philadelphia, Pa.	1898
Post, Guy Bates	Seattle, Wash.	1875
Powers, Tyrone	London, England	1869
Rambeau, Marjorie	San Francisco, Cal.	1884
Reed, Florence	Philadelphia, Pa.	1883
Rennie, James	Toronto, Canada	1890
Richard, Amy	Boston, Mass.	1880
Ring, Blanche	Boston, Mass.	1876
Roberts, Theodore	San Francisco, Cal.	1861
Robson, May	Australia	1868
Ross, Thomas W.	Boston, Mass.	1875
Rubens, Jose	Belgium	1886
Russell, Annie	Liverpool	1864
Russell, Lillian	Clinton, Iowa	1860
Ryan, Mary	New York	1886
Sanderson, Julia	Springfield, Mass.	1887
Scheff, Fritzi	Vienna	1879
Scott, Cyril	Ireland	1866
Sears, Zelda	Brockway, Mich.	1873
Selwyn, Edgar	Cincinnati, Ohio	1875
Shannon, Effie	Cambridge, Mass.	1867
Schildkraut, Joseph	Bukarest	1896
Sidney, George	New York	1876
Skinner, Otis	Cambridgeport, Mass.	1857
Sothern, Edward H.	New Orleans, La.	1864
Spong, Hilda	Australia	1875
Stahl, Rose	Montreal, Canada	1872
Starr, Frances	Oneonta, N. Y.	1886
Stevens, Emily	New York	1882
Stone, Fred	Wellington, Kan.	1877
Taliaferro, Edith	New York	1892
Taliaferro, Mabel	New York	1887
Tanguay, Eva	Holyoke, Mass.	1878
Taylor, Laurette	New York	1884
Tell, Alma	New York	1892
Tell, Olive	New York	1894
Tempest, Marie	London, England	1864

Terry, Ellen Alice	Coventry, England	1848
Thomas, Augustus	St. Louis, Mo.	1859
Thomas, John Charles	Baltimore, Md.	1887
Thompson, W. H.	Scotland	1852
Tinney, Frank	Philadelphia, Pa.	1878
Tobin, Genevieve	New York	1901
Tobin, Vivian	New York	1903
Toler, Sidney	Warrensburg, Mo.	1874
Trevor, Norman	Calcutta	1877
Truex, Ernest	Denver, Colo.	1890
Tynan, Brandon	Dublin, Ireland	1879
Ulric, Lenore	New Ulm, Minn.	1897
Valentine, Grace	Indianapolis, Ind.	1892
Varesi, Gilda	Milan, Italy	1887
Victor, Josephine	Hungary	1891
Wainwright, Marie	Philadelphia, Pa.	1853
Warfield, David	San Francisco, Cal.	1891
Warwick, Robert	Sacramento, Cal.	1878
Weber, Jos.	New York	1867
Welford, Dallas	Liverpool, England	1874
Westley, Helen	Brooklyn, N. Y.	1879
Whiffen, Mrs. Thomas	London, England	1845
Whiteside, Walker	Logansport, Ind.	1869
Wilson, Francis	Philadelphia, Pa.	1854
Winant, Forrest	New York	1888
Winwood, Estelle	England	1883
Wise, Tom A.	England	1865
Wood, Peggy	Philadelphia, Pa.	1893
Wycherly, Margaret	England	1883
Wyndham, Olive	Chicago, Ill.	1886
Wynn, Ed	Philadelphia, Pa.	1886
Ziegfeld, Florenz, Jr.	Chicago, Ill.	1867

NECROLOGY

June 15, 1921–June 15, 1922.

George Loane Tucker, actor and motion picture director, 49. Born Chicago; died Los Angeles, June 21, 1921.

Edward P. Temple, stage director, 60. General stage director for the Shuberts. Born New York; died New York, June 22, 1921.

George C. Hazleton, playwright, 53. Author of "Mistress Nell," adapter of Pierre Loving's "Aphrodite," co-author of "The Yellow Jacket." Born Boscobel, Wis.; died New York, June 24, 1921.

Frank Stammers, composer. Died New York, June 27, 1921.

Ralph Herz, actor, 42. Born Paris; died Atlantic City, N. J., July 12, 1921.

Enrico Caruso, operatic tenor, 48. Born Naples, Italy; died Florence, Italy, Aug. 2, 1921.

William G. Smythe, manager, 66. For twenty years executive in David Belasco's office. Producer of "My Friend From India," "The Man From Mexico." Died New York, Sept. 15, 1921.

Prof. Engelbert Humperdinck, composer, 67. Composer of "Hansel and Gretel." Died Berlin, Sept. 28, 1921.

William Dooley, acrobatic comedian, 39. Died New York, Sept. 29, 1921.

David Bispham, operatic baritone, 65. Born Philadelphia; died New York, Oct. 2, 1921.

Joseph Hart, vaudeville actor and producer, 59. Died New York, Oct. 3, 1921.

Frank N. Mandeville, conductor. Born Rochester, N. Y.; died New York, Nov. 6, 1921.

Claire Nagel (Mrs. Arthur Hammerstein), actress, 25. Born Buffalo, N. Y.; died Reno, Nev., Nov. 11, 1921.

Edith Kingdon Gould, actress, 60. Famous as member of Augustin Daly company previous to her marriage to George J. Gould. Died New York, Nov. 13, 1921.

Christine Nilsson, singer, 79. Famed as " Swedish Nightingale." Toured America, 1870-1892. Died Copenhagen, Nov. 22, 1921.

Ivan Caryll, composer. Composed " The Pink Lady " and other operas. Born Belgium; real name Felix Tilken; died New York, Nov. 29, 1921.

Sherrie Matthews, comedian, 53. Long member of the musical comedy team of Matthews and Bulger. Died New York, Dec. 8, 1921.

Victor Jacobi, composer, 37. Composed (with Fritz Kreisler) " Apple Blossoms." Born Hungary; died New York, Dec. 11, 1921.

Camille Saint-Saens, composer, 86. Born France; died Algiers, Dec. 16, 1921.

John C. Fisher, manager, 67. Producer, with Thomas W. Ryley, of " Florodora." Born Louisville, Ky.; died Chicago, Dec. 17, 1921.

Ada Gilman, actress, 67. Played with Forrest, Charlotte Cushman, Lawrence Barrett; member Daly company. Died Philadelphia, Dec. 18, 1921.

Sir John Hare, English actor, 77. Toured America in " A Pair of Spectacles " and " The Gay Lord Quex." Died London, Dec. 28, 1921.

Charles MacGeachey, manager, 62. Died New York, Dec. 24, 1921.

Rennold Wolf, playwright and dramatic editor *New York Telegraph*, 50. Born Ithaca, N. Y.; died, New York, Jan. 2, 1922.

A. Toxen Worm, manager, 55. Widely known as a creative press agent. Born Denmark; died Paris, Jan. 12, 1922.

John T. Kelly, Irish comedian, 70. Popular in vaudeville

and as member of old-time musical comedy team of Kelly and (Gus) Williams. First comedian to be engaged for Weber and Field's burlesque company. Born South Boston; died New York, Jan. 16, 1922.

Bert Williams, colored comedian, 49. Born New Providence, Nassau, British West Indies; died New York, March 4, 1922.

Joseph R. Grismer, actor and dramatist, 73. Part author and producer of "Way Down East," and many other plays. Many years shepherd Lambs' Club, New York. Supported many famous old stars and was leading man Grand Opera House and Baldwin stock companies, San Francisco, 1877. Born Albany, N. Y.; died New York, March 5, 1922.

Louis Vincent Defoe, dramatic critic, 52. On staff *New York Morning World* 23 years. Born Adrian, Mich.; died New York, March 13, 1922.

Harry Kellar, magician, 73. Born Erie, Pa.; died Los Angeles, Cal., March 9, 1922.

Samuel K. Hodgdon, vaudeville manager, 69. An executive in the Keith offices for forty years. Born Saco, Me.; died New York, April 6, 1922.

William Sampson, actor, 63. Died New York, April 6, 1922.

Harry Vokes, comedian, 56. Long member musical comedy team of Ward and Vokes. Died Lynn, Mass., April 15, 1922.

John G. Sparks, comedian, 70. Long with Harrigan and Hart. Died Brooklyn, N. Y., May 3, 1922.

Sylvia Thorne, singer, 55. With Aborn Opera company and Weber and Field's company. Died New York, May 9, 1922.

Eugenie Blair, actress, 54. Starred in west in "A Lady of Quality," "Zaza," "Mme. X" and other plays. Was with "Anna Christie" at time of death. Born Columbia, S. C.; died Chicago, May 13, 1922.

Emil Nyitray, playwright. Author of "The Typhoon"; part author, "My Lady Friends." Died Milford, Conn., May 20, 1922.

Sidney Ainsworth, actor, 50. Played in support of Maude Adams in "The Little Minister," later with Robert Edeson and John Barrymore. Went into pictures in 1909. Born England; died Madison, Wis.

Charles Osgood, manager, 63. For thirty years executive in Klaw & Erlanger offices. Died New York, May 26, 1922.

Barry Baxter, actor, 25. Prominent English juvenile; playing in "Bluebeard's Eighth Wife" at time of death. Born London; died New York, May 27, 1922.

Walter Jones, comedian, 48. Began career as tramp comedian in "1492." Born Connecticut; died Bensonhurst, N. Y., May 26, 1922.

Lillian Russell, singer, 61. Widely known on American stage, first in comic opera, later as member of Weber and Field's stock company; famed for her beauty and her kindliness. Born Nellie Leonard, Clinton, Ia.; died Pittsburg, Pa., June 5, 1922.

Henry Leone, actor and singer, 64. Played eight consecutive seasons in support of Lillian Russell at the Casino, New York. Died Mount Vernon, N.Y., June 9, 1922.

INDEX OF PLAYS AND CASTS

"Abie's Irish Rose" 550
"Above the Clouds" 491
"Advertising of Kate, The" 543
"Alias Jimmy Valentine" 475
"Ambush" 271, 493
"Anna Christie" 22, 454
"As Ye Mould" 444

"Bachelor's Night, A" 443
"Back Pay" 405
"Back to Methuselah" 517
"Bavu" 516
"Beware of Dogs" 429
"Billeted" 545
"Bill of Divorcement, A" 63, 438
"Blood and Sand" 422
"Blossom Time" 427
"Bluebeard's Eighth Wife" 421
"Blue Kitten, The" 494
"Blue Lagoon, The" 418
"Blushing Bride, The" 506
"Bombo" 437
"Bonbouroche" 469
"Bought and Paid For" 475
"Broken Branches" 521
"Bronx Express, The" 538
"Bulldog Drummond" 486

"Candida" 530
"Captain Applejack" 487
"Cat and the Canary, The" 507
"Chains of Dew" 540
"Charlatan, The" 537
"Chauve-Souris" 504
"Children's Tragedy" 440
"Chocolate Soldier" 476
"Circle, The" 311, 416
"Claw, The" 442
"Czarina, The" 502

"Daddy's Gone A-Hunting" 408
"Danger" 479
"Deluge, The" 499
"Demi-Virgin, The" 443
"Desert Sands" 510
"Detour, The" 400
"Don Juan" 414
"Dover Road, The" 237, 480
"Dream Maker, The" 466
"Drifting" 490
"Drums of Jeopardy" 553
"Dulcy" 96, 393

"Easiest Way, The" 413
"Elsie Janis and Her Gang" 495
"Elton Case, The" 415
"Everyday" 463

"Face Value" 485
"Fair Circassian, The" 474
"Fan, The" 434
"Fanny Hawthorne" 546
"Fedora" 508
"First Fifty Years" 525
"First Man, The" 519
"For Goodness Sake" 514
"Frank Fay's Fables" 507
"French Doll, The" 513
"From Morn 'Til Midnight" 548

"George White's Scandals" 388
"Getting Gertie's Garter" 390

" Get Together " 411
" Goat Alley " 387
" Go Easy, Mabel " 545
" Golden Days " 453
" Goldfish, The " 535
" Good Morning Dearie " 452
" Grand Duke, The " 451
" Great Broxopp, The " 462
" Great Way, The " 456
" Green Ring, The " 532
" Greenwich Village Follies " 407

" Hairy Ape, The " 524
" Hand of the Potter " 473
" Hero, The " 199, 412
" Her Salary Man " 469
" He Who Gets Slapped " 126, 492
" Hindu, The " 528
" Honors Are Even " 392
" Hotel Mouse, The " 526

" Idle Inn, The " 478
" Intimate Strangers " 454

" Julius Cæsar " 496
" Just Because " 529

" Kempy " 547
" Kiki " 470

" Lady Bug " 536
" Lancelot and Elaine " 420
" Law Breaker, The " 505
" Lawful Larceny " 489
" Letty Pepper " 533
" Like A King " 431
" Lilies of the Field " 433
" Love Dreams " 441
" Love Letter, The " 435

" Macbeth " 496
" Madame Pierre " 511
" Mad Dog, The " 457
" Madeleine and the Movies " 520
" Madras House, The " 450
" Main Street " 436
" Make It Snappy " 534
" Makers of Light " 551
" Man in the Making " 423
" Man's Name, The " 463
" March Hares " 392
" Marie Antoinette " 465
" Marjolaine " 496
" Married Woman, The " 482
" Mask of Hamlet, The " 399
" Merchant of Venice " 446
" Merry Widow, The " 412
" Mimic World, The " 397
" Montmartre " 509
" Mountain Man, The " 477
" Mr. Faust " 501
" Mrs. Warren's Profession " 516
" Music Box Revue, The " 426

" National Anthem, The " 497
" Nature's Nobleman " 461
" Nest, The " 346, 500
" Night Call, The " 539
" Night Cap, The " 394
" Nobody's Money " 397

" O'Brien Girl, The " 432
" Only 38 " 417

" Partners Again " 542
" Perfect Fool, The " 457
" Personality " 402
" Pigeon, The " 503
" Pinch Hitter, A" 554
" Pins and Needles " 503
" Poppy God, The " 404
" Pot Luck " 428

" Raymond Hitchcock's Pinwheel " 556
" Red Geranium, The " 544
" Red Pepper " 552
" Return of Peter Grimm " 424
" Right to Strike, The " 447
" Rivals, The " 555

" Romeo and Juliet " 497
" Rosa Machree " 494
" Rose of Stamboul, The " 523
" Rotters, The " 549
" Rubicon, The " 515

" Salome " 550
" Scarlet Man, The " 398
" Shadow, The " 538
" Silver Fox, The " 411
" Six Cylinder Love " 163, 402
" Six-Fifty, The " 448
" Skirt, The " 455
" Skylark, The " 388
" Some Party " 534
" Sonny " 396
" Sonya " 395
" Spring, The " 425
" Squaw Man, The " 484
" S.S. Tenacity, The " 488
" Straw, The " 459
" Suzette " 467
" Swords " 409

" Taboo " 531
" Taming of the Shrew " 446
" Tangerine " 391
" Tarzan of the Apes " 410
" Teaser, The " 389
" Thank You " 430
" Title, The " 460
" To the Ladies " 512
" Trilby " 481
" Triumph of X, The " 401
" Truth About Blayds " 527
" Twelfth Night " 445
" Two Blocks Away " 406

" Up the Ladder " 522

" Varying Shore, The " 472
" Verge, The " 461
" Voice from the Minaret " 500
" Voltaire " 528

" Wait 'Til We're Married " 426
" Wandering Jew, The " 449
" We Girls " 458
" What the Public Wants" 541
" Wheel, The " 403
" White Headed Boy " 419
" White Peacock, The " 483
" Wife With the Smile " 468
" Wildcat, The " 467
" Wren, The " 438

" Your Woman and Mine "518

" Ziegfeld Follies, 1921 " 388
" Ziegfeld Follies, 1922 " 555
" Ziegfeld Midnight Frolic " 464